THE SPREADING FLAME

THE
SPREADING FLAME

*The Rise and Progress of Christianity from its First
Beginnings to the Conversion of the English*

by

F. F. BRUCE, M.A., D.D.

*Rylands Professor of Biblical Criticism and Exegesis in the
University of Manchester*

*Wm. B. Eerdmans Publishing Company
Grand Rapids, Michigan*

FILIO FILIAEQVE

CONTENTS

PART III: LIGHT IN THE WEST

PREFACE

THE FIRST EDITION OF THIS WORK APPEARED IN THREE successive volumes of the "Second Thoughts Library", published by The Paternoster Press, London, in which I endeavoured to trace the course of early Christianity from its Palestinian beginnings down to the conversion of the English nation—*The Dawn of Christianity* (1950), *The Growing Day* (1951) and *Light in the West* (1952). In 1953 all three were reproduced in an omnibus volume by Messrs. Eerdmans of Grand Rapids, Michigan; it was for that edition that the title *The Spreading Flame* was devised. For the suggestion that a new British edition might be produced in one volume I am indebted to my friend Mr. B. Howard Mudditt, proprietor of The Paternoster Press. This has given me an opportunity to revise the work thoroughly, to correct a number of errors, to improve things which might have been better expressed, and to bring the account into line with the latest stages in research and discovery.

I am most grateful to readers and reviewers of widely divergent schools of thought for the generous reception which they have given to these studies. I did not expect that they would be recommended as handbooks in church history in theological colleges, but that this has happened in some places is certainly gratifying. My indebtedness to other writers in this field is immense, and nothing in these pages can be called an original contribution to knowledge; but the judgments are my own, and I have not consciously tried to sustain by historical argument positions antecedently held on less rational grounds. The scale of the treatment has made it necessary to select certain features and pass over others; and the principle of selection probably amounts to little more than my personal interests and preferences.

My thanks are due above all to my wife, for her help at every stage of the production of the work.

1958

F.F.B.

PREFACE TO PAPERBACK EDITION

For this edition a few revisions and updatings have been made, but the text remains essentially unaltered.

1981

F.F.B.

PART I

THE DAWN OF
CHRISTIANITY

*The Rise and Progress of Christianity from its
First Beginnings to the Fall of Jerusalem* (A.D. 1–70)

CHAPTER I

STRANGERS IN CORINTH

CORINTH IS AN ANCIENT CITY OF GREECE, SITUATED ON THE Isthmus of Corinth, and occupying an admirable position for commercial enterprise. It stands at the junction of land-routes north and south, and at the junction of sea-routes west and east. On the west lies the Gulf of Corinth (leading to the Ionian Sea and Western Mediterranean), where Corinth had the port of Lechæum; on the east lies the Saronic Gulf (leading to the Ægean Sea and Eastern Mediterranean), on which Corinth had the port of Cenchreæ.

For many centuries Corinth enjoyed great commercial and naval prosperity. Its reputation, as might be expected in a great seaport, was none too good on the moral side. Indeed, the Greeks had a verb to denote indulgence in the more abandoned forms of wantonness—*korinthiazesthai*, they called it, "behaving as they do in Corinth."[1]

Disaster came to Corinth in 146 B.C. By that time the Roman supremacy had been imposed upon the Greek lands, and in an attempt to throw off the Roman yoke Corinth took the lead. The Roman vengeance was savage. The Roman general Mummius razed Corinth to the ground, and the site lay derelict for exactly a hundred years. Then the fortunes of the city were restored. In 46 B.C. Julius Cæsar refounded Corinth with the status of a Roman colony and bestowed on it the proud title *Laus Iulia Corinthus*, "Corinth, the praise of Julius." A Roman colony was a little Rome planted in other lands amid a non-Roman population to be a centre of Roman life and to maintain the Roman peace. Along the great Roman roads, those military highways which ran from Rome to the various frontiers of the Empire, these colonies of Roman citizens were planted at strategic points and they played an important part in the imperial organization.

Nineteen years after Corinth was refounded by Cæsar, it became the capital city of the Roman province of Achaia, which comprised Greece south of Thessaly. As the city's fortunes returned, so did something of its old ill repute; *korinthiazesthai* remained a fitting description of sexual vice. This sort of activity, in fact, found

[1] Cf. Shakespeare, *I King Henry IV*, Act 2, Scene 4, line 13: "I am no proud Jack, like Falstaff, but a Corinthian, a lad of mettle, a good boy."

official religious sanction at Corinth: on the summit of the Corinthian acropolis (the Acrocorinthus) stood a temple of Aphrodite, the Greek goddess of love, whose worship here as in some other Greek cities was really a Hellenized form of the worship of the Syrian goddess Astarte, the Ashtoreth of the Old Testament. Nor did this goddess lack a Syrian consort in Corinth. At the foot of the Acrocorinthus the worship of Melicertes, the patron deity of navigation, was carried on. But Melicertes is simply a Greek way of pronouncing the name of Melkart,[1] the chief god or "baal" of the city of Tyre, whose cult was introduced into Israel in the ninth century B.C. when King Ahab married Jezebel, daughter of the ruler of Tyre and Sidon.

There were many other shrines in Corinth, dedicated to the worship of this or that divinity. But if we wished to find the greatest contrast to the cult of Aphrodite, with its ritual prostitution, we should have made our way about A.D. 50 to the place where the Jewish residents in this great commercial city came together on sabbath days and at other times to listen to the reading and exposition of their sacred writings. Here was a form of worship which combined a reasonable creed with a decent way of life. Here it was proclaimed that God was one, and not many; that He was holy, and not morally neutral; and that His law, which He had made known to men, required that they should exhibit in their lives that righteousness and mercy which distinguished His own character. True, it was maintained that He had revealed all this in a special way to the Jewish people, whom He had chosen as His own people; but He was not uninterested in other men, and they might share the fullest benefits of His revelation by taking upon themselves "the yoke of the kingdom of heaven"—entering the Jewish community as proselytes.

Gentiles who wished to become proselytes must be circumcised (if they were men) and undergo a purificatory baptism and offer a prescribed sacrifice. By these means they undertook the full observance of the Jewish law and became participators in all the religious and social privileges of the community of Israel.

The real test was circumcision, and this helps to explain why full proselytization to the Jewish religion was commoner among Gentile women than men. Men who were attracted to the monotheism and morality of the Jewish faith and way of life were largely content with a looser attachment to the synagogue. They attended divine worship there, and observed with more or less strictness some distinctive Jewish practices, such as refraining from work on the sabbath day or avoiding certain kinds of food. In particular, they would be expected to conform to certain ethical requirements which the Jewish rabbis regarded as binding

[1] Melkart is Phœnician *melk-qart,* "king of the city".

on the whole human race, since God had imposed them on Noah and his sons—abstinence from idolatry, murder and fornication. Those Gentiles who attached themselves in this loose way to the synagogue, without going so far as to become true proselytes, were called "God-fearers."

A fragment of one Corinthian synagogue of these days has actually been found; it is part of an inscription over a door which read, when it was complete, "SYNAGOGUE OF THE HEBREWS."[1] This may, indeed, have been the only synagogue in Corinth at the time with which we are dealing; at any rate, our literary evidence refers to one synagogue only.

To this synagogue Jews from all parts of the world made their way when they found themselves in Corinth. Here they could be sure of a welcome from their brethren; here they could find a haven from the pagan pollutions of the great city; here, too, they could listen to the reading and exposition of the same scripture lessons as they would have heard in their home synagogues.

Early in the year 50 an interesting Jewish couple made their way to the synagogue in Corinth. They had lived in Rome for some years, but lately an outburst of rioting among some of the Jews of Rome had given the Emperor Claudius the not unwelcome opportunity to impose restrictions on the Jewish community there which were tantamount to their expulsion. The edict of expulsion had no long-lasting effect; many of the Roman Jews, however, had to find a home elsewhere for a time, and among those who found their way to Corinth were the couple we are speaking of, a leather-worker called Aquila and his wife Prisca. Aquila was not a Roman Jew by birth; he was born in Pontus, on the Black Sea coast of Asia Minor. His wife—known to her friends by her more familiar name Priscilla—seems to have belonged to a higher social class than her husband; she may have been connected with the noble Roman family called the *gens Prisca*. This couple appear to have been associated with a new movement in Judaism which had occasioned the rioting at Rome; but more of this anon.

Aquila and Prisca had not been in Corinth long when another Jewish leather-worker came to the city, not from the west but from the east, from the province of Cilicia. As he practised his trade, he soon made the acquaintance of Aquila. They began to work together, and found that they had more in common than the fact that they belonged to the same craft. For the new-comer was a prominent figure in the new movement with which Aquila and his wife were connected. He joined them in attending the synagogue in Corinth, and here he was not long in making himself heard.

[1] A. Deissmann, *Light from the Ancient East* (1927), pp. 15ff.

The new-comer was not only a leather-worker; he was also a great rabbi. He was now between forty and fifty years old, but in his youth he had received a thorough training in rabbinical learning at Jerusalem in the school of the greatest rabbi of the day, Gamaliel the Elder. That a rabbi should support himself by a manual trade was regarded as right and proper, for it was reckoned unfitting to receive money for imparting sacred lore. Hillel, a great rabbi of an earlier day, the teacher of Gamaliel, had declared: "He who makes a worldly use of the crown of the divine law shall waste away." A later rabbi said: "Do not make the divine law a crown with which to magnify yourself, or a spade to dig with." "Hence," said other rabbis, "it may be inferred that whosoever derives a profit for himself from the words of the divine law helps on his own destruction."[1] But even teachers of the divine law must eat and drink, and it was recommended that to do this they should learn and practise a manual occupation.[2] So it was with this new-comer to Corinth.[3]

Such a learned visitor would not be left long without an invitation to contribute to the edification of the audience in the synagogue, and this the new-comer did with the utmost readiness, although he betrayed traces of nervousness at the same time. But he did some very curious things in the synagogue. As he read the sacred lessons, or heard them read, he would (we are told) interpolate words not found in the scrolls. Sometimes these lessons contained references to one through whom God in future days was to do great things for the Jewish people, and indeed for mankind at large. When such passages were read, the new-comer would insert words of explanation which suggested that this coming one of whom the holy writings told had actually come in recent days. If this were really so, it was the best of all good news; but some details of the career of this recent figure in whom the holy writings were said to have found their fulfilment were so strange, and indeed scandalizing, that many listened to the rabbi with deepening misgivings. Others, however, listened with growing pleasure to what he had to say, and believed that his news was true. This was especially so with many of the Gentile God-fearers who attended the synagogue.

So it went on sabbath by sabbath. After a few weeks the rabbi was joined by two friends whom he had left behind in the more northerly province of Macedonia. When they arrived, they brought some supplies which relieved him of the necessity of

---

[1] *Pirqe Aboth* I, 13; IV, 7. See p. 43, n. 1.   [2] *Pirqe Aboth* II, 2.
[3] The Greek word used to describe his manual occupation means etymologically "tent-making"; but in the first century A.D. it had the wider sense of "leather-working". (Similarly a "saddler" with us does much more than make saddles.) The rabbi's trade was closely connected with the chief manufacture of his native province, *cilicium*, a material of goat's hair used for making cloaks, curtains, etc.

supporting himself by his leather-working, and so he was able to give all his time and attention to teaching. At last the party in the synagogue which disagreed with him told him that he could not be allowed to go on with his strange teaching in their midst; to their mind it was blasphemous nonsense.

Now the rabbi had to find another place in which to teach. Nor had he to look far. One of the God-fearers who had listened to him with pleasure, a Roman citizen bearing the name Gaius Titius Justus, lived next door to the synagogue, and he placed his house at the rabbi's disposal. Here, then, was established a rival meeting-place, to which many members of the rabbi's former synagogue audience now came, and continued to pay eager attention to what he had to say. Large numbers of other Corinthians also flocked to hear him. Those who believed his message were formed into a community similar in some ways to that which continued to meet next door, but distinct from it in other ways. In this new community no distinction was made between Jews and Gentiles. Both were admitted on equal terms. Neither circumcision nor sacrifice nor an undertaking to observe the Jewish law was required of any. For those who entered the community, Jews and Gentiles alike, there was an initiation ceremony which took the form of baptism with water. There was also a repeated ceremony in which the members of the community expressed their common fellowship; this was a simple meal of bread and wine to which a special significance was attached. The holy writings continued to be read and expounded as in the synagogue, but expounded with special reference to the one in whom (as the rabbi maintained) they had recently found their fulfilment. A high ethical standard was inculcated; in particular, those moral requirements which the Jews believed God had imposed on the sons of Noah were strictly enjoined; idolatry, murder or fornication would inevitably exclude a member from the fellowship. But the standard of morality to which the rabbi appealed was not so much a written law-code as the life and character of the person in whom, as he claimed, God had fulfilled His ancient promises.

When at last the ruler of the synagogue next door himself became a convert and joined the new rival body, the synagogue authorities felt that the time for more drastic action had come, and they made representations to the Roman governor of the province. They knew that theirs was not the first synagogue to be faced with this situation; correspondence with Jewish communities in other cities of the Greek world revealed that this rabbi had done much the same thing in a number of places, and had got into serious trouble for his pains. Perhaps it would do no harm if they could get him into trouble here in Corinth. So they charged him before the governor with propagating a form of religion which was not permitted by law. A religion which had not secured a licence for its practice under Roman law was regarded as illicit. The charge was a serious one, if it could be substantiated. But before we come to the result of the charge, we had better be more explicit about the rabbi and his teaching.

The rabbi who caused such a stir in the Jewish community of Corinth was a native of the Greek city of Tarsus, in southern Asia Minor. He was born into an orthodox Jewish family, and as his father was a Roman citizen, he inherited this distinction, a rare one among eastern Jews. In Jewish circles he bore the name of Saul, but in the Gentile world he was commonly known by his Roman cognomen Paullus, Anglicized as Paul.[1] How about the year 33 he relinquished the dazzling prospects which a distinguished pupil of Gamaliel might have looked forward to, and became a leading proponent of the new teaching which split the synagogues in Corinth and other places, must be the subject of a later chapter. At the moment we are more interested in the message than in the messenger. What was his message, and why did it cause such an upheaval?

Fortunately we are not left in doubt about the main outline of his message. About two years after he left Corinth he had occasion to write a letter to the community which he had founded there, and at certain points in the letter it was necessary to refer to some of the chief features of what he had taught them when he led them out of the synagogue and formed them into a rival congregation.

From these references we can gather this much. The message centred round a coming deliverer predicted in the sacred scriptures of the Jewish people. By the beginning of the Christian era this coming deliverer was generally referred to as the "Messiah." This word really means "anointed," and indicated that this deliverer was to be specially consecrated for the exercise of his proper functions, as a king was consecrated by anointing for the exercise of his sovereignty or a priest for the exercise of his sacred office. In Greek-speaking circles the Semitic title Messiah was not generally used; it was replaced by the Greek verbal adjective *christos* (Anglicized "Christ"), which similarly means "anointed."

Well, said Paul, this deliverer, the Messiah, has actually come. Paul identified Him with a man named Jesus, a teacher whose sayings he regarded as supremely authoritative. It was not, however, primarily as a teacher that Paul spoke of Him. Had it been so, the Jewish colonies in Corinth and elsewhere might not have felt the same objection as they did to the account which Paul gave of Him. What really gave offence was that, as Paul himself insisted, this Jesus, whom he identified with the Messiah, had died

[1] See p. 81 below.

a violent death; He had, in fact, been crucified. Far from trying to gloss over this scandalous fact, Paul went out of his way to emphasize it, although he knew very well that in doing so he ran the risk of alienating his Greek and Hebrew hearers alike. That anyone should acclaim as a supreme teacher one who had not sufficient wisdom to save himself from so shameful and horrible a death was, to Greek minds, sheer folly. But that anyone should acclaim as God's Messiah one who had died by crucifixion was, to Jewish minds, worse than folly; it was plain blasphemy. A suffering Messiah was foreign enough to current Jewish ideas, but a crucified Messiah was a contradiction in terms. The Messiah was one upon whom the divine blessing rested in a unique degree, whereas the form of death that Jesus died was an evident sign that the divine curse rested on Him; for it was clearly laid down in the holy law: "He that is hanged is accursed of God."[1] Yet Paul did not try to avoid this paradox; he made it one of the central points of his proclamation, and added that the Messiah endured this death for the sins of other men, not for His own. This, he said, was in strict accordance with the account of the coming Messiah given in the Hebrew scriptures. This statement must have puzzled and shocked his Jewish hearers. (As we shall see, it depended on an identification which Jesus Himself made of the Messiah with another figure portrayed in the Hebrew scriptures.)

But this was not the end, said Paul. The Messiah was buried, but rose from death on the third day (as the Hebrew scriptures had also foretold) and appeared alive to a large number of people at various times. In the letter which he wrote to his converts at Corinth two years later, Paul reminds them of those who had seen and recognized Jesus alive after His death and burial; they included Peter, the leading figure among those who had been Jesus' closest companions, then the whole group of twelve to which Peter belonged, then more than five hundred of His old followers (and of those, said Paul, the majority are still alive to tell the tale). Jesus' own brother James was another who saw Him thus; on another occasion He appeared alive to all those whom He had commissioned as His special envoys in earlier days, "and last of all," Paul added, "He appeared to me also."[2]

This is certainly an amazing story. It demands the most watertight attestation if it is to be seriously considered. Where did Paul get it from? Did he evolve it out of his inner consciousness? Or was he giving a local habitation and a name to an old figure of Hebrew mythology in order to present him as an acceptable lord and saviour of a new mystery cult—a Lord Jesus to set up as a rival to the Lord Serapis and others? Paul alone could speak of the occasion when he claimed to have seen for himself the crucified

---

[1] Deuteronomy 21 : 2 .   [2] 1 Corinthians 15 : 1ff.

Messiah alive again from the dead; but he affirmed that the others who had similarly seen Him all told the same story. Indeed (apart from the incident which fell within his own experience) Paul says that the message which he passed on to his hearers in Corinth was one which he had in turn received himself; he was a link in the chain of testimony. And we shall see that two of Paul's earliest informants were the two most prominent people in his list of witnesses to the Messiah's resurrection—Peter and James.[1]

In this letter which he wrote to his Corinthian converts Paul reminds them of something else which he had received and imparted—something which, he declared, went right back to the Messiah Himself. The Lord Jesus (as Paul regularly calls Him) had been the victim of an act of treachery. On the very night in which this act of treachery took place, He was partaking of a meal with His closest companions, when He suddenly gave them some of the bread and wine on the table and told them to accept these as tokens of His body which He was giving up for them and of His blood which was to be the seal of a new covenant which God was making with them. He further requested them to go on doing this in remembrance of Him, and (adds Paul) "every time that you eat this bread and drink the cup you proclaim the Lord's death until He comes." This was the origin of the meal which formed the centre of the new community's life and fellowship in Corinth and in every other place where there were similar communities. Besides, the very language which Paul uses in reference to this meal suggests that the life of the new community not only looks back to the Messiah's death and triumph over death, but also looks forward to an event in the future: the words "you proclaim the Lord's death until He comes" indicate that He was expected to return at some time in some fashion.[2]

Not only this fellowship rite of the new community, but also its initiation rite, is mentioned by Paul in this letter. We infer that this rite took the form of baptism into the Messiah's name; at any rate, when Paul has occasion to remonstrate with his readers for forming cliques called by his own name and the names of other teachers, he asks ironically: "Was Paul crucified for you? Or was it into Paul's name that you were baptized?"[3] As "Christ" should obviously be substituted for "Paul" in the former case, the same substitution is suggested in the latter.

We have thus been able to gather some idea of the teaching and practice which Paul's Jewish opponents at Corinth regarded as constituting an illicit religion. For they would not allow that it was Judaism in any form. But when they arraigned him before the governor of Achaia on this charge, he ruled that the question was one of internal Jewish concern. Paul seemed to him (so far as

[1] See p. 87 below.   [2] 1 Corinthians 11 : 23ff.   [3] 1 Corinthians 1 : 13.

he troubled to hear the case) to be propounding a variant type of the Jewish religion, not a different religion altogether, and he declined to adjudicate in such a matter. This was quite satisfactory from Paul's point of view; it meant in effect that he was acquitted of the charge of propagating a forbidden religion. In his view, the faith that he was inculcating was the true fulfilment of the "hope of Israel," the timely fruition of the Jewish religion which already enjoyed the protection of Roman law.

It is a matter of interest, by the way, that the Roman governor who made this decision was Lucius Junius Gallio, brother to the distinguished philosopher Seneca, who was at this time tutor to Nero, the Emperor's stepson and future successor. An inscription at Delphi, in central Greece, recording a proclamation made by the Emperor Claudius between the end of A.D. 51 and the following August, makes it probable that Gallio became proconsul of Achaia at the beginning of July, A.D. 51.[1] After a year in office he left his province owing to a fever and went on a cruise for his health. It was probably about the beginning of his governorship that the case of Paul was brought before him.

Encouraged by Gallio's decision, Paul continued for several more months in Corinth. At last, after a year and a half's stay in all, he left with Aquila and Prisca, and visited Ephesus on his way to Palestine. Aquila and Prisca stayed in Ephesus. There they met another Jew who was making for Corinth. This was a native of Alexandria in Egypt, called Apollos. Apollos, like Paul, was a man of great learning; like Paul, too, he caused a stir in the synagogues by arguing from the sacred writings that Jesus was the Messiah. He had an accurate knowledge of the story of Jesus, but he had acquired his knowledge along another line of transmission than that which Paul represented. He had not heard, for example, of baptism into the name of Jesus; the baptism with which he was acquainted was an older form, associated with a preacher named John, who had baptized many people in Palestine in the days before Jesus began His public activity; this baptism was a token of repentance rather than of initiation into the community of the Messiah. But before Apollos left Ephesus for Corinth, Aquila and Prisca supplied the deficiencies in his information (telling him, no doubt, much of what they themselves had heard from Paul). Then, when he set out across the Ægean, they gave him a letter of introduction to the new community in Corinth.

Apollos reached Corinth a few months after Paul had left, and

[1] The title "proconsul" was given to the governors of those Roman provinces which required no standing army and were therefore under the nominal control of the Roman Senate. Achaia was such a senatorial province from 27 B.C. to A.D. 15 and again from A.D. 44 onwards. Provinces which required the presence of a standing army were under the direct control of the Emperor and governed by an imperial legate.

not only made contact with the new community there, but held disputations with the Jews as well, maintaining that the ancient prophecies concerning the Messiah found their complete fulfilment in Jesus.

The learning of Apollos, which probably bore the stamp of Alexandrian culture, made a deep impression on some members of the new community at Corinth. "Here is a man," they said, "who knows a lot more than Paul; Paul taught us elementary things compared with what we have learned from Apollos. Let those who will remain content with Paul's teaching; as for us, we enroll ourselves as disciples of the school of Apollos." Not that there was any feeling of partisan rivalry between Paul and Apollos. Paul, in particular, while he deprecated party feeling in the Corinthian community, regarded Apollos as watering the seed which he himself had planted, acknowledged him as an authentic envoy of the Messiah, and encouraged him to stay among these Corinthians and give them all the help he could.

But the community was to have no lack of teachers. For hard on the heels of Paul and Apollos came men from Palestine who were closely associated with those who had been personal companions of Jesus before His death. It may even be that Peter, the leader of Jesus' personal companions, paid a personal visit to Corinth. At any rate, the visit of these Palestinians gave occasion for the emergence of a third group in the new community at Corinth. This group considered that, while Paul and Apollos were certainly followers of Jesus in a sense, they were not to be compared with His earliest followers. "Now," said they, "we are in direct touch with the original envoys or 'apostles' selected and commissioned by the Messiah himself. Let others regard themselves as disciples of Paul or Apollos; we belong to the school of Peter, the prince of the apostles, the one on whom the Messiah conferred special authority to make decisions which would be ratified in heaven."

Paul, who by this time had returned from his Palestinian visit and was active in Ephesus, across the Ægean, kept in close touch with his friends in Corinth, and was dismayed by all this talk of rival schools. The idea of some regarding themselves as in a special sense his own disciples was just as distasteful as the idea of others claiming Apollos or Peter as distinctively their leaders. Paul and Apollos and Peter, he wrote, belong to you all equally. If you want a name to call yourselves by, what is wrong with the name into which you were baptized—the name which covers you all? Christ is not divided; His name must not become the perquisite of any clique or party. Let Him be your leader, and acknowledge no other!

All this is very interesting, but consider now where these

strangers in Corinth came from. We have the couple from Rome, the rabbi of Tarsus, the scholar from Alexandria, and the visitors from Palestine. From all directions they came to Corinth, between the years 50 and 54, and all of them were already connected with this new movement which was turning the Jewish communities throughout the Roman Empire upside down and was beginning to make its revolutionary impact on the pagan world as well.

What was this new movement, and how did it originate? What supplied its driving force? Whence did it derive its popular appeal? Who was this Jesus with whom it was all bound up? Was He really the promised Messiah of Israel, as these strangers in Corinth maintained, or were they mistaken, as the synagogue authorities for the most part asserted? How did He come to fall foul of the ruling powers and come to such a tragic death? What did they mean by saying that He died for the sins of others? And, above all, what was all this about His returning to life on the third day and appearing alive to so many witnesses? To answer these questions we must begin by going a long way back in history.

CHAPTER II

WHEN THE TIME WAS RIPE

IN A FAMOUS PHRASE PAUL DECLARES THAT CHRISTIANITY appeared on earth when the time was ripe for it: "when the fulness of the time came, God sent forth his Son."[1] Whether we look at the Jewish people or the Greco-Roman world of the first century A.D., we can understand something of what he meant. Politically and religiously the world was ready for the gospel at that time as it had not been before. The greater part of the civilized world was politically united, but the old classical religions were bankrupt. Many people had recourse to the popular mystery cults in their search for liberation from evil powers and assurance of well-being in the after-life. Others, as we have seen, were attracted to the Jewish religion, but it laboured under the disadvantage of being too closely tied to one nation. When the Christian message began to be proclaimed among the peoples of the Roman Empire, it showed a capacity to satisfy both the craving for salvation which the mystery cults professed to meet and the ethical ideals which, as many Gentiles believed, were realized in the Jewish way of life even more than in Stoicism.[2]

The one writer above all others in the New Testament who is concerned to set the story of Christian origins in the context of contemporary history saw this plainly, and expresses it in the words with which he begins the story of Jesus. "In those days the Emperor Augustus issued a decree for the enrolment of the whole world."[3] Augustus, after long-lasting civil strife, had attained supreme power in the Roman Empire and imposed the Roman peace on a war-weary world. And in consequence of the decree which he issued and the particular way in which it was carried into effect in a petty vassal-principality on the Asiatic fringe of the Empire, the birth of Jesus took place in the Judæan city of Bethlehem. Augustus never heard of Jesus, who was scarcely out of His teens when Augustus died. But the achievement of

---

[1] Galatians 4 : 4.

[2] Stoicism is the name given to the philosophical system first taught by Zeno, a Cypriot philosopher (336–264 B.C.), who migrated to Athens and taught for many years in one of the *stoai*, or colonnades, of the market-place there. It inculcated a lofty ethical standard, in which special emphasis was laid on the control of the passions by reason. Leading Stoics in Roman times were the philosopher Seneca, the slave Epictetus, and the Emperor Marcus Aurelius.

[3] Luke 2 : 1.

Augustus played no small part in the ripeness of time for the work of Jesus and His followers. And the successors of Augustus were destined to hear more and more of Jesus, until after three centuries had gone by one of those successors acknowledged His supremacy. "When you see this orb set under the cross, remember that the whole world is subject to the power and empire of Christ, our Redeemer."[1]

Yet the birth of Jesus was as obscure as anyone's birth could be, and His days were not passed in the blaze of world publicity. He spent His life in a remote and unimportant province of the Empire, and only rarely did He cross the frontiers of that province. He did not court the attention of the world. He concentrated His activity on the Jewish people in Palestine, and it was only for two or three years at the end of His life that He played any public part among them.

What then was His world-significance? How did the faith which He fostered and the community which He founded spread so rapidly throughout the world?

For an answer we must go back to Abraham. It is from him, in a sense, that the rise of Christianity is to be dated. "The gospel", says Paul, "was preached to Abraham."[2] Historians from Eusebius in the fourth century A.D. down to recent times have understood that what is called church history really begins with him. Arthur Penrhyn Stanley, appointed to the Regius Chair of Ecclesiastical History at Oxford in December, 1856, burst into his mother's room the morning after he had accepted the appointment, exclaiming: "I have settled my first course. I shall begin with Abraham; he is the true beginning of ecclesiastical history."[3]

The piece of territory in south-western Asia which Professor Breasted taught us to call the Fertile Crescent, stretching from the Persian Gulf to the frontier of Egypt, between the mountains on the north and east, the desert to the south, and the Mediterranean on the west, was the centre of great migrations of peoples in the centuries following 2000 B.C. Mountaineers from the north and east, desert-rangers from the south, sea-rovers from the west, pressed into it. Amid these confused waves of wanderers we have the record of one man who, with a few retainers, set out from Mesopotamia and settled in the south of Palestine about 1700 B.C. According to our records, there was something distinctive about

[1] British Coronation Service.

[2] Galatians 3 : 8.

[3] A rabbinical comment on Isaiah 51 : 1f. (where Israelites are told to "look to the rock from which you were hewn . . . Abraham your father"), runs thus: "A certain king desired to build and to lay foundations; he dug ever deeper, but found only morass. At last he dug and found a rock (*petra*). He said, 'On this spot I will build and lay the foundations.' " (*Yalqut* 1 : 766; the parallel with the New Testament passage in Matthew 16 : 18 hardly needs to be pointed out.)

this man's migration; it was closely bound up with a religious motive. "The God of glory", we are told, revealed Himself to this man, and the impulse derived from that revelation sent him away from his native land and ancestral worship and brought him to the new land of his adoption. "In you and in your progeny", the word of revelation assured him, "blessing will come to all the nations on earth."[1]

The descendants of this man Abraham in the third generation went down from Palestine to Egypt in a time of famine and settled down to a pastoral life in the Wadi Tumilat, near what we know today as the Canal Zone. But the building frenzy of the Egyptian king Rameses II (1301–1234 B.C.) drew them from their free pastoral life and conscribed them in his forced labour gangs. This bondage they endured for several decades, until under the leadership of one Moses they made their escape from Egypt in circumstances which could have no other meaning for them than that, when all hope was gone, the God of their fathers had intervened miraculously and decisively on their behalf. A period of nomad life in north-west Arabia followed, during which they were solemnly constituted as the nation of Israel, bound by covenant to the God of their fathers who had chosen them as His own people and delivered them from their slavery in Egypt. The terms of this covenant had a markedly ethical character; they insisted that as Israel's God was righteous and merciful, so also must His people Israel be.

The people who had escaped from Egypt as an undisciplined crowd of slaves marched out of north-west Arabia in the next generation as a well-organized federation of tribes bent on the conquest and occupation of the land of Palestine where their ancestor Abraham had lived as an alien. The process of conquest and occupation was long drawn out; it was completed about 1000 B.C. under David their king, who seized the opportunity afforded by the weakness of the contemporary empires in Mesopotamia and Egypt to win an empire for Israel, stretching from the Gulf of Akaba on the south to the Upper Euphrates on the north. This empire, however, was short-lived; towards the end of the reign of David's son Solomon it fell to pieces, and even the home territory itself was split into two kingdoms, each acknowledging (formally at least) the God of Israel. Both these small kingdoms came to an inglorious end—the one at the hands of the Assyrian Empire in 721 B.C. and the other at the hands of the Babylonians in 587 B.C.

Politically the history of Israel had been disastrous. But the spiritual seed sown in the days of Abraham and Moses was not extinguished. In the days of the two kingdoms a succession of

[1] Genesis 12 : 3; 22 : 18.

men had arisen, spokesmen of Yahweh,[1] the God of Israel, recalling the nation to the terms of the covenant which he had made with them and pointing forward to a glorious future, when the knowledge of God, communicated to Israel through Moses and the prophets (as these spokesmen are usually called), would spread out from Israel to cover the whole world so that the blessing promised by God to all mankind through Abraham's progeny might be realized. Nor did these hopes cease to be proclaimed with the cessation of national independence.

The high water mark of the hope of Israel is to be found in the second part of the book of Isaiah, where the character of Israel's world mission is expressed more clearly than anywhere else in the Hebrew writings. In these chapters the nation of Israel is addressed as the "servant of Yahweh", called to make Him known to the world.

But Israel has not been an obedient servant; the task of communicating the knowledge of God to other nations is therefore entrusted to another who is similarly called the servant of Yahweh. This servant is to make known the divine law to the Gentiles and establish divine righteousness on earth; he is to restore Israel to God and bring divine illumination to all mankind:

> It is too light a thing that you should be my servant
> To raise up the tribes of Jacob and bring back Israel's refugees:
> I will also give you as a light to the nations,
> That my salvation may reach to the ends of the earth.[2]

Here the servant who undertakes Israel's task is intimately associated with Israel and yet distinguished from her. In him the faithful remnant of Israel is reduced to a single individual. In the carrying out of his task he is to suffer contempt, unjust judgment, and death; but by his suffering he will achieve his object, and blessing and liberation for multitudes will be the outcome of his death.

This was not, however, the only form which the hope of the future took. Alongside the idea of the servant of Yahweh we have to set the messianic idea.[3] The kings of Israel had not been abso-

---

[1] The form Yahweh is probably familiar enough nowadays to be used even in a non-technical work. The vowels of the name were forgotten in a time when the name was thought to be too holy to be pronounced, but it is pretty certain that the pronunciation was "Yahweh", or something very like it. The traditional English form "Jehovah" represents the consonants of Yahweh (Jahveh) combined with the vowels of another word which was substituted for Yahweh in the public reading of the Hebrew Bible.

[2] Isaiah 49 : 6.

[3] Perhaps these are not two ideas but two ways of stating the same idea. C. R. North, in his recent book *The Suffering Servant in Deutero-Isaiah* (1948), holds (rightly, in my judgment) that the servant whose sufferings are portrayed in Isaiah 52 : 13–53 : 12 was from the first intended to be identified with the messianic king of Isaiah 11 : 1–10, who is to spring from the house of David. But this identity was forgotten, and appeared as something new and perplexing when Jesus revived it.

lute monarchs; they ruled as the representatives of God. Each king was the Lord's anointed (the Messiah of Yahweh), deriving his sovereignty from the heavenly King, whose vicegerent he was, and to whom he was responsible for the manner in which he exercised this delegated rule. When the royal house of David fell in 587 B.C., the contemporary prophets Jeremiah and Ezekiel pictured the crown as remaining without a wearer "until he comes whose right it is"[1]—a greater David of the future, one who should be in the fullest sense the anointed one of the God of Israel, and restore and surpass the vanished glories of earlier days.[2]

The national hope takes yet another form in the visions of Daniel, where the promise is given that pagan domination is not to endure for ever; it will pass away and in its place "the God of heaven shall set up a kingdom that shall never be destroyed . . . and it shall last for ever."[3] Although Israel's kings have fallen, Israel's God has not abdicated his sovereignty; pagan emperors like Nebuchadnezzar of Babylon also hold their power by divine permission: "the Most High rules in the kingdom of men and gives it to whomsoever he will."[4] The pagan monarchies are depicted in the guise of wild beasts, but when the eternal kingdom is set up it will be given to "one like a son of man" and its authority will be exercised by the holy ones of the Most High.[5]

The idea of this coming kingdom took a strong hold on the imagination of the Jewish people in the closing centuries B.C., when Babylonian domination had given place to Persian, and Persian to Greco-Macedonian. Their eager expectation was stimulated by the mad attempt made by the Macedonian king of Syria, Antiochus IV, to abolish the Jewish religion. He did succeed in abolishing the temple worship at Jerusalem for three years (167–164 B.C.) and establishing in its place the cult of a pagan deity, Olympian Zeus, which the Jews called "the abomination of desolation."[6] But Judas Maccabæus and his brothers, members of the priestly Hasmonean family, led the nation to arms against the oppressor and secured national independence for a further brief period of eighty years, until the Romans imposed their sovereignty on Palestine in 63 B.C. This period of independence under the native Hasmonean dynasty seemed at first to many to be the dawn of a golden age. But the Hasmoneans proved to be almost as tyrannical as many of their pagan masters had been, and the Roman conquest in some ways brought relief to the pious members of the nation.

---

[1] Ezekiel 21 : 27. [2] Jeremiah 23 : 5; 30 : 9; Ezekiel 34 : 23f.; 37 : 24f.
[3] Daniel 2 : 44. [4] Daniel 4 : 17.
[5] Daniel 7 : 13f., 18, 27. [6] 1 Maccabees 1 : 54. (Cf. p. 102.)

WHEN THE TIME WAS RIPE

The persecution under Antiochus also led the pious people in Israel to attach much more importance to the idea of resurrection. In those days obedience to the law of God no longer guaranteed length of days; it was more likely to bring swift and painful death. The idea of resurrection is not entirely absent from earlier Old Testament writings (Jesus, we remember, found it implied in God's description of Himself as the God of Abraham and Isaac and Jacob),[1] but from this time onwards we find a more continuous and explicit insistence on it. The story of the martyrdom of the seven brothers and their mother in 2 Maccabees 7 makes the nature of this hope abundantly clear. One of the brothers addresses the tyrant: "You, vile wretch, set us free from this present life; but the King of the universe will raise us up to an eternal renewal of life since we have died for His laws." And another brother, holding out his hands to be cut off, says: "From heaven I received these . . . and from heaven I hope to recover them again." So, with reference to these and other martyrs, an early Christian writer says that "they were tortured, not accepting the deliverance [which they could have won by forswearing their religion], in order that they might receive a better resurrection."[2] The resurrection and the advent of the divine kingdom were closely associated in thought henceforth.

This whole complex of ideas was very much in the minds of the Jewish people during the closing decades of the pre-Christian era. We can trace them, for example, in the curious body of literature known as the Book of Enoch, one section of which, written about 100 B.C., presents a majestic being called "the Son of Man," arriving in the full exercise of His messianic glory, to execute judgment and administer universal sovereignty. We can trace them in another form in the days when the Roman conquest had put an end to the brief spell of Jewish independence under the Hasmoneans, in the collection of poems known as the Psalms of Solomon, where all hope is placed in the coming Messiah of David's line who is to put down the oppressors of Israel and restore His people's fortunes.

> He will have the nations to serve him under his yoke,
> And he will glorify the Lord with the praise of all the earth;
> He will purify Jerusalem in holiness, as it was from the beginning,
> That the nations may come from the ends of the earth to see his glory,
> Bearing gifts for her sons that were utterly weakened,
> And to see the glory of the Lord with which God has glorified her;
> And he himself is a righteous king over them, taught by God,

[1] Mark 12 : 26f., alluding to Exodus 3 : 6.
[2] Hebrews 11 : 35.

And there shall be no unrighteousness in their midst all his days,
For all will be holy, and their king is the anointed Lord.[1]

Others saw the only hope of Israel in the conscientious performance of the divine law according to the traditional interpretation
of it which had grown up through successive generations. If all
Israel kept the whole law perfectly for one day only, it was believed, Messiah would come. Some of these banded themselves
together in local fellowship-groups to encourage one another in
the study and practice of God's commandments. Others thought
that this could best be achieved in isolation from their fellow-
Israelites who were not so particular about these things, and so
they withdrew to the wilderness to live under a strict community-
rule and make ready for the new age. Among these were the
sectaries of Qumran of whom we have learned so much lately
through the discovery of the "Dead Sea Scrolls."[2] And yet others
considered that only by their strong right arm could deliverance
come; they were the men of violence who aimed at seizing and
establishing the divine kingdom by force.

All these currents and cross-currents of thought were in the
air. As the last pre-Christian century came to an end and the new
era dawned, there were many in Israel who were looking for the
kingdom of God, the consolation of Israel, the redemption of
Jerusalem, to use the various phrases in which the nation's hope
was expressed. We can appreciate, therefore, the excitement
which ran through the country in the fifteenth year of the
Emperor Tiberius,[3] when the prophetic figure of John the Baptist
appeared suddenly in the Jordan valley, proclaiming the urgent
necessity of repentance in view of the near approach of "The
Coming One." The race of prophets had been extinct for four
hundred years, but here was a man with all the marks of the
prophets of olden time, whose words carried a rare note of
conviction and authority.

Not only did John call the people to repentance, but he insisted
that those who paid heed to his words should give evidence of
their repentance by submitting to a rite of baptism which he
administered in the river. To those who knew the sacred writings,
this baptism may have recalled certain prophecies of the new age,
when "a fountain shall be opened to the house of David and to
the inhabitants of Jerusalem for sin and for uncleanness,"[4] and
God would sprinkle clean water upon them and they would be

---

[1] Psalms of Solomon 17 : 32–36. The last words, "the anointed Lord" (Greek
christos kyrios) are the same as those spoken by the angel to the shepherds near
Bethlehem in the well-known nativity story: "a Saviour, who is *Christ the Lord*"
(Luke 2 : 11).

[2] See my *Second Thoughts on the Dead Sea Scrolls* (1956), pp. 99ff.

[3] About A.D. 28.

[4] Zechariah 13 : 1.

clean.[1] But others no doubt saw a further significance in John's baptism. Gentiles who were admitted to the Jewish nation as proselytes had, among other things, to undergo a purificatory baptism. But why should true-born Jews have to be baptized? Because, John insisted, ordinary birth was in itself of little account. It was no use to say "Abraham is our father," as if that made any difference. If God were so disposed, He could turn the very stones of the ground into children of Abraham. A new beginning must be made. John does not seem to have talked about a *new birth*, but the idea is implicit in his action and words. And there was no time to lose, he urged; he himself was simply there to prepare the way for the Coming One, who would make a clean sweep of everything in the nation that was false and unworthy, just as the farmer with the winnowing fan separates the chaff from the wheat on his threshing-floor, storing the wheat in his barn and making a bonfire of the chaff. They must therefore make sure that they belonged to the wheat and not to the chaff, for the winnowing was to start very soon.

John's period of prophetic activity was intense but short. After a few months he fell foul of Herod Antipas, who ruled Galilee and Southern Transjordan from 4 B.C. to A.D. 39. Herod Antipas was a son of Herod the Great, who had reigned over all Palestine as Rome's vassal from 37 to 4 B.C. When Herod the Great died (a year or two after the birth of Jesus) his kingdom was divided by the Emperor Augustus between his sons, of whom Antipas was one. Antipas, no doubt, felt concern over John's activity on political grounds. When a man began to attract great crowds of people, he might very well start an insurrection. Others had done that very thing in recent times. John might do it, too, and Antipas would be responsible to Rome for not maintaining proper order in his realm. On the other hand, John was popular; he was widely venerated as a prophet. Antipas had to be cautious, because a rash step against John might precipitate the very insurrection he was anxious to prevent. But he soon had more particular grounds for coercing John. Some years earlier Antipas had fallen in love with his sister-in-law Herodias, for whose sake he had divorced his wife, the daughter of the king of Nabatæan Arabia, lying east of Syria and Transjordan. This example of profligacy in high places demanded prophetic denunciation, and John publicly rebuked the noble pair for their illicit union. This aroused the anger of Herodias even more than of Antipas, and John was arrested and imprisoned in the grim Transjordanian fortress of Machærus. There he lay for some months, after which he was put to death.

His death filled many with horror, and when Antipas was worsted in battle a few years later by his indignant ex-father-in-

[1] Ezekiel 36 : 25.

law, they nodded their heads and said that this was obviously a divine judgment on him for his treatment of John.[1]

But John's imprisonment and death did not mean the end of his work. He had made better preparation than perhaps he realized for the work of the Coming One. For it was after John was thrown into prison that Jesus came into Galilee, announcing good news from God: "The appointed time has now fully come, and the kingdom of God has drawn near: repent, and believe in the good news."[2]

[1] The information given in the New Testament about John is supplemented by the first century Jewish historian Josephus in his *Jewish Antiquities*, XVIII, 5, 2.

[2] Mark 1 : 14f.

CHAPTER III

A LIGHT FOR THE NATIONS

THE LATE DR. W. R. INGE, DEAN OF ST. PAUL'S, LONDON, WAS once invited to write a Life of Christ for a series of handbooks published by a well-known firm, and sent his answer on a post card to this effect: "As there are no materials for a life of Christ, I regret that I cannot comply with your request."[1]

His reply was perhaps not so paradoxical as might appear at first sight. The life of Christ lasted for well over thirty years, but apart from the birth narratives in the gospels of Matthew and Luke, and Luke's account of the visit which He paid to the temple in Jerusalem at the age of twelve, the New Testament gives us no details of His life outside the last two or three years, and even in them the incidents recorded would not cover more than about forty days. For the last week, it is true, and especially for the two days preceding His death, the narratives are quite full; but if we were asked to write a biography of any other figure of history with no more materials than these, we might well reply with Dean Inge's negative terseness.

The four Evangelists, in fact, were not biographers. Yet many readers of their works feel that they know Christ very well as a result of their reading. And they are justified in so feeling, for although the Evangelists do not provide us with a biography of Christ in the ordinary sense of the word, they do present us with a vivid and unforgettable picture of Him, to which each of the four contributes distinctive features. And this picture is not seen so well by reading a harmony in which all four gospels are combined to form one continuous story,[2] as by reading the gospels separately and allowing each of the four to make its own special contribution to the composite picture of Jesus which they unite to portray.

Yet the scarcity of the material has not deterred people less cautious than Dr. Inge from writing Lives of Jesus. The frequency with which these come from the press proves, firstly, how unsatisfying each such attempt is, and, secondly, how perennially

[1] Douglas Jerrold, *Georgian Adventure* (1937), p. 309. A similar story was told by Dean Inge himself in the *Evening Standard* of August 14th, 1944.
[2] The earliest harmony of this kind, called the *Diatessaron* (a musical term meaning "harmony of four"), was compiled by an Assyrian Christian named Tatian about A.D. 170. See pp. 285f.

B

fascinating a subject the life of Jesus is. But in the end these books very often tell us more about their authors than about Jesus: as Professor T. W. Manson puts it, "By their Lives of Jesus ye shall know them."[1]

Although biographical materials are so scanty, however, we should not despair of ever knowing anything about Jesus. There have in recent years been signs of an unwarranted pessimism in this regard, and that not so much on the part of people called modernists as in some representatives of neo-orthodoxy. Here are some expressions of this pessimism: first, a couple from the Marburg scholar, Rudolf Bultmann:

> One thing we must admittedly forego: the character of Jesus, the clear picture of his personality and his life is for us no longer recognizable. But that which is more important is, or is becoming, ever more clearly recognizable—the content of his message.[2]

And again:

> I do indeed think that we can now know almost nothing concerning the life and personality of Jesus, since the early Christian sources show no interest in either, are moreover fragmentary and often legendary; and other sources about Jesus do not exist.[3]

And here is Professor R. H. Lightfoot, concluding his Bampton Lectures at Oxford in 1934:

> It seems, then, that the form of the earthly no less than of the heavenly Christ is for the most part hidden from us. For all the inestimable value of the gospels, they yield us little more than a whisper of his voice; we trace in them but the outskirts of his ways.[4]

In a book published fifteen years later than his Bampton Lectures—*The Gospel Message of St. Mark* (1950)—Professor Lightfoot reached more positive conclusions, and protested against the widespread misunderstanding of the words just quoted: the allusion which they contain to Job 26 : 14, he said, ought to have shown that he was concerned to contrast the relatively small knowledge available to men with the boundless immensity which lies beyond their grasp (p. 103). But, taking the words as the expression of a viewpoint held by many theologians today, we

---

[1] *The Interpretation of the Bible* (ed. C. W. Dugmore, 1944), p. 92.

[2] *Erforschung der synoptischen Evangelien* (1930), pp. 32f.

[3] *Jesus and the Word* (1935), p. 8. See N. B. Stonehouse, "Rudolf Bultmann's Jesus," in *Paul before the Areopagus and other NT Studies* (1957), pp. 109ff.

[4] *History and Interpretation in the Gospels* (1935), p. 225. It is interesting to find an uncompromising "modernist" like the late C. J. Cadoux comment: "I am not prepared to admit that the Gospels show us but the outskirts of Jesus' ways and enable us to hear little more than a whisper of his voice. And I submit that the general and undesigned coherence of the resultant story constitutes a powerful confirmation of the general soundness of the method that has been followed. . . . That the facts are unascertainable. . . . I roundly deny—and I deny it on historical grounds, which any investigator can test for himself" (*Life of Jesus* [Pelican Books, 1948], pp. 209, 211). Compare his larger book, *The Historic Mission of Jesus* (1941), pp. 10f.

may well ask whose form it is that we discern so clearly and compellingly in the gospels, if it be neither the earthly nor the heavenly Christ. The answer given by some is that it is the Christ of the faith of the early Church. So it is, of course; but the Christ of the faith of the early Church was not created by that faith (in spite of all that we have been told about a "creative community"): a church which by its faith could create the Christ of the gospels would be a greater and more inexplicable miracle than that which our earliest Christian records set before us—a church brought into being by the Christ whom the gospels portray. There is no vacuum between the story of Jesus and the story of the early church: the original members of this new society were men who had known Jesus and spent much time in His company. If some theories of the rise of Christianity which are proffered to us nowadays are true, then the personal disciples of Jesus "must have been translated to heaven immediately after the Resurrection,"[1] so complete is the break which they postulate between Jesus and the Church. No such break is indicated by the only records of those days which have been preserved to us.

These records are based on the Christian message as it was proclaimed by the disciples of Jesus in the years following A.D. 30. Only when the generation which had actually seen and known Jesus was about to pass away did the need for written reports of that message begin to be felt. Our gospels are the transcript of the apostles' preaching and teaching.[2] And that is why they are not biographies, for the primitive Christian message was not concerned with the biographical interest of Jesus' life, but with certain outstanding events through which the salvation of God was made available to men and women.

Some writers make up for the lack of detailed information about the first thirty years of the life of Jesus by imaginative reconstruction. This kind of reconstruction has a very ancient lineage: the earliest examples of it are the apocryphal gospels.[3] A few reasonable inferences may be drawn from *obiter dicta* in the New Testament narrative. We gather, for example, that He was brought up with four brothers and some sisters, and that probably when Joseph died Jesus took his place as the family breadwinner: "Is this not the carpenter?" people asked.[4] He lived the life of a pious Jew, attending the synagogue regularly on the sabbath day, as Luke assures us His custom was.[5]

Or we can set those years against their historical background.

[1] Vincent Taylor, *The Formation of the Gospel Tradition* (1935), p. 41.
[2] See C. H. Dodd, *The Apostolic Preaching and its Developments* (1936); *History and the Gospel* (1938).
[3] These may be most conveniently consulted in M. R. James's *Apocryphal New Testament* (1924), pp. 1ff.
[4] Mark 6 : 3.   [5] Luke 4 : 16.

A child born in Palestine in the closing years of the reign of Herod the Great did not grow up amid such scenes of peace as are pictured in Milton's *Ode on the Morning of Christ's Nativity*. The land was seething with discontent; the death of Herod in 4 B.C. was the signal for "myriads of troubles," Josephus tells us,[1] in both Judæa and Galilee, and these were ruthlessly quelled by the Romans. Nine years later took place the insurrection led by Judas of Galilee "in the days of the enrolment."[2] This too was crushed in blood, but the fires of revolt were only banked up, ever threatening to break forth, until they blazed up at last in the Jewish War of A.D. 66–70, which brought about the destruction of Jerusalem and its temple. Nazareth, the home town of Jesus, was no remote village, but a city overlooking the main highway from Egypt to Syria. Along this road passed the Roman armies as they went about their various duties, including the punitive suppression of this or that revolt. When Jesus talked to His disciples about taking up their cross, He did not use the expression metaphorically as we do nowadays. The cross was too familiar a reality in Palestine in those days to be referred to in any other than a grimly literal way. When Quintilius Varus, governor of Syria, put down a revolt in Judæa in 4 B.C., he crucified two thousand people.[3] And the rising of Judas the Galilæan took place about the time when Jesus, as a boy of twelve, paid His visit to Jerusalem. The whole point of this rising was the burning question. "Is it right to pay tribute to Cæsar or not? Shall we give, or shall we not give?" "No!" said Judas and his followers, who developed into the party of the Zealots, "we have no king but God!"—and the popular sympathy was with Judas, although few joined in open revolt. So it was no academic question that was presented to Jesus when this matter of paying tribute was submitted to Him; the dilemma with which He was confronted was a very practical one. If He said that tribute should be paid to Cæsar, He would forfeit the people's good will; if He said it should not be paid, He could be denounced to the Roman governor.

The chief priests at Jerusalem did their best to maintain relations of mutual toleration with the Roman power. This they were able to do in large measure by their wealth. Caiaphas, in particular, succeeded in remaining in office for eighteen years, during the last ten of which Pilate was procurator of Judæa. It looks very much as if these two had established a *modus vivendi*.

The party of the Sadducees, to which the chief priests belonged, dominated the Sanhedrin, the supreme Jewish court. But the party of the Pharisees, who were in a minority in the Sanhedrin,

---

[1] *Antiquities* XVII, 10 : 4.
[2] Acts 5 : 37; Josephus, *Jewish War*, II, 8 : 1; *Antiquities*, XVIII, 1 : 1.
[3] Josephus, *Antiquities*, XVII, 10 10.

were so influential with the people in general that their views could not be ignored. The party of the Pharisees included most of the "scribes," the popular exponents of the divine law. In those days the scribes were mainly divided into two schools, called after two illustrious rabbis of the previous generation, the "house of Shammai" and the "house of Hillel" respectively. Of these the house of Hillel favoured a more liberal and lenient interpretation of the law than did the house of Shammai. When Jesus emerged from the obscurity of His earlier years He, too, became known as a rabbi, but He could not be accounted for in terms of any known school of His day.

The public life of Jesus began with His baptism. While John the Baptist was proclaiming his message of repentance by the Jordan, Jesus came from Nazareth to be baptized by him. In the light of later developments, we can see in Jesus' desire to be baptized a consciousness of His life-mission and a sense of deliberate identification with His people. The gospel story tells how, as He came out of the water, He was hailed by a heavenly voice[1] which said: "Thou art my Son, my beloved, in thee I am well pleased."[2] The importance of these words for our understanding of Jesus' messianic consciousness and mission cannot be overestimated. A sense of divine vocation and of filial relationship to God may certainly be traced in the reply which He gave to Mary when He was discovered in the temple at the age of twelve;[3] but our entire ignorance of His thought between that time and His baptism precludes us (if we are wise) from making any assertion about His messianic consciousness during those "hidden years." But the heavenly voice which He heard at His baptism brings together two passages of Old Testament scripture—Psalm 2 : 7, "Thou art my Son; (this day have I begotten thee;)" and Isaiah 42 : 1 "(Behold my Servant, whom I uphold;) my chosen one, in whom my soul delights."[4] The heavenly voice attaches the second part of the Isaianic passage to the first clause of the allocution in the Psalm. We know that in the time of Jesus, Psalm 2 was interpreted messianically; it was agreed that the person addressed by God in the words "Thou art my Son" was the coming Messiah of David's line.[5] To Jesus, who knew that He belonged to the

---

[1] This kind of heavenly voice is mentioned in rabbinical writings as the Echo or *Bath Qol*, i.e., "the daughter of the voice [of God]"; it was regarded as a means of conveying the divine will in the days when the prophetic office had ceased.

[2] Mark 1 : 11.

[3] Luke 2 : 49; the words, rendered "wist ye not that I must be about my Father's business?" in our Authorized Version, probably mean "where else would I be than in my Father's house?"

[4] One Greek version of this Isaianic passage, quoted in Matthew 12 : 18, runs: "Behold my Servant whom I have chosen; my beloved, in whom my soul has found delight."

[5] It is so interpreted in the seventeenth "Psalm of Solomon" (c. 50 B.C.). See p. 29.

royal house of David,[1] these words were a divine confirmation of His Messiahship. But the words that followed showed what the character of His Messiahship was to be; they came from the first of the great "Servant songs" of the book of Isaiah, and made it clear that the Messiahship to which Jesus was called in that moment was to be fulfilled in terms of the prophecy of the obedient and suffering Servant who was to be the hope of Israel and the Gentiles alike.[2] At the same time, Mark tells us, "he saw the heavens rent,[3] and the Spirit like a dove coming down upon him."[4] This gives a further point of contact with the passage from Isaiah: the words quoted above from Isaiah 42 : 1 are immediately followed by the clause, "I have put my spirit upon him."

Whether the Isaianic servant of Yahweh had previously been interpreted messianically is uncertain. In the Targums, or Aramaic paraphrases of the Hebrew Bible, which preserve a long-standing oral tradition, although they were not written down (according to the usual account) until some centuries after this time, the passages which speak of the Servant's exaltation are applied to the Messiah, but those which speak of his humiliation are applied to the nation of Israel.[5] There are, however, traces in rabbinical tradition of a messianic interpretation even of the passages which speak of the Servant's suffering; and some have found traces of a similar interpretation in a manuscript of Isaiah from Qumran. But what is of chief importance is the fact that the heavenly voice did identify the Servant with the Messiah of Psalm 2, and that Jesus did consistently understand and interpret and fulfil His messianic role in terms of the Servant prophecy, not excluding those parts of it which describe the Servant's humiliation and death.

If we bear this in mind, we shall not think, as some have done, that Jesus' expectation of suffering and death began at a later period in His ministry. If He did not speak about it to His disciples until their confession of His Messiahship at Cæsarea Philippi showed that they were in some limited degree ready for it, that does not mean that He had not Himself foreseen it long before.

After the baptism He retired to the wilderness of Judæa for

[1] Cf. Romans 1 : 3, a reference independent of the Gospel genealogies.

[2] This is adumbrated in the *Nunc Dimittis* of the aged Simeon who took the child Jesus in his arms; the words "mine eyes have seen thy salvation . . . a light to lighten the Gentiles, and the glory of thy people Israel," echo the Isaianic Servant songs (Luke 2 : 30, 32). Four "Servant songs" are usually distinguished in the book of Isaiah: (*a*) 42 : 1-4; (*b*) 49 : 1-6; (*c*) 50 : 4-9; (*d*) 52 : 13-53 : 12.

[3] A probable allusion to Isaiah 49 : 1: "Oh that thou wouldest rend the heavens, that thou wouldest come down."

[4] Mark 1 : 10.

[5] So also in the Septuagint, the Greek version of the Old Testament produced at Alexandria before the Christian era, Isaiah 42 : 1 is paraphrased: "Jacob my servant, I will support him; Israel my chosen, my soul has accepted him."

some weeks, and there His obedience to the heavenly voice was put to the test. The insistent temptations, with their refrain "If you are the Son of God," refer clearly enough to the messianic salutation "Thou art my Son." Was he to achieve His Messiahship by methods which, however much they chimed in with popular and traditional expectation,[1] fell short of that high vocation to which the heavenly voice pointed? No: God's will had been plainly revealed,[2] and this will He would obey, even if the way of obedience was the way of suffering.

The next months were mostly spent in southern Palestine, in contact with the Baptist and his followers, with occasional visits to Galilee.[3] When the Baptist was imprisoned, in the autumn of A.D. 28, Jesus went north to Galilee and commenced His public ministry in that region. He now called into His company some young Galilæans whom He had met by the banks of Jordan as disciples of John; these formed the nucleus of His twelve apostles. As the apostolic company was increased, it included some remarkable contrasts. The inclusion of a man who collected taxes for the Roman overlords or for their vassal Herod Antipas gave occasion for unfavourable comment. The inclusion of a Zealot, one of those who sought to hasten the divine kingdom by violence and gave no quarter to the Romans or their creatures, is equally noteworthy. Matthew's inclusion must have called for a good deal of forbearance on the part of the fishermen in the company (as Dr. Christie remarked, "if ever cursing was justified it was when such as Peter the fisherman cursed Matthew the publican"[4]); but that the same company should have been able to contain both Matthew the tax-collector and Simon the Zealot was a miracle. Of the twelve only one, Judas the man of Kerioth,[5] appears to have been a Judæan.

The earliest period of Jesus' Galilæan ministry, as He went round the countryside proclaiming the arrival of the appointed time and the messianic age, healing the sick and relieving the demon-possessed, was marked by great popular enthusiasm. The

[1] For example, the temptation to leap down from the pinnacle of the temple has been compared with a passage in a rabbinical commentary or *midrash* which says: "When King Messiah is revealed he comes and stands upon the roof of the holy place; then will he announce to the Israelites and say 'Ye poor, the time of your redemption is come' " (*Pesiqta Rabbati*, 162a).

[2] Not only by means of the heavenly voice and the body of prophecy lying behind it, but also in the Old Testament writings in general, as witness the passages from the book of Deuteronomy with which Jesus rebutted the temptations.

[3] For this earlier period we have a valuable source of information in the earlier chapters of the fourth Gospel, which deal with a time when "John was not yet cast into prison" (John 3 : 24).

[4] W. M. Christie, *Palestine Calling* (1939), p. 39.

[5] Iscariot (Greek *Iskariotes*) probably represents Hebrew *Ish-Kerioth* "the man of Kerioth," a place in the south of Judæa (cf. Joshua 15 : 25). Codex Sinaiticus in John 6 : 71, and Codex Bezæ everywhere in the fourth Gospel, have *apo Karyotou* ("from Kerioth") in place of *Iskariotes*.

synagogues of the district round the Sea of Galilee were open to Him, and people listened eagerly to His teaching.

The teaching of Jesus was accompanied by "mighty works," as they are called in the gospels—works not to be explained in terms of known natural laws. The presence of these works in the record is a stumbling-block to many readers. Dr. Klausner looks forward to the day when Jesus' ethical code will be "stripped of its wrappings of miracles and mysticism" and "the Book of the Ethics of Jesus will be one of the choicest treasures in the literature of Israel for all time."[1] Dr. Klausner is a Jewish scholar; but there are Christians who share his desire to free the record of the teaching of Jesus from these "accretions" which prevent people from appreciating as they should the beauty of His words. Something of His ministry of healing may be allowed to remain, but even that, they hold, has been exaggerated.

We must not, however, judge the testimony of the first-century Christian records by our preferences. In the eyes of Jesus' contemporaries, His works attested the authority of His teaching. "What is this?" they asked as He began His ministry in Capernaum. "A new teaching, with authority! He even commands the demons and they obey Him."[2] The mighty works are not just miracles for miracles' sake; they are signs of the presence of the divine kingdom, the evidence that the powers of the age to come are now at work in the world. The demon-possession which forms so prominent a feature of the gospel narrative is particularly rife because the kingdom of evil realizes that the advent of the divine kingdom confronts it with a mortal threat which it must muster all its powers to resist.[3] Those who knew the writings of the prophets could recognize in the works of Jesus the things that the prophets had foretold of the messianic age.

So the earliest proclamation of the good news after the death of Jesus described Him as "a man accredited by God among you by mighty works and wonders and signs which God wrought through him, as you yourselves know full well"—the followers of Jesus were not inventing these accounts; they knew that their hearers were perfectly conversant with the sort of thing that Jesus did. Those who declined to accept the messianic claims of Jesus did not deny His miracles; the facts were too well known. They were wrought by superhuman power, to be sure; but while His disciples and many others regarded them as manifestations of the divine activity, His theologically-minded opponents ascribed

---

[1] J. Klausner, *Jesus of Nazareth* (1929), p. 414.
[2] Mark 1 : 27.
[3] On the subject of demon-possession see J. L. Nevius, *Demon Possession and Other Themes* (1897); W. M. Alexander, M.D., *Demonic Possession in the New Testament* (1902); A. R. Short, M.D., F.R.C.S., *Modern Discovery and the Bible* (1943), pp. 89ff.; *The Bible and Modern Medicine* (1953), pp. 109ff.

them to the power of Baal-Zebul, lord of the demons.[1] In later Jewish controversy with Christians, the same position is maintained. It does not meet the Christian appeal to the evidential quality of the miracles of Jesus by denying that they ever took place but by arguing that they were performed by sorcery.[2] Sorcery is also the explanation given by Celsus, a philosophic critic of Christianity in the second century.[3]

As late as A.D. 133 a Christian apologist named Quadratus, writing a defence of Christianity to the Emperor Hadrian, could refer to the miracles of Jesus as facts which the opponents of Christianity did not dispute, and mentioned that some of the people whom Jesus had raised from the dead had lived on until his own day.[4]

The miracles of Jesus recorded by the canonical gospels are not haphazard events. As distinct from the miracles described in the apocryphal gospels, they are "in character"; they are all of a piece with the rest of the life and work of Jesus.[5] This is because the canonical gospels, unlike the others, are the written deposit of the apostolic witness to Jesus. The miracle-stories formed an integral part of the primitive Christian message. When Peter on the day of Pentecost referred to the mighty works by which God had accredited the mission of Jesus,[6] or later in the house of Cornelius described how He "went about doing good and healing all who were under the domination of the devil,"[7] the sort of miracles which the gospels record would have been exactly the sort which he might relate to illustrate his statements.[8]

As Jesus continued His work, misgivings began to arise. The common people heard Him gladly, but others began to feel uneasy about His failure to conform to the accepted standards of rabbinical practice and precept. The company that He kept at times was particularly shocking; He seemed to have no objection to consorting with outrageous offenders against the current social and moral codes. And there was something about His teaching that was quite disturbing to the exponents of the traditional law.

---

[1] Baal-Zebul was an ancient Canaanite deity, mentioned in the Ras Shamra tablets (fifteenth century B.C.); his name meant originally "lord of the high place." The form Baal-Zebub (or Beelzebub), "lord of flies," may have been intended as a derogatory pun.

[2] See Klausner, op. cit., pp. 18ff., for rabbinical references.

[3] Origen, Against Celsus, I, 38; II, 48.

[4] Eusebius, Ecclesiastical History, IV, 3.

[5] On the acted parable of the barren fig tree, which has been thought an exception, see my Are the NT Documents Reliable? (1950), pp. 72f.

[6] Acts 2 : 22.

[7] Acts 10 : 38.

[8] On the question of the Gospel miracles the two most illuminating books I know are D. S. Cairns, The Faith that Rebels (1929), and Alan Richardson, The Miracle-Stories of the Gospels (1941). Nor, of course, should Miracles, by C. S. Lewis (1947), remain unmentioned.

"He taught as one having authority, and not as the scribes";[1] instead of quoting venerated precedents, He set them aside in favour of His own interpretations: "You have heard that it was said to them of old time . . . but *I* say unto you[2] . . ."

The two chief rabbinical schools of the day, we have said, were those of Hillel and Shammai. Many stories were related to illustrate the differing viewpoints of these two great rabbis. The most famous is the story of the would-be proselyte who went to Shammai and invited him to summarize the whole law while the inquirer stood on one leg. The severe Shammai drove the man away indignantly. But when he approached the milder Hillel with the same request, he received the answer: "What is hateful to yourself, do not to your neighbour. That is the whole law; everything else is a commentary on that; go and learn it."[3]

It is natural that the teaching of Jesus should be compared with what has been preserved of the teaching of Shammai and Hillel. Hillel's summary of the law, of course, reminds us at once of the Golden Rule enunciated by Jesus.[4] And in general, as we might expect, Jesus' teaching has more parallels with the teaching of the liberal Hillel than with Shammai's. The school of Shammai was probably dominant among the Pharisees in the days of Jesus, and we think naturally of its adherents when we read Jesus' denunciations of those who laid heavy burdens on men's shoulders without moving a finger themselves to lighten the load.[5]

But we should not press too close a parallel between Jesus and Hillel. In one point, indeed, Jesus agreed with Shammai more than with Hillel. Hillel made divorce easy; Shammai made it difficult; Jesus probably forbade it altogether.[6]

But the very reason for which Jesus probably forbade divorce illustrates the basic principle of all His teaching. The law of Moses, admittedly, authorized divorce. This, said Jesus, was a concession to the hardness of men's hearts. He did not blame Moses for making the concession; Moses had to legislate for the situation with which he was faced. But it was not God's ideal, and

---

[1] Mark 1 : 22.

[2] Matthew 5 : 21, 27, 31, 33, 38, 43.

[3] Babylonian Talmud, tractate *Shabbath*, 31a. It has often been pointed out that Hillel's Golden Rule is negative, while that of Jesus is positive. The Jewish writer Ahad Ha-Am made much of this, insisting that the positive form was alien to the true spirit of Judaism (*Essays in Zionism and Judaism* [1922], p. 235). But in point of fact the positive form is found in Maimonides, while the negative form is found in the "western" text of Acts 15 : 20, 29, and in the early second-century *Teaching of the Twelve Apostles*, I, 2.

[4] "Whatever you wish that men would do to you, do so to them; for this is the law and the prophets" (Matthew 7 : 12).

[5] See p. 73, n. 3, below.

[6] Mark 10 : 11f.; Luke 16 : 18. The "excepting clauses" in Matthew 5 : 32; 19 : 9 which appear to make fornication the one ground for divorce, may well use that word (Greek *porneia*) to denote marital relations within forbidden degrees; cf. p. 110 below.

nothing less than God's ideal was good enough for Jesus' followers, the citizens of the new kingdom. What God's ideal was might be discovered by going back to first principles and finding out what God intended when He instituted marriage. That was made plain by the Genesis narrative which told how He who made them in the beginning made them male and female, so that man and wife become "one flesh." Moreover, the Jewish law of divorce was weighted to the disadvantage of the wife, who could not divorce her husband, although he might put her away for a variety of reasons, against which she had no effective right of appeal. Jesus' pronouncement may thus be viewed, in addition, as a characteristic instance of His defence of the under-privileged.

The accumulated interpretation of centuries—the oral law, the "tradition of the elders"—Jesus swept aside as obscuring the original purpose of God in giving instruction to His people. His whole approach was poles apart from the casuistical approach of the rabbis. This was so, pre-eminently, with His attitude to the sabbath law.

When Jesus first healed a man in the Capernaum synagogue on the sabbath day, any questionings which might have arisen were swallowed up in amazement at His power; but as in one way and another He disregarded the traditional conventions of sabbath observance, opposition from the custodians of the traditional law began to develop. The rabbinical practice of surrounding the written precepts of the Mosaic law by a "hedge" of detailed interpretation was not in all respects a bad thing—certainly not in so far as it was designed to adapt these precepts to a changing manner of life. But there was a tendency to interpret the written and oral regulations woodenly, and to regard the tithing of mint and anise and cummin as being (in practice) of equal importance with the great requirements of justice and mercy. A rabbi of a later date gave the advice to pay as much attention to a "light" precept as to a "heavy" one, "for thou knowest not the recompense of reward for each precept."[1] Jesus, on the other hand, viewed the regulation in the light of the purpose which it was intended to serve, and had no scruples in disregarding it if its observance would not promote or would actually hinder that purpose. As for the sabbath law, "the sabbath was made for man, and not man for the sabbath"[2] and therefore the healing of a sick person on that day was perfectly justifiable, even if the healing could safely have been postponed to the next day. The same principle applied to the disciples' plucking and rubbing the ears of corn, actions which

---

[1] *Pirqe Aboth*, II, 1. *Pirqe Aboth* ("Sections of the Fathers") is a tractate of the Mishnah, a collection of maxims ascribed to various rabbis between the third century B.C. and the third century A.D.
[2] Mark 2 : 27.

were criticized as being species of reaping and grinding. It had not been to prevent that sort of thing that God commanded His people to keep the sabbath day holy.

The cleavage which began over the sabbath question was widened when Jesus was heard assuring people that their sins were forgiven. That God could and did freely forgive the repentant was acknowledged; Jesus was criticized because, as Montefiore put it, "he claimed to himself the exclusive prerogative of God."[1] In this as in His interpretation of the sabbath law He was tacitly making messianic claims for Himself. "The Son of man is lord of the sabbath";[2] and the Son of man, divinely ordained to execute judgment, must as a corollary have the authority to pronounce acquittal.[3] There is a messianic ring, too, about the rejoinder which He made to those who complained about his disciples' neglect of religious fasting. "Can the wedding guests fast," He asked, "so long as they have the bridegroom with them?"[4]

Before long, the fame of Jesus went out far beyond Galilee, and a delegation of scribal experts from Jerusalem came to observe His activities. Their opposition speedily became sharper than that of the Galilæan rabbis. In disputation with them, Jesus broke with another traditional set of rules when He laid down the principle that all kinds of food were clean in themselves.[5] And He emphasized the breach by applying to His opponents the words of God in Isaiah 29 : 13: "In vain do they worship me, teaching as their doctrines the precepts of men."

The scribal party, on their side, made the breach with Jesus final by attributing His demon-expelling power to the aid of the lord of the demons. "How can Satan cast out Satan?" asked Jesus; and He added His solemn warning about the sin against the Holy Spirit—that deliberate closing of their eyes to the light by ascribing the work of God to the power of Satan, which by its very nature is irremediable.

Now that the breach with the scribal party was complete, Jesus could no longer count upon a platform for His teaching in the synagogue, but must avail Himself of the mountain slope and the lakeside, where the people still flocked to hear Him.

About this time He sent out His twelve closest disciples—His

[1] C. G. Montefiore, *The Synoptic Gospels* (1927), I, p. 78.
[2] Mark 2 : 28.
[3] Daniel 7 : 13f. (cf. 1 Enoch 69 : 27: "And he sat on the throne of his glory and the sum of judgment was given unto the son of man"); Mark 2 : 10.
[4] Mark 2 : 19.
[5] Mark 7 : 19: "This he said, making all meats clean." In view of the tradition, well attested externally and internally, which makes Mark's Gospel depend on Peter's preaching, we may see in these words the comment of Peter on the teaching of Jesus in this context, not properly understood by Peter himself until his experience on the housetop in Joppa recorded in Acts 10 : 9ff.

apostles or "emissaries"—two by two to carry His message farther afield throughout Jewish Palestine, and the proclamation of the kingdom was accompanied in their case as in His by the exorcizing of demons and the healing of the sick. During this mission Herod Antipas began to take a keen interest in Jesus. John the Baptist, whom he had lately ordered to be beheaded, had surely (he thought) come to life again in this new teacher. So, when the apostles returned, Jesus took them apart to an unfrequented spot on the shores of the Sea of Galilee, but even there the crowds followed Him, and after He had fed them with loaves and fishes they attempted to crown Him king by force. They had to be positively discouraged by "hard sayings," showing something of the true nature of Jesus' kingship. So "hard" did these sayings prove that, as John the Evangelist tells us, "from that time many of His disciples turned back, and walked no more with Him."[1]

It was now April in A.D. 29. Six months of public ministry in Galilee had gone by,[2] and a period of more private and intensive instruction for his disciples was necessary, to prepare them for what lay ahead. For this they must go away where they could have adequate freedom from distraction, so, leaving Palestine, they walked northward in the direction of the Phœnician territory and back by way of Cæsarea Philippi (the modern Banias), near the source of the Jordan, the capital of the principality of Philip, another son of Herod the Great. It was at Cæsarea Philippi that Peter, acting as spokesman for the others, declared that Jesus was the Messiah. A year and more had gone by since Andrew, by the banks of the Jordan, had run to find his brother Simon and bring him to Jesus saying "We have found the Messiah."[3] But then, they were relying on the testimony of John the Baptist; now, as Jesus said, it was no human being but God himself who had revealed the truth to Peter. That they should have this deepened conviction of His Messiahship, in spite of the many ways in which He disappointed popular expectation, was to Jesus a cause of joyful thanksgiving.

And now He went on to tell them things about His messianic mission that they had never dreamed of—the suffering and rejection, the dying and rising again. In the light of all this, following Him as disciples was a much graver matter than they had previously realized. He would not have them follow Him under a misapprehension: "if any man wishes to come after me, he must deny himself—renounce all personal hopes and ambitions—and

---

[1] John 6 : 6off.
[2] On the chronological questions, *The Chronology of the Public Ministry of Jesus*, by Dr. George Ogg (1940), may be consulted with profit.
[3] John 1 : 41.

take up his cross and follow me." And as we have seen, when He said "take up his cross" He was not speaking figuratively. The followers of a man who had set out on the road to a cross could expect no other goal for themselves. But the prediction of suffering and death was balanced by a vision in advance of the glory that was to follow, when on the mount of transfiguration three of the apostles beheld "the kingdom of God come with power."[1]

Now the Feast of Tabernacles of the autumn of A.D. 29 drew on, and Jesus went up to Jerusalem—not publicly, with the pilgrim crowds, but privately, when the feast had already begun. He preached to the festal crowds in the temple courts, and stayed in the vicinity until December, when at the Feast of Dedication[2] He renewed his public exhortation. His scribal opponents charged Him with blasphemy "because," said they, "you, a mere man, give yourself out to be God."[3] An attempt to arrest Him was unsuccessful, for He left Jerusalem and spent a few months in retreat with His disciples near the place where John the Baptist had formerly baptized. But the decisive clash was not to be long delayed.

[1] Mark 9 : 1; it is no accident that this verse introduces the transfiguration story. See A. M. Ramsey, *The Glory of God and the Transfiguration of Christ* (1949), pp. 101ff.
[2] The Feast of Dedication (*Chanukkah*) celebrates the rededicating of the Jerusalem temple in 164 B.C. after its desecration by Antiochus Epiphanes.
[3] John 10 : 33. In the "Synoptic" record, too, He insists that men will be judged at the last by their response to Him and His teaching (cf. Mark 8 : 38; Matthew 7 : 21ff.; 10 : 32f., etc.).

CHAPTER IV

THE LIGHT SHINES IN THE DARKNESS

ARCHBISHOP WILLIAM TEMPLE ONCE REMARKED: "WHY ANYONE should have troubled to crucify the Christ of Liberal Protestantism has always been a mystery."[1] This may be doubted. The Christ of liberal Protestantism, the teacher of a purer ethical monotheism than any hitherto known, the preacher of the divine Fatherhood, the author of the Sermon on the Mount, the cleanser of the temple, must have been quite a difficult person for the authorities to tolerate, especially the sacerdotal authorities. We may counter Dr. Temple's epigram with one from Dr. Inge, equally exaggerated in its own way: "A priest is never so happy as when he has a prophet to stone."[2] But Dr. Temple was right to this extent, that it was not chiefly those elements in the gospel portrait of Jesus which appealed to liberal Protestantism that made the cross inevitable.

The Jesus of the thorough-going eschatologists, finding that the divine kingdom did not come when He expected its arrival, determined to force the pace of time, threw Himself upon the wheel of history and was broken on it.[3] He went out of His way to confront the authorities with a challenge that could not be ignored, in order to compel the divine intervention. But there was no intervention, and He died on the cross, crying out that God had forsaken Him. Out of His failure, indeed, came a triumph that He could never have dreamed of, but no such hope brightened His last hours.

The Jesus of the revolutionary theorists[4] met His death in conflict with the Roman occupation forces and the quisling Sadducees. His followers did their best to support His cause with armed force, but were overwhelmed and scattered. But if one thing stands out clearly in the gospel narrative, it is that many who had once placed their hopes in Jesus as their liberator from the alien

---

[1] *Readings in St. John's Gospel* (1940), p. 24.

[2] W. R. Inge, *Things New and Old* (1933), p. 48.

[3] Compare the memorable account in A. Schweitzer, *Quest of the Historical Jesus* (1911), pp. 368f.

[4] Compare such a reconstruction as that monument of perverse ingenuity, Robert Eisler's *The Messiah Jesus and John the Baptist* (1931). A very different type of book, written from a generally orthodox viewpoint, but emphasizing the element of political revolution, is Conrad Noel's *Life of Jesus* (1937). A marxist interpretation was presented by Karl Kautsky in his *Foundations of Christianity* (1925).

yoke were disillusioned because this was the very thing that He refused to do. He deliberately renounced the way of force and chose the way of obedience and suffering. Barabbas proved more popular than Jesus simply because Barabbas was the sort of man the crowd wanted—a man who was ready to engage in violent insurrection for the national cause.

Jesus was all that the liberal Protestants have claimed for Him, but He was more. He did envisage the advent of the divine kingdom, as the consistent eschatologists claim, and regarded Himself as the Son of man ordained to inaugurate that kingdom, but He had no thought of forcing the hand of God. He had freely chosen the path that inevitably led to the cross, because that path was the Father's will for Him, and only by the suffering of death could He bring in the kingdom in its fulness and make its blessings available to men. And while He renounced the political and military ideal, He did, when occasion required, agree that He was the Messiah, the predestined king and liberator of the people of God, but a Messiah with a difference—a Messiah whose progress to His investiture must be by way of humiliation and death.

Early in A.D. 30 a notable miracle performed by Jesus not far from Jerusalem—the restoration to life of Lazarus of Bethany, a man who had been four days in the grave—caused much excitement in Judæa and grave concern to the Sanhedrin. A meeting of the supreme court was convened to discuss the situation. "Something will have to be done," they said. "This man is doing so many works of this kind that if we let him alone, he will unite the whole nation round himself. We know what the result of that will be. The heavy hand of Rome will come down on the whole nation, and we ourselves shall not escape the general destruction."

The high priest, *ex-officio* president of the Sanhedrin, listened cynically to his colleagues' agitated talk. When they had finished he addressed them concisely and bluntly. Sadducees were noted for their neglect of the formal courtesies,[1] and Caiaphas was no exception. "You don't know what you are talking about," he declared. "You ought to consider an alternative to the destruction of the whole people, which you fear so much. Why should not one man die, rather than let the nation perish?" The suggestion was not lost on the court. The solution to their problem became clear. If the presence of Jesus constituted a threat to all that they counted worthy of survival, then Jesus must die. The question was how best to bring about His death. They must avoid going about the business in such a way as to ensure the very thing they were most anxious to prevent—a rebellion in support of the popular champion. An opportunity must be awaited; if possible, an opportunity must be created.

[1] Cf. Josephus, *Jewish War*, II, 8 : 14.

But for the present Jesus sought the quietness of a remote spot with His disciples, waiting for the coming Passover season. Then, about a week before the sacred festival, they made their way to Jerusalem. In the vicinity of Jericho they fell in with a large body of pilgrims coming from Galilee to keep the Passover in the holy city. These hailed Jesus with enthusiasm, and the enthusiasm increased as they approached their journey's end.

Then, when Jerusalem was but a few miles away, Jesus did a strange thing. He sent two of His followers to borrow an ass from a man in the village of Bethany, in accordance with a pre-arranged plan. They brought the ass to Jesus, and He sat upon it and so rode the remainder of the way to Jerusalem.

Once upon a time the ass had been the beast on which judges and kings rode in Israel. But since Solomon's time the horse had replaced the ass for this purpose. When, however, a prophet of later days drew a picture of the coming king presenting himself to his people, he portrayed him as riding not on a horse but on an ass, like the rulers of Israel in days of greater simplicity.[1]

> Rejoice greatly, O daughter of Zion;
> Shout, O daughter of Jerusalem:
>   Behold, thy king is coming unto thee.
> He is righteous, and brings salvation;
> Lowly, and riding on an ass;
>   Yea, on a colt, the foal of an ass.

Jesus accordingly presented Himself to the people of Jerusalem as their king, and at the same time indicated what manner of king He was: no military conqueror mounted on a war-horse, or drawn in a chariot like an imperial potentate, but Zion's promised Messiah, coming to her in lowliness and peace, bringing her the gift of true liberation, if even at this late hour the opportunity might be seized.

The crowd, however, saw the messianic implication of His action without grasping its real inwardness. They hailed their king with exultation but with little appreciation of the true character of His kingship. So also did the pilgrims who had already reached Jerusalem and now went out at the news of His approach to greet Him and escort Him to the "city of the great king." They saluted Him in words drawn from an ancient processional psalm: "God save the King," they sang; "Blessed is he who comes in the name of the Lord." These were the words with which in days of old a triumphal king was welcomed home. But the king who now came to His own had but little joy in the enthusiasm with which He was greeted. As the procession reached the summit of Mount Olivet and the city lay spread out before their eyes, He wept over it. Had Jerusalem but recognized even

[1] Zechariah 9 : 9.

now the only way of peace, there was still hope for her salvation; but, as it was, that way was ignored. They would not have Him as the only kind of king He was prepared to be, and the alternative to which they shut themselves up was one of violence and ruin, in which city and citizens alike would be overwhelmed.

The leaders of the Sanhedrin, watching the triumphal progress of Jesus to the capital, saw little of the sorrow of the king, but marked the enthusiasm of His retinue. "What's the use?" they asked. "We can do nothing; the whole world is following him." Their determination to take drastic action was renewed the following day when Jesus entered the outermost court of the temple—the Court of the Gentiles—and ejected the vendors of sacrificial animals and those who exchanged other kinds of money for the imageless coinage which alone was acceptable for temple purposes; and forbade the use of the court as a business thoroughfare. His avowed reason for this action was the fact that all the mercantile traffic in this part of the sacred precincts prevented the temple from fulfilling its proper function as "a house of prayer for all the nations."[1] But the authorities were more alarmed than ever. How could they possibly find an opportunity to put Him out of the way?

The opportunity came sooner than they expected.

Two or three days before the Passover Jesus attended a feast at Bethany at which a woman poured over His head a flask of ointment of quite extraordinary value. The extravagance (as it appeared) took people's breath away, and some criticism was voiced. Jesus warmly defended the woman's action. Had she kept the ointment and used it to anoint His dead body at the time of burial, no one would have complained. Why complain, then, when she chose by this means to display her devotion to Him while He was yet alive? When we remember that, according to John, this woman was a sister of Lazarus, whom Jesus had raised from the dead, we can appreciate something of the gratitude that prompted her action. But Jesus saw in her action more than that; it was to Him a symbolic anticipation of His burial anointment, and so fraught with the utmost significance. He himself knew that He would not escape with His life this time, as had happened more than once before; here was one at least whose attitude was in harmony with the thoughts that were uppermost in His mind.

But another member of the supper party reacted very differently. John tells us that the apostle Judas Iscariot was foremost in complaining against the waste of the ointment. But in Judas's eyes it was not simply waste. The woman had deliberately anointed Jesus king—as truly as ever Samuel anointed Saul and David—and Jesus had accepted and defended her tribute.

[1] So Mark 11 : 15ff.

The character of Judas has fascinated many students of the gospel story. Most commonly he has been pictured as a near-zealot, who was disappointed when he saw that Jesus had no intention of establishing His kingdom by violence, and betrayed Him to His enemies either out of resentment or in order to force His hand. But certain aspects of the story give some colour to Miss Sayers' very different portrayal, according to which Judas repudiated the idea of a politico-military Messianism and feared that Jesus had allowed Himself to be carried away by those who wished to use Him for political ends. Whatever the truth may be, Judas made his way to the chief priests and offered to bring Jesus into their power.

The leaders of the Sanhedrin had already come to the conclusion that, while Jesus must be arrested at the earliest opportunity, the Passover season was no time to do it, as the populace would certainly create a riot. But they changed their minds when Judas showed them how to achieve their aim under circumstances which would not involve a popular disturbance. He promised to guide a band of temple police to the secluded spot where he knew Jesus would be found late on the following day.

And so it turned out. On Thursday evening of that week Jesus kept the commemoration feast[1] with His disciples in the house of a friend in Jerusalem. Towards the end of the meal Judas slipped out of the house, not before he had received private but pointed intimation from Jesus that the purpose of his departure was not unknown.

In the conversation that followed Judas's departure, Jesus spoke words calculated to prepare and strengthen His companions for the crisis which was almost upon them. Realizing something of the danger of which He spoke, they declared that they would stand by Him and, if necessary, defend Him with their lives. But He knew how unready they really were to meet the test.

Leaving the house as evening advanced, He went with them to a place on the slope of Olivet remembered ever since as the Garden of Gethsemane. There, withdrawing from the others, He faced in spirit the ordeal that lay before Him and accepted it in its immediate horror, as He had accepted it long ago, as being the

[1] It is highly probable that Jesus and His disciples, in keeping the passover feast, followed a different calendar from that which regulated the temple services; the chief priests ate the passover on *Friday* evening (cf. John 18:28). A strong case, but one that falls short of conviction, has been made for the view that Jesus ate the passover on *Tuesday* evening and was arrested in the early hours of Wednesday morning, although He was not crucified until Friday. This reconstruction resolves the apparent conflict between the Synoptic and Johannine accounts of the earlier events of Holy Week, makes room for all the movements which took place between Jesus' arrest and crucifixion, and allows the legal procedure to conform with the prescriptions of the Mishnah. See A. Jaubert, *The Date of the Last Supper* (Eng. tr. 1965).

Father's will for Him. Rising from prayer, He had barely time to warn His companions when the police, guided by Judas, were upon them. After a brief and ineffectual attempt at resistance, Jesus' companions ran away, and He himself was hurried off to the high priest's palace.

A preliminary inquiry was held in the house of Annas. Annas had been high priest from A.D. 6 to 15. Although he was deposed in the latter year, he continued to enjoy great prestige. He was father-in-law of Caiaphas, who was now high priest, and he was senior ex-high priest. From the house of Annas Jesus was taken to the palace of Caiaphas, where a special session of the Sanhedrin was convened at short notice. It has been held that such a session was illegal, but this is doubtful. Obviously there may be occasions when a court must hold an emergency session; and the view that the Sanhedrin could not legally meet at night is based on the Mishnah tractate *Sanhedrin*,[1] which is an idealized reconstruction of the period before A.D. 70, committed to writing about the year 200. This tractate further informs us that capital cases were tried by twenty-three judges;[2] if this is an accurate account of procedure in the time of Christ, then we need not suppose that all seventy-one members of the Sanhedrin were summoned on this occasion.

The real illegality of the proceedings lay in the fact that the leaders of the Sanhedrin had previously decided that Jesus must die. The unexpected opportunity which Judas supplied made it necessary to convene the emergency court and secure the necessary witnesses in haste. Those witnesses who remembered Jesus' words about destroying the temple and building another in three days told their story so badly and disagreed from each other so much that their evidence could not be admitted. A threat to destroy the temple, had it been substantiated, would indeed have been a charge of the most serious kind. But matters had to be hastened, as certain arrangements had been made for the subsequent ratification of the predetermined sentence. The high priest, therefore, as presiding judge, adopted the dubious expedient of making the accused incriminate Himself. He adjured Him to give a true answer to the question: "Are you the Messiah, the Son of the Blessed One?"

Probably he did not expect the answer which he received. It satisfied him beyond his wildest hopes. "I am," said Jesus; and then went on to say: "And you will see the Son of man sitting at the right hand of the Power, and coming with the clouds of

[1] "In capital cases the trial takes place in daytime and the verdict is given in daytime. . . . In capital cases a verdict of acquittal may be reached the same day, but a verdict of conviction not until the following day. Therefore such a case is not tried on the eve of a sabbath or festival" (Mishnah, *Sanhedrin*, IV, 1).
[2] Mishnah, *Sanhedrin*, IV, 1.

heaven."[1] Here was an explicit claim to be the Messiah who in Psalm 110 : 1 receives an invitation from God to sit at His right hand, and also to be the Son of man who in Daniel 7 : 13f. approaches the throne of God to receive universal and everlasting dominion. The case was clear; the crime was obviously blasphemy; there was nothing for it but the death penalty. So the court agreed.

According to the Mishnah,[2] the crime of blasphemy involves the utterance of the ineffable name of God—the name now believed to have been pronounced Yahweh. But it is not suggested that Jesus did this. We should not press His words "I am" in the sense of a divine title here;[3] they simply indicate an affirmative reply, expressed in Matthew's account by the synonymous phrase "Thou hast said."[4] Jesus, in fact, seems on this occasion to have used the term "The Power" (Hebrew *ha-geburah*) as a surrogate for the divine name, in conformity with current practice.[5] But it is certain that before A.D. 70 blasphemy involved more than the utterance of the ineffable name. The Son of man in Daniel's vision was regarded by some schools of Jewish interpretation as a divine being, the peer of the Most High.[6] The claim to be this Son of man might well be construed as blasphemy. One point does not seem to have been seriously considered—the possibility that Jesus' claim might be well founded. The judges were no doubt quite convinced that it was unfounded, but some of them —and those the most influential—were more interested in finding a legal plea for getting rid of Him than in arriving at the real truth.

Who were these judges? An attempt has been made to distinguish between two Sanhedrins at this time—a political body, dominated by the pro-Roman high-priestly party, and a religious body, controlled by leading rabbis.[7] Now it is plain that the

---

[1] Mark 14 : 62.

[2] "The blasphemer is not guilty until he have expressly uttered the Name. . . . When the trial is over . . . all are sent out of the room except the chief witness, and it is said to him, 'Say expressly what you heard.' He does so, whereupon the judges stand up and rend their clothes" (Mishnah, *Sanhedrin*, VII, 5).

[3] In Exodus 3 : 13ff., where the name *Yahweh* is revealed to Moses, it is associated with the Hebrew verb *ehyeh*, "I am."

[4] Matthew 26 : 64.

[5] "The Blessed One," the expression used by the high priest, was another such surrogate. Compare its later expansion, "The holy one, blessed be He."

[6] In the earliest known Greek version of Daniel 7 : 13, "one like a son of man . . . was present *as an ancient of days*." This is not a translation of the Aramaic original, but an interpretation, and so all the more significant in the light of the present question. (Similarly in Revelation 1 : 13ff., "one like a son of man"— clearly the exalted Jesus—is described in terms of Daniel's vision of the Ancient of Days.) See pp. 265f.

[7] E.g. by the Jewish scholar Adolf Büchler in *Das Synhedrion in Jerusalem* (Vienna, 1902), and more recently by Solomon Zeitlin in *Who Crucified Jesus?* (Philadelphia, 1942), where it is argued that the pro-Roman political Sanhedrin was the only section of the Jewish nation responsible for the execution of Jesus. A thorough examination of Zeitlin's thesis by N. B. Stonehouse appears in *Paul before the Areopagus and Other NT Studies* (1957), pp. 41 ff. The theory of two Sanhedrins is also

Mishnah regards a religious Sanhedrin as existing before A.D. 70, under the presidency of one of the great rabbis of the day.[1] If there were in fact two separate Sanhedrins, then there is no doubt that the political Sanhedrin was the one which sentenced Jesus to death. But we can regard the Mishnaic picture only as the projection back into those earlier years of the new Sanhedrin as reconstituted by Yohanan ben Zakkai after the fall of Jerusalem. The Sanhedrin as it existed before that time is frequently referred to in the New Testament in terms of its constituent elements— chief priests and elders and scribes.

Can we then make any distinction between the various elements in the Sanhedrin in the matter of Jesus' condemnation? According to John, whose narrative here suggests that he had access to reliable inside information, two members of the court, Joseph of Arimathæa and Nicodemus, performed the burial duties for Jesus after His death on the cross. Luke tells us that Joseph had not voted for the condemnation of Jesus, and probably the same is implied by John with regard to Nicodemus. But we cannot be sure if they were present or not at the meeting in the early hours of that fateful morning. Jesus Himself laid the prime guilt at the door of Caiaphas ("he who handed me over to you has the greater sin," he said to Pilate[2]); and Caiaphas himself, we may be sure, would have been quite ready to admit responsibility for an action which, whatever its strict legality, was to his mind in the best interests of church and state. It is conceivable that certain members of the Sanhedrin whose concurrence could not be relied upon did not receive a summons to the emergency session, especially if twenty-three judges sufficed on such an occasion. But while the high-priestly party took the lead in procuring Jesus' condemnation, there is no evidence that such Pharisaic elders as may have been present opposed it. Indeed how could they, without admitting that He was Messiah? When He made His reply to the high priest's adjuration, they must have regarded it as blasphemous and therefore undoubtedly deserving the death penalty—unless they accepted His claim as true. And this they had no thought of doing.

But the high priest's plan was not fully revealed as yet. He could, of course, secure ratification from the Roman governor of a death sentence passed for blasphemy,[3] as Jewish religious law

maintained by J. Z. Lauterbach, in the *Jewish Encyclopædia*; it is opposed by W. Bacher in Hastings' *Dictionary of the Bible*, while Israel Abrahams, in the *Encyclopædia of Religion and Ethics*, gives the arguments for both views without taking sides (art. *Sanhedrin* in all three works).

[1] Mishnah, *Chagigah* II, 2.
[2] John 19 : 11.
[3] Rabbinical tradition agrees with the New Testament (John 18 : 31) that at this time the Sanhedrin had no authority to administer capital punishment (Babylonian Talmud, *Sanhedrin* 41a; Jerusalem Talmud, *Sanhedrin* I, 1; VII, 2).

was protected by the Empire; but the governor was not likely to be pleased at being troubled over a matter that could easily wait. It was necessary to the high priest's plan that the matter should be despatched as speedily as possible. The governor might not be interested in blasphemy, but he could not ignore a charge of insurrection. The air was charged with the spirit of insurrection already; indeed, two or three leaders of a recent outbreak were due for execution that day. Even if it was a public festival, the public execution would do no harm, the Romans considered; it would serve as a grim warning to the thronging crowds of pilgrims, just in case they might have ideas of staging a riot, as could always happen when so many of them were together.

So to Pilate Jesus was brought (in accordance, no doubt, with a hastily improvised arrangement between the high priest and the governor).[1] The messianic claim might be blasphemy in the ears of the Jews, but it could be made to sound very differently in the ears of the Roman procurator. "This man claims," they said, "to be king of the Jews." And Pilate might be expected to send him to the cross with little ado. But Pilate temporized. His temporizing strikes us as strange; something like the conversation which John narrates between Pilate and Jesus is necessary to explain Pilate's reluctance, reported by the Synoptists, to pronounce the death sentence. This conversation convinced Pilate that Jesus used "king" and "kingdom" in no ordinary sense. The man was plainly a dreamer, a visionary, with His talk of the "kingdom of truth" whose servants renounced the use of force. Even so, visionaries can be dangerous. Some further motive for Pilate's uneasiness suggests itself, and Matthew's story of his wife's dream and warning message deserves more serious consideration than it sometimes receives. Dreams were uncanny things, and must not be disregarded. If all stories were true, Julius Cæsar came to grief on the Ides of March in 44 B.C. because he disregarded his wife's dreams of the preceding night. It was too plain, besides, that the high-priestly party had some spite against this strange visionary. So Pilate pronounced him not guilty. But his verdict was unacceptable, and he could not afford to offend the Jewish leaders too deeply. The Emperor Tiberius would not be lenient if it came to his ears that his procurator had acquitted a man who claimed to be king in Judæa. Pilate's temporizing was unavailing. When he tried to release Jesus as a concession to the crowd that had gathered outside his residence, he found that they wanted someone else—Barabbas, who was awaiting execution for his part in the recent rising. It was plain to them that Jesus was no Messiah after their heart; they had no time for so obviously passive a Messiah. So Pilate bowed to the

[1] Cf. Frank Morison, *Who Moved the Stone?* (1944 edition), pp. 36ff.

high-priestly insistence, re-echoed as it was by the crowd, and sent Jesus away to be executed.

It is unnecessary to suppose that those who cried "Crucify Him" on Good Friday were the same as those who had cried "Hosanna" on Palm Sunday. The people who cried "Hosanna" were Galilæan pilgrims; those who clamoured for His death were a city mob, incited by the chief priests. The Galilæan pilgrims were disillusioned, no doubt, but they need not be credited with such a *volte-face* as this. To the Jerusalem populace the temple was a chief source of livelihood, and one who spoke and acted so freely with regard to the temple as Jesus did must necessarily incur their hostility.[1]

Jesus was not the first or the last to die because His death seemed expedient to certain highly-placed interests. Of all the parallels which history offers to His death, perhaps that of Socrates comes nearest. And yet there is a gulf between the two, quite apart from the contrast which the grisly narrative of the crucifixion forms to the peaceful scene where the old philosopher talks with his friends until the hour comes to drink the hemlock, and then dies quietly and painlessly.

For Jesus Himself did not think of His death primarily as an act of folly and injustice on the part of his opponents. It was all that, but it was more. He had long since accepted this as the way of obedience. It was implied in His baptism and in His response to the wilderness temptations. The role which He was to fulfil was that of the suffering Servant, obedient to God even unto death, and by His death bearing the sin of many and achieving deliverance and victory for them.

When His disciples, looking forward eagerly to the establishment of the coming kingdom, discussed the positions which they hoped to occupy in it, He emphasized that His kingdom was one

---

[1] It is particularly important to note that it is this Jerusalem mob, egged on by Jesus' persecutors, which Matthew represents as saying "His blood be on us and on our children." C. G. Montefiore had only too good ground for what he said of the "oceans of human blood, and a ceaseless stream of misery and desolation" for which this phrase has been responsible—or rather, we should say, a perverted application of this phrase, as anti-Christian as it is anti-Jewish. But it does not follow that the phrase is "a horrible invention," expressing the evangelist's "bitter hatred," as Montefiore thought (*The Synoptic Gospels*, II, p. 346). Matthew, in recording the crowd's imprecation, is not thinking beyond the disaster of A.D. 70. There is no reference whatever here to the Jewish people at large. To imagine that all Jews of A.D. 30, or any Jews of later time, have some special responsibility for the death of Christ, beyond what is shared by all those whose "base self-love and guilty pride" perpetuate the sins that brought His death about, is tragic and criminal folly. There is no difference in substance, though there is in atmosphere, between these words reported by Matthew and the words which, according to Luke, Jesus addressed to the weeping women of Jerusalem who bewailed His fate on the *via dolorosa*, when He bade them weep not for Him but for themselves and their children, in view of the horrors that were to come upon their city. Both utterances found ample and awful fulfilment in the horrors of the siege and destruction of the city forty years later.

in which service was the sole qualification for honour and advancement. "For even the Son of man," He added, "did not come to be served by others but to be a servant, and to give his life a ransom for many."[1] And again, on the night before His death, as He sat at supper with His disciples, He showed very plainly how He regarded the impending events when He broke bread and gave it to them as the token of His body, about to be given in sacrifice for them, and asked them likewise to drink a cup of wine in His memory. "This," said He, "is my covenant blood, which is shed for many."[2]

Moses, long centuries before, had ratified with sacrificial blood the covenant between God and Israel by which Israel became thenceforth the people of God. But now the people of God must be reconstituted, and the new covenant must be ratified by a greater sacrifice. The prophet, too, had declared of the suffering Servant:

> All we like sheep have gone astray,
> We have turned every one to his own way,
>   And Yahweh has placed on him the iniquity of us all.

> .   .   .   .

> When his soul is made a guilt-offering,
> He will see his posterity and prolong his days,
>   And Yahweh's pleasure will prosper in his hand.

> He will see light after his soul's travail and be satisfied;
> By his knowledge my servant will indeed make many righteous,
>   And their iniquities he will bear.[3]

And this Jesus accepted as His peculiar task. In His suffering He offered up His life for the sins of His people, to bring them salvation by His death.

But as he hung upon the cross, deserted by His followers, crying "My God, why hast thou forsaken me?", none of those who stood by could have expected to see the far-reaching blessings which the prophet foresaw as the sequel to the Servant's death. It was the end of all that. His enemies said it with satisfaction; His friends with sorrow. But it was not the end. It was a new beginning.

[1] Mark 10 : 45.
[2] Mark 14 : 24.
[3] Isaiah 53 : 6, 10f. The reading of v. 11, "he will see light," is that of the Septuagint, confirmed by the two Hebrew manuscripts of Isaiah from Qumran Cave 1; a possible variant rendering is "he will cause light to appear."

CHAPTER V

THE DARKNESS DID NOT PUT IT OUT

JESUS WAS CRUCIFIED AT THE PASSOVER SEASON IN A.D. 30. NOT one of His followers went along with Him to share His death, for when He was arrested their nerve failed, in spite of the earlier protestations that they would stand by Him to the death. The leading disciple, who had made the loudest and most emphatic protestations of unfailing loyalty, the one who had previously been the first to confess Him as the Messiah, broke down completely when put to the test. He mingled with the servants in the courtyard of the high priest's palace, curious to know what would become of his Master, hoping that he would pass unnoticed in the crowd by night. His Galilæan accent, however, attracted attention, and when someone claimed to recognize him as one who had been with Jesus at the time of His arrest, he swore repeatedly and insistently that he had never set eyes on the man.

If it was on men like these that Jesus depended to carry on His work after His death, they looked like being broken reeds.

Seven weeks after the Passover came the Feast of Pentecost, the ancient feast of the firstfruits of wheat harvest. It was one of the three great pilgrimage-festivals of the Jewish year (the other two being Unleavened Bread and Tabernacles[1]), and large numbers of Jews from outside Palestine were present in Jerusalem for its celebration in the year of which we are speaking. On the festival day (Sunday, May 28th, A.D. 30) a number of people in Jerusalem, consisting of both natives and visitors, were attracted by the unusual behaviour of a small group of men in the temple precincts. These men suddenly burst out in ascriptions of praise to God in other forms of speech than their own, which some of the visiting Jews recognized as languages and dialects with which they were acquainted in their homelands. A modern psychologist would identify the phenomenon with one form of what is called *glossolalia*, utterance which is partially or wholly uncontrolled by one's conscious mind.[2] A translation of the New Testament account of

---

[1] Unleavened bread (associated with Passover) fell in spring; Pentecost, seven weeks after it, and Tabernacles in autumn.

[2] Prophecy is another form of such utterance; the differentia of *glossolalia* is that the utterance is in a tongue of which the speaker has no command in normal circumstances.

the phenomenon, as it was manifested on the day of Pentecost, into modern jargon, would probably say that their speech was temporarily under the control of their subliminal consciousness, which in turn was subject at that moment to the influx of divine power. But the New Testament account itself is most adequate, and is sufficiently intelligible to most of us: "They were all filled with the Holy Spirit, and began to speak with other tongues, as the Spirit gave them utterance."[1]

The crowd of onlookers was not quite sure what the cause of this behaviour was, some suggesting that it was the result of strong drink, when one of the group turned and faced them, and began to address them. He assured them that the strange behaviour of himself and his companions was due, not to strong drink, but to the onrush of the Spirit of God upon them, in accordance with an ancient prophecy which announced such an outpouring of divine grace "in the last days"—in the time of fulfilment. And this time of fulfilment had arrived, for (he went on) "Listen to this, men of Israel. You yourselves know all about Jesus of Nazareth, a man accredited to you by God by means of the mighty works and wonders and signs which God performed through Him among you. This man you handed over to Gentile sinners, and by their hands you nailed Him to a cross and thus put Him to death."

The boldness of this accusation was astonishing, especially when the speaker added that all that Jesus of Nazareth suffered thus happened "in accordance with the predetermined counsel and foreknowledge of God."[2] But perhaps the most astonishing thing of all was the fact that the body of men on whose behalf this statement was made consisted of those disciples of Jesus who had forsaken Him at His arrest, while the man who acted as their spokesman was Peter, the disciple whose nerve had failed so ignominiously in the high priest's courtyard. Their nerve had certainly returned. But what had happened to produce the change?

Peter himself went on to announce what had happened. After reminding his audience of the execution of Jesus, he went on: "But God raised him up, loosing the bonds of death, for it was not possible that death should hold him fast."

Here was an astounding assertion. But how was it to be substantiated? Peter quoted Old Testament scriptures to the effect that the Messiah would not be abandoned to the abode of the dead nor allowed to undergo the corruption of death, but that he

---

[1] Acts 2 : 4. Of course in those cases where the subliminal consciousness is held to be *en rapport* with a spiritual power, the character of that power can only be deduced, if at all, from the nature and effect of the resultant phenomena.

[2] Acts 2 : 23. The "predetermined counsel and foreknowledge of God" were expressed in Old Testament scripture.

was to be enthroned at God's right hand until universal victory was his.[1] True (his hearers might have responded), but what have these scriptures to do with Jesus of Nazareth? This, said Peter, that Jesus has actually fulfilled the conditions of Messiahship which they lay down. When he and his associates asserted that Jesus had risen from the grave and triumphed over death, this was no pious assertion of faith; it was a matter of personal testimony. Each one of them had actually seen Jesus alive after His crucifixion and burial. "God has raised this Jesus from the dead, and of this we are all witnesses. . . . Therefore, let the whole house of Israel be well assured that this very Jesus whom you crucified has been invested by God as Lord and Messiah."

The first proclamation of the good news after the death of Jesus was based on the claim that He had risen from the dead. But for the belief of Peter and his associates that Jesus had so risen, they would never have begun to proclaim Him as Lord and Messiah. A dead Lord? A crucified Messiah? The idea would have been as absurd to Peter and his friends as to any other Jew. But the Lord was risen, no longer dead; the Messiah once crucified was exulted above the universe. And in this exaltation they saw the divine vindication of the very claim for which Jesus had been condemned to death. Asked by Caiaphas if He were indeed the Messiah, He replied that He was. His claim was adjudged untrue and blasphemous, and they condemned Him to death. But, said these disciples of His, God knew that His claim was true and He reversed the Sanhedrin's sentence and its execution by raising Jesus from death.

Right from the beginning, then, the apostolic preaching was bound up with the resurrection of Jesus. As it began, so it continued. Whatever differences developed in later days between various groups of Christ's followers, here was something on which they remained united—Peter the first of the apostles and James the brother of Jesus and Paul the missionary to the Gentiles. Recounting the basic facts of the gospel story—the death, burial and rising of Jesus, and His resurrection appearances to various people—Paul says: "Whether therefore it be I or they [Peter, James, and the rest], this is what we proclaim, and this is what you believed."[2] Moreover, he went on (and Peter and James and the rest would have agreed with him), if this resurrection claim is untrue, then there is no Christian gospel, no message of hope or salvation; our faith is the sheerest vanity, and we have sacrificed all for nothing, most wretched of mortals that we are.

The truth of Christianity, in fact, is inseparable from the truth of the apostolic assertion that Jesus the crucified rose again from the dead. This assertion therefore calls for serious examination.

[1] Psalm 16 : 10; 110 : 1.   [2] 1 Corinthians 15 : 11.

That a man should come to life again the third day after his death is certainly improbable; but, in the view of those who knew Him, it was impossible that *this* Man should *not* come to life again. The question is not, "Can a man rise from the dead?" but "Did *Jesus* rise from the dead?" There was so much else unprecedented about Him that it might well be expected that there would be something unprecedented about the end of His days on earth.

But this must be emphasized. It was not the disciples' conviction that their Master could not be held by the power of death that gave rise to their insistence that in fact He had not been held by it. On the contrary, it was only when they were convinced by overwhelming evidence that He had indeed come to life again that they realized how impossible it was that He should have remained dead, and how foolish they had been not to grasp this before.

The earliest witnesses of Christ's resurrection were the men and women who had known and loved Him. They had believed in Him, but their faith had received a great shock when they saw Him led unresistingly to the cross and fastened to it. Now their faith was revived in new and greater strength by the assurance that He had conquered death. Their evidence may be gathered from the four gospels and from the list of witnesses of the resurrection given by Paul at the beginning of 1 Corinthians 15, though many interesting sidelights appear elsewhere in the New Testament, especially in the reports of early Christian speeches preserved in the Acts of the Apostles. The difficulties experienced in an attempt to dovetail these accounts together are just the sort of difficulties inherent in most cases where several eyewitness accounts of an incident have to be pieced together to form a comprehensive narrative. Even so, a reasonable and self-consistent narrative can be built up from the reports which have been preserved, as has been especially well demonstrated by Henry Latham in *The Risen Master* (1901).

The earliest evidence stresses two facts: (1) that the grave in which Jesus was laid after His crucifixion on Friday night was empty the following Sunday morning, and (2) that He himself was seen alive very soon after by a variety of eyewitnesses, both in Judæa and in Galilee.

The empty tomb is not so unimportant as is sometimes thought. Had His body still been lying in it, then the appearances of the risen Master must be set down as hallucinations and nothing more. Dr. C. J. Cadoux has said: "Once the disciples were convinced by the visions they had had that Jesus was alive and active despite His death on the cross, their belief that His tomb must therefore be empty would follow inevitably as the night the day, whether there was any actual evidence for it or not."[1] But this overlooks some of the realities of the situation. As soon as the story began to get about that something mysterious had taken place at the tomb that Sunday morning, numbers of people would inevitably walk out to the place to see for themselves. The story which the chief priests set afoot, that the disciples had stolen the body of Jesus, itself presumes an empty tomb.

On the other hand, the empty tomb does not prove the resurrection. The women who first found it empty simply thought that their Lord's body had been removed elsewhere.[2] To quote a recent American writer: "The early Christians did not believe in the resurrection of Christ because they could not find his dead body. They believed because they did find a living Christ."[3] In the earliest apostolic preaching they did not say "We found His grave empty" but "We saw Him alive." But they *imply* that His grave was empty. Peter, addressing the crowd on the day of Pentecost, said "David's sepulchre is with us to this day," meaning that the bones of David still lay within it; the corollary is that no relic of the body of Jesus remained in *His* sepulchre. So, too, when Paul includes the burial of Christ as one of the basic facts in the gospel he proclaimed, between His death and resurrection, he implies a real continuity between the body that was buried and the body that was raised, even if "it was sown a natural body and raised a spiritual body."[4]

It is a commonplace nowadays that Jesus' triumph over death can be understood as a spiritual resurrection, operative in the lives of His followers, no matter what happened to His body. "The inner light," says Dr. Inge, "can only testify to spiritual truths. It always speaks in the present tense; it cannot guarantee any historical event, past or future. It cannot guarantee either the gospel history or a future judgment. It can tell us that Christ is risen, and that He is alive for evermore, but not that He rose again the third day."[5] It is safe to say that such an argument would have carried little weight in Jewish circles in the first century A.D. Nor was it the sort of argument which the apostles used. While they did claim that they were energized by the power of Christ's risen life, what they emphasized in their public preaching

[1] *The Historic Mission of Jesus* (1941), p. 284.
[2] The contents of the tomb, however, told a clearer story; when the beloved disciple viewed the arrangement of the grave-clothes and the head-wrap, "he saw, and believed" (John 20 : 8).
[3] C. T. Craig, *The Beginning of Christianity* (1943), p. 135.
[4] I Corinthians 15 : 44. Paul here used adjectives derived from the Greek words for "soul" (*psyche*) and "spirit" (*pneuma*). He "declares that a change from a 'natural' body to a 'spiritual' body is the appointed destiny of Christian believers, and since he speaks of Christ as the 'first-fruits of them that sleep,' he obviously believed the same wonderful change to have taken place in Christ's body. In his own phrase, the body of humiliation had become the body of glory"(A. M. Hunter, *St. Mark*, p. 151).
[5] *Christian Mysticism* (1899), p. 326.

was that Christ rose again on the third day and was seen alive by them. What they meant, and what their hearers, friendly and hostile alike, understood them to mean, was that Jesus of Nazareth, who had died on the cross and been placed in a tomb, returned to life the third day thereafter and left the tomb untenanted. That was their basic affirmation; and it was supported very soon by the evidence publicly provided that the name of Jesus was still as potent in the accomplishment of mighty works through His disciples as it had been when He himself was active in bodily presence among them.[1]

The gospel records make it plain that the first witnesses, both of the empty tomb and of the risen Lord, were women. But this fact was not insisted on in the apostolic preaching, as the reports of that preaching in Acts and in the New Testament epistles indicate. This is quite intelligible. Outside Christian circles, the evidence of women would have been dismissed as of little value. Had it been adduced, it would have been ridiculed as the fantasies of excitable females.[2] But the responsible leaders of the young Christian movement affirmed emphatically and repeatedly that they themselves had seen Jesus alive again after His passion, and that not once but several times, over a period of some weeks. Nor were they the only ones to see Him; He was similarly seen alive by more than five hundred people, and the majority of these were still alive as witnesses to what they had seen a quarter of a century later.

What are we to make of this claim? Those who made it were charged with imposture in the earliest days of Christianity, and this charge has been repeated frequently since then,[3] but it is rarely made nowadays.[4] It is morally and psychologically incredible that such men as the apostles and their associates could have been deliberate deceivers. Men and women who are prepared to die for what they affirm are usually sincere in affirming it, even if they are sincerely mistaken. The genuineness of the "resurrection faith" is generally conceded to-day even by those who deny the "resurrection fact"; they agree that the early disciples honestly believed that Jesus was alive again, even if they themselves do not believe it.

---

[1] Acts 3 : 6, 16; 4 : 10–12.

[2] This objection was voiced by Celsus in the second century (see Origen, *Against Celsus*, II, 55).

[3] H. S. Reimarus, about 1778, in the *Wolfenbüttel Fragments*, argued that the disciples, disinclined to return to their old employments, since thay had learned that preaching pays (!), stole the body of Jesus, waited fifty days till it should be unrecognizable and then began proclaiming His second coming.

[4] The Jewish scholar, J. Klausner, remarks that "*deliberate imposture* is not the substance out of which the religion of millions of mankind is created"; he supposes that Joseph of Arimathæa removed the body secretly from his own tomb and placed it in an unknown grave (*Jesus of Nazareth*, p. 357).

But what gave rise to the "resurrection faith" if it was not the "resurrection fact"? If the resurrection appearances are regarded as purely subjective, they do not seem to conform to the conditions which normally govern such experiences. The disciples were not expecting to see their Master. Whereas such experiences are often the result of people's seeing something else and mistaking it for the object on which their mind is concentrated, the gospel records tell how the disciples saw their risen Lord and mistook Him for someone else—the gardener, or an unknown fellow-traveller.[1] The atmosphere of gloom and despair in which they lived between the arrest and the resurrection was not such an atmosphere as gives rise to visions of this kind. Again, the experiences happened to increasing numbers of people over a period of forty days, and then stopped.[2] Had they been purely subjective, we should have expected them to continue indefinitely, and to affect still greater numbers of people.

This period of forty days, mentioned by Luke,[3] is responsible for the arrangement in the Christian calendar by which Ascension Day falls on the fortieth day from Easter. But the exaltation of Jesus to the right hand of God, which is really what Ascension Day commemorates, was not postponed for forty days after His triumph over death. (Incidentally, the "right hand of God" was as figurative an expression to first-century Christians as to those of the twentieth century and denoted universal supremacy in honour and authority.) In the primitive apostolic preaching the resurrection and ascension of Christ represented one continuous movement and together constituted His exaltation. (In John's account, indeed, the exaltation begins with the crucifixion.) The fortieth day was not the first occasion on which He vanished from the sight of His companions after His rising from the dead. Nor did the New Testament writers intend us to suppose that the intervals between His resurrection appearances were spent in some earth-bound state. These appearances, in which He condescended to their temporal conditions of life, were visitations from that exalted and eternal order to which His "body of glory" now belonged; and what happened on the fortieth day, when "a cloud received Him out of their sight,"[4] was that this series of frequent though intermittent visitations had now come to an end.

The question what happened to the body of Jesus is one to which a reasonable answer must be given in any case. If the

[1] This point is well made by R. A. Knox, quoted by Arnold Lunn, *The Third Day* (1945), p. 75.
[2] The subsequent appearance to Paul is an exception, as Paul himself indicates when he compares his conversion to an "untimely birth" (cf. p. 68).
[3] Acts 1 : 3.
[4] This expression is so similar to one found in the Transfiguration narrative (cf. Luke 9 : 34ff.) as to suggest that a comparison of the two narratives will promote the better understanding of both.

disciples' experiences were purely subjective, the body presumably lay somewhere where it could be produced. It was to the interest of the Sanhedrin leaders to produce it when the apostles began proclaiming that Jesus had risen from the dead, and under ordinary circumstances it was surely not beyond their power to produce it, or at least to procure certified evidence of its disposal. But the earliest counter-argument to the disciples' assertion that Jesus was alive again—the charge that these disciples had stolen the body—was in itself an acknowledgment that the body could not be produced. Loisy's idea[1] that the body of Jesus was thrown into the common criminals' pit in the valley of Hinnom or elsewhere is a good example of replacing an account for which there is early evidence (the burial in Joseph's tomb) by one for which there is no evidence at all. That is not the way to reconstruct history. And if the body had been disposed of thus, there was no need for the circulation of the story that it had been stolen by the disciples. The Sanhedrin, in fact, did not know what had happened to the body after its interment. If we ask why they did not sponsor a more convincing story than that of the disciples' theft, the answer probably is that, in view of facts that were commonly accessible at the time, they knew (as Arnold Lunn puts it) what they could get away with.[2] If Gamaliel, a respected member of the Pharisaic party in the Sanhedrin, could suggest even the theoretical possibility that the new Christian movement might be of God, then we may be sure that the Sanhedrin had no *conclusive* proof that the apostles' claim that Christ was risen was not true.

If they really believed that the disciples had stolen their Master's body, could they not have taken police action to recover it? A dead body is none too easy a thing to dispose of at any time, as many a murderer has found to his cost.

Or if, as Kirsopp Lake suggested,[3] the women went to the wrong tomb and found it empty, the simplest thing for the Sanhedrin to do when the apostles began to proclaim the resurrection of Jesus was to organize conducted tours to the real tomb and show His body still lying there. If, as others have suggested, the Sanhedrin itself or Joseph of Arimathæa or the gardener removed the body, it could have been produced at once, or evidence of its disposal could have been provided. But it was not, and there is no suggestion anywhere that anything of the sort was contemplated as practicable. We may, of course, bear in mind the point made by Reimarus, that the apostles did not start their public preaching until fifty days had elapsed, since by that time the body was un-

---

[1] A. Loisy, *The Birth of the Christian Religion* (1948), p. 90. But the idea had already been propounded by D. F. Strauss, as H. P. V. Nunn points out in *What is Modernism?* (1932), pp. 108f.

[2] *The Third Day*, p. 89.

[3] *The Resurrection of Jesus Christ* (1907), pp. 251f.

C

recognizable. The fourth evangelist, however, tells us that the body was embalmed by Joseph of Arimathæa and Nicodemus before being entombed;[1] and it is unlikely that he invented this story in order to forestall Reimarus's theory.

Perhaps, then, Jesus did not really die. Men have survived crucifixion, both then and in our own day, if they were taken down soon enough.[2] May not Jesus have swooned on the cross, and revived in the cool of the sepulchre? It was the business of the soldiers to make sure that He was dead, and it is unlikely that they were mistaken. Moreover, the reality of His death on the cross is vouched for in the most emphatic terms by one who explicitly claims to have been an eyewitness of the piercing of Jesus' side and the effusion of blood and water.[3] This writer's claim to be an eyewitness is borne out by the quality of his record: the crucifixion narrative of John 19 bears the convincing marks of first-hand ocular testimony.[4] The piercing of Jesus' side was intended to make sure that He was really as dead as He appeared to be.

But further, the sight of one who had just managed to survive the racking torture of crucifixion could not have had the effect on the disciples that the appearances of the risen Christ produced. The idea that Jesus did not actually die on the cross is perfectly suitable for imaginative fiction (as readers of George Moore's *The Brook Kerith* will readily acknowledge), but it has nothing whatever to do with the historic facts of the rise of Christianity.[5] This argument was adequately dealt with by D. F. Strauss[6]—not that his own view that the resurrection faith was a gradual growth in

[1] John 19 : 39f.

[2] Josephus (*Life*, 75) tells how at his request Titus commanded three of his former acquaintances to be taken down from their crosses; "two of them died under the surgeon's hands, but the third recovered." I have heard Professor Ferenc Kiss, of the Medical Faculty in Budapest University, describe a Hungarian who had been crucified by enemy soldiery after World War I, but was released in time and recovered.

[3] John 19 : 34f.

[4] "It must be remembered that, of the four evangels, St. John's is the only one that claims to be the direct report of an eyewitness. And to anyone accustomed to the imaginative handling of documents, the internal evidence bears out this claim" (Dorothy L. Sayers, *The Man Born to be King*, p. 33; see the whole passage from which these words are quoted, and also her *Unpopular Opinions* [1946], pp. 25–28).

[5] While George Moore's reconstruction may be the best-known presentation of this theory, it goes back to K. F. Bahrdt (1741–1792), whose views, published in several works, are summarized in Schweitzer's *Quest of the Historical Jesus* (1911), pp. 38–44. Bahrdt propounded the view that the Essenes stage-managed Jesus' so-called death and resurrection in order to destroy by spiritualizing the false messianic notions held by the people. This theory was developed by K. H. Venturini at the beginning of the nineteenth century.

[6] In *The Fair Haven*, Samuel Butler, with assumed *naïveté*, uses the fact of Strauss's rejection of this view as a sufficient argument against it, deliberately introducing this weak link into his chain of pretended evidence in support of the resurrection. The way in which Butler's irony deceived some of the very elect is amusing to read. He himself believed that Christ did not really die on the cross.

the disciples' minds is any more in accordance with the facts of the case. For the gospel of the resurrection was the sum and substance of the earliest apostolic preaching, less than two months after the death of Jesus; the main outline of the story, common property to all the strands of primitive Christian thought, is to be traced back to the very beginnings of the church's history, and it was, in fact, the resurrection faith which brought the church to birth (or rebirth) in the early summer of A.D. 30. Quite apart from the question of the resurrection fact, an ordinary critical examination of the New Testament records by the canons applicable to all such records makes this abundantly clear. The details of the passion and resurrection narratives were the first element in the apostolic message to be fixed, and they were so fixed very soon after the passion. The greater part of Paul's summary of resurrection appearances in 1 Corinthians 15 : 4-7, represents what he learned from Peter and from James the brother of Jesus, not more than five years after the crucifixion.

Peter was the first of the apostles to see Jesus in resurrection, and we may trace something of what that experience meant to him in words which he later penned: "Blessed be the God and Father of our Lord Jesus Christ, who according to His abounding mercy has begotten us again to a living hope by the resurrection of Jesus Christ from the dead."[1] But the other two men just mentioned are particularly interesting because they, too, received a similar experience, in spite of the fact that they had not previously believed in Jesus. All the others who saw the risen Christ had their former faith restored and reinforced thereby, but James and Paul became disciples of Jesus only from the time when He appeared to them in resurrection.

"The brothers of the Lord" are enumerated among the leaders of the church in 1 Corinthians 9 : 5, and their discipleship goes back to the period preceding the first Christian Pentecost.[2] But they were not disciples of Jesus during His public ministry, "for even his brothers," we read, "did not believe on him."[3] Strange, that they should have withheld their support from Him when He enjoyed comparative popularity, and given it freely on the morrow of disaster and defeat! Among these brothers of Jesus the outstanding figure is James. He appears in later days as the unquestioned leader of the Christian community in Jerusalem, and his pre-eminent holiness of life procured for him the title "James the Just" even from the non-Christian Jerusalemites. A man of his character is unlikely to have been a party to deceit, nor was he predisposed, as some think the disciples of Jesus were, to expect the resurrection of one whose messianic actions and claims he deplored. The condemnation and execution of Jesus were just

[1] 1 Peter 1 : 3.   [2] Acts 1 : 14.   [3] John 7 : 5.

what his brothers had feared all along. What wrought the revolution in James's attitude towards Jesus at this juncture, when the
worst had actually happened? Paul gives us the explanation
which he had received from James himself: "He appeared to
James."[1]

"And last of all," Paul goes on to say, "He appeared to me too,
as to one untimely born."[2] Paul's antecedents are well enough
known; he, at any rate, was not predisposed to believe in Jesus'
claim to be the Son of God, nor in the apostles' insistence that
God had vindicated that claim by raising him from the dead. The
revolution which took place in Paul's life outside the gate of
Damascus about A.D. 33 is a matter of history; the cause of that
revolution may be a matter of debate, but Paul's account of it was
that there and then he saw the risen Christ. It is an adequate
account; the more we examine the circumstances, the more inclined
we may be to go further and call it the only adequate account.
Paul's conversion, a notable historic landmark in its own right
(with which we shall have to deal in a later chapter), is also a
powerful testimony to the truth of Christ's resurrection. The
evidence which convinced a man like Paul of the out-and-out
wrongness of his former course, and led him so decisively to
abandon his most passionately cherished convictions for a movement which he had so vigorously opposed, but for which he was
thenceforth prepared to sacrifice everything—this evidence must
have been of a singularly cogent quality. George Lyttelton might
well declare, just over 200 years ago, that "the conversion and
apostleship of St. Paul alone, duly considered, was of itself a
demonstration sufficient to prove Christianity to be a divine
revelation."[3]

It may be difficult to believe that for once the grip of death was
broken and a dead man came back to life. Instances are recorded,
of course, in modern days of people who have come back to life
after lying dead for a few minutes—thirty at the very outside.
The gospels record a few miracles of raising the dead after a
longer period, but even so these were not resurrections but resuscitations. The life that was resumed was of the same mortal
order as before, and was terminable again by death. Only in a
limited sense could such resuscitations be represented as triumphs
over death. But the resurrection of Christ was not the resuscitation
of a corpse; it was proclaimed as a decisive conquest of death:

---

[1] I Corinthians 15 : 7.

[2] The Greek word *ektrōma*, which Paul uses, means an abortion or premature
birth. Paul's use of the word may refer to the painful abruptness with which he was
snatched from darkness to light. It is conceivable that he is giving a new significance
to a term of reproach hurled at him by those who refused to admit his claim to be a
true apostle.

[3] *Observations on the Conversion of St. Paul* (1747); cf. the section on Lyttleton in
Samuel Johnson's *Lives of the Poets*.

"Christ being raised from the dead dies no more: death has no more dominion over Him."[1]

What really happened? If we say that the resurrection of Christ was the transformation of His body into something of a new order altogether,[2] we are dealing with phenomena beyond our experience. But it is for our health to remember that all phenomena are not yet within our ken—that the known is, in fact, the the merest margin of the unknown. The resurrection body of Jesus, according to the gospel records, while it could be adapted to ordinary physical conditions, was not subject to them; it could be materialized and dematerialized at will. And this portrayal is in harmony with the Pauline doctrine of the spiritual body which is to replace the natural body, when "mortality is swallowed up by life."[3]

That a man should rise from the dead after three days is, as we have said, certainly improbable; but we are not concerned here with *a* man, but with *this* man. There are many other things recorded of this man which in isolation are equally improbable— His virginal conception, His life and works—but in Him all these improbabilities coincide. Does the coincidence of improbabilities amount to sheer impossibility, so that we conclude the picture is a cunningly wrought invention? Or is the picture that of God incarnate, in whom the "improbabilities" coincide like a threefold cord that is not quickly broken? That God incarnate should enter human life by a unique way ("conceived of the Holy Ghost and born of the Virgin Mary," as the ancient creed says) is not improbable, but perfectly fitting. That God incarnate should live a life of perfect holiness, marked by works of miraculous power and teaching of pre-eminent wisdom, is not improbable, but just what we should expect. That God incarnate should *die*—there is something in the highest degree amazing. Die He did, none the less; but this could not be the end. When we have seen this act in the drama of our salvation, we wait breathlessly for the sequel, and greet it as something divinely natural: this is the one "whom God raised up, loosing the bonds of death, because it was not possible that death should hold him fast."

[1] Romans 6 : 9.
[2] See the discussion of Paul's doctrine of the resurrection of Christ by K. Lake, *The Resurrection of Jesus Christ* (1907), pp. 18ff. Lake was far from agreeing with the conclusions of this chapter, but his exegesis of Paul's treatment of the subject is excellent, and worthy of such a great scholar as Lake was.
[3] 2 Corinthians 5 : 4.

CHAPTER VI

THE NEW COMMUNITY

C HRISTIANITY BEGAN AS ONE AMONG SEVERAL PARTIES IN first-century Palestinian Judaism, or so at least it appeared. Judaism before A.D. 70 was much more variegated than afterwards, and there was room within it for a great diversity of parties and schools, provided that all maintained the central loyalty to the Jewish faith in one God and to the Jewish way of life.

The party of the Nazarenes took its place among the others. Why its members were called Nazarenes is a matter of dispute. The word is derivable from a root which means "to observe" and may possibly mean the "observant people"—those who observe a certain way of life (compare the origin of the name "Methodists"). At any rate this may have been the sense in which people came to use it of the members of this party. But in actual practice the name Nazarenes was probably derived originally from Nazareth, the Galilæan home-town of Jesus. Jesus Himself was called "Jesus the Nazarene," and although various explanations are given of this title as applied to Him, it is probable that the traditional account is to be accepted, which regards "Jesus the Nazarene" as being synonymous with "Jesus of Nazareth."[1]

"Nazarenes," however, was probably not the name which they chose for themselves, although to this day it is the ordinary word for "Christians" in Hebrew and some other Semitic languages. The term "Christians" originated in a Gentile environment at a rather later date. But the followers of Jesus seem to have described themselves by various names in early days. Many of these names were redolent of Old Testament phraseology. "The saints" or "holy people" was a common name, implying that they regarded themselves as the pious remnant or true Israel. "The poor,"[2] another name, was not only economically apt (for the

---

[1] G. F. Moore's study "Nazarene and Nazareth," in *The Beginnings of Christianity*, edited by Foakes Jackson and Kirsopp Lake, vol. I (1920), pp. 426ff., gives a satisfactory account; see also to much the same effect W. F. Albright, "The Names 'Nazareth' and 'Nazoræan,' " in the *Journal of Biblical Literature*, LXV (1946), pp. 399ff.

[2] Hebrew *ha-ebyonim*, whence "Ebionites," a name used in later days by some Gentile Christians of certain Jewish Christians whom they charged with heresy. For a New Testament use of the term see Galatians 2 : 10, where "the poor" means practically the Jerusalem Church. See p. 93.

Jerusalem church appears to have been afflicted with chronic poverty in the first century) but was reminiscent of the adjectives "poor and needy" applied to the "saints" in the Book of Psalms— the "poor in spirit" of the Beatitudes. "Disciples" (of Jesus), "brothers," "friends," "believers," were other names in common use within their community. Their movement they referred to as "The Way." They themselves constituted a separate "synagogue" or community within the larger community of Judaism. But while the term "synagogue" enjoyed some currency among them for some decades, it was gradually ousted by its synonym *ekklesia*, the word translated "church" in the English Bible when it refers to the Christian community.

The Greek word *ekklesia* was one of the equivalents for Hebrew *keneseth* and Aramaic *kenishta*, "synagogue." But *ekklesia* has a Gentile as well as a Jewish background. In several Greek cities the *ekklesia* was the citizen body in its legislative capacity. (Thus the citizen body of Ephesus is referred to by the term *ekklesia*, "assembly," in Acts 19 : 39.) In the Septuagint, however, the Greek version of the Hebrew scriptures made at Alexandria in the closing centuries B.C., *ekklesia* was used to render the Hebrew word *qahal*, the "congregation" of Israel,[1] the nation in its theo-cratic character, organized as a religious community. The choice of this term was a further indication of the early Christians' con-viction that they were the legitimate successors of the true Israel, bound by God to Himself in covenant-relationship from the days when Israel first became a nation.

The party of the Nazarenes enjoyed considerable popularity in the early days in Jerusalem. When the apostles began to proclaim Jesus as the Messiah, crucified by man but raised from death by God and exalted to His right hand, they found many eager hearers, and the number of those who adhered to them increased rapidly. After a few weeks the number reached five thousand, and even then the increase continued.

Of the other Jewish parties only one seems to have been

---

[1] Another Hebrew word used in this sense in the Old Testament is *'edah*. The Septuagint always renders *'edah* by *synagogé*, it renders *qahal* sometimes by *ekklesia* and sometimes by *synagogé*. There is more than philological significance in the original identity of "church" and "synagogue." In Aramaic *kenishta* was used both in the wider sense of the whole "congregation" of Israel and in the narrower sense of a local congregation of Israelites. So, too, its Greek equivalent *ekklesia* as used by Christians has a double sense, referring to the universal church and the local church. The first and second occurrences of *ekklesia* in the Greek New Testament (Matthew 16 : 18; 18 : 17) display the universal and the local senses, respectively. The Greek *synagogé* is used of a Christian congregation in the New Testament in James 2 : 2 (and in the compound form *episynagogé* in Hebrews 10 : 25), and in some second-century writers (Hermas and Justin in Rome, Ignatius of Antioch, Dionysius of Alexandria), but it became almost entirely specialized in the sense of a Jewish congregation, while its synonym *ekklesia* became specializedi n the parallel Christian sense.

actively hostile to them. This was the party of the Sadducees, the party with which the high-priestly families were closely associated. The objections to messianic movements which had impelled the chief priests to get rid of Jesus continued to operate, and on the theological plane the Sadducees could not look with great favour on a religious group whose very existence was based on that very faith in the resurrection of the body which the Sadducees rejected as new-fangled and absurd.

Attempts were made by the Sadducees to supress the infant community, but they failed completely. Not only did the rapid increase of its adherents make suppression difficult; its popularity was very great, and even of the priests a considerable number attached themselves to the Nazarenes. (There were, of course, many priestly families in addition to the powerful and wealthy aristocracies from which the high priests were drawn.) Even in the Sanhedrin the Nazarenes found champions. When the high-priestly party tried to have them officially banned, a protest was voiced by no less a personality than the leader of the Pharisaic party, the illustrious Rabbi Gamaliel the Elder. His argument, in true Pharisaic style, was that every movement which was of divine origin would in the end be established,[1] and opposition to it would be opposition to God. If, on the other hand, as the chief priests held, the movement was subversive, it would peter out as other popular messianic movements had done in recent years.

The Pharisees, in fact, could find little fault with the Nazarenes. They did not flout convention. They were pious, observant Jews, honouring the law to the best of their ability. True, their belief that Jesus was the Messiah must have appeared preposterous to most of the Pharisees, but at least they based this belief on the resurrection of Jesus from the dead, and their emphasis on resurrection was a sign of grace. Some of the Pharisees even joined the new party. Not all Pharisees, to be sure, were so tolerant; there was one young Pharisee in particular, a pupil of Gamaliel, who discerned that the new community contained within itself a seed which when it sprouted would split the edifice of Judaism from top to bottom. But few realized this at the beginning—few even of the Nazarenes themselves. The inward implication of certain words of Jesus announcing the end of the temple-order was overlooked for the time being.

As a small party, then, within Palestinian Judaism, the Naza-renes had something in common with other parties. Like the Essenes, they laid great stress on purity of life and—to begin

---

[1] This sentiment is found in a well-known collection of rabbinical adages, *Pirqê Aboth* (IV, 14). "Every assembly which is in the name of heaven will in the end be established; but that which is not in the name of heaven will not in the end be established" (ascribed to the second-century Rabbi Yohanan, the sandal-maker).

with at any rate—practised a voluntary communism; but they showed few leanings towards the ascetic and coenobitic side of Essenism. The asceticism of James the Just (see p. 150) was noteworthy because it was exceptional. Some striking affinities have been traced between the early Christians and one Essene group— the covenanters of Qumran—but the differences are more fundamental than the points of resemblance.[1] The Nazarenes had this much in common with the Zealots, that they expected the establishment of the kingdom of God; but they differed from them in looking for this kingdom to come, not by their own violent action against Rome and Rome's creatures, but by the return of Jesus as the mighty Son of man, with power and great glory, on the clouds of heaven, to inaugurate the new age in its fullness. Attempts, like that of Dr. Eisler, to depict the Nazarenes as Zealots, must be pronounced failures. No doubt in the minds of many they were lumped together with other messianic movements which did pin their faith to force of arms;[2] but it is as plain as anything can be that the early Christians did not make headway by such means. They had a good deal in common with a number of apocalyptic sects, but they differed from them in the vital point that all their apocalyptic imagery, all their eschatological expectation, was centred in Jesus as the Messiah and interpreted in the light of His teaching and passion and triumph. The age of fulfilment, they believed, had already dawned with the advent of Jesus, and of the successive stages of His redemptive activity one only now remained to be accomplished in order to bring the new age to consummation.

The Nazarenes did make a tremendous appeal to the ordinary people among their contemporaries. The Sadducees and the great priestly families were cordially disliked. The Pharisees set up a standard of conformity to the law which only the religious élite could hope to attain. But the Nazarenes consisted mainly of ordinary people who, in the eyes of some Pharisees at least,[3] simply

---

[1] See my *Second Thoughts on the Dead Sea Scrolls*, pp. 123ff.

[2] This may have been helped out by the apparent coincidence of an unsuccessful insurrection with the events of the days preceding the crucifixion. This is a fair inference from the repeated definite article in the statement that Barabbas, before his release, "lay bound with the insurgents, those who had committed murder in the insurrection" (Mark 15 : 7).

[3] It is unwise to make sweeping generalizations about the Pharisees. There are seven types of Pharisee enumerated in the Talmud (Babylonian Talmud, *Sota* 22b; Palestinian Talmud, *Berakhoth* IX, 14b, and *Sota*, V, 20c), and of these only one, the "Pharisee from love," receives unqualified commendation. This proportion is more or less what we might infer from references to the Pharisees in the New Testament. Even the liberal Rabbi Hillel is quoted for the view that "no ignorant person is pious" (*Pirqe Aboth*, II, 6), with which we may compare the words of Pharisaic members of the Sanhedrin in John 7 : 49: "This multitude which is ignorant of the law is accursed." The attitude of the common people at that time may be judged from Peter's reference in Acts 15 : 10 to "a yoke which neither we nor our fathers were able to bear." According to Prof. H. Danby (*Studies in Judaism* [1922],

could not hope to be true keepers of the law. The Zealots and militant Messianists invariably came to grief at the hands of the Romans, and their risings always provoked horrible reprisals, in which the common people suffered most. The apocalyptists looked for the act of God which was just round the corner. But the disciples of Jesus proclaimed the act of God which had already begun in Christ, only one phase of which remained to be fulfilled. And in this Jesus everyone who truly repented received the assurance of the forgiveness of their sins—an assurance which but few of the common people could obtain by Pharisaic rule.

The Nazarenes met in each other's houses day by day for a communal meal in the course of which they remembered Jesus with thanksgiving as they partook of bread and wine. In these gatherings, too, those who had been with Jesus recounted their memories of Him and instructed the others in His teaching. In public they proclaimed to their fellow-citizens the good news of the divine act accomplished in the Messiah. Entry into the new community was solemnized by baptism "into the name of the Lord Jesus"; this baptism marked them off as His people. They met for prayer among themselves and also attended the appointed hours of prayer in the temple. In the earliest days they pooled their property and those who were in need were allotted supplies out of the common fund.

In this fellowship the common people—those who had moved the compassion of Jesus because they were like sheep without a shepherd—found new life and new hope; they were no longer leaderless, because if there was one thing more than anything else that was very real to the Nazarene community, it was the presence and power of Jesus. Though no longer with them in visible form, His presence was realized and enjoyed when they met together, and—more stupendous still—the mighty works which Jesus had performed as signs of the new age when He was on earth con-

p. 19), the extreme position which insisted on the fulfilment of every jot and tittle of the oral law was characteristic of the school of Shammai as opposed to the school of Hillel. It must be remembered that the rabbinical literature rarely reflects the conditions of the first century, especially the years before A.D. 70; and there is some evidence that at the end of the century a change took place in the conception of one's duty to observe the whole law. The change is associated with the influence of Rabbi Akiba, who is credited with the dictum that "the world is judged in mercy, and all is according to the amount of the work," i.e. according to the preponderance of good or bad in human actions (*Pirqe Aboth*, III, 19). "Sometimes he asserted God's mercy to be such that a single meritorious act will win a man admission to the future world" (L. Finkelstein, *Akiba*, p. 185). That means that one righteous act can weigh down the scale of merit, when a man's good and evil deeds are equally balanced, so that a 51 per cent righteousness, in effect, will open the way to Paradise. This is a very different viewpoint from that quoted in the New Testament in the Epistle of James (2 : 10), a work of about the middle of the first century: "Whosoever shall keep the whole law, and yet stumble in one point, he is become guilty of all." But we must remember that the New Testament writings are among the best contemporary evidence we have for the attitude to the law in Palestine for the first seventy years of the Christian era.

tinued to be performed by His disciples in His name, or (to put it more accurately) were performed by Him from heaven through His disciples. This manifest power of the name of Jesus made a deep impression on the populace of Jerusalem, and contributed materially to the increase of the community.

Nor was it only native Palestinian Jews who joined the new community. A number of Greek-speaking Jews whose family ties were with the lands of the "dispersion" also found their way among them. Dr. Klausner argues, indeed, that it was because so many Jews of the dispersion were half assimilated to Gentile ways already that they were so ready to embrace Christianity. This is doubtful. So far as the Jerusalem church was concerned, the Greek-speaking believers (or "Hellenists") were never properly absorbed into it. When trouble arose, as we shall see, it was chiefly the Hellenists who had to leave Jerusalem, and from their departure until the early decades of the second century the Nazarenes of Judæa were almost entirely "Hebrews"—native Aramaic-speaking Jews.

It was in connexion with the Hellenists that the first step towards providing an organization for the community was taken. The twelve apostles (including Matthias, who had been co-opted to fill the place of Judas Iscariot) were the natural leaders. The relatives of Jesus, who later played a leading part, were less prominent in the very early days. Before long we find "elders" appearing as the administrators of the community, on the analogy of the elders of other Jewish communities. Their authority increased in later years when the apostles became more "mobile." But the activity which most urgently required organization at the outset was the daily distribution to the poorer members of the community from the common pool of wealth. Complaints that the Hellenist widows were not being so generously treated in this matter as the Hebrews led to the appointment of seven men to have special charge of the distribution. The names of all seven are Greek, and one at least was not even a Jew by birth; he was a proselyte, Nicolas of Antioch. This may indicate that the community determined to allay the suspicions of the Hellenist members; but the seven probably served generally as leaders of the Hellenist section in the community. Two of them at any rate, Stephen and Philip, shone not only as almoners but also as preachers and teachers.

What did these early Nazarenes have in the way of literature? The Old Testament, of course, was their sacred book. For so regarding it they had the highest authority; Jesus Himself had constantly used it, appealed to it, treated it with the utmost veneration. The "Hebrews" would know it in the original Hebrew text or in the oral Aramaic paraphrases ("Targums") which they heard in the synagogues. The reading of the Hebrew scriptures in the synagogues was regularly accompanied in those days by the recitation of a paraphrase in the Aramaic vernacular of Palestine and the lands farther east. The Hellenists would know the Old Testament in the Greek Septuagint version.

But copies of the scriptures were not sufficient to go round. Some scriptures, however, were specially required for the proclamation of the good news. These were the passages which spoke of the coming of the Messiah, those to which they regularly appealed in support of their claim that Jesus was the Messiah because He had fulfilled messianic scripture. What some of these scriptures were may be discovered from a study of the sermons reported in the Acts of the Apostles as well as from Old Testament quotations in the Gospels and some other parts of the New Testament.

These proof-texts or "testimonies" were evidently collected in written form at a very early date. Whether or not such a collection may well have been the first Christian book, as the late Rendel Harris argued,[1] there are places in our New Testament writings which could well be explained by the influence of a "testimony book." When Matthew (27 : 9f.), for example, ascribes to Jeremiah the prophecy about the purchase of the potter's field with thirty pieces of silver which we find in Zechariah 11 : 13, we may infer that the "testimony book" had already combined that passage from Zechariah with the story of the visit to the potter's house in Jeremiah 18 : 1ff. Or when Mark begins his record of John the Baptist with the words "As it is written in Isaiah the prophet" (so in Revised Version), but before going on to quote the Isaianic passage in question ("The voice of one crying . . ." [Isaiah 40 : 3]) introduces a citation from Malachi ("Behold, I send my messenger before thy face . . ." [3 : 1]), we may envisage the juxtaposition of these two passages in an already-existent section of the testimony book dealing with John.

So, too, when Isaiah 53 is quoted of the sufferings of Christ, when Isaiah 6 : 9f. is quoted to explain the refusal of the majority of the Jews to recognize Him as the Messiah, when Psalm 16 : 10 is quoted of His resurrection, or Psalm 110 : 1 of His exaltation to God's right hand, we may see further traces of a primitive testimony book. The manner in which the testimonies were arranged may be illustrated by the combination of various Old Testament passages referring figuratively to a *stone*: the "stone which the builders rejected" (Psalm 118 : 22), the "stone cut out without hands" (Daniel 2 : 34f., 44f.), the "stone of stumbling

[1] J. R. Harris, *Testimonies*, I (1916); II (1920). A somewhat different conclusion from Rendel Harris's is reached by C. H. Dodd in his fine work, *According to the Scriptures* (1952).

and rock of offence" (Isaiah 8 : 14) and the "precious corner stone of sure foundation" laid by God in Zion (Isaiah 28 : 16) are in the New Testament identified with each other and together applied to the Messiah in a way which presupposes their having already been brought together thus in a testimony collection.[1]

If we try to trace this testimony collection back to its source, we shall find ourselves going back to the very beginnings of Christianity, back to Jesus Himself. We can find no more satisfactory account of its origin than the account of those occasions on which He "began at Moses and all the prophets" and interpreted to His disciples in all the scriptures the things which referred to Himself.[2] The messianic application of Old Testament prophecies which the earliest Christians used was that which they had learned from their Master himself. It was, in the first instance, His selected scriptures and His interpretation that were committed to writing—as some think, by the apostle Matthew. The collection and messianic interpretation of Old Testament prophecies continued increasingly as time went on (and, it must be said, became amazingly fanciful) until we come to the rich development found in Justin Martyr's *Dialogue with Trypho the Jew* (*c*. A.D. 135) and the *Testimonies against the Jews* formerly ascribed to Cyprian of Carthage; but the earliest form of such a collection is as primitive as anything in Christianity. When the church became predominantly Greek-speaking, testimonies were based on the Septuagint text and at times on Septuagint wording which mistranslates or distorts the Hebrew. The Jews, at whom in later times these testimonies were mainly aimed, rejoined (as Trypho did to Justin) that the original Hebrew was different. The Greek Christians, however, had their ready answer: the Jews, they said, had deliberately altered the Hebrew text to turn the edge of the messianic application![3]

Testimonies, however, were not the only thing to be written down in these early days. The teaching of Jesus was also committed to writing at an early date. His teaching was given in a form easily memorized, and may even have been written before His death. Professor B. S. Easton holds that "we have every reason to believe that the first tradition of the sayings-groups and the parables arose in Jesus' lifetime and under His personal direction; the earliest content of the tradition He himself required His

---

[1] Cf. Mark 12 : 10 (with Matthew 22 : 42, 44; Luke 20 : 17f.); Acts 4 : 11; Romans 9 : 32f.; 1 Peter 2 : 4–8.

[2] Cf. Luke 24 : 25–27; 44–47.

[3] Thus Justin quotes, as a prophecy of the Cross, a Septuagint reading of Psalm 96 : 10: "Say among the nations, The Lord reigned from the tree." The words "from the tree" are not, of course, in the Hebrew text, nor yet are they known from any manuscript of the Septuagint. They must have been inserted into the text known to Justin as a Christian gloss. But Justin charges the Jews with cutting them out of the Biblical text (*Dialogue with Trypho*, 73). See p. 278.

disciples to commit to memory."[1] If it be objected that this procedure was contrary to rabbinic practice, we must remember that Jesus was a rabbi with a difference; to many even outside the circle of His immediate disciples He was "a prophet mighty in deed and word," while to His disciples themselves He was still more: He was the Messiah himself. It was because the written form was suitable only for prophetic words that the rabbis refrained from using it; but this restriction could not apply to Jesus, acclaimed by His followers as the predicted "prophet like unto Moses."[2]

The need for communicating the teaching of Jesus to a rapidly growing community must in any case have led to the drawing up of summaries or digests of His teaching. Teachers or catechists themselves had to be trained quickly in order that they might instruct others. It is widely thought that one such collection of the teaching of Jesus, circulating perhaps in the church at Antioch and its daughter-churches, underlies our canonical gospels. The preface to Luke's Gospel plainly indicates that such written summaries of the doings and sayings of Jesus were in circulation when he wrote.

Then the good news itself took quite definite shape in the very early days of the community. An examination of the apostolic preaching reveals a fairly stereotyped pattern, and this same pattern forms the framework of our gospels, especially Mark and John. In particular the passion narrative can be traced in definite outline practically from the beginning. "On all grounds," says Professor C. H. Dodd, "it seems probable that in the Passion-narrative we are in close touch with the primitive tradition. The story was not produced either by the teaching of the early Church or by theological reflection upon it. It is the story that underlies the *kerygma*,[3] and provided the basis for the theology of the epistles."[4] It was not until nearly the end of the first Christian generation, when the original eyewitnesses could not be expected to survive much longer, that our gospels as such began to be written,[5] but the material contained in our gospels was, in oral form, and to some extent also in written form,[6] the common property of Christians from the earliest times.

The joy and exaltation of these early days found expression in praises to God. For their praises the primitive Christians had the Old Testament Book of Psalms ready to hand, and in several of

---

[1] *Christ in the Gospels* (1930), p. 41.
[2] Deuteronomy 18 : 15ff., quoted of Jesus in Acts 3 : 22f.; 7 : 37 (cf. John 1 : 21, 24; 6 : 14).
[3] The Greek word for "proclamation," frequently used of the apostolic message.
[4] *History and the Gospel* (1938), p. 84.
[5] See pp. 35, 139.
[6] Cf. Luke 1 : 1.

these psalms they found adumbrations of the advent and work of the Messiah. There is some reason to think that Greek-speaking Christians from an early date used Psalm 34 as a baptismal hymn; the opening words of verse 5, which the Septuagint renders "Come to him and be enlightened", are echoed in 1 Peter 2 : 4 ("to whom coming . . .") in what is probably a baptismal context, and "enlightenment" was a synonym for Christian baptism perhaps as early as New Testament times (cf. p. 195).

But the reference to "spiritual songs" in the New Testament epistles suggests that many Christians found a new song in their mouths, springing up spontaneously by the power of the Spirit of Christ within them. Something of this sort, for example, seems to have happened to Paul when he suddenly leaves his necessarily pedestrian directions on church order in 1 Corinthians 12 and 14 and soars to the high reaches of poetry in his hymn in praise of heavenly love. Nor are his other letters free from passages which seem to be snatches of early Christian hymnody. Such are the baptismal lines of Ephesians 5 : 14:

> Awake, O sleeper,
> And rise from the dead,
> And Christ shall shine upon thee.

So, too, the great passage on the humiliation of the Christ in Philippians 2 : 6ff. and the summary of Christian belief in 1 Timothy 3 : 16 ("He was manifest in flesh . . ."), illustrate the fact that to these early believers the great doctrines of Christianity were no theological abstractions but matter for inspired rejoicing.[1] The prologue to the fourth gospel ("In the beginning was the Word...") has also been looked upon as an early Christian hymn: with the exception of certain prose insertions by which it is dovetailed into the beginning of John's narrative it is, in fact, of poetic form.[2] And the collection of second-century Christian hymns curiously known as the "Odes of Solomon" shows that hymns with the same high Christology and the same distinctive style as we find in the fourth gospel were current in the churches in the neighbourhood of Palestine.[3] High Christology and "Johannine" style are already present in a saying of Jesus recorded in Matthew 11 : 25–27 and Luke 10 : 21 f., and usually regarded as having been part of the sayings collection called "Q":

[1] It is interesting to recall that the *Quicunque Vult* (the so-called "Athanasian Creed") is really a canticle, not a creed. "The Church's confession of faith," said James Denney, "should be *sung*, not signed."

[2] Cf. J. R. Harris, *The Prologue to St. John's Gospel* (1917); C. F. Burney, *The Aramaic Origin of the Fourth Gospel* (1922), pp. 28ff.

[3] These odes are extant in Syriac. When Rendel Harris discovered them in 1909, and expressed the opinion that they dated from the first century, the German scholar, Adolf Jülicher, is reported to have remarked: "Then all our criticism of the Fourth Gospel is *kaput*."

> Thanks be to thee, O Father,
> Lord of heaven and earth,
> That hast hidden these things from the wise,
> And revealed them to babes.
> Yea, Father (thanks be to thee),
> For so it was pleasing to thee.
> All is delivered to me from the Father,
> And none knows the Son but the Father;
> Nor does any know the Father but the Son,
> And he to whom the Son would reveal him.[1]

This leads up in the Matthæan account to the comfortable words" (in similar rhythm):

> Come unto me, all ye weary and burdened,
>   And I will refresh you.
> Take my yoke upon you
>   And learn of me;
> For meek am I, and lowly of heart,
>   And ye shall rest your souls.
> For my yoke is easy,
>   And my burden, light.[2]

But this has brought us beyond those early days in Jerusalem, when the Nazarenes were growing in numbers daily, praising God for His grace in Christ, walking in the apostolic teaching, rejoicing in the fellowship, proclaiming the good news abroad, and enjoying widespread goodwill.

[1] C. F. Burney, in *The Poetry of Our Lord* (1925), pp. 171f., gives an Aramaic retroversion of this passage which shows not only characteristic poetical rhythm but even rhyme. Indeed, a great part of the teaching of Jesus shows similar features, as is shown in this book of Burney's, as it was earlier shown by Bishop John Jebb of Limerick in *Sacred Literature* (1820). "Since Jesus appeared to His contemporaries as a prophet, and prophets were accustomed to give oracles in verse, it is credible that we have here something approaching His *ipsissima verba*" (C. H. Dodd, *History and the Gospel*, pp. 89f.).

[2] Burney, *op. cit.*, pp. 144f.

CHAPTER VII

THE RABBI OF TARSUS

THE GREAT RABBI GAMALIEL HAD AMONG HIS DISCIPLES ONE
who, according to a passage in the Talmud, gave his
master a good deal of trouble, manifesting "impudence in
matters of learning." But his name is not given; he is remembered
simply as "that pupil." Dr. Klausner sees in this passage a veiled
reference to Saul of Tarsus, later pre-eminent in the Christian
movement as Paul the apostle.[1] If his identification is right, then
the "impudence" which "that pupil" is said to have displayed
towards his venerated teacher is a projection back into his earlier
days of his subsequent course of life (as it appeared in the eyes of
Jewish orthodoxy).

It was in the later twenties of the first century that this young
Jewish citizen of Tarsus in Cilicia came to Jerusalem to be enrolled among the disciples of Gamaliel. The young man bore the
name of Saul, perhaps because his parents, who belonged to the
tribe of Benjamin, wished to give him the name of an illustrious
member of that tribe in ancient times—Saul, the first king of
Israel. They were distinguished Jews of Tarsus, belonging indeed
to the élite of the citizen body, for Saul's father was a Roman
citizen. Whence he acquired his citizenship we do not know. He
may very well have received it as a reward for services rendered
to a Roman commander like Pompey or Antony. In any case,
Saul was born a Roman citizen, and valued the privilege very
highly. As a Roman citizen, he had a Roman name, consisting of
three parts: *praenomen, nomen gentile* and *cognomen*.[2] What his *praenomen* (first or personal name) and *nomen gentile* (family name) were
we can only guess; his *cognomen*, however, was Paullus, by which
(in its English form Paul) we usually call him.

In the family circle, however, he was known by his Jewish
name Saul. Tarsus was a great Greek city, but this family did not
speak Greek at home, but Aramaic, the Palestinian vernacular.

[1] See J. Klausner, *From Jesus to Paul* (1944), pp. 310f., where references to other
literature are given, over and above the passage in the Babylonian Talmud, *Shabbath*
30b.

[2] The threefold Roman name may be illustrated from the full names of such famous
Romans as Gaius Julius Cæsar, Marcus Tullius Cicero, Lucius Cornelius Scipio. If
Paul's name was (say) Lucius Aemilius Paullus, that would link him with a distinguished Roman family; but we have no means of determining what the first two
parts of his Roman name were.

So they regarded themselves not as "Hellenists" but as "Hebrews" (Paul calls himself a "Hebrew son of Hebrew parents"[1]), in a linguistic as well as in an ethnic sense. And much as Paul valued his Tarsian citizenship (Tarsus being, as he said himself, "no mean city"), much, too, as he valued his free birth as a citizen of Rome, there was something which was of greater value in his eyes, and that was his Hebrew ancestry and traditions and upbringing. When, as a youth, he made the journey to Jerusalem to be educated at the feet of Gamaliel, the greatest rabbi of the day, instead of prosecuting his studies in the University of Tarsus, it was with the firm ambition of outstripping his fellows in expert knowledge and practice of the Jewish religion and in zealous adherence to the ancestral traditions. And he bade fair to achieve this ambition; he drank in eagerly the lore taught by Gamaliel, and in addition to the study of the law he probably learned more of Greek culture in Gamaliel's school than he had been permitted to acquire in Tarsus.[2] A distinguished career as a master in Israel lay before him. The Pharisaic school of thought, as expounded by his great teacher, commended itself to his mind, and he ardently embraced its tenets, including in particular the resurrection hope. His correspondence of later days which has survived bears ample testimony to his familiarity with rabbinic modes of thought and exegesis.[3] If the study and practice of the divine law according to the traditional interpretation constituted the way of acceptance by God and a share in the life of the age to come, then Paul's chance of this attainment was a high one. Endowed as he was with a powerful will, he could not see what he believed to be the right course without following it. In regard to the standard of righteousness prescribed by the oral law he was, on his own later testimony, blameless; and he succeeded in maintaining a good conscience in respect of his duty towards God and his fellow-men. Yet, despite this good conscience and meticulous devotion to the commandments, there were within him misgivings only half realized. There was a struggle between a strong self-will on the one hand and the desire to do the will of God on the other. Although the desire to do the will of God won every time, so far as outward action went, the young man became aware of increasing inward dissatisfaction, and nothing that he had learned in the rabbinical school was of any help in allaying it.

An opportunity arose, however, of throwing himself into a course of vigorous action which gave him, while it lasted, little time to attend to these inner questionings. The Nazarene move-

[1] This is the sense of the phrase in Philippians 3 : 5, rendered "an Hebrew of the Hebrews" in the Authorized Version of our Bible.
[2] See W. L. Knox, *Some Hellenistic Elements in Primitive Christianity* (1944), p. 33.
[3] See W. D. Davies, *Paul and Rabbinic Judaism* (1948), and E. P. Sanders, *Paul and Palestinian Judaism* (1977).

ment, as we have seen, was making headway in Jerusalem between the years 30 and 33, and enjoyed the general good will of the populace, in spite of efforts made by the Sadducean party to intimidate its leaders. Gamaliel might temporize, but on this point at least his pupil agreed with the Sadducees, though on theological rather than political grounds. To Paul, the Nazarene claims were too absurd to deserve serious attention. The man whom they acclaimed as Messiah had died upon a cross. Whether he merited that death or not was of minor importance; the fact that he did die thus was what really mattered, for it proved one thing decisively—that he could not be the Messiah. Was it not written in the law that a man who was hanged was accursed by God?[1] Jesus was hanged, and was therefore subject to the divine curse; it followed inevitably that he could not be the Messiah, who was the object of unique divine favour.

But the growth of this Nazarene party became too serious to be ignored. It was not only unlearned Galilæans who were propagating this blasphemy; priests and scholars too were being carried away. In the synagogue where the Cilician Jews met in Jerusalem quite a stir arose as another young man, a Hellenistic Jew who had embraced these beliefs, repeatedly emphasized that the crucified Jesus was indeed the Messiah—and more than that, that He was the inaugurator of a new order which was destined to supersede the present order in Israel, with its holy temple and sacrificial ritual. These were but temporary institutions and were now obsolete. A new age had dawned, in which the crucified Jesus was king. The Galilæan disciples might still go up to the temple to perform their devotions and otherwise behave as observant Jews; but this young Hellenist saw that the two religions were really incompatible. The new had come to stay; the old, therefore, must go.

This young man was Stephen, whom we have already met as one of the seven leaders of the Hellenist section in the Jerusalem church. As Paul listened to him, he realized that the new movement was dangerous as well as blasphemously ridiculous. This Stephen was no Galilæan peasant, but a most persuasive disputant; it was difficult to counter his arguments, and besides, in addition to his logical power, there was a disturbing charm about him which tempted one to believe that here was a man of whom the truth had taken hold, that the Spirit of God who formerly spoke through the prophets was speaking through him. But of course that could not be; this Jesus of Nazareth of whom Stephen spoke so much had been proved by the manner of his death to be under the curse of God and therefore could not possibly be the

[1] Cf. Deuteronomy 21 : 22f. with Acts 5 : 30; 10 : 39; and especially with Galatians 3 : 10–14.

Messiah. If those people went about saying that he had risen from the dead, it was probably deliberate deceit on their part and not simply self-deception. In any case, the movement revealed itself as a threat to all that Paul had learned to hold dear, and it must be opposed. As Paul saw the situation, the patience and moderation which Gamaliel counselled were not the qualities which the hour demanded. Stephen was right in this at least, that the new movement could not be reconciled with the old tradition. Paul, a zealot for the ancestral traditions of his nation, must take more drastic action than his teacher thought wise.

Stephen's assertion that the temple and the priesthood and everything associated with them were doomed to extinction formed the basis of a charge of blasphemy brought against him before the Sanhedrin. When called upon to make his defence he simply reiterated the arguments which he had used in the synagogue,[1] and at last he was hustled out of the council chamber and stoned to death. Paul thoroughly approved of this proceeding, and showed his approval by guarding the clothes of the witnesses in the case, who (in accordance with Jewish practice) acted as chief executioners.

The case of Stephen now gave the Sanhedrin an opportunity to pursue a policy of repression against the Nazarenes with popular support (for the people of Jerusalem would not tolerate a threat to the temple). Into this repression Paul threw himself zealously. If something about the look in Stephen's eyes as he faced his accusers and excutioners made an impression on Paul, he sternly thrust this impression down and threw himself into the work of harrying the Nazarene community—especially, we may gather, its Hellenist members. The effect upon the persecuted community was decisive; many of them left Jerusalem for other parts of Judæa and some even crossed the boundaries of Palestine into Syria and Phœnicia and other neighbouring states and provinces. Even there, Paul determined, the leaders among the refugees must be sought out and brought back to Jerusalem for suitable judgment at the hands of the Sanhedrin. So from synagogue to synagogue he went, hunting down the refugees and doing his best to make them renounce their faith publicly by declaring Jesus to be accursed. The leaders in the synagogue had certain powers of coercion over members who would not come to heel, and these powers were put into operation.

The writ of the high priest would be respected by synagogues

---

[1] The two main planks in Stephen's argument (preserved for us in Acts 7) were these: (1) the sacrificial order was never meant to be permanent; that was why God directed Moses to have a movable tent as the national sanctuary; a building of stone and mortar, such as Solomon built, being restricted to one spot, was a departure from the divine ideal; (2) the nation of Israel had always rejected God's messengers, and this rejection had recently culminated in their rejection of the Messiah Himself.

outside Palestine; so, armed with letters from Caiaphas, Paul made his way into Syria, in order first of all to secure the persons of leading Nazarenes who had sought refuge in Damascus, and send them back to Jerusalem. The high priest's religious authority was upheld by the Roman power, since this made for a measure of quietness among Jews throughout the Empire. In particular, the new movement could be represented as hostile to the temple prerogatives which were protected by imperial law. To Damascus, then, Paul went, and it was as he approached its ancient walls that the revolution took place which changed him from an implacable opponent of the new movement into its most ardent champion. Attempts have been made to account for his conversion in psychological terms; Paul's own account was that a blinding light shone upon him and his companions, and that in that moment he himself saw Jesus of Nazareth alive before him and heard His voice. The companions saw the light indeed, and heard Paul speaking, but they did not see the person whom Paul saw nor did they hear the voice that Paul heard. But to Paul the voice spoke distinctly, addressing him in the Aramaic tongue that he used to speak at home: *Sha'ul, Sha'ul, ma att radephinni?* "Saul, Saul, why are you persecuting me? To keep on kicking out against the goad is hard for you."[1] And as Paul in wonder asked the speaker who he was, he heard him say, "I am Jesus the Nazarene, the very one whom you are persecuting."

Blinded by excess of light, Paul was led by his companions into the city. On the third day he was visited by a devout Jew of Damascus, Ananias by name, one who had learned to call Jesus "Lord". This visit was the occasion for the restoration of Paul's eyesight, and with the return of his natural vision came a new understanding of his present condition and recent experience. Ananias, acting as the mouthpiece of Jesus, commanded Paul to get himself baptized and told him that he was to be the chosen bearer of the good news to both Jews and Gentiles.

When Paul had recovered from the physical effects of his experience and carefully considered all its implications, he lost no time in acting upon them. He went to the synagogues to which he had been accredited by the high priest's letters, but played a very different part from that which he had set out to play. He proclaimed boldly and with conviction that Jesus of Nazareth was the Messiah, the Son of God.

[1] The nearest parallel of modern times to the conversion of Paul is the account of Sadhu Sundar Singh's conversion after a period of determined hostility to Christianity. "At 4.30 a.m. . . . I saw a great light. . . . I saw the form of the Lord Jesus Christ. . . . I heard a voice saying in Hindustani, 'How long will you persecute Me?' . . . The thought then came to me, 'Jesus Christ is not dead but living and it must be He Himself'" (B. H. Streeter and A. J. Appasamy, *The Sadhu*, pp. 5–7). To the best of his remembrance he did not then know the story of Paul's conversion.

But how? Was the old argument no longer valid, that Jesus, by being "hanged on a tree", had incurred the divine curse? No, it was still valid. But something else must now be taken into the reckoning. Those who claimed that Jesus had been raised from the dead were proved true witnesses, for Paul had now seen the risen Lord for himself and heard Him speak. Jesus, raised from the dead, was manifestly the object of the divine approval. God had reversed the curse involved in His death. Why then should He suffer the death on which the divine curse rested? Sooner rather than later the answer must have come to Paul, as he expressed it some years later in his letter to the churches of the province of Galatia. The law pronounces a curse on all who fail to keep it wholly: "Cursed is he who does not continue in all that is written in the book of the law to perform it." And this curse Jesus took upon Himself, being free from its necessity by reason of His perfect obedience to the divine law: "Christ has redeemed us from the curse of the law by becoming accursed on our behalf, as it is written, 'Cursed is everyone who hangs upon a tree'."[1] The *form* of the argument was such as Paul was perfectly familiar with in the rabbinical schools, but no rabbi had ever been so audacious as to formulate this particular argument—that the Messiah himself should assume the curse denounced upon the breakers of God's law in order to liberate them from that curse. But Paul's conclusion was inevitable; that Jesus was indeed the Messiah He was now sure, but Jesus had died an accursed death. The scandal of the cross, at which Paul had stumbled for so long, was resolved into the saving act of God.

Whether Paul at this stage connected his explanation of the Messiah's death with the statement in Isaiah 53 : 10 about the Servant's becoming a guilt-offering is not certain; but this idea appears later in Paul's statement that Christ was "made sin" (that is, "became a sin-offering") on our behalf that we in Him might be vested with God's righteousness[2]—and that, by the way, is a further echo of the Isaianic passage, where the Servant "makes many righteous."

But this is certain, that the suppressed questionings and dissatisfactions of his inmost being were brought to the surface to find their answer in Christ. The law demanded—and from Paul received—conformity to its requirements, but this, he felt, affected his external life only. The limitations of the law appeared when he attempted to carry out such an inward injunction as "Thou shalt not covet". The very existence of such a commandment, once it was brought to his attention, had stirred into life a latent tendency to covetousness, the very thing that it forbade.

[1] Galatians 3; 10–13, quoting Deuteronomy 27 : 26 and 21 : 23.
[2] 2 Corinthians 5 : 21.

The commandment was good, but it could not help him to obey it. Now, however, he learned that what the law could not achieve, because of the weakness of his human nature, God accomplished by sending His Son in human nature as a sin-offering for men. The work of Christ had the effect of implanting in those who were united to Him by faith the desire and the power to carry out the law's requirements, not by painstaking conformity to an external standard, but by the operation of the Spirit of Christ within.

How much of all this Paul settled for himself in the days following his conversion we cannot say; but probably the main outlines of his later teaching took shape very quickly. Both in Damascus itself and in the neighbouring territory of the Arabian king Aretas IV, Paul now proclaimed his new-found faith, and the opposition grew so severe that his life was threatened. The Damascene Jews who were scandalized by his doctrine enlisted the co-operation of King Aretas's representative in Damascus, and at his instance the city gate was watched day and night to seize the trouble-maker. So, as Paul himself narrates, "I was let down in a basket through a window in the city wall, and thus I escaped his hands".[1]

It was now the third year since Paul had set out for Damascus, and on his return to Jerusalem he tried to get in touch with the followers of Jesus. This was naturally a matter of some delicacy, as his former activity was not forgotten. His overtures were suspect as those of an *agent provocateur*. But Barnabas, a Levite from Cyprus, and a leader in the Nazarene community, who probably had some previous acquaintance with Paul and knew his character, lent his good offices and Peter showed hospitality to Paul for a fortnight. It appears from Paul's own account that the chief reason for his return to Jerusalem at this time was to make Peter's acquaintance and ascertain from him as much as he could about Jesus.[2] A record of the conversations which the two men had with each other during that fortnight would make interesting reading. "We may presume", as Professor Dodd says, "they did not spend all the time talking about the weather";[3] nor did that topic monopolize Paul's conversation with James the brother of Jesus, whom he also met on that occasion. He met none of the other apostles at that time, and it is no accident that, in his famous summary of the appearances of the risen Christ, the only persons whom he mentions by name as being granted such appearances are Peter, James and himself. These interviews with Peter and James were most important for Paul; the main outlines of the apostolic message as it had been proclaimed from the day of

[1] 2 Corinthians 11 : 32f.
[2] Galatians 1 : 18.
[3] *The Apostolic Preaching and Its Developments* (1936), p. 26.

Pentecost onward were made clear to him, so that he could thenceforth assure his hearers and readers that he was imparting to them what had been imparted to himself in the first instance: "whether it be I or they [the original witnesses of the resurrection], this is what we proclaim". There were not two or more divergent accounts of the good news circulating in the apostolic age, but one and the same account, whether propagated by Paul, Peter, James, or anyone else. Whatever differences might or might not arise later between Paul and the others, they were agreed about the basic facts which constituted the gospel.[1]

Paul considered that his immediate duty was to bear witness to his faith in Jesus as the Messiah in those circles where he had formerly opposed Stephen; but their reaction against him was swift and violent. Paul was in their eyes a traitor to the cause of truth; by his *volte-face* he tacitly condemned those who had previously followed him enthusiastically as their leader in the campaign of suppression. He himself relates[2] how he fell into a trance while praying in the temple and had a vision of Jesus, who told him to leave Jerusalem, because his witness would not be accepted. Paul protested that he was a particularly valuable witness, because the people of Jerusalem knew his earlier record as a persecutor and his approval of the death of Stephen. But the Lord repeated His command to depart, adding: "I am going to send you far away to the Gentiles."

In these words of the risen Lord to Paul we may catch an echo of the Servant's mission: "I will also make you a light to the Gentiles." Paul was now to be the chief instrument in the inauguration of this part of the Servant's task.

That Paul's testimony was not going to be accepted in Jerusalem was made very evident by an attempt upon his life. His friends got him away safely to Cæsarea on the coast, and there he took ship for his native Tarsus. No doubt the Nazarenes breathed more freely when he had gone. He had caused them much anxiety in his persecuting days, and now that he, too, had become a follower of Jesus they were to have a good deal more anxiety of other kinds because of him.

There follow several obscure years spent by Paul in Tarsus and the surrounding parts of the province of Syria-Cilicia, faintly illuminated by a few hints dropped here and there in his letters. He was evidently disinherited by his family,[3] and suffered the indignity of "forty stripes save one" at the hands of synagogue

---

[1] When Paul claimed to have received his gospel by revelation, independently of the other apostles (Galatians 1 : 11ff.), he is thinking not of the salvation-bringing events themselves so much as of their implication, particularly with regard to the position of Gentiles in the gospel economy (cf. Ephesians 2 : 3).

[2] Acts 22 : 17–21.

[3] Cf. Philippians 3 : 8.

authorities more than once.[1] Towards the end of this period of
his life he underwent the experience which he describes as being
caught away into paradise and hearing unutterable words
("whether in the body, I do not know; or whether out of the body,
I do not know; God knows"[2]), and which left him with a recur-
ring physical affliction which he found to be for his spiritual
benefit. What the affliction was has been a subject of varied
speculation—malaria, epilepsy, stammering, ophthalmia have all
been suggested—but it is not too fanciful to think that it was this
malady that gave his traducers at Corinth in later days occasion to
say in scorn that his bodily presence was weak and his speech
contemptible.[3]

But these experiences were preparing Paul for his true life-
work, to which he was introduced about the year 45 when his old
friend Barnabas turned up in Tarsus and discovered his where-
abouts. Barnabas had come from Antioch in Syria specially to
look for Paul, for there was work to be done in Antioch, and
Paul was the man to do it.

[1] 2 Corinthians 11 : 24.
[2] 2 Corinthians 12 : 1–10.
[3] 2 Corinthians 10 : 10.

CHAPTER VIII

ANTIOCH ON THE ORONTES

IN NORTH SYRIA, FIFTEEN MILES UP THE RIVER ORONTES, LAY the city of Antioch.[1] It was founded in 300 B.C. by Seleucus Nicator, a general of Alexander the Great, to be the capital of the Macedonian dynasty which Seleucus established in Syria. When Syria was incorporated in the Roman Empire in 64 B.C., Antioch received the status of a free city, and it became the capital of the Roman province of Syria. Like other chief cities of the Macedonian empires, it was an important centre of the Jewish dispersion. Here Jew and Gentile met; here, too, the sophisticated Greeks of the coastal territory met the nomads of the interior. Here was a place where people of different races and religions were thrown together and had many of their rough corners rubbed off. And here Christianity was firmly planted and underwent a remarkable development about ten years after the birth of the new community in Jerusalem.

It all resulted from the persecution which broke out on the morrow of Stephen's death. Some of the believing Hellenists who left Jerusalem at that time made their way to the chief centres of Hellenist Jewry in the neighbouring lands—Cyprus, Phœnicia, Syria—and some arrived in Antioch. There some daring spirits, men of Cyprus and Cyrene, took a great step forward. If the gospel message was so good for Jews might it not be good for Gentiles, too? At any rate they would try. So they began to tell the good news to Gentiles, and their enterprise met with immediate success. The Gentiles took to the gospel story as something that exactly suited their case, and many of them believed in Jesus.

So revolutionary a course could not be concealed; news of the Gentile response reached the ears of the apostles at Jerusalem. The shock was no doubt softened for them by a recent experience which Peter had had in a Gentile home at Cæsarea.[2] But this busi-

---

[1] The results of excavations in Antioch from 1932 to 1939 have been published in four volumes, *Antioch-on-the-Orontes*, edited by G. W. Elderkin, R. Stillwell and F. O. Waage (Princeton, 1934–48). See also an article by B. M. Metzger, "Antioch-on-the-Orontes," in *The Biblical Archæologist* for December, 1948.

[2] See pp. 99ff. Paul, by this time, was back in Tarsus, and there is evidence that he, too, was evangelizing Gentiles in his home province of Cilicia, but the Jerusalem authorities were not in direct contact with him as they were with Antioch.

ness at Antioch seemed to be moving on a scale which they had not envisaged, and they sent a trusted delegate to make investigations. The man they sent was Barnabas; they could not have made a better choice. When he came to Antioch he recognized that this was the work of God, and was delighted at what he saw. He encouraged his fellow-Cypriots and the men from Cyrene to carry on, and the work developed rapidly, until Barnabas felt the need of a colleague to share the responsibility of supervising it. But who had the necessary qualifications? Many excellent Jewish Christians would be unable to discard traditional prejudices sufficiently to take a wholehearted part in a mission to Gentiles. There was one man, however, whom Barnabas had in mind; and he made it his personal business to hunt this man out and enlist his support. This was Paul, the Tarsian, who had been active for some years now in his native city and the surrounding district and had already had some experience in evangelizing Gentiles.

Paul, then, returned to Antioch with Barnabas, and helped him in the building up of a strong Christian church. It is no longer anachronistic to use the term "Christian," for it was in Antioch that the Nazarenes received this name from the Gentile population. Jews would not have given them a name containing the element "Christ" (the Greek equivalent of Messiah), for that would have been tantamount to admitting that Jesus, whose followers these people were, was indeed the Messiah. To Gentiles, however, Christ was merely a name (if rather an odd one), with none of the religious associations which it had for Jews; and so, as they heard these people talk so much about their Lord and Saviour as *Christos*, they called them *Christianoi*, "Christ's people."

Other leaders of the church at Antioch were a Cyrenean named Lucius, Simeon, who bore the Latin surname, *Niger*, or "Black" (identified by some with Simon the Cyrenean who carried the Cross for Jesus), and Manaen (the Greek form of Menahem), who had been brought up at the court of Herod the Great and was a close boyhood associate of Herod Antipas. About this time, too, a young Greek physician named Lucas (Anglicized as Luke) became a member of the church at Antioch,[1] and to him historians of early Christianity owe a quite special debt; for we should be immeasurably worse equipped for our task if he had not in later years composed a history of the beginnings of Christianity in two volumes, which appear in the New Testament as "The Gospel

[1] That Luke was a native of Antioch is stated by the Anti-Marcionite prologue to his gospel about A.D. 170, and by Eusebius (*Ecclesiastical History*, III, 4) early in the fourth century; this tradition is supported by some internal evidence in his writings, and especially by the "Western" text of Acts, which in Acts 11 : 28 reads "when *we* were gathered together."

according to St. Luke" and "The Acts of the Apostles" respectively.[1]

In those days there were commonly heard in the Christian communities people called prophets, who were liable at any time to rise in church meetings and utter words immediately inspired by the divine power which took possession of them. In later times they became rarer, partly because the churches became suspicious that not all who claimed to practise the prophetic gift were genuine prophets, partly because the growth of ecclesiastical organization left little room for such unarranged ministry, and partly, no doubt, because their numbers were actually less. But we meet quite a number of them in the earlier years, and in fact such super-normal manifestations are not unparalleled at the outset of a great religious movement.[2]

One of these prophets, a visitor from Jerusalem, Agabus by name, suddenly declared in a meeting of the church at Antioch that famine conditions were to prevail in all lands. We know, in fact, from the Roman historian Suetonius that the reign of the Emperor Claudius (A.D. 41–54) was marked by a succession of bad harvests;[3] and so far as Palestine is concerned, Josephus relates that it was beset by famine about A.D. 46, and that the Jewish queen-mother of the kingdom of Adiabene on the Tigris bought corn in Egypt and figs in Cyprus to relieve the wants of the Jews in Palestine.[4] It was about this time, too, that the church of Antioch, having collected a sum of money for their Palestinian friends in response to the prophecy of Agabus, sent Barnabas and Paul to carry this gift to the church at Jerusalem.

Barnabas and Paul made use of the opportunity which this visit to Jerusalem afforded to discuss with the leaders of the mother church the question of evangelizing Gentiles. The discussion was conducted in a brotherly spirit. The Jerusalem leaders—the apostles Peter and John, and James the brother of Jesus—agreed that God had manifestly called and qualified Barnabas and Paul for spreading the good news among Gentiles; to their minds, the success that attended their work was an obvious token of the divine approval. It was recognized that the primary call of the Jerusalem leaders, on the other hand, was to

[1] The two parts of Luke's history were separated in this way when the four gospels were gathered together into one gospel collection about the end of the first century. Formerly his history would have been entitled *Luke to Theophilus* (Parts I and II).

[2] This prophetic gift was similar to, but not identical with, the gift of tongues mentioned on pp. 58f. It survived in the Syrian churches till the end of the first century, when the treatise called the *Didache* reveals how attempts were made to control it: it was revived in the second century in Asia Minor among the Montanists, and similar manifestations are recorded at various periods in the history of the church. See pp. 214ff.

[3] Suetonius, *Life of Claudius*, XVIII, 2.

[4] *Antiquities*, XX, 2 : 5.

evangelize Jews. They therefore shook hands over this, in token of mutual fellowship in the matter. Only, said the Jerusalem leaders, go on remembering "the poor"; and, of course, Barnabas and Paul heartily agreed; as Paul says in his report of the discussion, "this was the very thing I had made it my business to do";[1] this was, in fact, the prime object of their visit to Jerusalem at that time.

There is reason to believe that some at least of the Jerusalem leaders regarded Barnabas and Paul's undertaking to remember "the poor" as an acknowledgment of the Jerusalem church's right to receive a sort of tribute from the Gentile Christians (much as the Jerusalem temple exacted an annual contribution from Jews throughout the world). Paul, for his part, regarded the undertaking as a voluntary act of grace and fellowship. However, the present agreement was satisfactory so far as it went. When the Antiochene delegates returned to Antioch, they took with them from Jerusalem Barnabas's young cousin John, who also bore the Roman name Marcus (Mark).

It was now plain to Barnabas and Paul that they could carry on their mission to Gentiles with the fullest liberty and not be afraid of misunderstandings arising with the Palestinian leaders. And before long they had an opportunity of wider activity in their chosen work. One day in a meeting of the Antiochene church a prophet arose and uttered words in which his hearers recognized a divine oracle: "Set Barnabas and Paul apart for me, for the work which I have called them to." It was the voice of the Holy Spirit; it must not be disobeyed. The work to which these two leaders of the church were called was, of course, the Gentile mission; this was now to be prosecuted over a wider field. So the two men were released from their local responsibilities in the church to carry out this work.

Westward from the Syrian coast lay the island of Cyprus, a Roman province, Barnabas's native land. In the decision to evangelize this island we may trace the mind of Barnabas. With them went John Mark. He was a useful companion because there were certain phases of the story of Jesus of which he had special knowledge—especially the events leading up to the crucifixion.

But the Gentile mission must not be carried out haphazardly. The missionaries had a fixed plan of operation. The important cities lying along the great highways of empire should be the special object of their attention; if the gospel could be planted in them, it would spread out to the surrounding territory. But where would they find their Gentile hearers? In the first instance, among those Gentiles who, sabbath by sabbath, went to the Jewish synagogue. There were many Gentiles throughout the

[1] Galatians 2 : 10. See p. 70.

Roman world in those days who found in the Jewish synagogue-worship a pure and attractive monotheistic religion to which paganism offered nothing comparable. Most of these Gentiles did not go so far as to become proselytes; they did not accept circumcision and the obligation to keep the whole Jewish law (ceremonial as well as ethical) which incorporation in the Jewish community required. But they attended synagogue, and some of them kept the sabbath as a day of rest and observed the Jewish food laws. They were known as "God-fearers." On their part a certain acquaintance with the Old Testament background of the gospel could be reasonably presumed, as they heard the law and the prophets read week by week in the synagogues.

Besides, it was only right (in the eyes of Barnabas and Paul) that they should make the synagogue their first base of operations in evangelizing any city. For the Jews, as the people of God, had the right to hear the good news first, not only for their own sakes, but in order that they might actively fulfil Israel's appointed mission to carry the good news to the Gentiles. Barnabas and Paul, in their work of Gentile evangelization, did not wish to dispense with Jewish co-operation; they earnestly desired it. Rarely, however, was their desire realized; for the most part, the Jewish communities declined the good news, whereas the God-fearers accepted it avidly as the very thing they were waiting for.

Barnabas, Paul and John Mark passed through Cyprus from east to west. At Paphos, its western capital, they had an interesting encounter with Lucius Sergius Paullus, the proconsul of the province. Sir William Ramsay presented some evidence suggesting that certain members of this man's family in later generations were Christians[1]—an interesting footnote to Luke's statement that Sergius believed the message which the missionaries brought.[2]

From Paphos the missionaries took ship again and sailed to Perga, a port on the south coast of Asia Minor. If Cyprus was dear to the heart of Barnabas, Asia Minor for a similar reason was dear to Paul's. And in Asia Minor it is Paul who seems to take the lead. It may have been for this reason that John Mark left them at this point and went home to Jerusalem. Possibly he had not bargained for this extension of their tour and did not like the way in which his cousin Barnabas seemed to be slipping into the second place.[3] Paul, at any rate, thought there was no justification

[1] *The Bearing of Recent Discovery on the Trustworthiness of the New Testament* (1915), pp. 150ff.

[2] Acts 13 : 12.

[3] Dr. S. C. Carpenter, in the *Daily Telegraph* for October 2, 1948, told how one of the Exeter Cathedral choristers, in an examination answer, accounted for Mark's seeming desertion by suggesting that a message reached him to this effect: "Will John Mark, of Jerusalem, believed to be in Perga of Pamphylia, return at once to Jerusalem, where his mother, Mary Mark, is seriously ill." Paul would certainly have regarded his departure more leniently in such circumstances as these!

for Mark's departure and considered that he had let them down. The two missionaries now went up country into the Roman province of Galatia, and visited the town of Antioch. This Antioch may be distinguished from Syrian Antioch by its fuller name Pisidian Antioch (it was so called because it was near the border of the region of Pisidia, but it was not "in Pisidia," as the Authorized Version says at Acts 13 : 14). Pisidian Antioch was a Roman colony, situated on one of the great Roman roads through Asia Minor. A Roman colony was a community of Roman citizens planted at a strategic point of communications, to safeguard the interests of Rome in that outpost of empire. Paul's missionary eye picked out these strategic outposts and envisaged them as strategic centres in the spiritual kingdom which he was proclaiming and extending. Roman colonies played an important part in his successive plans of campaign.

The synagogue in Pisidian Antioch was attended by a large number of Gentiles. On the first sabbath after their arrival in the city, Barnabas and Paul attended the synagogue. When the scripture lessons had been read, they were invited by the rulers of the synagogue to address the congregation. Paul stood up to speak, and his sermon is summarized by the historian, probably to give readers a sample of the type of sermon which Paul regularly preached when he had a synagogue audience before him. He outlined the history of Israel from the time of the divine deliverance of the people at the Exodus and carried the story on to the reign of David. Then, with a reference to the promise that the Messiah, the deliverer of Israel, would be born of David's line, he announced that this deliverer had actually come in the person of Jesus, whose well-attested resurrection, following upon His crucifixion, proved Him to be the Messiah foretold in Hebrew scripture. Paul's address ended on the twofold note of the proclamation of forgiveness offered through Christ to all who believed in Him and the warning of disaster for those who failed to heed the message of deliverance.

This proclamation greatly attracted the God-fearers in the congregation. They spread the news around among their friends, and next sabbath the Gentile population turned up at the synagogue in such numbers as almost to crowd out the Jews. The Jews expressed their annoyance; and Paul announced that, as they reckoned themselves unworthy of the life of the coming age whose advent he proclaimed, he would henceforth concentrate on the Gentiles. This he did; and when a number of these confessed their acceptance of Jesus as Lord and Deliverer, he formed them into a new community of believers in Jesus—as we should say, a Christian church. Thus was established a pattern of procedure which was to be repeated regularly in city after city. The

Jews naturally disliked this kind of activity. They regarded the formation of God-fearers into a separate community as a poaching on their preserves. They had naturally hoped that those God-fearers would one day go the whole way with them and enter the Jewish community as proselytes. Now this hope was frustrated by Paul's action. His reply to their complaint was that, if they had availed themselves of the opportunity to accept the good news themselves, then they could have fulfilled their true mission of evangelizing the God-fearers and other Gentiles. The Deliverer, in whom the hope of Israel found its incarnate fulfilment, had appeared on earth for this very purpose. But if they would not discharge this responsibility, then it had to be discharged without them, for the mission of the Servant was clearly worded:

> I will make you a light to the Gentiles,
> That my salvation may reach to the ends of the earth.

The Jewish community in its resentment stirred up trouble and Barnabas and Paul had to leave. They went on to Iconium (the modern railway junction of Konya), where similarly they founded a separate community of Jews and God-fearers who believed the gospel. But they soon had to leave Iconium in the same way as they had left Pisidian Antioch. So, leaving the Phrygian region of the province, they entered the region of Lycaonia. There they came to the city of Lystra, another Roman colony. Here the healing of a lame man by Paul made a great impression on the indigenous non-Roman population, and provoked an outburst of religious enthusiasm. That district in mythological narrative had once been favoured by a visit from two deities corresponding to the Greek Zeus and Hermes, the king of the immortals and his chief herald. They had been entertained unawares by an aged couple named Philemon and Baucis, who in the sequel were suitably rewarded for their hospitality. Now (said the natives to one another) these two gods were here again. They must be paid divine honours. In fact, archæological research in the vicinity of Lystra has made it clear that Hermes and Zeus were worshipped in association with each other here.[1] The apostles did not at first tumble to what was afoot, as the natives were speaking their Lycaonian vernacular. But when their preparations for sacrifice were well advanced, Paul and Barnabas, horror-struck, expostulated with them. It was no use telling these pagans about the covenant with Abraham or the promises made to David; but they could and did tell them of the one living and true God who had revealed Himself in creation and providence.

Their stay in Lystra was interrupted by a visit from their opponents from Iconium and Pisidian Antioch; these stirred up a riot

[1] Cf. my *The NT Documents: Are They Reliable?* (1960), pp. 95f.

in which Paul, so lately acclaimed as the messenger of the immortals, was almost lynched. From Lystra they went on to Derbe, a town some sixty miles farther east, and there, too, they planted a Christian group. But with Derbe they reached the eastern frontier of the Roman province, so now they retraced their steps through Lystra, Iconium and Pisidian Antioch, encouraging the young communities to persevere and placing them on a stable footing by appointing elders to take charge of them. Every Jewish community throughout the empire had its elders, who looked after the welfare of their fellows, and similar administration was necessary for the Christian communities, to be exercised by those who possessed the requisite qualifications.

So they made their way back to the coast, telling the Christian message as they went. Then they took ship at Attalia (modern Antalya) and landed in Seleucia, at the mouth of the Orontes. Thus, after an adventurous circular tour, they arrived back at Syrian Antioch, and were able to tell the Christians there of all that happened during their journey, and how the Antiochene church now had several daughter-churches in Asia Minor.[1]

[1] It is not certain if churches had actually been planted in Cyprus as well.

CHAPTER IX

ADVANCE IN PALESTINE

IT WAS NOT ONLY THE LANDS OUTSIDE PALESTINE THAT BENEFITED from the dispersion which followed the death of Stephen. Of the other leaders of the Hellenist group in the Jerusalem church, Philip now displayed the gifts of an evangelist in a remarkable degree.

Between Judæa and Galilee lay the region of Samaria, populated by Israelites who followed a separate tradition of worship and teaching from the Jews. The division between Samaria and Judæa in New Testament times perpetuated the Old Testament division between Israel and Judah. This division, which can be traced back to the morrow of the Hebrew conquest of Canaan, was not properly healed during the united monarchy of David and Solomon, and became open again after the death of Solomon, when the kingdom of Israel was divided. The breach was not healed even after the Persian kings permitted the exiles of Israel and Judah to return to Palestine; the Israelites of Samaria offered their co-operation to the returning Judæan exiles, but their offer was declined, largely on the ground that those who made it were a mixed race. For, in the eighth and seventh centuries B.C., when the Assyrian kings deported the upper classes of the population of Samaria, they replaced them by colonists from other parts of their empire. These colonists soon gave up their foreign worship and became indistinguishable from the Israelites among whom they lived, but the Judæans never ceased to regard the people of Samaria as half-breeds racially and religiously.

When the Samaritans' offer to share in restoring the worship at Jerusalem was not welcomed, they built their own temple on Mount Gerizim, a mountain hallowed in early Israelite story. The Hasmonean kings conquered the Samaritans and destroyed their temple, and this did not make for greater amity between the two groups. When the Romans added Palestine to their empire, the Samaritans were liberated from the Jewish yoke; but the gospel records bear ample witness to the unfriendly relations which continued to exist between them.

But when the persecution broke out after Stephen's death, Philip made his way to one of the cities of Samaria and proclaimed the good news there. The Samaritans, too, shared the messianic hope; their expectation was specially centred on the "prophet like Moses" of Deuteronomy 18 : 15, whom they called the *Ta'eb*, or "restorer." Now Philip told them that this "restorer" had come in Jesus of Nazareth, whom the religious rulers of Judæa had rejected and handed over to the Romans for execution; and his words met with widespread acceptance. Many of the people in that place believed the good news which he announced.

The apostles in Jerusalem, who seem to have remained immune from the persecution (perhaps because they were differentiated in the popular mind from Stephen and the Hellenists), heard of Philip's success. They regarded themselves as responsible for exercising a general supervision over the new movement wherever it might expand to, and two of their leading men, Peter and John, visited Samaria and confirmed the new converts in their faith. They had already been baptized into the community of believers in Jesus; now that the two apostles came and laid their hands on them, they began to manifest the same spiritual gifts as had marked the first Christian Pentecost in Jerusalem. In this connexion we are first introduced to the enigmatic figure of Simon the sorcerer, who showed a professional interest in the gifts of the Spirit and tried to buy the power to impart them.[1]

Philip's next assignment was with an Ethiopian proselyte, treasurer to the queen-mother of Nubia, who was returning home from Jerusalem. Philip encountered him near Gaza as he was reading in his chariot the Isaianic prophecy of the suffering Servant, and used the words that he was reading as a text from which to tell him the story of Jesus. The treasurer believed and was baptized by the roadside, and continued joyfully on his southward way. Philip then turned north along the Palestinian coast, evangelizing the places he passed through, until he arrived at Cæsarea, the provincial capital. There he settled down, and it is no doubt to Philip that the Christian community at Cæsarea owed its inception.

But Philip was not the only visitor to those parts. Peter embarked upon an evangelistic enterprise in the semi-Gentile towns of the Plain of Sharon, in western Palestine, to which some Christians had already found their way. The chief centres of Peter's activity were Lydda and Joppa (Jaffa). While he was in the latter place he received an invitation from a Roman centurion of

[1] Simon Magus claimed to be a sort of divine incarnation. In the fictional narratives of the *Clementine Homilies* and *Clementine Recognitions* he appears as the untiring adversary of Peter at Antioch and Rome. This literature, which is Judaistic and anti-Pauline, uses Simon as a pretext for an attack on Paul. Justin Martyr's statement that Simon was worshipped as a god in Rome may be due to the misreading of an inscription in honour of an old Sabine deity Semo. But Simon's followers, the Simonians, survived to the third century at least.

Cæsarea to pay him a visit. This centurion, Cornelius by name, was another of those Gentiles belonging to the class called God-fearers. For a Jew to enter a Gentile's house was a breach of the laws of ceremonial purity, and the very idea would naturally be so abhorrent to Peter that he would not have accepted the invitation had he not, on the very day when it reached him, had the lesson impressed upon him in the course of a trance-vision that God recognized no ceremonial distinction between "clean" and "unclean," whether in respect of food laws or with regard to human beings. Thus prepared, Peter accepted the invitation, and with six Jewish Christians of Joppa he went to Cæsarea and found a large company of Gentiles gathered in Cornelius's house to hear him. The narrator has summarized Peter's words for us as follows:

> God sent His message to the children of Israel—the message of peace through Jesus the Messiah, the universal Lord. You know what took place, for that message was spread abroad through the whole land of the Jews, beginning in Galilee, as a sequel to the baptism which John the Baptist proclaimed. It is the message about Jesus of Nazareth, anointed as Messiah by God with the Holy Spirit and divine power. He went about doing good and healing all those who were under the control of the devil, for God was with Him. We apostles can bear personal witness to all that He did in the whole land of Palestine and in Jerusalem. There they put Him to death, hanging Him up on a gibbet; but God raised Him from death on the third day and caused Him to appear alive—not indeed to the people as a whole, but to eyewitnesses whom God had previously chosen for that purpose. Yes, we actually ate and drank with Him after He rose from the dead. And He commanded us to announce and testify to the people that He is the one whom God has appointed to be Judge of the living and dead alike. For He is the one to whom the prophets of old bear witness, that everyone who believes in Him will receive forgiveness of sins through His name.

Of course, there was much in this which ordinary pagans would not have understood, because the whole background of thought would have been foreign to them. But these were not ordinary pagans; being God-fearers, they knew a good deal about the Hebrew scriptures and the messianic hope; and as Peter spoke, they were convinced of the truth of his words, and suddenly manifested the characteristic spiritual gifts of Pentecost, proclaiming the mighty works of God in new tongues as the apostles themselves had done on that earlier occasion. Peter and his companions were astonished, but they recognized the sovereign grace of God at work in the hearts of the Gentiles. They had no option but to acknowledge the *fait accompli* with which they were confronted, and Peter directed that these Gentile believers should be baptized, just as he had commanded the Jewish believers in

Jerusalem to be baptized on the day when he first announced the good news after his Master's departure.

This preaching of Peter in the house of the Gentile Cornelius probably preceded the preaching to Gentiles at Antioch, but by no very great interval of time. Later, at the Council of Jerusalem, Peter claimed that he was the first to make the gospel known to Gentiles.

On his return to Jerusalem, Peter had to defend his unprecedented breach of convention to his fellow apostles. To have entered a Gentile house and eaten with the occupants was something which demanded explanation. But Peter simply recounted the clear course of divine guidance which had led him to take this step—otherwise as unthinkable to him as to them—and as he described how the Holy Spirit had taken possession of these Gentiles, the others felt that they, too, had no choice but to accept the manifest good pleasure of God. But Peter's departure from Jewish convention and the other apostles' acquiescence in his action had further repercussions both inside and outside the Christian movement. For the present, however, Jews and Christians alike in Palestine had something else to think about.

The end of the year 40 was marked by an incident which caused great consternation throughout the Jewish world. From the time of Augustus it was customary that sacrifices should be offered daily in the temple at Jerusalem on behalf of the Emperor—the Emperor himself made provision for this to be done. The Emperor Gaius, however (better known by his nickname Caligula), who succeeded Tiberius in 37, was not satisfied with this. His great power went to his head and gave him an exaggerated notion of his status: he asserted his divinity and claimed appropriate recognition. The Emperors were already accorded divine honours by their eastern subjects, who had been accustomed to "divine" rulers for centuries. But the Jews, naturally, formed an exception, and this irked Gaius. It was not enough that sacrifices should be offered *for* him; he required that they be offered *to* him.[1] At Jamnia, in western Judæa, the Gentile population set up an altar to Gaius; the Jewish inhabitants, who formed the majority of the town's population, promptly pulled it down. When news of this reached Gaius, he retaliated by ordering that his statue be erected in the temple at Jerusalem. Knowing very well that the Jews would resist this order to the death, he commanded Petronius, imperial legate of Syria, to march to Jerusalem with two legions to enforce the order.

[1] Compare the Emperor's retort to a deputation of Alexandrian Jews who assured him that sacrifices of prayer and thanksgiving were offered for him in the Jerusalem temple: "That is all very well; you have offered sacrifice, but it was to someone else, even if it was on my behalf. What good is that? You have not offered sacrifice to *me*." (Philo, *Embassy to Gaius*, 357.)

The ensuing consternation must have affected the Christians of Palestine as much as it did the Jews in general. Petronius marched south and came as far as Ptolemais (Acre), where he was besieged by deputations of Jews, who assured him that their nation would die as one man sooner than allow this outrage. Petronius replied, however, that he had no option: his duty was to carry out the Emperor's orders.

It was very probably at this critical moment that the Christians of Palestine remembered some words of their Master which seemed to have a direct bearing on this situation. These words portended a destruction of the temple and widespread tribulation following just such a profanation as now seemed imminent, and warned the disciples to flee from Judæa "when you see the 'abomination of desolation' standing where he ought not to be."[1] That this warning was committed to writing about this time and perhaps circulated as a broadsheet has also been inferred from the parenthesis which follows this quotation: "let the reader understand" (i.e., let him understand what is being referred to here).

In the event, it turned out that this crisis was not the fulfilment of these words of Jesus; the danger was averted. Thirty more years were to pass before the desolation overwhelmed the city and temple. But the crisis left a deep mark on the thought of the early church, and the broadsheet circulated at that time provided a form of words which we can trace in Christian writings later in the century—not only in the Book of Revelation, but in the Pauline correspondence. For example, in his second letter to the Thessalonian Church (written in A.D. 50), Paul tells his readers that the second advent of Christ will be preceded by a widespread revolt against the divine government, when "the man of lawlessness is revealed, the son of perdition, who opposes and exalts himself against every so-called god or object of worship, going so far as to take his seat in the temple of God, proclaiming himself to be God."[2] He reminds them that he told them this when he was with them a few months before. And there is a clear connexion between his picture of lawlessness incarnate enthroned in the temple of God and the earlier reference to the "abomination of desolation" standing where he ought not.

In A.D. 40, however, Petronius temporized, being genuinely unwilling to execute the Emperor's mad command. While he procrastinated, urgent representations were made to Gaius himself by his great friend Herod Agrippa, a grandson of Herod the

[1] This expression, first found in Daniel 9 : 27; 11 : 31; 12 : 11, is applied in 1 Maccabees 1 : 54 to the altar of Zeus which Antiochus Epiphanes erected in the temple in 167 B.C. In Mark 13 : 14 (from which the words of Christ quoted above are taken) the Greek construction indicates that the abomination is regarded as masculine. (See p. 28.)
[2] 2 Thessalonians 2 : 3f.

Great, whom he had made king of the former tetrarchies of Philip, Lysanias and Antipas in Transjordan and Galilee. So great was Gaius's friendship for Agrippa that he granted his request to the extent of writing to Petronius to say that, if the statue had already been erected, it must remain, but if not he was to take no further action.

But Petronius had by this time written to the Emperor to say that it was impossible to carry out his order except by exterminating the Jewish people. Gaius, therefore, sent him a second letter ordering him to commit suicide as the penalty for his insubordination. Before Petronius received this second letter, however, news came that Gaius had been assassinated.

Gaius's successor Claudius (41–54) continued to show favour to Agrippa, and added Judæa to his existing kingdom. From 41, therefore, to Agrippa's death in 44, Judæa was ruled not by a Roman procurator but by a Jewish king. Though he was a member of the Herod family (which was of Edomite origin), the Jews remembered that he was a descendant of their own Hasmonean dynasty (through his grandmother Mariamme), and he, for his part, assiduously courted their good will.

The Mishnah tells us that when he read the "law of the kingdom"[1] (as a Jewish king must do) at the Feast of Tabernacles in a sabbatic year (presumably in October, A.D. 40), he wept when he came to the words: "Thou shalt not set a stranger over thee, who is not thy brother"; but the people called out repeatedly: "Be not dismayed; thou art indeed our brother!"[2]

This is that "Herod the king" who, according to Acts 12 : 1, "stretched forth his hands to vex certain of the church." In the persecution that followed Stephen's death some ten years previously, the apostles had been immune; but now the apostles were the main target of attack. James the son of Zebedee was beheaded and Peter was imprisoned, with the approval of the people of Judæa. Yet the popular displeasure was not apparently directed against all the Nazarenes indiscriminately; James the brother of Jesus and those who followed his lead appear to have enjoyed general good will for almost two decades more. If we ask why the apostles should now be singled out for attack, the answer may be found in the wider phase of apostolic activity which had recently set in with Peter's visit to the Gentile Cornelius in Cæsarea. Although the other apostles acquiesced in Peter's action, the news of what he had done was not restricted to them; and the action of their leader in consorting with Gentiles must have been viewed with suspicion by the stricter Jewish Christians, while it completely alienated the non-Christian Jews.

[1] Deuteronomy 17 : 14–20.
[2] Mishnah, Soṭah, VII, 8.

Peter, however, made his escape from prison during the Passover celebrations of A.D. 44. He had then to go into hiding for some time, going perhaps to Antioch. Agrippa died suddenly in the summer of that year, in the course of a festival which he had organized at Cæsarea in honour of the Emperor,[1] and Judæa reverted to procuratorial government. Claudius did consider whether he might not appoint Agrippa's son, Agrippa the younger, as his father's successor, but was persuaded not to do so because of the son's youth (he was seventeen years old at the time).[2] It was, therefore, safe for Peter to return to Jerusalem, but from this time forward the leadership of the Jerusalem church passes increasingly into the hands of James the brother of Jesus.

Even at the time of Peter's imprisonment, James appears to have occupied a special position. When Peter escaped, we are told, he went to the house of Mary (mother of the evangelist John Mark), which seems to have served as a meeting place for one group of the Christian community. To the company gathered there, who had been busy praying for his release, Peter made known his escape, and before leaving them to go elsewhere, he said, "Tell James and the brethren." By A.D. 44, then, James seems to have attained a position of leadership and to have had a following of his own.

Two years later came the visit to Jerusalem of Barnabas and Paul, bearing gifts from the Antioch church to relieve the need of the mother church in the famine then prevailing. Referring to this visit at a later date, Paul says that he and Barnabas had an interview with those who were reputed "pillars" in the Jerusalem church: James, Peter and John (the son of Zebedee)—and he mentions them in that order.[3] But James on that occasion concurred with Peter and John in giving Paul and Barnabas "the right hand of fellowship" on the understanding that these two should evangelize the Gentile lands while the others concentrated on bringing the gospel to the Jews.

Besides, from the middle forties onwards, Peter and the other apostles were increasingly absent from Jerusalem; James was always there. His role seems to have been the administration of the large and growing Nazarene community at Jerusalem, in conjunction with a council of elders. The Christian elderhood was no doubt modelled on the Jewish self-perpetuating sanhedrins—whether the supreme Sanhedrin of Jerusalem or the lesser sanhedrins of Jewish communities elsewhere.

James therefore, occupied this responsible position a few years

---

[1] Cf. Acts 12 : 20–23 with Josephus, *Antiquities*, XIX, 8 : 2.

[2] Some years later the younger Agrippa received as a kingdom the territory over which his father had reigned before 41. He is the King Agrippa who appears at a later stage in Luke's history, Acts 25 : 13–26 : 32. See p. 154 below.

[3] Galatians 2 : 9.

later when a critical decision had to be made on the status of Gentile converts in the Christian movement. The success of the Antiochene mission, which meant that there might soon be more Gentile Christians in the world than Jewish Christians, made such a decision urgently necessary. And it was in considerable part thanks to James's practical wisdom that a serious problem, which might have brought about an unbridgeable cleavage in primitive Christianity, was settled in a spirit of concord.

CHAPTER X

THE COUNCIL OF JERUSALEM

THE INTRODUCTION OF GENTILES INTO THE CHRISTIAN
community presented many of the older Jewish Christians
with a problem. It was not easy to agree on a solution.
Misgivings arose, as we saw, within the apostolate itself when
Peter visited the house of the Roman Cornelius and led him and
his household to the knowledge of Christ; and if these were
allayed for the time being, the problem arose again in a more
acute form with the wholesale entry of Gentiles into the church
at Antioch and then into her daughter churches founded by
Barnabas and Paul in the course of their missionary tour.

For some of the Jerusalem Christians—those in particular
whose affiliations were with the Pharisaic party and who are described as being "zealots for the law"[1]—the church was little more
than a new party within the commonwealth of Israel, albeit a
party which embodied the hope which all Israel ought to have
welcomed. Their solution of the problem was simple enough.
They agreed that, since so many Jews had refused to accept Jesus
as the Messiah, Gentiles had to be incorporated into the messianic
community so that the full number might be made up. But these
Gentiles should be incorporated as proselytes; they should be
circumcised and be required to observe the whole Mosaic law.
Quite obviously, however, these conditions were not insisted on
by Christians outside Jerusalem. Peter, some years before, had
learned his lesson that no man should be called "common or unclean"; he had seen that God was as ready to accept believing
Gentiles as believing Jews, and there is no hint that he urged the
necessity, or even the desirability, of circumcision on Cornelius.
Moreover, when Paul and Barnabas visited Jerusalem about A.D.
46 as administrators of the famine relief fund,[2] they were accompanied by a young Greek member of the church of Antioch,
Titus by name.[3] But, although Titus was an uncircumcised Gentile, no one at that time raised the question of having him circumcised. The church of Antioch appears to have adopted this
liberal outlook from the start, and the new churches recently

[1] Acts 15 : 5; 21 : 20.
[2] Cf. pp. 92f.
[3] Galatians 2 : 3. Titus may have been Luke's brother.

formed in Asia Minor included not only Jews but an even greater number of Gentiles, who were not required to be circumcised or otherwise to observe the ceremonial Jewish law. There were, indeed, some Jews in those days who thought that the actual rite of circumcision might be neglected, provided that its spiritual significance were appreciated; but the vast majority of Jews, including so liberal a Jew as the learned Philo of Alexandria, insisted on circumcision as indispensable.[1] This was, no doubt, the attitude of the rank and file of the Nazarenes in Jerusalem. Therefore, unless the problem were thoroughly ventilated and discussed and settled, there was grave danger of a division between the churches of Jerusalem and Judæa on the one hand, and the church of Antioch with her daughter churches on the other.

This danger was increased by the action taken at Antioch by some emissaries from the Jerusalem church.[2] These men exceeded the terms of their commission (whatever it was), and took matters into their own hands by insisting that circumcision and obedience to the Mosaic law were necessary to salvation. Such men would naturally refuse all social fellowship with uncircumcised persons—and that included the common participation in their solemn meal of fellowship and thanksgiving—the "Lord's Supper" or the "Eucharist." So they introduced an awkward situation into the church at Antioch in regard both to the fundamental question of the way of salvation and the practical question of fellowship between Jewish and Gentile believers. Some who would have refused to compromise on the fundamental question were disposed to give way on the other.

Peter was in residence at Antioch when these visitors from Jerusalem arrived. When he first came to Antioch, he ate freely with Gentile Christians, as we might expect. But after the arrival of these visitors (one of whom appears to have brought him a special message from James), he withdrew from Gentile society and ate with Jews only—probably, he would have said, to conciliate the weaker consciences of his Jerusalem brethren. But it looked as if the prince of the apostles was forgetting, or even renouncing, the lesson which he had learned at Joppa and first put into practice at Cæsarea. The example of his concession was bound to have a disastrous effect on Jewish and Gentile Christians alike. Even Barnabas, who had lately returned with Paul from their missionary journey, was inclined to follow his example. Paul was

---

[1] Philo (*On the Migration of Abraham*, pp. 89–94) criticizes those who would give up the literal observance of ceremonial laws on the plea that it is enough to learn and practise their spiritual lessons: "nor, because circumcision signifies the cutting away of pleasure and all passions and the destruction of ungodly glory . . . let us do away with the law of the circumcision." Cf. also Josephus, *Antiquities*, XX, 2 : 4, where the Jewish instructor of King Izates of Adiabene advises him to worship God according to the Jewish religion without being circumcised.

[2] Acts 15 : 1; Galatians 2 : 12.

clear-sighted enough to see that in the long run the concession on the matter of fellowship compromised the basic principle that salvation was God's gift in Christ, to be received by faith. For ultimately the one valid reason for making circumcision a condition for social fellowship must be that it was necessary for salvation and membership in the new community. Peter's concession was the thin end of the wedge (although Peter did not intend it to be so); refusal to sit at table with uncircumcised believers would be followed before long by refusal to admit them to church membership or to regard them as recipients of God's salvation in Christ. No wonder, then, that Paul (to use his own language) "withstood Peter to his face,"[1] for his behaviour implied that circumcision, even if not a condition of entry into the community of the saved, was none the less necessary in practice. Peter himself did not really believe that it was necessary in either respect, and that is why Paul characterizes his conduct with the Greek word *hypokrisis*, "play-acting."[2] Peter seems to have taken the rebuke in good part, for we hear no more of such untimely appeasement on his side.

But the trouble was not confined to Antioch. Not long after, it broke out in the recently founded churches of the province of Galatia—in Pisidian Antioch, Iconium, Lystra and Derbe. These churches received visits from some Judaizing Christians who urged upon them (as something over and above what Barnabas and Paul had taught them) the necessity of adding to their faith in Christ circumcision and observance of the Jewish ceremonial law. In their innocence, these young churches were inclined to submit to this new teaching. But when the news of what was going on came to Paul at Antioch, he wrote an urgent letter[3] to his Galatian converts: "I am astonished that you are turning away so soon from him who called you and following another gospel." For such teaching, as he saw it, was a radical contradiction of the good news which brought deliverance from sin, and membership in the people of God, through faith in Christ alone, and not through conformity to legal requirements. It was a different gospel—not really a gospel at all. His letter, written at white heat, revealed his loving anxiety over these "new-born children," as he calls them, and his indignation at those who were troubling them thus.

The whole matter had to be put right immediately, and so the Antiochene Christians sent a deputation, including Paul and

[1] Galatians 2 : 11.
[2] Galatians 2 : 13.
[3] Readers who are interested in such matters will already have discovered my adherence to the school of interpretation which dates Paul's Epistle to the Galatians at this juncture and regards it as the earliest of his extant letters. For a fuller statement of this view see F. F. Bruce, *The Epistle of Paul to the Galatians*, NIGTC (1982).

Barnabas, to discuss it thoroughly with the leaders at Jerusalem. Thus, in A.D. 49, the momentous Council of Jerusalem met. The circumcision party had their say, but the contrary arguments were too strong to be confuted. Peter, perhaps profiting by Paul's recent plain speaking, reminded the council how God had clearly shown his pleasure in the conversion of Cornelius and bestowal of the Holy Spirit on him and his household. Barnabas and Paul related how God had impartially extended his blessing to Gentiles during their recent Anatolian mission. Finally, James (on whom the circumcision party may well have relied for support), in a judicial summing-up, agreed that, as God had plainly chosen Gentiles as well as Jews (a situation which he found foretold in Old Testament prophecy), they must not impose on Gentile believers conditions which God had obviously not required of them. James's ruling carried the day. It was decided that no other condition than faith in Christ should be imposed on Gentiles, as necessary either for salvation or for fellowship with their Jewish fellow-believers.

There remained, however, a practical difficulty. In most of the churches Gentile Christians had to live alongside Jewish Christians who had been brought up to observe certain food laws and to refrain, as far as possible, from intercourse with Gentiles. While there was no more question of requiring Gentiles to be circumcised and keep the ceremonial law, they would do well to respect the scruples of their "weaker" Jewish brethren (not all of whom could be expected to become as emancipated as Peter and Paul), provided that there was no compromise on matters of principle. Hence the council decided to recommend a *modus vivendi*. This recommendation was that they should abstain not only from idolatry itself (that was a matter of course), but from everything that had idolatrous associations, such as food that had been sacrificed to pagan deities; that they should conform to the Jewish practice of not eating blood (and that included meat from which the blood had not been properly drained); and that they should bring their sexual code into line with the Jewish marriage laws, which were based on the Old Testament. These were the terms of the letter which was taken from the council to Antioch by two members of the Jerusalem church, Judas and Silvanus (or Silas), as preserved in Acts 15 : 23–29:

> The brethren, both the apostles and the elders, to the brethren who are of the Gentiles in Antioch and in Syria and Cilicia, greeting. Since we have heard that some persons from us have said things that troubled you, unsettling your minds (although we gave them no such instructions), we have decided to send chosen delegates to you along with our beloved Barnabas and Paul—those men who have hazarded their lives for the name of our Lord Jesus Christ.

We are therefore sending Judas and Silas, and they themselves will tell you the same things by word of mouth. For it has seemed good to the Holy Spirit and to us to lay upon you no heavier burden than this: it is necessary to abstain from food sacrificed to idols, from blood, from strangled meat, and from unchastity.[1] If you keep yourselves from these things, you will do well. Farewell.

The receipt of this letter caused great satisfaction at Antioch. The necessary abstentions listed in the letter were such as the responsible leaders of the Antiochene church would have urged upon the Gentile Christians in any case.

It should be observed that there is no suggestion that the mother church had the authority to dictate to the autonomous churches of Antioch and Asia Minor; as Hort pointed out, no verb of command is used in the letter, although the Greek tongue has a plentiful supply of such words.[2] There is no thought here of a central or metropolitan authority to which the various churches must bow.

It is frequently supposed that Paul could not have accepted these recommendations; but in fact there is no good reason to believe that he would have found them objectionable. Where no compromise of principle was involved, Paul was the most conciliatory of men.[3] In his own letters he urges that those who are strong in faith and have thoroughly emancipated minds should voluntarily restrict their liberty in food questions and the like so as not to put a stumbling-block in the way of those with weaker consciences.[4]

The situation which gave rise to the whole controversy was a temporary one. It was no longer urgent after A.D. 70.[5] And after A.D. 135 the church of Jerusalem itself was a Gentile church. The terms of the apostolic decree became so meaningless to a later

---

[1] The word here rendered "unchastity" is *porneia*, the ordinary Greek word for "fornication." It may seem strange to have this included along with food laws, although many forms of sexual irregularity were regarded by contemporary paganism as little more reprehensible than excess in food and drink. But the avoidance of fornication in the ordinary sense of the term was part of basic Christian teaching, just as the avoidance of idolatry was. What is meant here is probably something more specialized. The Jewish laws of affinity were based on Leviticus 18. Gentile unions which contravened these laws would be classed as *porneia* by Jews. It was desirable that there should be one code of marriage laws for all Christians, and the code adopted was that already in operation among the Jews. The *porneia* prohibited in this letter should be understood in this sense.

[2] F. J. A. Hort, *The Christian Ecclesia* (1897), p. 82; see his whole discussion of the Council of Jerusalem, pp. 67ff. The authority of the apostles, of course, was not locally restricted, but that was because they were apostles; their superior authority was not shared by the Jerusalem church and its elders.

[3] Cf. Acts 16 : 3; 21 : 26; 1 Corinthians 9 : 19–22.

[4] Romans 14 : 1–15 : 6; 1 Corinthians 8.

[5] The terms of the letter were still observed in the province of Asia later in the first century, when the Apocalypse was written (cf. Revelation 2 : 14, 20), and in Gaulish churches as late as A.D. 177 (cf. Eusebius, *Ecclesiastical History*, V, 1, 26). Gaul was evangelized from Asia Minor.

generation that in the "western" text of Acts (a recension made early in the second century) we find them replaced by wholly ethical requirements—abstinence from idolatry, bloodshed and fornication[1]—with the addition of the Golden Rule in the negative form: "and whatsoever things you do not wish done to yourselves, do not to others."[2]

It was necessary to communicate the terms of the apostolic letter to the daughter churches of Antioch as well as to the Antiochene church. Of these, some were situated in the province of which Antioch was the capital—the double province of Syria-Cilicia, which was specially named in the letter. But it was desirable to make the letter known to the daughter churches farther afield, those recently founded in the province of Galatia, in order that they might see that the Jerusalem apostles and elders were at one with their own apostle Paul in condemning the action of the Judaizers who had been urging their views in those parts.

Barnabas and Paul, therefore who had come back from Jerusalem to Antioch with the bearers of the apostolic letter, decided to pay a visit to their churches in South Galatia. But when they were on the point of setting out, Barnabas proposed that they should take Mark with them, as they had done on the earlier occasion. Paul refused point-blank; he had not forgotten Mark's desertion in the course of their previous tour. Neither Barnabas nor Paul would give way, and the upshot was that instead of one missionary expedition from Antioch this time there were two. For Barnabas and Mark went to Cyprus, while Paul went to Asia Minor. He did not go alone, however. He had made the acquaintance of Silas, one of the bearers of the apostolic letter from Jerusalem to Antioch, and judged him to be a kindred spirit. In addition, Silas, like himself, was a Roman citizen,[3] and that was a very useful qualification for travellers through the provinces of the Roman Empire. So he fetched Silas from Jerusalem to be his new colleague. Paul and Silas therefore went through Cilicia and South Galatia, strengthening the Christian communities in those areas and leaving copies of the apostolic letter with them.

[1] These three abstentions were regarded by Jews as "Noachic" regulations binding on the whole human race (see p. 15 above).

[2] See p. 42 above, with n. 3.

[3] This is a fair inference from Acts 16 : 37f. Silvanus would be his Roman *cognomen* (cf. p. 81) and Silas his Jewish name.

CHAPTER XI

INTO EUROPE

AND WHAT NEXT? THE MAIN ROUTE RUNNING WESTWARD through Asia Minor had been evangelized from the Cilician Gates as far west as Pisidian Antioch. It led on to Ephesus, an ancient Greek city, now capital of the Roman province of Asia; and Ephesus was the natural goal for Paul and Silas to make for. But as they set their faces in the direction of Ephesus, they found their way barred. If the province of Asia was closed for the present, however, they could take a northward road from Pisidian Antioch which crossed the Sultan Dagh mountain range and ran to the frontier of the province of Bithynia. Here the roads diverged; one ran north to Nicomedia on the sea of Marmora, the capital of Bithynia, the other turned west to the Ægean port of Troas, just south of the entrance to the Dardanelles. The road into Bithynia was closed to them; to Troas, therefore, they made their way.

At Lystra Paul and Silas had taken into their company a young man named Timotheus (usually Anglicized as Timothy), a member of the Christian community in that town, the son of a Greek father and a Jewish mother. At Troas they were joined by Luke, the physician of Antioch, to whose narrative we are indebted for so much of our knowledge of Paul and his friends.

In the closing of the roads leading to Ephesus and Nicomedia the missionaries traced the guidance of the Holy Spirit. But when they came to Troas the guidance became positive; in a vision by night Paul saw "a certain Macedonian who stood and besought him, 'Come across to Macedonia and help us.' "[1] When he recounted this vision to his three companions, all agreed that it was a divine monition, and that their duty was to cross the north Ægean to the province of Macedonia.

Accordingly, they set sail and landed at the port of Neapolis (modern Kavalla). From there they went inland along the great Egnatian Road—the Roman highway through Macedonia and Illyricum from the Ægean coast at Neapolis to the Adriatic coast at Dyrrhachium (modern Durazzo)—until they arrived at the Roman colony of Philippi. Philippi had become a colony when Antony and Octavian settled their veterans there in 42 B.C. after

[1] Acts 16 : 9.

their victory over Brutus and Cassius, the assassins of Julius Cæsar. We have Luke's eyewitness account of their stay in this place. Here apparently there were not enough Jewish residents to constitute a proper synagogue,[1] but a number of women, both Jewesses and Gentile God-fearers, met for informal prayer by the bank of the river Gangites outside the city, and here the missionaries found the nucleus of the new community which they founded in Philippi. The leading spirit among these women was a God-fearer named Lydia, a native of Thyatira in Asia Minor, who traded in the purple dye for which her home town was famous.

The two leaders of the missionary party, Paul and Silas, were involved in trouble with the local authorities because of Paul's action in exorcizing the demon from a fortune-telling slave-girl. Unfortunately (from her owners' point of view) when he exorcized the spirit that possessed her he exorcized at the same time a profitable source of revenue for them, and they lodged a complaint before the chief magistrates of the colony that these visitors were causing trouble by illegal proselytizing. The chief magistrates, two in number, as in the city of Rome itself and all its colonies,[2] handed Paul and Silas over to their attendant lictors for a beating and sent them to prison for a night. But next morning, learning to their embarrassment that the victims of this summary "justice" were Roman citizens, they apologized to them and requested them to leave the city. The duty of protecting two unpopular Roman citizens was too much for them to assume. Timothy left Philippi with them, but Luke stayed behind.[3]

Continuing the journey along the Egnatian Road, Paul, Silas and Timothy made their next prolonged stay at Thessalonica, the capital of the province of Macedonia. Here they visited the local synagogue on three successive sabbaths, and Paul, demonstrating from the Old Testament scriptures that the Messiah was bound to suffer and rise again from the dead, argued that Jesus was therefore the Messiah. Some Jews and more God-fearers believed the good news, as usual, and were constituted into a new community;

[1] The quorum for a synagogue congregation was, and still is, ten Jewish men.

[2] From their number these collegiate magistrates were properly called *duumvirs*, but they affected the more grandiloquent title "prætors." The lictors who attended them bore the rods and axes (*fasces et secures*). The fussy self-importance of these colonial magistrates is well portrayed by Luke; there is also a humorous touch in his contrast between the citizen's complaint, "These men, *being Jews*, are causing our city a lot of trouble and teaching customs which we ought not to observe, *being Romans*," and the apostles' counter-charge the next day, "We have been beaten publicly and without having our case examined, *being Romans*." Paul and Silas were not only the leaders of the party, but probably distinctively Jewish in appearance by contrast with the Gentile Luke and half-Gentile Timothy.

[3] Luke is probably the "true yokefellow," specially addressed by Paul in his letter to the Church at Philippi (Philippians 4 : 3).

but before the missionaries had finished their work, the magistrates of the city[1] received information that these men were messianic agitators, such as had caused a deal of disturbance elsewhere in the Roman Empire where there were Jewish communities, and that they proclaimed a rival Emperor to him who ruled from Rome. Such a charge could not but be regarded with the utmost gravity. The friends whom the missionaries had made in Thessalonica, however, and from whom they had received hospitality, guaranteed that they would leave the city quietly and sent them away by night.

Even so, the infant Christian community in Thessalonica was the object of some active persecution, and their opponents—especially, we may suppose, the husbands of those leading women who had attached themselves to the missionaries—must have seized the opportunity of saying: "A fine lot of leaders they are! They come here and stir up trouble, but as soon as the place gets too hot to hold them, off they go and leave their dupes to face the music!"[2] The wonder is that in spite of it all the Christians of Thessalonica stood firm and actually began to propagate on their own initiative the message which they had believed. A few weeks later, when Paul wrote them a letter, he was able to say that the gospel had sounded forth from them throughout all Macedonia and Greece, and that their steadfast faith in God was a matter of common talk in other churches.[3] The modicum of eschatological teaching which they had received, to be sure, tended to go to the heads of some of their number, and these had to be warned that the "day of the Lord" was not yet here, so that it was too soon to give up their jobs. To live on the charity of others was not God's way for able-bodied Christians.[4]

From Thessalonica the missionaries turned south through Thessaly, and stopped at Berœa. Here they received a better welcome in the synagogue than they usually did. Quite a number believed the gospel; but those who had stirred up trouble in Thessalonica sent a delegation to Berœa, and Paul had to leave that city too. His Berœan friends escorted him to Athens, and from there he sent back a message to Silas and Timothy in Berœa asking them to join him as soon as possible.

Meanwhile he spent some days in Athens, waiting for them—

[1] These magistrates are called "politarchs" in Acts 17 : 6—a title not found in literature, but occurring on inscriptions as that of chief magistrates in Thessalonica and other Macedonian cities.

[2] Paul felt this keenly, but his hands were tied; his host Jason had, without consulting him, gone bail for his departure, and he could not return at present without compromising Jason. Paul saw a sinister agency at work in this situation. "We wished to come to you," he wrote, "and Satan hindered us." (1 Thessalonians 2 : 18).

[3] 1 Thessalonians 1 : 8.

[4] 2 Thessalonians 2 : 1ff.; 3 : 6ff.

Athens, the Eye of Greece, Mother of Arts
And Eloquence, native to famous wits
Or hospitable, in her sweet recess,
City or Suburban, studious walks and shades.

The great days of Athens were past, but she still enjoyed very high prestige by reason of her cultural reputation. She carried on her glorious traditions as the cradle of democracy, retaining her own institutions as a "free and allied city" within the Roman Empire. Here, as in the days of Pericles and Demosthenes, her citizens gathered in the Agora to debate the latest tidings; here flourished the great philosophical schools—Academic, Peripatetic, Stoic and Epicurean; here, too, were the great temples and statues of the gods, the Parthenon and others, the handiwork of Pheidias and Praxiteles and other sculptors of the first rank.

But to Paul's eyes the art of the violet-crowned city, dedicated as it was to pagan cults, made no appeal. On the contrary, the sight of the city full of images stirred the indignation of one brought up in the spirit of the Second Commandment. These were in his eyes so many vanities which men ought to abandon for the service of the living God. So he told those with whom he had an opportunity to speak. They greeted his arguments, however, with amused contempt. Using a word of characteristic Athenian slang, they summed him up as a *spermologos*, an intellectual cheap-jack who retailed scraps of learning which he had picked up here and there. The two predominant terms of his religious vocabulary, "Jesus" and *Anastasis* ("resurrection"), conveyed to their not very attentive minds something of the sense of "Healing" and "Restoration"; these were two new-fangled deities whom he was recommending for their worship, they supposed.

There was a venerable institution in Athens which took cognizance of matters of moral and religious import, and exercised some sort of control over public lecturers. This was the ancient court of the Areopagus, so called because it used to meet on an eminence of that name in Athens; now it met in one of the colonnades in the Agora. To this venerable court, then, Paul was escorted, and invited to give an *exposé* of his teaching.

Much of what Paul said before the Areopagus takes the form of common Jewish propaganda against paganism. But Paul infused into this something of the missionary spirit of evangelical urgency. He took as his "text" an inscription he had seen on an altar in the city, AGNOSTO THEO, "To the unknown God." Diogenes Laërtius, in his *Lives of the Philosophers*, tells how the Athenians once, during a pestilence, sent for Epimenides, the wise man of Crete, who advised them to release a number of sheep from the hill called the Areopagus, and offer sacrifices to the appropriate deity on each spot where any of these sheep rested. As a result, says Diogenes, "anonymous altars" were to be seen throughout Attica as late as the third century A.D. Other ancient writers confirm that altars to "unknown gods" were found at Athens.[1] It was no doubt one of these that Paul saw. He, however, chose to interpret the inscription as a dedication to the God whom he proclaimed: "What you worship unknowing, that I announce to you," he said. Then he went on to tell them of the God who revealed Himself in creation and providence, the God whose offspring all men were. No race could claim a superior origin over any other, as the Athenians did by their boast of autochthony; the poets whom his audience knew as well as he did himself emphasized this fact. His fellow-Cilician Aratus, author of a poem on natural phenomena, declared of the supreme God: "We are also His offspring." And Epimenides of Crete gave expression to the same truth in the words which he made Minos address to his father Zeus:

> They carved a tomb for thee, O holy and high one—
> The Cretans, always liars, evil beasts, slow bellies!
> But thou art not dead; forever thou art living and risen,
> For in thee we live and move and have our being.[2]

Parts of the speech might have appealed to the Epicureans and Stoics alternately. The Epicureans would have approved of the sentiment that God needs nothing from men, and the Stoics would have agreed that He is the source of all life. But then Paul went on to introduce his distinctively Christian message against this background. Hitherto, he said, God, by your own admission, has been an unknown God to you, and you have devised various forms of worship in your ignorance. And hitherto God has overlooked your ignorance. But the time for ignorance is now past, for God has made Himself known in a new way. Moreover, He has issued a command for universal repentance, for He has appointed a day for the righteous judgment of the world. The man through whom He is to execute this judgment has been designated; a sure token of His appointment to this high office is the fact that God has raised Him from the dead.

This sort of thing an Athenian audience could not be expected to take seriously. That the real personality of a man survives death all but the Epicureans would have readily agreed. But the

---

[1] Pausanias, *Description of Greece*, I, 1–4; Philostratus, *Life of Apollonius of Tyana*, VI, 3–5.
[2] The quatrain is preserved in a commentary on Acts by the Syriac bishop Isho'dad (c. 850) who probably got it from the works of Theodore of Mopsuestia (350–428). The second line of the quatrain is quoted in the New Testament in Titus 1 : 12. The Cretans were proverbial liars in the Greco-Roman world because they had the audacity to point out to visitors to their island the tomb of Zeus, the father of gods and men.

body was a prison-house or a coffin which the soul was only too glad to throw off. Immortality, yes; resurrection, no. Their great tragedian Aeschylus, describing the occasion when that very court of the Areopagus was instituted by the city's patron goddess Athene, had represented the god Apollo as saying:

> But when the earth has drunk up a man's blood,
> Once he is dead, there is no resurrection.[1]

The *Anastasis* proclaimed by Paul was even more absurd than they had thought at first. So the more polite members of his audience said, "That will do for to-day, thank you"; the less polite did not trouble to conceal their mirth. A handful of people were really impressed by what he said, including a member of the august court itself, Dionysius the Areopagite, to whom a body of pseudonymous literature of Neoplatonic character was ascribed in later centuries.

To the student of Athenian life and history, the whole story of Paul's visit to Athens rings true.[2] In no other city of the ancient world could things have happened just like that. "How this scene can ever have been explained as an invention," wrote Eduard Meyer, "is one of those things that I have never been able to understand."[3]

Paul had only been in Athens for a few days when his friends Silas and Timothy followed him there, as requested. He sent them back to Macedonia to inquire how the churches there were faring. In particular, he was anxious to learn the latest news of his converts in Thessalonica, and he sent Timothy there. He himself went to Corinth. There he met Aquila and Priscilla, fellow-believers, who had lately come from Rome, and when Silas and Timothy returned with encouraging news from Macedonia, he had a strong team of helpers. In Corinth, then, he settled for a year and a half, building up a large community of Christians, as we have seen in our introductory chapter.

---

[1] *Eumenides*, 647f. The word Aeschylus uses for "resurrection" is *anastasis*, the same as that used by Paul.

[2] Acts 17: 16–34. See B. Gärtner, *The Areopagus Speech and Natural Revelation* (1955).

[3] *Ursprung und Anfänge des Christentums*, III (1923), p. 105.

CHAPTER XII

PAUL AND HIS CONVERTS

PAUL'S CONVERTS AT CORINTH WERE A MIXED LOT. A FEW OF them were people of respectable antecedents. There was, for example, Crispus, the former member of the board of governors of the local synagogue; there was also Sosthenes, his colleague.[1] With these there were a number of other Jews and God-fearers, among the latter being Gaius Titius Justus, who gave Paul the hospitality of his house when he was turned out of the synagogue next door. There was Stephanas, possibly another God-fearer, and his family: these were Paul's first converts in the province of Achaia, and they took a leading part in ministering to the Corinthian church. Among the Gentile converts there was at least one outstanding man, Erastus, the city treasurer.[2] But in general the church at Corinth was drawn from the obscurer strata of the population. "Not many of you were wise according to wordly standards," Paul wrote to them later on; "not many were powerful, not many were of noble birth."

The Jews and God-fearers who joined the new community had a sound ethical background, inculcated in the synagogue. But it was otherwise with the majority of the Gentile converts. In one of his letters to them Paul, listing certain classes of people who by their own act exclude themselves from the kingdom of God, mentions "fornicators, idolaters, adulterers, homosexuals, thieves, covetous folk, drunkards, people who indulge in abusive language, robbers," and adds: "And some of you were like that, but you were cleansed and sanctified and justified in the name of the Lord Jesus Christ and in the Spirit of our God."[3]

In short, the Christian community at Corinth consisted of very largely the same sort of people as had been attracted to Jesus Himself in Palestine (making allowance for the difference in general ethical standards between the two places). Paul's descrip-

---

[1] That is, if the Sosthenes mentioned as a Christian in 1 Corinthians 1: 1 is identical with Sosthenes the ruler of the synagogue who was beaten by the Corinthian mob according to Acts 18 : 17.

[2] Cf. Romans 16 : 23. In 1929 a first-century pavement was uncovered at Corinth by American archæologists, bearing the inscription: ERASTVS PRO : AED : S : P : STRAVIT ("Erastus, curator of public buildings, laid this pavement at his own expense"). The reference is probably to the Erastus mentioned by Paul.

[3] 1 Corinthians 6 : 9-11.

tion of what the Corinthian Christians had once been strikes the authentic gospel note:

> Outcasts of men, to you I call,
> Harlots, and publicans, and thieves!
> He spreads His arms to embrace you all;
> Sinners alone His grace receives.

And in many places throughout the Gentile world this was the sort of material out of which the Christian churches were built. In the next century the philosopher Celsus contrasts the respectable "mysteries" with Christianity: the former say "Come all you of clean hands and prudent tongue," but Christianity says, "Everyone who . . . is a sinner, a fool, a child . . . everyone who is in misfortune, him will the kingdom of God receive."[1]

Such criticism, of course, is the boast of the true missionary, just as the complaint that Jesus Himself welcomed outrageous sinners and sat at table with them was freely admitted by Himself and acclaimed as His proper purpose in life: "it was sinners and not righteous people that I came to call."[2] But though the gospel invitation is distinctively for sinners, the purpose of the invitation is that they should be delivered from their sins. And how does this deliverance work out in practice?

This was the searching test with which the Corinthian community presented Paul. What was the best way to inculcate sound morality into such people? The Palestinian Christians for the most part would have said: "Tell them that unless they submit to the Jewish law, in addition to believing in Jesus as the Saviour, there is no hope for them." But this way was impossible for Paul, who had learned that all the law-keeping in the world could not bring assurance of salvation and peace with God, while obedient faith in Christ did so at once. When a man yielded his life to the living Christ and the power of His Spirit, then his inward being was changed and delighted to produce spontaneously the fruit of the Spirit, those graces which were manifested perfectly in Christ himself. Such a conception might work all right with people like Paul himself, who already knew and respected the moral law; but would it work with a body of immoral pagans such as had been swept into the church at Corinth? Paul believed that it would, and in the long run he was justified in his belief; but many other Christians thought he was impossibly optimistic, and they viewed with grave concern the lowering of ethical standards in the Christian movement through what appeared to them to be Paul's laxity. If you teach justification by faith alone, they argued, these people will imagine that once they have accepted Christ by faith

---

[1] Cf. Origen, *Against Celsus*, III, 59. This (like other anti-Christian arguments of Celsus) was later echoed by Julian the Apostate.
[2] Cf. Mark 2 : 14–17; Luke 15 : 1f., etc.

it does not really matter how they live. On the contrary, said Paul, if they really have accepted Christ by faith, they have accepted the way of Christ and the mind of Christ as well. The man who really loves God can do as he chooses, for if he really loves God he will choose to do the will of God. The difference in outlook between the Paulinists and the legalists (if we may call them so without prejudice) has endured in Christianity to our own day: the legalist thinks the Paulinist rash and unrealistic; the Paulinist accuses the legalist of treason to the foundation principle of the gospel of God's grace.

The trouble was made more acute for Paul by the way in which some of his converts played into the hands of the legalists. Some converts did imagine that everyday morality was a very secondary consideration compared with justification by faith. They have never lacked successors, who forget that the Christian is "under the law of Christ"[1] and that (as Paul taught) the righteous requirements of the divine law are fulfilled in the lives of those who are truly controlled by the Spirit of God.[2]

Now, to one brought up in the Jewish way of life, there was no breach of the law more offensive than that which was the besetting sin of Corinth. But it was very difficult to persuade an ordinary Corinthian that fornication was a sin at all. That it was a gross violation of the fundamental Christian law of love to one's neighbour had yet to be appreciated by several members of the Corinthian church. Just as some decent citizens to-day cannot understand why so many churchmen look sternly upon football pools and a glass of beer, so some Corinthian Christians must have thought that in condemning the proverbial "Corinthian behaviour" their stricter brethren had no other motive than a perverse love of interfering in other people's harmless pleasures. The trouble was accentuated by the conflicting sentiments voiced by some who aspired to leadership in the community. On the one hand there were the former members of the synagogue, who knew that fornication was a grave sin; on the other hand, there were some of the intelligentsia among the Gentile converts who took the view that, as the body was a relatively unimportant constituent in all that went to make up a human being, bodily acts were of comparatively little consequence.

Paul, hearing after his departure from Corinth that some of his converts were inclined to follow their pagan habits in this respect,

---

[1] I Corinthians 9 : 21; cf. Galatians 6 : 2. The law of Christ, be it noted, is not less difficult, but more difficult than the law of Moses. Those who talk loosely of the Sermon on the Mount as a cure for all ills ("If only all men would carry out the teaching of the Sermon on the Mount, what a happy world it would be"), do not always take adequate account of the fact that it sets a much higher standard for human behaviour than do the Ten Commandments.

[2] Romans 8 : 4.

wrote a letter to them on the subject.[1] Fornicators, he insisted, are bad company for Christians. Of course, one cannot help rubbing shoulders with them in the ordinary business of daily life, but the Christian circle itself must be kept free from this vice. If a man who ranks as a Christian brother is guilty of fornication, or certain other vices and crimes which bring the Christian name into disrepute, he must be excluded from the community and from social intercourse with its members. That may bring him to his senses. The Christian's body is the temple of the Holy Spirit; to use that body for fornication or the like is to commit sacrilege. God must be glorified by the body as well as by the spiritual part of the Christian's being.

At a later date, when Paul was in Ephesus, further information reached him about his Corinthian converts. He received a visit from some members of the household of a Corinthian lady named Chloe. These people told him that the elements of partisan strife had appeared in the community, and that cliques were being formed in the name of various leaders. Some regarded Paul as their leader and called themselves Paul's party; others, fancying themselves to be a little more intellectual than the others, called themselves the followers of Apollos, the learned Alexandrian Jew, who had come to Corinth soon after Paul's departure and carried on the good work that Paul had begun. Another group called themselves Peter's party. Who were they?

That they had Peter's explicit approval for so calling themselves is doubtful. Peter may have no more approved of their doing so than Paul and Apollos approved of the similar action of the groups that claimed their respective patronage. It is not at all certain that Peter himself had visited Corinth;[2] Paul does not suggest it in his correspondence with the church there, and he would very probably have expressed himself differently if Peter had come there in person.

We have actually to do with a freshly concerted plan to bring the Pauline churches into subjection to Palestine and to impose the yoke of the Mosaic law upon them. The earlier attempt, which had the churches of Syria and Asia Minor as its target, had been made in the name of James, but it had not met with conspicuous success. The name of James was one to conjure with in Palestine, but it did not carry such authority in the Gentile churches. James himself, at the Council of Jerusalem, disowned those who claimed

---

[1] This letter is referred to by Paul in 1 Corinthians 5 : 9. Some have thought that part of it is preserved in 2 Corinthians 6 : 14–7 : 1.

[2] Eduard Meyer, indeed, says: "How anyone has been able to doubt that Peter himself came to Corinth is one of the things that are incomprehensible to me" (*Ursprung und Anfänge des Christentums*, III, p. 441). But while he is right in saying that Peter "stands altogether on a level with Paul and Apollos" in 1 Corinthians 1 : 12 and 3 : 22, personal presence in Corinth is not emphasized in these passages.

to speak in his name. It is plain from the pseudo-Clementine literature of a later date that "Jacobean" Christianity, as we may call it, survived into the following centuries, but it does not play a central part in the growth of Christianity.

Far different, however, was it with the name of Peter. Peter was the leader of the twelve apostles who had been with Jesus during His ministry and had been specially commissioned by Him to make the gospel known worldwide. Peter was no narrow-minded Jewish particularist; he had played a leading part in the evangelization of Gentiles. A party which could claim Peter's name would be in a very strong position. And a number of propagandists claiming to act in Peter's name visited Corinth.

They did not begin, as their predecessors in Antioch and Galatia had begun, by insisting that circumcision and subjection to the ceremonial Jewish law were necessary for salvation. In a more subtle manner, they made it their primary aim to undermine Paul's authority. They did not contradict what Paul had taught; they rather represented his teaching as very elementary. Not that Paul was to blame for that; after all (they said), he was not one of the real apostles; he had not enjoyed the privilege of being trained in the school of Jesus as Peter and the other apostles had done. In fact, Paul was not really an apostle at all. Did he say that he was? But on what ground did he base his claim? Ah, a vision! But of course you never knew where you were with visions; anybody could say he had received a commission in a vision, but who was to prove it? Now, Peter and his companions were on a different footing; they had no need to appeal to visions, for they had received their commission from Christ in a more tangible form; there was no questioning the validity of *their* "orders." Paul was all right, of course; what he had taught them was good and true so far as it went, but they must go on from that. The foundation had been laid, but the superstructure had yet to be built, and here was where Peter's party came in. (Did they quote at this point "Thou art Peter, and upon this rock I will build my church"?)

And how (they asked) did Paul support himself? By his own craftsmanship? Ah! they thought as much. That proved that he was none too sure in his own mind that he was really an apostle. For Jesus had authorized the real apostles to receive material support from those for whose spiritual well-being they cared: "the labourer," He had said, "is worthy of his hire."[1] If Paul were fully convinced of his apostolic status, he would not hesitate to live at the expense of his converts. These arguments sounded plausible enough in the ears of some Corinthian Christians, and these regarded themselves as belonging to "Peter's party."

[1] Luke 10 : 7.

Then there appears to have been a fourth party at Corinth, whose members called themselves "Christ's party." It has, indeed, been held that the words "I am of Christ" or "I belong to Christ" in 1 Corinthians 1 : 12 may be Paul's retort to those who enrolled themselves under sectional names. In that case Paul says: "You call yourselves after various leaders, but I am Christ's: I recognize no leader apart from Him."[1] More probably, however, there really was a self-styled "Christ's party" at Corinth, and Professor T. W. Manson may well be right in thinking that it stood at the opposite extreme from the Peter party—that its members "were a group for whom Christ meant something like 'God, freedom, and immortality,' where 'God' means a refined philosophical mono- theism; 'freedom' means emancipation from the puritanical rigours of Palestinian barbarian authorities into the wider air of self-realization; and immortality means the sound Greek doctrine as opposed to the crude Jewish notion of the Resurrection."[2] Others have identified "Christ's party" with the extreme Judaizers.[3] In any case, whether this is so or not, it is certain that the church of Corinth did include a group which believed itself to be such a "spiritual" élite as Professor Manson describes.

In dealing with the situation at Corinth, therefore, Paul had to fight on two fronts. He had to be on his guard against subtle attempts to rob his converts of their Christian liberty, and also against a line of thought and teaching which would turn that liberty into a licence that took no account of the moral law. Amid the busy concerns of his life at Ephesus, therefore, he penned a letter to the Corinthian church, based (to begin with) on the reports brought to him by Chloe's people. He deprecates and condemns party-spirit; Christ is not divided, and His servants Peter, Apollos and Paul are meant to be equally at the service of all Christians and not to be mere party-leaders. The partisans are really impoverishing themselves. As for the intellectual aspira- tions of some members of the church, let them bear in mind that the very gospel to which they owe their new life is a very foolish message by the standards of current wisdom: a crucified Messiah, forsooth! But divine wisdom and power are very different from the human qualities which are graced by those names. As for those people who talk about going on to build a superstructure, let

[1] So K. Lake, *The Earlier Epistles of St. Paul* (1911), pp. 127f. This is the inter- pretation behind the first line of F. W. H. Myers' *St. Paul*: "Christ! I am Christ's! and let the name suffice you."

[2] *St. Paul in Ephesus*, III (Manchester, 1941), p. 20 (reprint from the *Rylands Bulletin*).

[3] This view (based in part on an interpretation of 2 Cor. 10 : 7) was maintained by F. C. Baur, whose paper on "The Christ Party in the Corinthian Church" (*Die Christuspartei in der korinthischen Gemeinde*) in the *Tübinger Zeitschrift*, 1831, part IV, pp. 61ff., inaugurated the literary activity of the Tübingen school of early church history.

them make sure first of all that they are building on the true foundation, for the only foundation that God recognizes is the one that He Himself has laid: Christ is the true foundation. And then, having found the true foundation, they must see to it that they use the right kind of material for the superstructure, for much of what some people would like to use for building will go up in smoke as soon as a fiery test is applied to it. Regard us all, then—Apollos, myself, and so on—as servants of Christ, stewards of the revelation which God has commissioned us to make known. We must be faithful stewards, but it is God who will have the last word to say about that. Meanwhile I am not over-concerned about the sort of judgment that you or any other mortals may pass upon me. Now I am sending Timothy with this letter; he will remind you of my teaching, and later on I will come to you myself. It is for you to decide what kind of visit you want me to pay you.

But at this juncture, before Timothy set out with the letter, three other members of the Corinthian church arrived at Ephesus with a letter for Paul. This letter propounded a number of questions on which Paul's judgment was sought.[1] In addition, the three bearers of the letter, Fortunatus, Stephanas and Achaicus, gave him an oral account of further developments at Corinth, some of them of a most disquieting nature. So the apostle proceeded to dictate much more of the letter that had been practically finished.

First, there was a scandal in the church which might well shock even the pagans of Corinth: a man was cohabiting with his father's wife. This was bringing the Christian name into public disrepute and the severest measures were called for: a church meeting must be held forthwith (and Paul would be with them in spirit) to excommunicate the offender. This was as necessary for his own spiritual health as for the community's. Then, a spirit of litigation was manifesting itself: Christians were going to law with each other before the secular courts. This public washing of dirty linen could do the Christian cause no good. If a man thought that his fellow-Christian was defrauding him, could he not suffer in silence? If not, let him at least get the dispute settled within the believing community and not go outside with it.

Then the ultra-spiritual party was going too far in its assertion of Christian liberty. "All things are lawful for me," they claimed, and especially so where the body was concerned. To the Christian, therefore, such matters as food and sex were morally indifferent. Not at all, Paul rejoined; the body belongs to Christ as much as the spirit does. Sex relations establish a permanent and vital bond

[1] See R. A. Knox's chapter, "The Corinthians' Letter to St. Paul", in his *Enthusiasm* (1950), pp. 9ff.

between the parties concerned. "All things are lawful?" Very good, but remember also that all things are not expedient, that it is best not to let anything gain control of you, that all things do not help to build up a sound Christian character either for yourself or for those with whom you live.

This then leads him on to discuss the questions raised in the Corinthians' letter.

May a Christian marry? Yes, says Paul. I think it best (he goes on) for people to remain celibate like myself, especially in view of the distressful times impending. To give hostages to fortune (but that is not a Pauline—or even a Christian—expression!) is to incur material anxieties from which the unmarried Christian is free. But the important point is what our Lord Himself has laid down: the wife must not leave her husband and the husband must not divorce his wife. These are unalterable commandments; what I add to these should be regarded as advice and permission, "and I think that I also have the Spirit of God."

Should a Christian eat food which has been sacrificed to idols? It depends, says Paul. Of course, you are intelligent men; you know that an idol has no real existence, and therefore food sacrificed to an idol is not really polluted; it remains as good food after as before. But your brother may not be so intelligent as you; he thinks the idol is real and that the food is really polluted; he may imitate your example and do irreparable harm to his conscience. Consideration for your weaker brother should take precedence over your own liberty.

Is Paul really an apostle? Have I not (he replies) seen Jesus our Lord? Others may doubt my apostolic status, but there can be no such doubt in Corinth; you yourselves are the evidence of my apostleship. If I deny myself certain rights, it is not because I have no title to them; I choose to forego them for the sake of the gospel I proclaim. I have no option whether I shall proclaim the gospel or not; that is an absolute obligation which rests upon me. But I can and do exercise my option of proclaiming it without making myself a charge upon those to whom I make it known. The interests of the gospel are paramount, and to them I subordinate everything.

Then he takes up the conduct of their church gatherings. These should be orderly, as befits the dignity of the Christian name. The Eucharist must not be profaned, whether by being taken in conjunction with idol sacrifices elsewhere or by being made an occasion for gluttony and drunkenness within the Christian circle. The inspirational utterances to which some of their members attached great value—the prophetic gift and speaking with strange tongues—must not be overrated; ministry must be intelligible and profitable for building up the church. The best spiritual gift is heavenly love, and at this point Paul bursts out in his beautiful hymn extolling the supremacy of this grace.[1]

Those who found the doctrine of the resurrection of the body too crude for their acceptance must remember that Christianity is founded upon resurrection—the resurrection of Christ. "If Christ is not risen, our faith is vain." All the same, resurrection must not be understood in a crassly carnal sense; flesh and blood do not inherit the eternal order. It is a natural body that dies; it is a spiritual body that rises again.[2]

Then he reminds them of the collection that he is organizing in his Gentile churches as a gift for the Jerusalem church. Paul attached great importance to this collection, as a token of fellowship between the churches of the Gentiles and the mother church in Palestine. Corinth is invited to make a contribution to it. The way to set about it, he says, is for each member to lay aside a certain sum week by week. Then, when Paul comes, there will be no need for a special collection; the money will be ready.

At last, then, he sent his letter. But it does not seem to have been sufficiently effective with the parties which were disaffected towards Paul, and Timothy himself would not be regarded as an impressive enough character to enforce his teacher's directions. A visit from Paul himself seemed the only course that would meet the situation. But Paul's visit brought the opposition to a head. He withdrew, and sent another letter, this time by the hand of Titus, in which he threw appeasement to the winds and dealt with his opponents in terms of unsparing severity, charging the church to take strong disciplinary action against those who refused his authority—or rather the authority of the Christ whose apostle he was.[3] So severe was this letter, that after it was sent, Paul began to wonder whether it had not been too severe, and he waited anxiously for Titus to return and report on its reception. He tried to do some missionary work in the district round Troas (for he had left Ephesus by now), but he could not settle, and set out for Macedonia. There he met Titus, and to his infinite relief he learned that a complete revulsion in his favour had taken place at Corinth. The severe letter had done its work. The anti-Pauline factions were in utter disgrace. The church as a whole had been stung to such a degree of grief and shame and indignation by his letter that they were now in danger of going too far in their proceedings against those who had led the opposition to Paul.

In the joy of relief Paul quickly sent them yet another letter.[4]

---

[1] 1 Corinthians 13 (cf. p. 79 above). It has often been pointed out that Paul's description of heavenly love is a portrayal of the character of Christ.

[2] See pp. 62, 69 above.

[3] It is widely believed that part of this letter has been preserved in 2 Corinthians 10–13.

[4] 2 Corinthians 1–9.

He rejoices over them; he assures them that he cherishes no personal resentment towards anyone for what had taken place, and he promises to pay them another visit soon. The atmosphere of reconciliation in which this letter is written provides the background for a statement of the ministry of reconciliation which those who preach the gospel exercise. But Christian ideals must be realized in practice, and he reverts to the matter of the collection for the impoverished church of Jerusalem. He had been spurring other churches on by telling them that Achaia—and that meant chiefly Corinth—was ready a year ago; he knows they will not let him down. "Under the test of this service, you will glorify God by your obedience in acknowledging the gospel of Christ, and by the generosity of your contribution for them and for all others; while they long for you and pray for you, because of the surpassing grace of God in you. Thanks be to God for his unspeakable gift."[1]

The difficulties of the Corinthian church were perhaps exceptionally great. But in measure they were reproduced in all the communities of Gentile Christians, and our detailed consideration of Paul's relations with his converts at Corinth may help us to grasp something of what he meant when, in addition to his other burdens, he speaks of "that which presses upon me daily, anxiety for all the churches."[2]

[1] 2 Corinthians 9 : 15.
[2] 2 Corinthians 11 : 28.

CHAPTER XIII

DIANA OF THE EPHESIANS

THE NAME OF THE GREAT GODDESS OF EPHESUS WAS NOT really Diana; Diana was a Roman goddess. The Greek-speaking Ephesians called their goddess Artemis. The Romans identified the Greek Artemis with their own Diana, and when the common version of the English Bible was produced there was an illogical fashion of following the Romans and giving Latin names to Greek deities.[1] But while the Greek-speaking people of Ephesus and the province of Asia called their great goddess Artemis, she was a very different goddess from the well-known Artemis of Greek mythology—the "queen and huntress, chaste and fair" of Ben Jonson's poem. Far from being a virgin goddess, she was really the ancient mother goddess of Asia Minor, worshipped in that land from time immemorial as mother of gods and men.

In Ephesus, however, she was called Artemis, and there she was worshipped with special veneration. Her temple was one of the seven wonders of the ancient world. An earlier temple had been burnt down (on the very day of Alexander the Great's birth, it was said) by a young man who said he did it to make a name for himself in history; but it was rebuilt in greater splendour. And the image of the goddess which this temple enshrined was no image graven by art and device of man; it was of heavenly workmanship, for had it not fallen from the sky?[2] No wonder, then, that the Ephesians were specially devoted to her worship and to the service of her temple. The city itself had acquired the title "Temple-warden of Artemis"[3] for its devotion to the goddess and her cult. So widely was her fame spread abroad that Greeks and barbarians in many lands joined in her veneration: "all Asia and

[1] Similarly in Acts 14 : 12 our common versions tells us that the Lystrans hailed Barnabas and Paul as Jupiter and Mercury, respectively; the Greek text has Zeus and Hermes. Cf. p. 96.

[2] Acts 19 : 35. Similar meteorites which became objects of worship were the Palladium (image of Pallas) at Troy, the image of the Great Mother taken from Pessinus in Galatia to Rome in 204 B.C., the image of Artemis at Taurica on the Black Sea, and that of Ceres at Enna in Sicily. Probably all these meteorites were thought to bear some resemblance to the female form.

[3] This title, mentioned in Acts 19 : 35, is also found on an inscription relating to Ephesus.

the world worshipped her"[1] and invoked her with the cry "Great Artemis of the Ephesians!"

Her votaries bought small shrines to dedicate in her temple, representing the goddess in a niche with her attendant lions. Such miniature shrines in terra-cotta have survived; Luke tells us also of silver shrines. An inscription found in the Ephesian theatre some years ago records how a Roman official presented a silver image of the goddess and other statues to be set up in the theatre on the occasion of a meeting of the citizen-body of Ephesus.[2]

The silversmiths of Ephesus seem to have regarded their guild as being under the special patronage of Artemis, in whose honour so many of their wares were manufactured. When, therefore, a threat to the supremacy of the goddess arose in Ephesus, they were sincerely indignant, with that special intensity of indignation which is manifested when religious and economic sentiments are simultaneously offended. The guild held an indignation meeting under the presidency of one of their number named Demetrius, and the indignation spread to their fellow-citizens, who organized a demonstration in the civic theatre, the usual place of assembly, revealed by excavation to have accommodated some 25,000 people. The demonstration was in honour of their goddess, whom they invoked continuously for two hours with the customary invocation "Great Artemis of the Ephesians!"—but it was directed particularly against those people who did not share their veneration for her, and that meant Jews and Christians. The town clerk who acted as liaison officer between the autonomous municipality and the Roman provincial government, was alarmed lest the proceedings might become so riotous as to bring down the heavy hand of Rome on the city, and with much ado he persuaded the assembly to disperse.

The anger of the Ephesian populace on this occasion was directed indiscriminately against Jews and Christians, although it was actually occasioned by the missionary activity of Paul and his colleagues. The local Jews tried to dissociate themselves publicly from the missionaries, but the crowd was in no temper to make fine distinctions between people who were at least agreed in their refusal to honour the great goddess. But it is plain that the Christian propaganda had been remarkably successful. Paul came to Ephesus in the autumn of A.D. 52, and the demonstration in the theatre took place in the spring of 55—quite possibly, as Principal G. S. Duncan has suggested, in connection with the Artemisia, the spring festival held in honour of the goddess.[3] We

---

[1] The *Realencyclopädie* of Pauly and Wissowa enumerates thirty-three places where Ephesian Artemis was worshipped.

[2] Deissmann, *Light from the Ancient East*, pp. 112f.

[3] G. S. Duncan, *St. Paul's Ephesian Ministry* (1929), p. 141.

need not doubt the accuracy of Demetrius's complaint, as reported by Luke, that the guild of silversmiths were likely to lose a substantial part of their livelihood by the diminution in the number of Artemis's worshippers. Nearly sixty years later, in Bithynia, a similar complaint was voiced, that the business of supplying fodder for sacrificial animals had declined through the spread of Christianity.[1]

Certainly the two and a half years that Paul spent in Ephesus left their mark on western Asia Minor. The Christianity established there at that time endured until the expulsion of the Greeks from those parts in 1923. Paul himself spent the greater part of the time in Ephesus itself, but his colleagues carried the gospel into other parts of the province of Asia, especially to the cities in the valley of the Lycus (a tributary of the Mæander, which finds its way to the sea near Ephesus). The seven churches of Asia, to which at a later time the Book of Revelation was addressed, were probably all founded at this time, and not these only, but others, such as Colossæ and Hierapolis, which played an important part in early Christian history.

There is some evidence that the knowledge of Christianity had reached Ephesus and the surrounding district even before Paul settled down there in the autumn of 52. It had not, however, been planted there by apostolic action, so that Paul's missionary work constituted no breach of his policy not to build on another man's foundation. Visitors from other parts of the Roman world were constantly coming to such an important city as Ephesus and settling there for longer or shorter periods, and among those visitors were some who had a measure of acquaintance with the gospel story. On leaving Corinth in the spring of 52, Paul crossed over to Ephesus with Aquila and Priscilla. There he started his usual practice of arguing with those who frequented the synagogue, and they were apparently willing to hear more, but for the present he could not wait as he was bound for Palestine. He left his two friends behind him, however, and they must have spoken to several people about the way of Jesus. When the Alexandrian Apollos visited Ephesus in the course of that summer, they found that his knowledge of the gospel story was less complete than theirs. They, therefore, made good the deficiencies in his knowledge, and he proved a powerful propagandist for the truth of Christianity, both in Ephesus and in Corinth, to which he later betook himself, "for he powerfully confuted the Jews in public, demonstrating by the scriptures that the Messiah was Jesus."[2]

Then, when Paul returned to Ephesus in the autumn of that year, he met a small group of people in the city who had a

[1] Pliny the Younger, *Letters*, X, 96. See p. 171.
[2] Acts 18 : 28.

limited acquaintance with the story of Jesus. Like Apollos, they had not heard of Christian baptism, nor yet of the Pentecostal gift of the Holy Spirit. They knew (like Apollos) the baptism of John the Baptist and had received that baptism. Yet it is hardly safe to regard them as nothing more than disciples of John.[1] It is more likely that they had derived their knowledge of Christianity from some Galilæan followers of Jesus, and that the gospel had not come to them through the apostolic channel running from Jerusalem *via* Antioch. That some followers of Jesus remained in Galilee and did not share in the Pentecostal experiences at Jerusalem and in the subsequent evangelistic enterprise based on that city is certain; but what they did is a matter for the writer of historical fiction rather than for one whose aim is to record what really happened, because there is no real historical evidence of the fortunes of these people. But it is natural to speculate; and when we find "disciples" in other parts, whether in Ephesus or Alexandria, who knew the story of Jesus but whose Christianity lacked those features which characterized the movement as it developed in Jerusalem from the first Christian Pentecost onward, we may envisage certain explanations as being more probable than others.

At any rate, the missionary enterprise of Paul and his friends in Ephesus proceeded at an extraordinary rate. Before the threat to the great civic cult developed, the gospel made its impact on lesser superstitions. Among these the practice of magic was a prominent feature of Ephesian life—so much so that a common name for scrolls inscribed with magic spells was "Ephesian letters." Luke gives us an interesting cameo of this sort of thing, when he describes converts bringing their magic scrolls and making a public bonfire of them, divulging the secret meaning of the spells in order to render them ineffective.[2]

We have not had preserved to us as many details as we should like of the two and a half years that Paul spent in Ephesus. Luke, who was not in Ephesus with him, gives us little beyond the account of the purveyors of magic and the description of the riotous demonstration of the Artemis-worshippers. He does tell us, however, that after Paul had spent three months debating in

---

[1] In Acts 19 : 1 these people are called simply "disciples," and when Luke uses this term absolutely it is synonymous with "Christians." They may have been converts of Apollos.

[2] We gather from examples of such scrolls which have survived that the ineffable name of the God of Israel was much thought of as an unusually potent spell. This explains the curious incident related in Acts 19 : 13-16 of a Jewish "high priest" who practised exorcism in Ephesus. The Jewish high priests possessed the knowledge of the true pronunciation of the ineffable name. Of course, this man Sceva was a mountebank; Luke would have put his description as "high priest" within quotation marks had this device been used in that day (he probably advertised himself as "Jewish High Priest" on a placard outside his shop).

the synagogue, such opposition was aroused that he withdrew and hired the lecture-hall of a man named Tyrannus[1] and continued his instruction there. One variety of the New Testament text tells us that he taught there from 11 a.m. to 4 p.m.[2] We gather that he spent the earlier—and perhaps the later—hours of the day earning his living by working at his usual manual occupation.[3] Probably Tyrannus himself used the lecture-hall before 11 a.m. Paul's hearers must have been infected with his own enthusiasm, as more people would normally be asleep in Ephesus at 1 p.m. than 1 a.m.

But all was not plain sailing, although the work was attended with such success that the gospel spread through the whole province of Asia. The missionaries were exposed more than once to serious hazards, and Paul's life was on at least one occasion as good as lost. Not only were there the dangers aroused by the affronted devotees of Artemis, and others which sprang from Jewish opposition; danger of a more direct character also assailed him. There is a curious passage in one of his letters where he writes: "If (as men put it) I fought with wild beasts at Ephesus, what good does it do me if there is no resurrection of the dead?"[4] This is shown by the very way it is expressed to be a figure of speech and not to be understood of literal exposure to lions in the arena; but the reference must be to some danger which could aptly be described under such a figure. Another passage in his letters refers to trouble which he had to endure in the province of Asia: "we were so utterly and unbearably crushed that we despaired of life itself," he writes; "we felt that we had received the death sentence; in ourselves we found no hope, so we placed our hope in God who raises the dead, and in truth He did deliver us from so awful a death."[5]

Sometimes the reading of Paul's letters is tantalizingly like listening to one end of a specially thrilling telephone conversation; the people at the other end know the context in which the speaker's words are to be understood, but as we do not, we have to fill in the gap in our knowledge as intelligently as we may. So it is with reference to the perils which beset the apostle in Ephesus. At the end of his stay there Paul can speak of himself as having suffered frequent imprisonments;[6] and it is extremely likely that one if not more of these imprisonments must be dated during his Ephesian ministry. A number of scholars, indeed, have

[1] Was this his real name, we wonder, or did his pupils call him this?
[2] The "western text" adds at the end of Acts 19 : 9, "from the fifth hour till the tenth" (reckoning, of course, from sunrise).
[3] Cf. Acts 20 : 34.
[4] 1 Corinthians 15 : 32.
[5] 2 Corinthians 1 : 8–10.
[6] 2 Corinthians 11 : 23.

maintained the opinion that the imprisonment referred to by Paul in his letter to the church at Philippi was an imprisonment endured in Ephesus.[1]

This imprisonment, he says, has worked out for the progress of the gospel, and therefore he is able to rejoice in it. It has actually increased the courage and boldness of the other Christians, and it has enabled the good news to penetrate Government House itself.[2] He expects to be released, but even if things turn out otherwise and his life is to be "poured out as a libation" on the sacrificial offering of his converts' faith, he will continue to rejoice. In fact, so far as his personal welfare is concerned, death would be clear gain; it would mean immediate entrance into the presence of the exalted Christ. But it is better for his friends' and converts' sakes, he says, that he should go on living down here a little longer.

The atmosphere of this letter to the Philippians, however, does not suggest the desperate situation referred to above in which he and his companions gave up all hope of life and greeted their deliverance as a veritable miracle of resurrection. This more serious crisis may be connected with a political episode in the history of the province of Asia.

Readers of Luke's account of the demonstration staged in the Ephesian theatre by the worshippers of Artemis will remember the generalizing terms in which the town clerk, calming his excited audience, tells them that the law-courts are available if they wish to prefer a charge against anybody. And, he adds, "there are proconsuls."[3] But why the plural? There was only one proconsul in the province. Yes; but what if there was an interregnum: if one proconsul had died and his successor had not yet arrived? Might not a speaker in that case be less definite and use what grammarians call the "generalizing plural"?

Nero had succeeded to the imperial power in October, A.D. 54. He was a great grandson of the Emperor Augustus, and so, as it happened, was the man who was proconsul of Asia at the time, Marcus Junius Silanus. Nero's mother Agrippina saw in Silanus a possible rival to her son, and had him assassinated. The assassins were a Roman knight named Helius and a freedman named Celer, who administered the Emperor's personal affairs in Asia.[4]

[1] Philippians 1 : 7, 13.
[2] Philippians 1 : 13; the word here rendered "Government House" is a Greek form of Latin *prætorium*. On the commoner view that Philippians was written in Rome, the reference here is taken to be the headquarters of the Emperor's Prætorian Guard in Rome. But the word means the headquarters of the prætor or chief magistrate; it is used in Mark 15 : 16 and John 18 : 28 of Pilate's headquarters in Jerusalem. There is, however, no record of the use of *prætorium* for the headquarters of the proconsul of a senatorial province, such as Asia was.
[3] Acts 19 : 38.
[4] Dr. Duncan (*op. cit.*, pp. 102ff.) suggests that the plural term "proconsuls" may

Tacitus records that Silanus was the first victim of the new reign.[1]

If, as Dr. Duncan suggests, Silanus had extended his protection to Paul at the time of an earlier crisis, that very fact might make Paul's position specially delicate when Silanus had been put out of the way, especially if Helius and Celer exercised the chief authority in Asia during the ensuing proconsular interregnum.

However that may be, Paul survived all the dangers that beset him in Ephesus. By the end of his stay there he had evangelized both shores of the Ægean Sea, and the Christian cause in those lands could march forward without his presence. He looked farther afield for new worlds to conquer for the kingdom of Christ, and cast his eyes westward to Spain, where as yet the gospel had not been made known.[2] The western Mediterranean must be evangelized as thoroughly as the eastern. At the moment, however, he was engaged in organizing a collection for the Jerusalem church in his churches on both sides of the Ægean, as we have seen already; and he intended to visit these churches to receive the money and go with it to Jerusalem, accompanied by delegates from the contributing churches. When he had discharged this duty in Jerusalem, he would be free to go to Spain, and he looked forward eagerly to visiting Rome on the way there.

actually refer to Helius and Celer: "may it be that the two agents of the murder exercised proconsular authority until the arrival of the new governor?" This suggestion had already been made by H. M. Luckock in *Footprints of the Apostles as Traced by St. Luke in the Acts*, II (1897), p. 189, and was adversely criticized by W. M. Ramsay in *The Expositor*, VI, 2 (1900), pp. 334f.

[1] Tacitus, *Annals*, XIII, 1. Several other members of the Silanus family had fallen foul of the imperial court. That makes it the more natural that Luke, who maintains an apologetic motive throughout his narrative, should have judged it politic not to mention any protection that Paul might have received from Silanus; such mention would have the opposite effect to what was intended.

[2] Paul's policy of planting the Gospel in virgin soil (Romans 15 : 20) made it out of the question for him to think of evangelizing Italy or Egypt, as Christianity had already been planted in Rome (certainly) and Alexandria (probably).

CHAPTER XIV

CHRISTIANITY AT ROME

WHEN HE LEFT EPHESUS, PAUL CROSSED THE ÆGEAN AND spent some time in Macedonia and Greece before going to Jerusalem to discharge his business there. He passed the winter of A.D. 56–57 in Corinth, and while he was there he wrote a letter to the Roman church to prepare them for his projected visit to the imperial city on his way to Spain.

I have often intended to visit you (he writes), but have been prevented up to now. I long to see you all, so that both you and I may impart to each other some spiritual blessing. As it is, I want you to know that you are constantly in my thoughts and prayers, and that I thank God for the extent to which your faith and loyalty are subjects of world-wide renown. I have seen some fruit as a result of my activity in other parts of the Gentile world, and I should like to see some among you as well. As I have proclaimed the good news elsewhere, I am ready to proclaim it in Rome, too; for I am in no way ashamed of the good news. . . . Not that I think of settling down as a missionary in Rome, for that would be building on another man's foundation—the very thing I have always avoided doing. And as for taking the place of a teacher among you, I know very well that you are well able to teach one another. But from Jerusalem to Illyricum I have proclaimed the good news and planted churches, and now my work in these parts is finished. The next place on my missionary programme is Spain. First of all, however, I must go to Jerusalem to discharge a service to the people of God there; but when I have done that, I hope to set out for Spain and break my journey at Rome, so that I may find refreshment in your company and be sped forth by you on my further journey.[1]

Thus he wrote to the Christians in Rome, and expanded his letter by setting before them a full statement of the Christian message as he understood and proclaimed it. It was three years before his hope of seeing them was realized, and in what unexpected fashion he arrived there we shall see later.

But it is plain from the way in which he wrote that the Roman church was not a recent growth. When, then, was it formed; and who was the "other man" whose foundation it was?

We have no explicit account of the origin of the Roman church. We have to reconstruct the story from various literary and

[1] A summary of Romans 1: 8–16 and 15 : 14–29.

archæological references. But these give a more coherent outline than might be expected. The archæological study of Roman Christianity has this advantage over that of Jerusalem: that there has been no breach of continuity at Rome from apostolic days. There is an unbroken line of tradition going back from our own day to the middle of the first century A.D. The diverse elements in this tradition, of course, have to be critically analysed and appraised for what they are worth; but at least they exist.

Among the crowds who had come to Jerusalem for the Feast of Pentecost in A.D. 30, we read, were "visitors from Rome, both Jews and proselytes."[1] Whether any of these were among the three thousand who believed Peter's message on that occasion and were baptized, is not recorded. But the fact that these Romans are the only European contingent mentioned in the list of visitors may have more significance than appears on the surface. In any case, all roads led to Rome, and once Christianity was established in the coastlands of the Levant, it must inevitably be carried to Rome. "By the autumn following the Crucifixion it is quite as possible that Jesus was honoured in the Jewish community at Rome as that He was at Damascus."[2]

There was a Jewish colony at Rome in the second century B.C., and this was augmented by those Jews who were brought from Palestine in 62 B.C. to grace Pompey's triumph, and later set free. In 59 B.C. Cicero, defending an official who had incurred Jewish hostility by forbidding the sending of temple contributions from the province of Asia to Jerusalem, pretended to be apprehensive of the Jews in Rome, and dropped his voice lest the Jewish crowd outside the courtroom might overhear him: "for you know how numerous they are, how united, how influential in public assemblies."[3]

Successive Emperors safeguarded Jewish rights and privileges, both in Rome and elsewhere in the Empire. We find the names of several synagogues in Rome mentioned in inscriptions—the synagogues of the Campenses, Augustenses, Agrippenses, Suburenses, and Volumnenses, the synagogues of the "Hebrews" and of the "Olive Tree". In the name of the last-mentioned synagogue some scholars think they have a clue to what lies behind Paul's parable of the olive tree in Romans 11: 16–24.

But it seemed desirable at times to clean up the city by expelling Oriental incomers, and among these Jews were naturally included. The most famous expulsion of Jews from Rome is that of A.D. 49,

---

[1] Acts 2 : 10.
[2] F. J. Foakes Jackson, *Peter, Prince of Apostles* (1927), p. 195. The anonymous fourth-century Christian called "Ambrosiaster," in the preface of his commentary on the Epistle to the Romans, says: "They had embraced the faith of Christ, after the Jewish rite, although they saw no sign of mighty works nor any of the apostles."
[3] Cicero, *Pro Flacco*, 66.

which involved Aquila and Priscilla, who at that time made their way to Corinth and met Paul there. One historian, Dio Cassius, says of the edict uttered at this time by the Emperor Claudius:

> As the Jews had again increased in numbers, but could scarcely be expelled from the city without a tumult because of their multitude, he did not actually drive them out, but forbade them to meet in accordance with their ancestral customs.[1]

If that means that they were forbidden to hold synagogue meetings, the edict was tantamount to one of expulsion. Another writer, the biographer Suetonius, says that Claudius "expelled the Jews from Rome because they were indulging in constant riots at the instigation of Chrestus."[2] This last reference is specially interesting. This Chrestus was conceivably a troublesome character in Jewish circles in Rome at the time; but the way in which Suetonius mentions him makes it more likely that the riots resulted from the recent introduction of Christianity among the Jews of Rome. Suetonius, writing seventy years later, may have looked up some record of these riots and inferred wrongly that Chrestus, whose name appeared as the leader of one party, was actually in Rome in the time of Claudius. ("Chrestus" was a variant spelling of "Christus" in Gentile circles.) It looks as if Aquila and Priscilla were Christians before they came to Corinth, though it is outrunning the evidence to suppose, with Harnack, that they were foundation members of the Roman Church.[3]

A year or two later (A.D. 52), a writer named Thallus (formerly a freedman of the Emperor Tiberius) wrote a history of Greece and its relations with Asia from the Trojan War to his own day. In the third book of this history he referred to the preternatural darkness which covered Palestine on the day of the crucifixion of Jesus, and explained it as due to a solar eclipse—wrongly, of course, as a solar eclipse could not take place at the full moon.[4] But it is worth noting that about the middle of the first century A.D. the traditional story of the death of Christ was known in non-Christian circles at Rome.

In the year in which Paul wrote his letter to the Roman church (A.D. 57), Pomponia Græcina, the wife of Aulus Plautius, conqueror of Britain,[5] was charged before a domestic court with having embraced a "foreign superstition."[6] Colour was given to

---

[1] *History*, LX, 6.

[2] *Life of Claudius*, 25 : 4.

[3] And joint authors of the Epistle to the Hebrews. See *Zeitschrift für neutestamentliche Wissenschaft*, I (1900), pp. 16ff.

[4] The Passover season, at which Jesus was crucified, fell at the full moon following the vernal equinox. The Christian chronologer Julius Africanus (A.D. 221) pointed out this flaw in Thallus's argument.

[5] Plautius reduced southern Britain to a Roman province in A.D. 43.

[6] Tacitus, *Annals*, XIII, 32.

this charge by the fact that for fourteen years she had worn mourning garb and avoided the society which a lady of her rank would naturally seek. She was acquitted of the charge and continued for the rest of her life to enjoy the respect of her acquaintances in spite of her retiring ways. It may well be that her "foreign superstition" was, in fact, Christianity.[1]

Some details of the membership of the Christian community at Rome in that year can be gathered from the personal greetings sent by Paul to various people at the end of his letter.[2] These would be people whom Paul had met here and there throughout the eastern world and who were now in Rome. The list includes the names of some very early Christians. We find, for instance, a couple called Andronicus and Junia, who (says Paul) "are well known among the apostles and were Christians before myself."[3] This pair were thus possibly foundation members of the church; they had perhaps been Hellenist members of the Jerusalem church in its earliest days. Whether Paul means that they were themselves apostles in a sense (as eye-witnesses of the risen Christ?), or that they were well known *to* the apostles is uncertain; he knew what he meant and so did his first readers, but to us in our ignorance his language here is ambiguous. One wonders, too, if the Rufus mentioned in this list is one of the sons of Simon the Cyrenean who carried the cross of Jesus.[4] If so, it was probably at Antioch that his mother played the part of a mother to Paul. One of Paul's colleagues in the Antiochene church, we remember, was Simeon surnamed *Niger*; and Simeon is simply a more genuinely Jewish form of Simon.[5] It does look as if some very interesting Christians had found their way from different parts to Rome by the beginning of 57.

The next landmark in the history of the Roman church is Paul's arrival in the city in or about February of the year 60. As Paul was conducted along the Appian Way from Puteoli to

[1] It is unlikely to have been Judaism, which was well known as a *religio licita* and affected by several Roman ladies. The phrase "foreign superstition" is quite general, but, as H. Pitman says in a comment on the Tacitus passage, "the retirement and sobriety of a Christian might well appear a kind of 'perpetual mourning' to the dissolute society of the Neronian period." This surmise receives some support from the fact that the crypts of Lucina, one of the oldest Christian cemeteries, going back to *c.* A.D. 140, contain inscriptions commemorating members of the *gens Pomponia*, one of whom (*c.* A.D. 200) was named Pomponius Græcinus, possibly a collateral descendant of this Pomponia.

[2] I accept the Roman destination of the last chapter of the Epistle to the Romans. But it is widely held, on grounds which cannot be ignored, that this chapter was directed to Ephesus. See C. H. Dodd, *The Epistle to the Romans* (1932), *ad loc.*; T. W. Manson, *St. Paul's Letter to the Romans—and Others* (Rylands Bulletin reprint, 1948), pp. 12ff.

[3] Romans 16 : 7. Paul calls them "my kinsfolk and fellow-prisoners."

[4] Romans 16 : 13: "Greet Rufus, elect in the Lord, and his mother and mine." Mark's Gospel (written at Rome) identifies Simon the Cyrenean as "the father of Alexander and Rufus" (15 : 21).

[5] Acts 13 : 1; see p. 91 above.

Rome by the courier-force in whose custody he was, some Christians in Rome learned of his approach and set out to meet him and give him something like a triumphal escort back to Rome. The sight of these friends some forty miles from Rome cheered the apostle considerably.

Paul came to Rome in this way because he had been charged by his Jewish opponents at Jerusalem with the serious offence of violating the sanctity of the temple. There was considerable delay in bringing him to trial, and at last, fearing that the procurator of Judæa might be swayed by a desire to favour the Sanhedrin leaders, Paul's prosecutors, Paul exercised his right as a Roman citizen and appealed to be tried by the Emperor in Rome. He spent two years in Rome awaiting trial, and enjoyed the company of a number of friends and fellow-workers—Luke and Aristarchus, who had accompanied him to Rome, and others, among whom Mark merits special mention.

Since the time of the cleavage between Barnabas and Paul, when Paul and Silas went to Asia Minor and Barnabas and Mark to Cyprus, Mark had become attached to the apostle Peter. In the fifties of the first century, Peter appears to have embarked upon a ministry more extended geographically than he had undertaken up to that time. Mark travelled with him as his interpreter and general aide-de-camp. Some time between 55 and 60, according to a reading of the evidence which seems to me very probable,[1] Peter and Mark visited Rome. When Peter left the city, Mark stayed behind, and the Roman Christians persuaded him to record in writing the story of Jesus as they had heard it from Peter's own lips (or through Mark's interpretation). This was the origin of the gospel according to Mark; and when Luke visited Rome in A.D. 60 along with Paul he found Mark's record of great usefulness in the drawing up of his own narrative of the rise of Christianity.

Paul's case probably went against his prosecutors by default at the end of 61. The chief priesthood at Jerusalem would realize that, since their charges were regarded as unfounded by impartial judges in Palestine, they were even less likely to convince the authorities in Rome.[2] So (on our interpretation of the evidence)

[1] See T. W. Manson, *The Life of Jesus*. 2. *The Gospel of Mark* (Rylands Bulletin reprint, 1944), pp. 12ff. The anti-Marcionite prologue to Mark's Gospel (c. A.D. 170) says that this Gospel was composed in Italy after Peter's departure; Manson wisely suggests that we have been over-hasty in taking "departure" here to mean "death" (as it has been taken from Irenæus onward).

[2] J. V. Bartlet, however, argued that the prosecutors gave notice within the eighteen months' time limit of their intention to proceed with the case, that they reached Rome early in 62 and successfully prosecuted Paul as a disturber of the peace of the provinces, that the original readers of Acts knew from Nero's record what the inevitable result of such a prosecution before him would be (the more so in view of Poppæa's Jewish sympathies), and would not need to be told explicitly of Paul's condemnation and execution (*Expositor*, VIII, v [1913], pp. 464ff.).

Paul left Rome on his release from custody[1] and shortly after his departure Peter paid a further visit to the capital. Here, about A.D. 63, he wrote, with the collaboration of Silvanus, the letter to the churches of north-west Asia Minor which appears in the New Testament as the first epistle of Peter.[2] The greeting which Peter sends to these Anatolian churches from "the (church) that is in Babylon, elect together with you," is a greeting from the church in Rome;[3] in the same sentence he adds a greeting from "Mark, my son."[4]

This letter contains warnings of a "fiery trial" which is soon to overtake Christians, and of a situation in which Christians may be subjected to suffering not for any overt act of law-breaking but simply for bearing and acknowledging the name "Christian." This situation was fast developing, and the conditions in which an apostle like Paul had been able to count upon the protection of Roman law in his missionary work were passing away.

When the proconsul Gallio, twelve years before, had refused to listen to the charges brought against Paul by his Jewish opponents in Corinth, he did so because he regarded the whole dispute as an internal Jewish concern. Judaism might be a contemptible Oriental superstition, but it was protected by law; it was a licensed cult (*religio licita*). So long as Christianity could be regarded as a movement within Judaism, it profited by the protection which Roman law extended to the Jewish faith and way of life. But in the sixties it was no longer possible to regard Christianity (outside Palestine) as simply a variety of Judaism. This was in large measure the result of Paul's own policy and activity, which drew a clear line of demarcation between Christianity and the Judaism of the synagogue. When the Christian

---

[1] Clement of Rome, in his letter to the Corinthian Church (*c.* A.D. 95) speaks of Paul as "having reached the farthest bounds of the West" (5 : 7); but this does not necessarily mean Spain. (See P. N. Harrison, *The Problem of the Pastoral Epistles* (1921), pp. 107f.) Eusebius (*Hist. Eccl.*, II, 22) reports that Paul was released at the end of his two years' custody and that his condemnation and execution took place on the occasion of a later visit paid by him to Rome.

[2] See E. G. Selwyn, *The First Epistle of St. Peter* (1946), for a full exposition of this setting of the letter. F. W. Beare, in a commentary on the epistle published in 1947, holds that it is a pseudonymous production of A.D. 112 or thereabouts, when Pliny's governorship of Bithynia was marked by some official action against Christians. See pp. 168ff.

[3] This interpretation of the clause is explicit in Eusebius (*Hist. Eccl.*, II, 15); it is maintained with no dissentient voice in pre-Reformation writers and by the majority of modern interpreters. The alternative views, such as that the greetings were not sent from a church but from a Christian lady (preferably Peter's wife; cf. 1 Corinthians 9 : 5), and that the "Babylon" mentioned was the city on the Euphrates or a fort of that name in Egypt, are much less probable (especially on archæological grounds) than the view adopted here.

[4] Mark may not have spent the whole interval between Peter's two Roman visits in Rome; on this arrangement of the evidence there is room for Eusebius's account that Mark evangelized Egypt and founded the church of Alexandria, where Annianus took over the supervision from Mark in A.D. 62 (*Hist. Eccl.*, II, 16, 24).

communities throughout the empire consisted largely of Gentiles, who had not taken the steps required of proselytes to Judaism and, in particular, had not submitted to circumcision, it was evident that these communities could not be looked upon as Jewish. The Jews themselves would be foremost in dissociating themselves from these new nondescript communities. And from A.D. 62 onward Jewish influence was present in the imperial court itself; the Empress Poppæa, whom Nero married in that year, was a friend of Jews.[1]

Christianity thus stood revealed as a movement not recognized or licensed by law—a *religio illicita*. It was not, like Judaism, the religion of a nation, but of the off-scourings of society. A Roman satirist of a later generation complained of the way in which the filth of the Orontes discharged itself into the Tiber;[2] and Gentile Christianity, which arose on the banks of the Orontes, was to the Roman mind simply another of these disgusting Asiatic cults. It was in accordance with Roman tradition to take severe measures against these eastern cults, which acted as a disintegrating and revolutionary ferment in Roman society.[3] Christianity, besides, was generally unpopular. Judaism, too, was unpopular; but Christianity had the added disadvantage of not being a permitted religion. The Roman power might at any time take police measures to suppress this new movement, and, so far as a spectator at the time could tell, the suppression would be effective and permanent.

So we come to the year 64, when Rome was devastated by a great fire. We need not inquire into the cause of the fire; most probably it arose by accident, like the Great Fire of London in 1666. Once such a fire started, it would find plenty of fodder in the congested buildings of the city. But rumour was not content to ascribe the fire to accident, and some curious reports began to circulate. Some men who ought to have been checking the conflagration were seen (it was said) actively helping it on, and when challenged they said they had their orders. The Emperor himself was suspected of starting the conflagration. There is no proof of this; even if he "fiddled while Rome burned," that does not make him an incendiary.[4] In fact, he threw himself actively into the

---

[1] Josephus (*Life*, 3) tells how, when he visited Rome in 63, he was introduced to Poppæa by a Jewish actor and was befriended by her. Tacitus (*Annals*, XVI, 6) says that on her death in A.D. 65 Poppæa was not cremated in the customary manner, but buried "after the fashion of foreign royalty." Josephus (*Antiquities*, XX, 8, 11) indicates that she was a God-fearer.

[2] Juvenal, *Satires*, III, 62.

[3] Precedents for the suppression of such cults go as far back as 186 B.C. when, in accordance with a decree of the senate, the cult of Bacchus was checked.

[4] Tacitus, though hostile to Nero, is more objective than Suetonius, who depended largely on court gossip. Tacitus says that *rumour* described Nero as singing of the fall of Troy while he watched the blaze (*Annals*, XV, 39); Suetonius gives the report out as a fact. Indeed, Suetonius states with no reservations that Nero set the city on fire (*Life of Nero*, 38); cf. Pliny the Elder, *Natural History*, XVII, 5.

organization of relief for those who had suffered in consequence
of the fire. But when he found that the finger of rumour pointed
to him as the instigator of the fire, he did not like it. The people
would not cherish kindly feelings towards one who was believed
to have destroyed their homes and their living, too. So Nero
looked about for scapegoats, and had no difficulty in finding
some. The sequel may be told in the words of Tacitus, who obviously had no sympathy with the scapegoats, but knew that
there was no evidence to connect them with the fire.

> Therefore, to scotch the rumour, Nero substituted as culprits,
> and punished with the utmost refinements of cruelty, a class of men
> loathed for their vices, whom the crowd styled Christians. Christus,
> from whom they got their name, had been executed by sentence of
> the procurator Pontius Pilate when Tiberius was emperor; and the
> pernicious superstition was checked for a short time, only to break
> out afresh, not only in Judæa, the home of the plague, but in Rome
> itself, where all the horrible and shameful things in the world collect
> and find a home. First, then, those who confessed themselves
> Christians were arrested; next, on their disclosures, a vast multitude
> were convicted, not so much on the charge of arson as for hatred
> of the human race. And their death was made a matter of sport:
> they were covered in wild beasts' skins and torn to pieces by dogs;
> or were fastened to crosses and set on fire in order to serve as
> torches by night when daylight failed. Nero had offered his gardens
> for the spectacle and gave an exhibition in his circus, mingling with
> the crowd in the guise of a charioteer or mounted on his chariot.
> Hence, in spite of a guilt which had earned the most exemplary
> punishment, there arose a feeling of pity, because it was felt that
> they were being sacrificed not for the common good but to gratify
> the savagery of one man.[1]

In spite of his contemptuous hatred for this pernicious superstition, as he calls it, Tacitus plainly implies that the charge of arson
broke down and that the Christians were victimized on general
principles, "for hatred of the human race." We must remember
that almost the whole of social life in all its strata was bound up
with practices which to the Christians were idolatrous and forbidden. The Jews also regarded these practices in this light and
abstained from social intercourse with Gentiles on that account;
but it was taken for granted that Jews were like that, and after
all their attitude was legalized. But Christians had no racial or
legally recognized reason for being anti-social; their attitude was
put down as sheer hatred of humanity, and humanity considered
itself justified in retaliating.

Tacitus's account of the persecution is corroborated by Suetonius who, in the course of his *Life of Nero* (but not in connection
with his narrative of the fire), remarks:

[1] *Annals*, XV, 44.

Punishment was inflicted on the Christians, a class of men addicted to a novel and baneful superstition.[1]

From the Christian side we have the words of Clement, a leader in the Roman church in the following generation, in the course of his letter to the Corinthian church (c. A.D. 95):

By reason of jealousy and envy the greatest and most righteous pillars of the church were persecuted, and contended even unto death. Let us set before our eyes the good apostles. There was Peter who, by reason of unrighteous jealousy, endured many toils, not one or two, and having witnessed thus went to the place of glory appointed for him. By reason of jealousy and strife Paul showed by his example the reward of patient endurance. After he had suffered imprisonment seven times, been driven into exile, been stoned; after he had preached in the east and in the west, he won the noble renown which was the result of his faith, having taught righteousness to the whole world and reached the farthest limits of the west; and when he had borne his testimony before the rulers, he departed thus from the world and went unto the holy place, having proved a noble pattern of patient endurance. Unto these men of holy life was gathered a vast multitude of the elect, who through many indignities and tortures, being the victims of jealousy, set a brave example among ourselves. By reason of jealousy women were persecuted, and after they had endured cruel and unholy insults by having to enact the parts of Dirce and the daughters of Danaus, they safely reached the goal of the race of faith, and received a noble reward, despite their physical weakness.[2]

The sufferings of the apostles and others are ascribed by Clement to jealous envy and spite because this is the vice against which he is warning his readers, and he is anxious to find awful examples of the disastrous results of jealousy. But it is clear enough that the "vast multitude of the elect" who joined the apostles in martyrdom "through many indignities and tortures" should be identified with the "vast multitude" of Christians who, according to Tacitus, were put to death with such accompaniments.

Furthermore, a natural inference from Clement's language is that Peter and Paul met their ends about the same time and under the same general circumstances. Paul's association with Rome and his death there have not been seriously doubted. Peter's association with Rome and his death there, unfortunately, have been confused by dogmatic controversy reflecting opposite ecclesiastical interests. With this, however, we have no concern. If we consider the question in the light of historical and archæological evidence, we are led to the conclusion that Peter, like Paul, spent some time in Rome and died there. This is how the German

[1] Suetonius, *Nero*, 16 : 2. See p. 165.
[2] 1 Clement 5 : 2–6 : 2.

Protestant scholar Hans Lietzmann (by no means a traditionalist!) summed it up:

> All the early sources about the year 100 become clear and easily intelligible, and agree with their historical context and with each other, if we accept what they clearly suggest to us, namely, that Peter sojourned in Rome and died a martyr there. Any other hypothesis regarding Peter's death piles difficulty upon difficulty, and cannot be supported by a single document. I cannot understand how, in face of this state of things, there can be any hesitation in accepting the conclusion.[1]

On the other hand, this does not involve us in accepting all the later accounts about Peter's association with Rome, including the tradition (preserved by Eusebius and Jerome) which ascribes to him a twenty-five years' episcopate there, from A.D. 42 to 67. In the earlier part of that period we find him at Jerusalem and Antioch; as for the later part, there is no hint that he was in Rome either when Paul wrote his letter to the Roman church early in 57 or when Paul arrived at Rome at the beginning of A.D. 60 to spend two years in custody there. On this point a French Roman Catholic scholar, Jacques Zeiller, may well be quoted:

> How long had St. Peter lived in Rome before his martyrdom? Here we must confess an almost complete ignorance. The so-called tradition of the twenty-five years of Peter's Roman episcopate rests on no historic data. . . . But of Peter's life in Rome we know for certain only the last act, his martyrdom.[2]

The continuous tradition of the Roman church ascribing its foundation to Peter might go back to Roman visitors who heard Peter preach in Jerusalem in A.D. 30 and returned to the capital to form a "Nazarene" community within the Jewish fold. But this community, after its expulsion in consequence of the "Chrestus" riots of A.D. 49, very probably was constituted anew a few years later on the occasion of Peter's first visit to Rome. The Christian writer Lactantius, at the beginning of the fourth century, evidently preserves a more accurate tradition of the twenty-five years' ministry of Peter when he says that the apostles "were dispersed throughout the world to proclaim the gospel . . . and for twenty-five years, until the beginning of Nero's reign, they laid the foundations of the church throughout all the provinces and cities. *Nero was already Emperor when Peter came to Rome.*"[3]

Nero's accession in A.D. 54 may well have seemed a favourable

[1] *Petrus und Paulus in Rom* (1927), p. 238.
[2] J. Lebreton and J. Zeiller, *The History of the Primitive Church*, I (1942), pp. 238f., 242.
[3] Lactantius, *On the Deaths of Persecutors*, 2. If there is any truth at all in the tradition of Peter's controversy at Rome with Simon Magus (cf. Eusebius, *Hist. Eccl.*, II, 14), it is probably to be dated about this time.

opportunity for reconstituting the community that had been scattered as a result of his predecessor's edict five years previously, and a visit by the leader of the twelve apostles would have been the very thing needful to consolidate the church. Aquila and Priscilla apparently returned to Rome about this time too.[1] And Peter's part in re-establishing the Roman church would at once illuminate Paul's insistence with which he wrote to that church two or three years later that he would refuse to build on another man's foundation.

But Paul's presence in Rome and his death there have not been forgotten by the Roman church, which honours him as a joint founder alongside Peter.[2] A Roman presbyter named Gaius, writing about 200, declares that the "trophies" of Peter and Paul are to be seen on the Vatican hill and the Ostian road respectively.[3] By "trophies" he meant memorials marking either their tombs or the places where they suffered martyrdom. In any case, their bodies would probably be buried near the places where they were put to death, and the "trophies" more probably marked their tombs. Thus the traditions commemorated to this day by the basilica of St. Peter and the church of *San Paolo fuori le mura* go back to the end of the second century at least. The bodies of executed criminals were normally given up to their friends for burial under Roman law, and it is not surprising that the places where the two apostles were buried should be known to Roman Christians a century and a half later.[4]

The inferences that we may legitimately draw from literary evidence bearing on this subject are supported by archæological evidence as well. During the rebuilding of St. Peter's in the sixteenth and seventeenth centuries, excavations led to the discovery of a number of bodies wrapped in linen winding-sheets and placed in stone coffins. With these were found some stone chests filled with burnt bones and ashes. An account of the discovery was written at the time (1626) by a canon of St. Peter's named Ubaldi, and deposited in the archives of the Vatican, where it lay

---

[1] They were in Ephesus with Paul for some time after 52, but are back in Rome at the beginning of 57 (cf. Romans 16 : 3ff.), if our view of the destination of the last chapter of the epistle to the Romans is right.

[2] Ignatius, in his letter to the Roman church (*c*. A.D. 115), writes: "I do not *command* you, like Peter and Paul" (4 : 3). Irenæus (*Against Heresies*, III, 3) refers to the Roman church as founded "by the two most glorious apostles, Peter and Paul" (*c*. A.D. 180).

[3] As recorded by Eusebius, *Hist. Eccl.*, II, 25.

[4] There is a further tradition that the bodies of Peter and Paul rested at one time on the site now marked by the basilica of St. Sebastian on the Appian Way. The tradition appears in the *Calendar of Liberius*, the *Liber Pontificalis*, and an inscription of Damasus (bishop of Rome, 366–384), and is attested by *graffiti* on the site. One theory is that the apostles' bodies were removed there during the persecution under Valerian in 258 (see p. 183), and restored to their original tombs in the time of Constantine.

forgotten until the end of the nineteenth century.[1] It was once supposed that the bodies wrapped in linen were those of early bishops of Rome, and that the ashes were those of some of the Christians who met their death in Nero's gardens in A.D. 64.[2]

It was in the belief that not only the relics of the martyrs in general, but the body of Peter in particular, had been buried here that the Emperor Constantine, at considerable trouble, erected the basilica of St. Peter on the slope of the Vatican hill—the basilica which was demolished in the fifteenth century to make way for the present St. Peter's. As we have seen, the presbyter Gaius claimed more than a century before Constantine that the "trophy" of Peter could be pointed out in this area. In the course of excavations beneath the crypt of St. Peter's, carried out in 1941 and the following years, a funerary monument was discovered, belonging to the middle of the second century A.D., which is almost certainly to be identified with the "trophy" of Peter mentioned by Gaius.[3]

The distinction which tradition makes between the two apostles in the manner of their death, in that Peter was crucified[4] while Paul was beheaded, is very likely to be true; Paul, unlike Peter, was a Roman citizen, and would therefore be executed in a less ignominious fashion. But the blood of the Christians, as Tertullian said, proved to be seed.[5] Christianity was not suppressed, either by this or by any of the subsequent attempts to root it out; and the church in Rome continued to flourish with increasing vigour and to enjoy the respect of Christians everywhere as a church "worthy of God, worthy of honour, worthy of congratulation, worthy of praise, worthy of success, worthy in purity, pre-eminent in love, walking in the law of Christ and bearing the Father's name."[6]

[1] R. Ubaldi, *Relazione di quanti à occorso nel cavare i fondamenti per le quattro colonne di bronzo eretto da Urbano VIII all' altare della basilica di S. Pietro.* This *relazione* was taken from the Vatican archives and published by Mariano Armellini in *Le chiese di Roma* (1891), pp. 697ff. An English translation of the pertinent parts of the report is given by Mgr. A. S. Barnes in *St. Peter in Rome* (1899), pp. 315ff. (In general, however, it must be pointed out that Mgr. Barnes's books on this subject are marked by serious inaccuracies.)

[2] It was formerly thought that the southern walls of Constantine's basilica of St. Peter rested on the northern walls of Nero's circus, which was probably oriented east and west. But the recent excavations have made it clear that the circus must have been situated some distance farther south.

[3] See J. M. C. Toynbee and J. Ward Perkins, *The Shrine of St. Peter and the Vatican Excavations* (1956), pp. 127ff.

[4] The story of Peter's being crucified head downward is to be found in Origen (preserved by Eusebius, *Hist. Eccl.*, III, 1). Although Seneca (*Consolation to Marcia*, 20), is a witness to this mode of crucifixion, the manner in which Peter's execution has been portrayed in the apocryphal *Acts of Peter* and in Christian art is improbable.

[5] Tertullian, *Defence of Christianity (Apologeticus)*, 50: "*semen est sanguis Christianorum.*"

[6] Ignatius, *Letter to the Romans*, preface.

CHAPTER XV

PALESTINE: THE END OF THE BEGINNING

W E HAVE NO CONTINUOUS ACCOUNT OF THE PROGRESS OF Christianity in Jerusalem after the apostolic council of A.D. 49. What information we have shows that the chief authority in the church of that city continued to be wielded by James. The fact that he enjoyed the consistent respect of the people of Jerusalem suggests in itself that he kept the law like other observant Jews; in fact, he is recorded to have been outstanding for his ascetic life. James was no bigot; while he kept the law himself, he refused to side with the extremists who wished to impose it on all Gentile converts to Christianity. But he was the leader of a community in Jerusalem which was regarded as a party within the Jewish fold—the party which believed that the Messiah had come in the person of Jesus of Nazareth and which envisaged itself as the true Israel, the Israel within the larger Israel. In this community there were thousands who could be described as "zealots for the law,"[1] and James was their accepted leader.

The character of James's ministry may be gathered from the letter in the New Testament which bears his name. His authorship of this letter has been doubted, but if we regard the elegant Greek form in which it has come down to us as a literary revision of his work, we shall probably be near the mark.[2] The letter is the work of a man who has caught the spirit of the Sermon on the Mount, the very wording of which is echoed at times. There is also more than a touch of the Old Testament prophet in the letter, especially in the denunciation of the heartless rich who are bidden to lament the miseries which are soon coming upon them. It is no accident that James was the chosen leader of a community whose members liked to describe themselves as "the poor." The letter contains practical instruction on the way to face trials and tempta-

[1] Acts 21 : 20.

[2] F. C. Burkitt suggested that the Epistle of James in the form in which it has come down to us is "a free Greek rendering of an original Aramaic discourse made by James . . . to some Jewish-Christian community, very likely that of Jerusalem itself," and that it was rescued from oblivion and given its present form by the Gentile-Christian Church which was established in Jerusalem after A.D. 135 (*Christian Beginnings* [1924], pp. 65ff.). But if James himself thought of making his discourse available to a wider circle of readers he might easily employ a Greek stylist for the purpose, as Josephus did for his *Jewish War*.

tions, on the nature of true righteousness, on the control of the tongue, on the true wisdom. The community addressed meets in a synagogue, but a synagogue of people who acknowledge Jesus as Lord and Messiah, and ascribe to him the title "The Glory."[1] James is particularly insistent that faith, to be of any real use, must be a working faith. The temptation to think that this insistence is a covert attack on Paul is natural, but must be met by the consideration that James says nothing on this point with which Paul would not have cordially agreed; for the faith that Paul commends is "faith that operates through love."[2] What James is attacking is rather the idea that orthodox belief will save a man apart from considerations of moral conduct.[3]

It is true, however, that curious accounts of Paul's teaching and conduct in his Gentile evangelization made their way to Palestine. Paul himself has to denounce those who slanderously misrepresent his gospel as teaching "Let us do evil, that good may come."[4]

Paul paid two visits to Jerusalem after the apostolic council. The former of these was a brief visit in the summer of 52 between his extended stays in Corinth and Ephesus. All that we are told by Luke about this visit is that he landed at Cæsarea and went up (to Jerusalem, that is) and saluted the church.[5] But common report at Jerusalem made him out to be a renegade from the law for which he had once displayed such zeal. When he arrived in Jerusalem on his last visit, in May, A.D. 57, with the delegates who were bearing the gifts from the Gentile churches to their brethren at Jerusalem, James and the other elders of the mother church welcomed Paul and his companions. Then they said to him, "You see, brother, how many thousands of Jewish believers we have, all zealots for the law. Now they have been told that you teach the Jews of the dispersion to stop following Moses, and to give up circumcising their children and observing our ancestral customs." So they urged him to join some of their number who were discharging a temporary Nazirite vow in the temple,[6] in order that everyone

---

[1] James 2 : 1; render so rather than "the Lord of glory," as in our common version. The implication is that Jesus is the presence of God manifested with His people, as the *shekhinah* was the divine presence dwelling in the midst of Israel in earlier days. This is a remarkable contact between the Epistle of James and the fourth gospel, where also Jesus is presented as the incarnate *shekhinah* (John 1 : 14).

[2] Galatians 5 : 6.

[3] It is noteworthy that the two examples of working faith which James adduces from the Old Testament—Abraham's sacrifice of Isaac and Rahab's harbouring of the spies—recur in the anonymous Epistle to the Hebrews.

[4] Romans 3 : 8.

[5] The "western" text of Acts 18 : 21 represents Paul as intending to keep a feast at Jerusalem on this occasion (perhaps the Passover).

[6] A vow which involved the shaving and dedication of one's hair and the offering of certain sacrifices. The regulations are found in Numbers 6 : 1–21 and in the Mishnah tractate *Nazir*.

might see that he himself, contrary to report, was an observant Jew. Obviously James and his colleagues made a distinction between Gentile Christians in outside lands, who were explicitly excused from Jewish ritual requirements by the decision of the Council of Jerusalem, and Jewish Christians in those lands, whom they expected to go on keeping the law just as the orthodox members of the Jerusalem church did. What Paul's views were on the proper course for Jewish Christians to take in this matter is a question not so simply answered as is sometimes supposed. He himself, at any rate, did on occasion conform to ancestral practices, in accordance with his stated policy, "To the Jews I became as a Jew, in order to win Jews."[1]

On this occasion it was thought that Paul's participation in a ritual cleansing would satisfy the suspicious Jerusalemites that he really was a good Jew. But in the event his appearance in the temple courts for this purpose was the occasion for a riot in which he was nearly lynched. The rumour got about that he had taken a Gentile into the sacred precincts with him, thus aiding and abetting a trespass which automatically incurred the death penalty. Notices in Greek and Latin were fixed to the barriers separating the outer court of the temple from the inner courts, forbidding Gentiles to penetrate farther on pain of death;[2] and so careful were the Romans to conciliate Jewish religious scruples that they authorized the execution of Roman citizens for this offence.[3] Paul was rescued from the rioting mob by the timely intervention of the military tribune in charge of the cohort stationed in the Fortress of Antonia which overlooked the temple. An inquiry was held into the charge of sacrilege preferred against Paul; when proof was not forthcoming, the tribune sent him to the provincial capital, Cæsarea, to the procurator Antonius Felix.[4] A deputation from the Sanhedrin pursued the case against Paul in the presence of Felix, but without success. Felix, however, kept Paul in custody, and left him there when he was relieved of his procuratorship in 59. When his successor Porcius Festus found Paul on his hands, and listened to the renewal of the Sanhedrin's case against him, Paul availed himself of his right as a Roman citizen and appealed from the provincial court to the supreme tribunal of the Emperor at Rome. To Rome therefore he was sent in the

[1] 1 Corinthians 9 : 20. See the whole passage, verses 19–22.
[2] One of these inscriptions, found in Jerusalem in 1871, is now in Istanbul; another, found in 1935, is to be seen at Jerusalem.
[3] Compare the speech of Titus reported by Josephus in the *Jewish War*, VI, 2, 4.
[4] After holding a subordinate office in Samaria from 48 to 52, Felix was promoted to the procuratorship of Judæa in the latter year—an unprecedented honour for a freedman. His promotion was due to the great influence exercised at the imperial court by his brother Pallas. Felix also married above his station—he had three wives, all princesses; the third mentioned in Acts 24 : 24, was Drusilla, younger daughter of Herod Agrippa I.

autumn of 59, and after being forced by storm and shipwreck to winter in Malta, he arrived at Rome in February, A.D. 60.

We do not gather from Luke's narrative that the Jerusalem church took active steps in Paul's defence either at the time of his arrest in Jerusalem or during his two years' detention in Cæsarea. It is dangerous to argue from silence, but, to judge from the general character of the Jerusalem church, it is quite likely that they breathed a sigh of relief when Paul was removed to Cæsarea, and thought that his detention there and subsequent departure for Rome were all for the best. His presence in Jerusalem could only disturb the reasonably tolerant relations subsisting between the Nazarenes and the general populace.

What happened to Paul's Gentile friends who accompanied him to Jerusalem we do not know, except that two of them, Luke and Aristarchus, set sail with him from Cæsarea in 59. No doubt the gifts which they brought from their churches were welcome, even if Paul's object in organizing the collection (the welding more closely together of the Jerusalem church and the Gentile churches) was not realized.

In the year 61 the procurator Festus died in office. A successor, Albinus, was appointed, but an interval of three months elapsed between the death of Festus and the arrival of Albinus in Palestine. In that interval the high priest Hanan (Ananus) saw an opportunity to take certain action which he judged desirable. "So," Josephus tells us, "he convened a council of judges and brought before it the brother of Jesus the so-called Christ, whose name was James, together with some others. Then, having charged them with breaking the law, he had them stoned."[1]

A fuller narrative by Hegesippus, a second-century Christian writer of Jewish descent, has been preserved for us by Eusebius.[2] According to Hegesippus, James's ascetic life and strict devotion to prayer and temple-worship earned him the reverence of the Jerusalem populace, who called him "James the Just" and "Bulwark of the People." He won many Jews to the Nazarene fellowship by his manner of life and his earnest testimony to Jesus as the "door of the sheepfold" and the true way to life.[3] At last a deputation from the Sanhedrin waited on him, demanding an answer to the question, "What is the door of Jesus?"[4] Angered by his response, they set him on a pinnacle of the temple and repeated their question. He replied, "Why do you ask me again about Jesus the Son of man? He sits at the right hand of the mighty Power in heaven, and He will come on the clouds of

---

[1] *Antiquities*, XX, 9, 1.
[2] *Hist. Eccl.*, II, 23. See p. 273.
[3] Cf. John 10 : 7, 9; 14 : 6.
[4] That is, the door of which Jesus spoke (John 10 : 7, 9), or perhaps "the door of salvation."

heaven." This led many of the surrounding multitude to glorify God and cry "Hosanna to the Son of David." The rulers then realized their mistake in affording James such an opportunity for public witness, and they began to shout in protest, "Oho, even the 'just one' has fallen into error!"[1] Then they seized him and threw him down and began to stone him, since he did not die from his fall. James, like Stephen, prayed for his murderers, and one of the priests, a Rechabite, called out "Stop! What are you doing? The 'just one' is praying for you." But a fuller lifted up the club which he used in his daily work and brought it down on James's head, thus killing him. So James bore his testimony in death, and was buried on the spot, beside the sanctuary. And immediately thereupon, says Hegesippus, Vespasian besieged them.

The limitations in Hegesippus's narrative are patent. He seems to believe, for example, that the siege and destruction of Jerusalem, which belong to the later years of the decade, were the direct and immediate sequel to the murder of James, whose continuous intercessions for the Jewish people[2] were thus brought to a violent end. There are legendary embellishments[3] (such as the reference to the pinnacle of the temple) and signs of a re-modelling of the story to emphasize points of similarity to the passion of Jesus and the martyrdom of Stephen. But we can clearly deduce from the narrative that James was put to death by stoning in a manner not unlike that prescribed in the Mishnah, according to which the person under sentence of death was thrown down from the place of stoning.[4]

The high priest and his party were probably alarmed by the growth of violent messianic movements, which bade fair to embroil the whole nation with the Roman power; and demanded that James should disown Nazarene Messianism. It was his refusal to do this that led to his death.

---

[1] Thus, says Hegesippus, they fulfilled the prophecy of Isaiah 3 : 10, which runs in the Septuagint (quite differently from the Hebrew): "Let us do away with the just one, for he is a nuisance to us" (cf. also James 5 :6).

[2] James, says Hegesippus, knelt so long and often in prayer for the people that the skin of his knees became as hard as a camel's.

[3] The most obvious legendary embellishment represents James as exercising priestly functions and having the right to enter into the sanctuary proper. This may be a literalist misunderstanding of the belief held by some Jewish Christians that James and his successors in the leadership of the church of Jerusalem were the true high priests of the new Israel.

[4] "Four cubits from the stoning-place the criminal is stripped. . . . The drop from the stoning-place was twice the height of a man. One of the witnesses pushes the criminal from behind, so that he falls face downward. He is then turned over on his back. If he die from this fall, that is sufficient. If not, the second witness takes the stone and drops it on his heart. If this cause death, that is sufficient; if not, he is stoned by the whole congregation of Israel" (Mishnah, *Sanhedrin*, VI, 3f.). This is no doubt in part the idealizing reconstruction of a later period, but it does present features of similarity to the narrative of Hegesippus.

When the new procurator arrived, Hanan was deposed from his little brief authority and replaced by Joshua the son of Damnai. As for the Nazarenes, their next leader was another member of the same family, Simeon the son of Clopas,[1] who lived on into the reign of Trajan (98–117), when he died a martyr's death at an advanced age.

There may, however, have been some lapse of time between the death of James and the appointment of his cousin Simeon as leader of the Nazarenes. The death of James must have been a devastating blow for the community which he led, and many of them, particularly those who were zealots for the law, must have begun to wonder whether, after all, they were right in espousing a cause which was widening the breach between themselves and their fellow-Jews. Jesus, whom they acknowledged as the Messiah, had been gone a long time; there was no sign of His return on the clouds of heaven in power and great glory to vindicate the cause of His chosen ones. The temple, whose downfall He predicted, still stood as stable as ever; the appointed sacrifices continued to be offered day by day upon the altar. Hostile as the priesthood—especially the high priesthood—was to their community, it was still carrying out ordinances which they themselves believed to be divinely ordained.

Nor was it only the Nazarenes of Jerusalem who had such thoughts around this time. In other cities too there were Christians of Jewish origin who were tempted by the deferment of their hopes and the heat of persecution to turn back to the fold which they had left, instead of pressing on with Christ.

In the midst of these questionings one such group of Jewish Christians received a communication from a friend whose name has been forgotten. He was, we may judge, a Jewish Christian of Hellenist (Alexandrian?) origin, associated possibly with those Hellenists who had formed part of the early Jerusalem church and had left Jerusalem in the persecution that followed Stephen's death. Now he wrote to steady those who were wavering and imbue them with the necessary patience. Did the coming of Jesus seem deferred? Let them cheer up; yet a very little while and the Coming One will come and make no delay. Above all, they must withstand the temptation to return to Judaism; that was the sin of apostasy which by its very nature was irremediable, for (as they had already acknowledged) there was no other name in the world but the name of Jesus in which salvation could be found. Not only was such apostasy sin; it was folly. For the system which retained its venerable attraction was an empty shell, void of all real substance. The sacrifices which were still offered daily were

---

[1] Clopas, according to Hegesippus, was a brother of Joseph the father of James (Eusebius, *Hist. Eccl.*, III, 11): cf. John 19 : 25 (R.V.).

an obsolete survival; Christ by His one perfect sacrifice for His people's sin had rendered all further sin-offerings superfluous. The same held good of the priesthood; Christ was enthroned at God's right hand and there exercised a heavenly and everlasting high priesthood on behalf of His people; the Jerusalem priesthood —inferior in any case—was now obsolete. A material temple should not be specially attractive to worshippers who had access by faith into the heavenly sanctuary, not merely into the court but into the very holy of holies itself, where their exalted high priest was in permanent session by virtue of His own sacrifice. The Jerusalem functionaries might still go through the motions of the old rite, but their acts had no validity in the sight of God— and in any case the whole order was on the eve of disappearance. The writer quotes the words of God in the ninety-fifth Psalm:

Forty years long I was grieved with this generation,
And said, "They are a people who are far astray at heart,
And they have not learned my ways."
Therefore I uttered an oath in my wrath:
"They shall never enter into my rest!"

In the forty years mentioned in the psalm (the forty years which the Israelites spent in the desert between Egypt and Canaan) he sees an adumbration of another forty years' period that is even now nearing its conclusion—the forty years' grace allowed to the city of Jerusalem after the death of Christ. Had not Jesus Himself predicted the circumstances surrounding the complete overthrow of the temple buildings and added, "This generation shall not pass till all these things are fulfilled"? The time was nearly up. What folly, then, it would be for believers in Jesus to go back to an outworn system which was under the doom of imminent dissolution! But these things need not disturb them: the whole material order must be shaken, in order that the unshakable things might endure, and so be clearly seen to be unshakable. The writer and his readers had received "a kingdom that cannot be shaken"; above all, in Christ Himself they had much more than all those things which they had lost or were about to lose. Whatever else might change, "Jesus Christ is the same, yesterday and to-day and forever."

The document which urged these considerations upon its Christian readers was the one which we know as the Epistle to the Hebrews. The authorship of this epistle is an ancient problem which has not been solved to this day; but the problem of the identity of the community to which it was addressed is equally difficult and even more important. The epistle has an abiding message in every age for Christians who are tempted through lack of faith to "fall away from the living God." But in the first instance it appears to have been composed about A.D. 63 for a com-

munity of believers whose hope was growing faint and who
were inclined to give up their Christian meetings and return
to the synagogue.[1]

The issue was not long delayed. Misrule on the part of the
Roman procurators of Palestime combined with the mounting
resentment among the Jewish people to fire the tinder which was
already very dry.[2] As for the Palestinian Jews, the situation passed
more and more into the hands of anti-Roman extremists. The
moderate party in Jerusalem, led by the chief priests, saw how
matters were going, and appealed for help to the Jewish king
Agrippa II, who ruled in northern Palestine and Transjordan.[3]
Agrippa sent reinforcements to the moderate leaders, but for all
that they could do, the extremist party had full control of Jerusalem by September, A.D. 66, after annihilating the Roman garrison.
In addition, they controlled the eastern Negev, Galilee and parts
of Transjordan.

Elsewhere the Jewish revolt was the signal for anti-Jewish
riots and massacres. The Jewish population of Cæsarea was
almost exterminated, and there were similar outbreaks in Damascus and Alexandria.

The situation in Jewish Palestine was beyond the capacity of
the procurator Florus; his superior officer Cestius Gallus, imperial
legate of Syria, had to take action. He marched south with the
twelfth legion and a number of other troops, but when he
attempted to storm the fortified area of the temple, he was re-
pulsed. Seeing that the place was too strong to be taken with such
resources as he commanded, he withdrew, and lost a considerable
portion of his army on the retreat.

This success, as it appeared to the Jews, filled them with false
optimism. The extremists' policy seemed to have been justified;
Rome itself could not stand against them. And, indeed, it might
have appeared that Rome was likely to have too many troubles
nearer home to be much concerned with Palestine. But the structure of the empire was sound, whatever Nero's antics might be;
and the appointment of Vespasian, a tried soldier of Sabine stock,
to take charge of affairs in Palestine, spelt the beginning of the end
for the defenders of Jerusalem. In 67 he quenched the rebellion
in Galilee—and incidentally acquired a curious friend and sup-

---

[1] See W. Manson, *The Epistle to the Hebrews* (1951), for the view that the community in question should be located in Rome.

[2] Gessius Florus succeeded Albinus as procurator in A.D. 64. The spark which
actually started the conflagration was Florus's attempt, at a moment when Jewish
resentment against Rome was high, to enforce by armed strength a demand of
seventeen talents from the temple treasury which had been refused. The resistance
offered to this attempt was the first act of the revolt, which soon became a formal
state of war when the daily sacrifice on behalf of the Emperor was terminated.
(see p. 101).

[3] See p. 104 above.

porter in Josephus, who had been in charge of the Jewish forces in Galilee. After defending the fortress of Jotapata until further resistance was useless, Josephus escaped to a cave with forty others. When this refuge was about to be stormed in its turn, the occupants arranged a suicide pact. Josephus found himself one of the last two survivors and persuaded the other that they might as well give themselves up to the Romans as kill each other. He then contrived to win Vespasian's favour by predicting his elevation to the imperial purple, and was attached to the general headquarters of the Roman army in Palestine for the rest of the campaign.[1]

Some of the bolder spirits from the Galilæan revolt made their escape to Jerusalem, and their admission to the doomed city added to the internal strife which made the last days of the second temple so outstandingly horrible.

In the early summer of 68 Vespasian was approaching Jerusalem when news of Nero's death arrived. The ensuing civil war in Rome nerved the defenders of Jerusalem with fresh hope; it looked from their viewpoint as if Rome and the empire were in the throes of dissolution.[2] But dissension within Jerusalem constantly increased, and yet all the time one party of Zealots, under Eleazar, member of a high-priestly family and captain of the temple, maintained themselves within the precincts of the temple and saw to it that the sacrificial ritual continued to be carried out.

Meanwhile Vespasian and his son Titus watched from Cæsarea the progress of events at Rome. On July 1st, A.D. 69, Vespasian was proclaimed Emperor at Alexandria by the renegade Jew, Tiberius Julius Alexander,[3] governor of Egypt, whose example was speedily followed by the armies at Cæsarea and Antioch, and then by those between the Adriatic and Black Seas. The command of the Palestinian forces was given to Titus, while Vespasian, after the triumph of his cause in Italy, returned to Rome to take control of the empire and restore to it a new stability. By the end of 69 all Judæa had submitted except Jerusalem and three strongholds overlooking the Dead Sea. In the spring of 70 Titus pro-

---

[1] This was Josephus's interpretation of the messianic hope (*Jewish War*, VI, 5 : 4). Josephus became a pensioner of the imperial family for the rest of his life, during which time he wrote his historical works.

[2] From the revolt of Vindex in Gaul early in 68 to the accession of Vespasian the empire was torn by civil war. Between Nero's death (June 9, A.D. 68) and the capture of Rome by Vespasian's troops on December 21, 69, three emperors ruled in turn— Galba, Otho and Vitellius—each of whom, like Nero, came to a violent end. The destruction and carnage in Rome itself, especially towards the end of Vitellius's brief spell of power, may well be reflected in the language of the book of Revelation announcing the downfall of "Babylon the great"; just as the belief in Nero's return to power (or even to life) is reflected in the description of the beast whose death-stroke was healed (Revelation 13 : 3; 17 : 8, 11).

[3] This Alexander, a nephew of Philo of Alexandria, was procurator of Judæa from 46 to 48. He was an apostate from his ancestral religion.

ceeded to besiege Jerusalem in grim earnest. It is amazing to think that the Jews outside Jerusalem were so confident in the triumph of the nationalist cause that on the very eve of the investment great numbers of pilgrims went up to the city to keep the Passover in accordance with the annual custom. Their presence within the walls once the siege began added to the scale of the tragedy. By May half the city was in the hands of the Romans. Titus then offered the defenders terms, but these were contemptuously refused, and the siege went on. On July 5th the Fortress of Antonia, overlooking the temple, was stormed. Twelve days later the daily sacrifices ceased, after being offered on that spot continuously from Solomon's time except during the Babylonian captivity and the brief profanation of the temple under Antiochus Epiphanes. Their final cessation must have been a heavy shock to the morale of many of the defenders. Step by step the Romans advanced, until on August 8th the temple itself went up in flames. Many more days passed before resistance was completely extinguished in the ruined city; and the revolt as a whole was not brought to an end until April 15th, A.D. 73, when the garrison of Masada, a rock-fortress on the western shore of the Dead Sea, committed mass-suicide rather than surrender.

According to Josephus, Titus wished to save the temple, but was unable to prevent his soldiery from venting their vengeful wrath on the structure which had been the core of the resistance during the siege. This was no doubt the account which Titus wished to be believed in the cooler reflection of later years, and Josephus, the grateful client of the Flavian dynasty, gave it the required publicity.

But an interesting variant has come down to us in a fragment of Tacitus's *Histories* preserved by Sulpicius Severus.[1]

> Titus first took counsel and considered whether he should destroy so magnificent a work as the temple. Many thought that a building which excelled all mortal works in sacredness ought not to be destroyed, for if it were saved, it would serve as a token of Roman moderation, whereas its destruction would display an eternal mark of savagery. But others, on the contrary, *including Titus himself*, expressed the opinion that the temple ought most certainly to be razed, in order that the Jewish and Christian religions might more completely be abolished; for although these religions were mutually hostile, they had nevertheless sprung from the same founders; the Christians were an offshoot of the Jews, and if the root were taken away the stock would easily perish.

Whatever Titus himself thought, there were no doubt many who cherished this hope. But they were doomed to disappointment. The temple had outlived its usefulness. Christianity, of

---

[1] Sulpicius Severus, *Chronicle* II, 30 : 6.

course, was essentially free from the trammels of the old sacrificial system; but so was all that was best in Judaism. And from the doomed city two groups of people had made their escape to perpetuate in different ways two distinct lines of the Abrahamic tradition.

According to Eusebius, the members of the church in Jerusalem left the city "before the war" (perhaps after the withdrawal of Cestius Gallus) and removed to the city of Pella in Transjordan (one of the cities of the Greek confederation called the Decapolis). This, he says, was done "in accordance with a certain oracle which had been delivered by revelation to their leaders."[1] In Pella, then, the Nazarenes took up their abode.

Meanwhile there was another exodus from Jerusalem. The dominion of the priestly families and the Sanhedrin was no more, but the party of the Pharisees—or at any rate one section of the party—was capable of undertaking the necessary work of reconstruction, and this they did from their new headquarters at Jamnia in western Palestine. Here the Sanhedrin was reconstituted on a spiritual basis, under the presidency of rabbis instead of chief priests. The leading spirit in this fresh move was one John (Yohanan) the son of Zakkai, who is said in rabbinical tradition to have been smuggled out of Jerusalem in a coffin during the siege, with the connivance of Titus.

In the lands outside Palestine, the decade which ended with the year 70 marked the close of the period when Christianity could be regarded as simply a variety of Judaism. By 64, as we have seen, they were clearly differentiated at Rome. The differentiation took a little longer in Palestine (where practically all Christians were of Jewish birth), but from A.D. 70 onward the divergence of the paths of Jewish Christianity and orthodox Judaism was decisive.

An observer in the middle forties of the first century might have concluded that the new movement had come to stay. He might even have considered the possibility that it would spread within Judaism until it had covered the whole Jewish world. By the middle fifties he would have seen, to his surprise, that it was spreading swiftly through the Gentile world and was being eagerly accepted by Gentiles. He would have shaken his head, however, in the middle sixties, as he saw it coming into conflict with the imperial police. That would put an end to it. If only it had been content to remain a leavening influence within Judaism! But the events of the later sixties and early seventies decided that, though

---

[1] Eusebius, *Hist. Eccl.*, III, 5. This oracle is not identified by Eusebius with Jesus' warning that those in Judæa should flee to the mountains when they saw the "abomination of desolation" (Mark 13 : 14), although he does identify the "abomination of desolation" with the profanation and destruction of the temple.

the struggle might be long, the Roman Empire and not Christianity would capitulate in the end. By the mere fact of surviving the first round Christianity ensured its ultimate triumph. On the other hand, reconstituted Judaism decisively repudiated the Christian way and closed the synagogue door against it. Henceforth the main stream of Christianity must make its independent way in the Gentile world. And so the light which was lit by the Servant shone more widely among the nations, as the news of the salvation which He brought advanced to the ends of the earth.

PART II

THE GROWING DAY

*The Progress of Christianity from the Fall of Jerusalem
to the Accession of Constantine (A.D. 70–313)*

CHAPTER XVI

THE THINGS THAT ARE NOT CÆSAR'S

IF WE TAKE SERIOUSLY THE PAULINE CONCEPTION OF THE Christian Church as the Body of Christ, then Church History may be regarded as the continuation of the story of Jesus. That is to say, Jesus, who began to act and teach on earth in the years immediately preceding A.D. 30, has continued to act and teach since that year by His Spirit in His servants; and the history of Christianity ought to be the history of what He has been doing and teaching in this way down to our own times—a continuous *Acts of the Apostles*. But this is not how Church history is usually viewed or presented. There is much truth in the words of the late Dean Inge:

> The real history of Christianity is the history of a great spiritual tradition. The only true apostolical succession is the lives of the saints. Clement of Alexandria compared the Church to a great river, receiving affluents from all sides. The great river sometimes flows impetuously through a narrow channel; sometimes it spreads like a flood; sometimes it divides into several streams; sometimes, for a time, it seems to have been driven underground. But the Holy Spirit has never left himself without witness; and if we will put aside a great deal of what passes for Church history, and is really a rather unedifying branch of secular history, and follow the course of the religion of the Spirit and the Church of the Spirit, we shall judge very differently of the relative importance of events from those who merely follow the fortunes of institutionalism.[1]

But the difficulty for the would-be historian is this: it is relatively easy to trace the fortunes of a visible institution, whereas the course of a great spiritual tradition is much more elusive. And yet, the two are so closely interwoven that it is impossible to treat of the one without constant reference to the other.

The light which was lit by the obedient Servant, who triumphed through suffering, did indeed shine more widely among the nations, as the news of the salvation which He brought advanced to the ends of the earth. Yet it is possible for the lamp to be so grimy that the light is obscured; it is possible for the messenger to distort the message that he bears, or to act in such a way as to impair its credit. And this has happened at

[1] W. R. Inge, *Things New and Old* (1933), pp. 57f.

times to the good news at the hands of the community to which it has been entrusted. But when that happens, it is more important to trace the fortunes of the message than to enlarge on the misbehaviour of the messenger.

During the period with which this second part of our story deals, however, there is little need to disentangle the spiritual tradition from the visible institution, to draw distinctions between the message and the messenger. These two and a half centuries are centuries of constant hostility towards the Christian Church on the part of the imperial power, a hostility that at times broke out into savage repression; and in such an age the "Church of the Spirit," as Dr. Inge calls it, does to a very large degree coincide with the visible institution. It is after 313, rather than before it, that the tension between the two begins to be really felt.

Titus, the conqueror of Jerusalem, followed his father Vespasian as Roman Emperor in A.D. 79, but died two years later. As he left no son to take his place, he was succeeded by his younger brother Domitian, who held the supreme power for fifteen years. Vespasian was hailed as "the restorer of the world" because of his great services in mending the disjointed state after the civil strife that followed Nero's death. Titus had those qualities that make a ruler popular with the great mass of his subjects, and was acclaimed as "the darling of the human race." Both these rulers were deified after their death by a grateful people—a posthumous honour which had been accorded to Julius Cæsar, Augustus, and Claudius. Domitian, however, did not wait until after death to assume divine honours; he had a keen sense of the dignity of his position even in life, and liked to be styled *dominus et deus noster*, "our Lord and God." And it was as well that he did not wait for posthumous deification, for this honour was denied him. Domitian did not share the popularity of his father and brother. His natural moroseness was in sharp contrast to the geniality of Titus, and during the second half of his reign in particular he became increasingly suspicious—not without good reason. He knew that he had enemies in the Roman senate, and executed a number of senators by way of precaution.

Among those who thus fell victims to the imperial suspicion were a few whose names are specially interesting to us. Most outstanding of these was the emperor's own cousin Flavius Clemens, consul in the year 95. Flavius Clemens, together with his wife Flavia Domitilla, Domitian's niece, was put on trial for "atheism, for which many others also were condemned who had drifted into Jewish ways."[1] Clemens and some others were put to death;

[1] Dio Cassius, *History* (Epitome), LXVII, 14.

THE THINGS THAT ARE NOT CÆSAR'S

others had their property confiscated; Domitilla was banished to the island of Pandateria, off the Campanian coast. The treatment of Clemens and Domitilla is the more striking because Domitian had actually designated their two young sons as his heirs. What happened to the boys we can only guess; they disappear from history.

But the charge brought against Clemens and the others is interesting; it appears to have involved a mixture of Judaism and atheism. That Domitian took some repressive action against the Jews we know from other sources; he taxed them severely, increased the penalties for proselytization, and was on guard against a fresh Jewish rebellion.[1] But it is improbable that the action which Domitian took against his relatives and other members of the nobility had much to do with his Jewish policy. Probably his real reason for proceeding against them was fear lest they might try to remove him; but he procured their condemnation by the senate on grounds of which that body would take cognizance. What were these grounds? What was this curious combination of Judaism and atheism? Could it, by any chance, have been Christianity?

That is the traditional explanation, indeed, and some colour has been lent to it in the eyes of some by the description which the Roman writer Suetonius gives of Clemens as "a man despised by all for his inactive life."[2] His "inactive life" may denote a withdrawal from the public activities normal in one of his station, and such a withdrawal may have been due to Christian scruples; but other reasons are conceivable. At any rate, he did serve as consul. Some stronger argument must be adduced if we are to have any confidence that the traditional account is true, and that Christianity had by this date penetrated to such exalted ranks of Roman society.

The really solid grounds for concluding that the charge brought against the noble pair was actually, if not explicitly, that of Christianity are of an archæological nature, and have to do with the history of one of the oldest Christian burying-places in Rome, the so-called Cemetery of Domitilla on the Via Ardeatina. There is inscriptional evidence that the land beneath which this burying-place was hollowed out belonged originally to Flavia Domitilla and her family. This Christian cemetery, "the earlier parts of which date back to the beginning of the second century," says a classical scholar who has subjected these early Christian traditions to severe criticism,[3] "appears to have continued in use, with successive extensions, till at least into the fourth century,

[1] See p. 268.
[2] Suetonius, *Life of Domitian*, 15 : 1.
[3] E. T. Merrill, *Essays in Early Christian History* (1924), p. 168.

and, as containing the tombs of martyrs, to have been visited for purposes of devotion much longer. It seems quite unlikely, if not impossible, that it should have been permitted in immediate connexion with Domitilla's own family burial-place, and in her own probable lifetime, if she had not herself been a Christian."

Another very early Christian burying-place in Rome is the Cemetery of Priscilla, called (no doubt) after the lady who owned the land. This cemetery, situated on the Via Salaria, contains a crypt belonging to the noble Roman family whose members bore the name Acilius Glabrio. It is certainly a very striking coincidence (if it is no more) that another of Domitian's victims about the year 95 was one Acilius Glabrio who had been consul four years earlier. He, too, was implicated in the charge of "Judaism and atheism"; but, over and above that (we are told), he had had the imprudence to display his prowess as a lion-killer with a skill which the Emperor envied.[1]

Christianity was no longer confined to the lower strata of the Roman population, as it had been in Nero's time, a single generation before. It had survived the initial attempt to suppress it, and was beginning to infiltrate into the most noble families, even into the imperial family itself. "What a change!" says Harnack. "Between fifty and sixty years after Christianity reached Rome, a daughter of the Emperor embraces the faith, and thirty years after the fearful persecutions of Nero, the presumptive heirs to the throne were brought up in a Christian house."[2]

One of the most intriguing might-have-beens of history suggests itself here: what would have happened if Clemens and Domitilla had lived on, bringing up their sons in the Christian faith, and if the boys in due course had mounted the imperial throne? Certainly our present story would be a very different one from what it is. Two hundred years and more had to elapse before a Christian Emperor sat on the throne of Augustus, and for the greater part of those two hundred years Christianity had to make headway against imperial opposition which from time to time took the form of savage persecution.

What were the reasons for this opposition? First of all, from the sixties of the first century onward, Christianity was clearly recognized as a distinct religion from Judaism, and it consequently ranked as an illicit cult in the eyes of the law. Nor was it the sort of religion that could easily win official permission for its observance. The official recognition accorded to the Jewish religion made it possible for Jews to practise their own distinctive

---

[1] Dio Cassius, *loc. cit.*

[2] *Princeton Review* I (1878), p. 269. This Domitilla was rather the granddaughter of the Emperor (Vespasian); her mother, Vespasian's daughter, bore the same name Flavia Domitilla.

rites and to enjoy exemption from a variety of civil and military duties involving some contact with idolatry; but then Judaism was the religion of a distinct subject-nation of the Empire. Christianity was not the religion of any particular nation, nor could it invoke long-established custom; it appeared to be a vulgar innovation whose religious aspect was probably a mere façade concealing something worse. Above all we must remember the general unpopularity of the Christians: "a class of men loathed for their vices," says Tacitus;[1] "a novel and baneful superstition," Suetonius calls their religion.[2] They were obviously atheists, since they worshipped no visible god; they were unsociable and haters of the human race, because they abstained so largely from the ordinary forms of social intercourse. The interest which the imperial police began to take in their meetings from 64 onward made them gather in secret; this in turn was interpreted in the worst sense. They would not meet in secret, it was argued, unless they had something shameful to hide. Stories began to circulate about the ritual cannibalism and ceremonial incest which were believed to go on at their meetings. Such a crowd of wretches were plainly worthy of extermination, and any repressive measures that were taken against them by authority could be sure of popular approval.

The first action taken against the Christians by the imperial power was that which followed the Great Fire of Rome in A.D. 64.[3] Although it was admitted that on this occasion the Christians were mere scapegoats to divert popular suspicion from Nero himself, yet the fact that the Christians of Rome, rather than any other group, were selected as scapegoats indicates that Nero knew he could safely exploit the general ill will with which these people were regarded by their pagan neighbours.

Nero's action served in a general way as a precedent for later rulers who saw fit to institute severe measures against the Christians. A situation arose in which Christians considered that they were being persecuted for the bare fact of being Christians, "suffering for the name," as the First Epistle of Peter put it.[4] It does not appear, however, that there was at this time a provision of Roman Law explicitly declaring Christianity to be a crime. The evidence is inadequate for a certain conclusion on this point. In any case, as the Christian profession was held to be essentially bound up with practices which were themselves illegal, a Christian was in constant danger of suffering for his profession whenever police powers were put into operation against him. He

---

[1] *Annals*, XV, 44.
[2] *Life of Nero*, 16 : 2. The word translated "baneful" could also convey to Roman ears the suggestion of black magic.
[3] See pp. 141ff.
[4] 1 Peter 4 : 16.

would say he was suffering "for the name"; the imperial authorities would say that he was suffering for crimes invariably associated with the name; but the difference was of technical rather than practical import.

When Nero, deposed by the senate in 68, committed suicide to escape the ignominious death to which that body had condemned him, many of his eastern subjects refused to believe that he was really dead. Throughout his reign he had enjoyed great popularity in his eastern provinces. For some twenty years after his death, therefore, the belief persisted that he had not really died but gone into hiding, probably beyond the Euphrates, and that he would return one day at the head of an army of Parthians to recover his dominions and rule once more as Emperor. Naturally, several opportunists profited by this widespread belief to set themselves up as pretended Neros, but none of these pretenders had any success worth mentioning. After 88, the last year in which one of these pretenders is known to have arisen, the belief that Nero was still alive was generally given up; but it was replaced by the belief that one day Nero would return from the realm of the dead and regain his sovereignty. This later belief in a *Nero redivivus*, which can be traced right on almost to the end of the second century, was not only a subject of hope to pagans in the eastern empire, but also a subject of dread to Christians, who identified *Nero redivivus* with the last Antichrist. There is a possible allusion to this identification in the book of Revelation, where the seven heads of the monster on which the scarlet woman (the city of Rome) sits are explained, not only as being the seven hills of Rome, but also as being "seven Emperors: the five have fallen, the one now is, and the other has not yet come. When he comes, he must continue for a little while. And the beast that was, and is not [i.e. the last Antichrist], is himself both an eighth and also one of the seven."[1] The characteristically allusive language of this form of literature makes it difficult to identify the Emperors intended with certainty. It is likely that the five who had fallen were Augustus, Tiberius, Gaius, Claudius and Nero; and that the reigning Emperor was Vespasian. In any case, it is clear that the last persecutor and Antichrist is represented as having had a previous incarnation in one of the first seven Roman Emperors. Nero? Very probably; but we should spare a thought for Gaius, who wished to have divine honours paid to his image in the temple at Jerusalem, and whose action may have coloured the language in which Paul describes Antichrist in his second letter to the church of Thessalonica.[2]

The book of Revelation, at any rate, reflects the great change

[1] Revelation 17 : 9–11.
[2] 2 Thessalonians 2 : 4 (see p. 102).

that had taken place in the relations between Church and Empire since the time of Paul. Paul could confidently look to the imperial administration to protect his legitimate activity in proclaiming Jesus as the true fulfilment of the age-long hope of Israel. Indeed, the true interpretation of an obscure passage in the letter to which we have just referred may be that he regarded the Roman Emperor—or the Roman Empire—as the power which hindered the last Antichrist from coming into the open: "you know what is restraining him now so that he may be revealed in his time."[1] But now the imperial order itself is the persecuting power, and shows itself clearly as the precursor of Antichrist. It is henceforth open war between the Empire and the Church—a war in which victory is assured to those Christians who maintain their confession steadfastly, even to death itself.

Little can be said with certainty about the date of the book of Revelation except that it belongs to the period of the Flavian Emperors, bounded by the years 69 and 96. Second-century tradition assigns it to the latter part of that period, but some of its internal features suggest an earlier dating, in the reign of Vespasian (A.D. 69–79). It is introduced by seven short covering letters addressed to leading churches in the Roman province of Asia, from which we gather that the persecution which Peter foresaw in 63 as soon to break out in western Asia Minor had begun. The writer himself was a victim of this persecution; he was in exile on the island of Patmos, possibly doing forced labour in the marble quarries. The province of Asia was outstanding for its devotion to the Emperor and the Empire; here, in Pergamum, one of the great cities of the province, had been established since 29 B.C. a temple consecrated to the worship of "Rome and Augustus." This is possibly what is referred to when the letter in Revelation addressed to the Pergamene church describes it as dwelling "where Satan's throne is."[2] And later in the same book, when John describes the fierce monster of the persecuting power as followed by another beast of lamb-like appearance but dragon-like voice, which commands men to pay divine worship to the former beast,[3] it is not difficult to conclude that the imperial cult of Asia sat for the portrait of the second beast.

This outbreak of persecution is traditionally assigned to the reign of Domitian (A.D. 81–96). It was probably intensified under him, but it began before his accession. But tradition has exaggerated Domitian's personal role as a persecutor. There is a curious tale of his interviewing two members of the family of

[1] 2 Thessalonians 2 : 6.
[2] Revelation 2 : 13. Some think the reference is to the worship of the healing god Asklepios at Pergamum under the guise of a serpent (compare the badge of the R.A.M.C.).
[3] Revelation 13 : 11ff.

Jesus (grandsons of His brother Judas) because they claimed descent from the royal line of David, and dismissing them when he found them to be simple peasants quite uninterested in secular kingship.[1] But whatever factual basis there may be for this legend, it probably reflects imperial precautions against a resurgence of Jewish nationalism rather than an investigation of Christian claims.

Domitian's most interesting association with Christianity, and probably the real basis for his traditional reputation as a persecutor, may be seen in the action which he took against his relatives and other Roman nobles who were convicted of atheism with a Jewish colouring. In some cases at any rate this appears to have meant Christianity. But this action of Domitian was really part of his general proceedings against people of senatorial rank whom he suspected of conspiring against him.

This increasing suspiciousness naturally proved his undoing; those who feared that they might be its next victims (the Empress included) determined to forestall him and he was assassinated in 96. It is not, perhaps, without significance that the man who struck the fatal blow was Stephanus, Domitilla's steward. The next Emperor was an elderly senator named Nerva, whose short but statesmanlike reign of two years was marked by the reversal of several of Domitian's tyrannical measures: his acts include Domitilla's release from the island of Pandateria and John's from the island of Patmos.

Nerva instituted a provision for the imperial succession which ensured a series of good emperors for several generations; this was the formal adoption as his son of the man whom he judged most fitted to take his place. Nerva's choice was Trajan. Trajan had been Acilius Glabrio's colleague in the consulship in 91, and the diverse fortunes of the two men were foretold in that year in a manner that reminds one of Joseph's dream-interpretations to Pharaoh's butler and baker.

Trajan's reign (98–117) was marked by a policy of imperial expansion; the frontiers of empire were pushed beyond the Rhine, Danube and Euphrates. Only the expansion beyond the Danube had any lasting effect; the Roman civilization in the new province of Dacia has left its mark in the name, language and general culture of the land and people of Romania.

In 112 Trajan sent as governor of the province of Bithynia, in north-west Asia Minor, a literary figure named Pliny—usually called Pliny the Younger to distinguish him from his uncle of the same name, a famous natural historian, who had lost his life in the eruption of Vesuvius in 79. The younger Pliny shows himself in his governorship as the perfect civil servant of caricature, un-

[1] Eusebius, *Hist. Eccl.*, III, 20, quoting the second-century writer Hegesippus.

willing to take the most ordinary step on his own initiative, the complete "red tapeworm" of antiquity, to use Sir Compton Mackenzie's happy expression. When any decision had to be taken in his province, he wrote home to consult the Emperor. For instance, after some serious outbreaks of fire in the chief cities of Bithynia, he thought it would be a good thing to organize fire brigades, but solicited the Emperor's opinion first. Trajan's reply is surprising but instructive. It is best, he says, that the business of putting out fires be left to private enterprise. Let each householder, so to speak, have a bucket of water and a stirrup-pump ready for emergency. The trouble with fire brigades or anything of the sort is that, no matter what the ostensible purpose of any such organization may be, it will inevitably deteriorate into a political club with subversive aims.[1]

This suspicion of clubs or secret societies—*collegia*, as the Romans called them—was of long standing and not without justification, as the course of Roman history had shown. And it helps to explain the objections which prudent administrators like Trajan felt towards Christianity. Not being a recognized cult, it could not justify its meetings on religious grounds; apart from any other objections, therefore, these meetings fell under the general ban imposed on unlicensed *collegia*. One form of *collegium*, however, was commonly permitted. That was a burial club; and Christians therefore found it expedient to organize their communities in such a way as to enjoy the freedom which friendly societies of this particular kind enjoyed in law.

All this helps us to understand the inquiry sent by Pliny to Trajan when he found that Christianity was spreading in his province, and the reply or "rescript" which Trajan sent back. As governor, Pliny had the sole right of sentencing inhabitants of the province to death (with the proviso that, if they were Roman citizens, they might appeal to the Emperor). At the beginning of his period of office, he ordered the execution of several Christians who refused to renounce their faith; but he realized that there were so many of them in his province that he decided to apply to the Emperor for a ruling, instead of relying on his own discretion. Here is the correspondence.

PLINY TO TRAJAN.

My Lord: It is my custom to refer to you everything that I am in doubt about; for who is better able either to correct my hesitation or instruct my ignorance?

I have never been present at trials of Christians; consequently I do not know the precedents regarding the question of punishment or the nature of the inquiry. I have been in no little doubt whether some discrimination is made with regard to age, or whether the

[1] *Epistles of Pliny*, X, 33 and 34.

young are treated no differently from the older; whether renunciation wins indulgence, or it is of no avail to have abandoned Christianity if one has once been a Christian; whether the very profession of the name is to be punished, or only the criminal practices which go along with the name.

So far this has been my procedure when people were charged before me with being Christians. I have asked the accused themselves if they were Christians; if they said "Yes," I asked them a second and third time, warning them of the penalty; if they persisted I ordered them to be led off to execution. For I had no doubt that, whatever kind of thing it was that they pleaded guilty to, their stubbornness and unyielding obstinacy at any rate deserved to be punished. There were others afflicted with the like madness whom I marked down to be referred to Rome, because they were Roman citizens.

Later, as usually happens, the trouble spread by the very fact that it was being dealt with, and further varieties came to my notice. An anonymous letter was laid before me containing many people's names. Some of these denied that they were Christians or had ever been so; at my dictation they invoked the gods and did reverence with incense and wine to your image, which I had ordered to be brought for this purpose along with the statues of the gods; they also cursed Christ; and as I am informed that people who are really Christians cannot possibly be made to do any of those things, I considered that the people who did them should be discharged. Others against whom I received information said they were Christians and then denied it; they meant (they said) that they had once been Christians but had given it up: some three years previously, some a longer time, one or two as many as twenty years before.[1] All these likewise both did reverence to your image and the statues of the gods and cursed Christ. But they maintained that their fault or error amounted to nothing more than this: they were in the habit of meeting on a certain fixed day before sunrise and reciting an antiphonal hymn to Christ as God, and binding themselves with an oath—not to commit any crime, but to abstain from all acts of theft, robbery and adultery, from breaches of faith, from denying a trust when called upon to honour it. After this, they went on, it was their custom to separate, and then meet again to partake of food, but food of an ordinary and innocent kind. And even this, they said, they had given up doing since the publication of my edict in which, according to your instructions, I had placed a ban on private associations. So I thought it the more necessary to inquire into the real truth of the matter by subjecting to torture two female slaves, who were called "deacons"; but I found nothing more than a perverse superstition which went beyond all bounds.

Therefore I deferred further inquiry in order to apply to you for a ruling. The case seemed to me to be a proper one for consultation, particularly because of the number of those who were accused. For

[1] Twenty years before Pliny's governorship would take us back to Domitian's reign.

many of every age, every class, and of both sexes are being accused and will continue to be accused. Nor has this contagious superstition spread through the cities only, but also through the villages and the countryside. But I think it can be checked and put right. At any rate the temples, which had been well-nigh abandoned, are beginning to be frequented again; and the customary services, which had been neglected for a long time, are beginning to be resumed; fodder for the sacrificial animals, too, is beginning to find a sale again, for hitherto it was difficult to find anyone to buy it. From all this it is easy to judge what a multitude of people can be reclaimed, if an opportunity is granted them to renounce Christianity.

TRAJAN TO PLINY.

My dear Secundus:[1] You have followed the correct procedure in deciding the cases of those who have been charged before you with being Christians. Indeed, no general decision can be made by which a set form of dealing with them could be established. They must not be ferreted out; if they are charged and convicted, they must be punished, provided that anyone who denies that he is a Christian and gives practical proof of that by invoking our gods is to win indulgence by this repudiation, no matter what grounds for suspicion may have existed against him in the past. Anonymous documents which are laid before you should receive no attention in any case; they are a very bad precedent and quite unworthy of the age in which we live.[2]

If Pliny was not sure of the precise position of Christians in the eyes of Roman law, we need not be surprised if we find ourselves sharing his uncertainty. It is noteworthy, too, that Trajan does not refer Pliny to any previous enactment or other precedent. A good deal of interesting information emerges incidentally from Pliny's letter. Christianity must have been advancing swiftly in that part of Asia Minor, if religious and economic interests were suffering to the extent that he indicates. The customary rumours about the ritual cannibalism that went on at Christian meetings are no doubt hinted at in the witnesses' insistence that the food eaten at those meetings was of an ordinary and innocent kind. And there are further references to Christian liturgical practice which we shall look at in due course.[3]

Pliny appears to have been satisfied that there was no ground for the vulgar charges of incest and cannibalism brought against Christians. But he was convinced that, if Christians were innocent of these "criminal practices" which were widely held to be inseparable from their profession, the contumacy which they showed in refusing to renounce Christianity at his bidding was itself a capital offence.

[1] Pliny's full name was Gaius Plinius Secundus.
[2] The two letters are preserved in the *Epistles of Pliny*, X, 96 and 97.
[3] See pp. 192, 198, 241.

It is easy to criticize Trajan's ruling, as Tertullian did later in his *Defence of Christianity* (2 : 8): "What a decision, how hopelessly entangled! He says they must not be ferreted out, implying that they are innocent; he orders them to be punished, implying that they are guilty!" But "entangled" as the ruling was, Trajan no doubt thought it the most reasonable and expedient course in the circumstances. Christians, if they were convicted and refused to give up their illegal association, were to suffer the due penalty; but no special effort should be made to harry them; they were not so dangerous to the state as all that.

An illustrious Christian who suffered for his faith in Trajan's reign was Ignatius, bishop of Antioch in Syria, who was sent to Rome about the year 115 to be exposed to the beasts in the arena. The circumstances of his condemnation can only be guessed at; his chief importance lies in seven letters which he wrote during his journey under armed guard from Antioch to Rome.[1]

Trajan's policy towards the Christians was followed by his successors Hadrian (117–138) and Antonine (138–161). A rescript of Hadrian to Minucius Fundanus, proconsul of Asia, in 124, echoes the general sense of Trajan's rescript to Pliny:

> I have received a latter addressed to me by your illustrious predecessor, Serenus Granianus, and his report, I think, ought not to be passed over in silence, lest innocent people be molested and an opportunity for hostile action be given to malicious accusers. If the provincials, then, plainly wish to support this petition of theirs against the Christians by bringing some definite charge against them before the court, let them confine themselves to this action and refrain from mere appeals and outcries. For it is much more just that, if anyone wishes to bring an accusation, you should examine the allegations. If then anyone accuses them and proves that they are doing anything unlawful, you must impose a penalty in accordance with the gravity of the crime; but if anyone brings such accusations simply by way of blackmail, you must sentence him to a more severe penalty in proportion to his wickedness.[2]

The genuineness of this document has been questioned, but on inadequate grounds. In insisting that accusations against Christians must be judicially investigated, and that anything in the nature of popular clamour must be severely discouraged, Hadrian was following the precedent of Trajan. By insisting that the accusers should lay specific charges before the proconsular court according to the procedure laid down for private prosecutors, he

---

[1] See pp. 190, 203ff.
[2] Cited in Greek by Justin, *Apology* I, 68; Eusebius, *Ecclesiastical History*, IV, 9 : 1, and in Latin by Rufinus. Arguments for its genuineness are presented by W. M. Ramsay, *The Church in the Roman Empire* (1893), pp. 320ff.; E. T. Merrill, *op. cit.*, pp. 202ff.; against, by H. Lietzmann, *The Founding of the Church Universal* (1950 ed.), p. 160. Lietzmann fails to see that the purpose of the rescript was not the toleration of Christians but the protection of pagans against false accusation.

discouraged vexatious or frivolous accusations, for Roman law imposed severe penalties on prosecutors who wasted the courts' time with charges which could not be substantiated. The rescript by no means implies that one could profess Christianity with immunity, provided that he did not infringe the law in any other respect. For there was one fundamental matter in which Christians were constantly liable to come into conflict with the law. The state religion of Rome had long since become a matter of political formality, but occasional participation in the formality was a recognized way of proving one's loyalty. We have seen how Pliny required those who said they had never been Christians or that they had ceased to be so to prove the truth of their assertion by paying divine honours to the state gods and to the Emperor's image, and also by cursing Christ.

Some imperial officials might not insist on the cursing of Christ; people might reverence Him and as many others as they pleased provided that they showed themselves loyal subjects of the Empire. And they could easily prove their loyalty by an act of homage to the state religion, and especially by acknowledging the divine character of the Emperor, who was regarded as the personal embodiment of the sovereign state. But this, of course, Christians steadfastly refused to do. Their refusal was shared by the Jews, but the authorities had long since exempted the Jews from such requirements, because the Jewish religion—the recognized religion of a subject-nation within the Empire—so demanded. Christianity, however, was not recognized as the religion of any national group. Christians must therefore conform or take the consequences. It was beside the point for Christians to argue that the malicious tales circulated about them were false, that they were neither incendiaries, cannibals, nor practisers of incest, that they were, in fact, loyal citizens. Deeds, not words, were required by the state; and if they were in fact loyal citizens, as they protested, there was a simple way of demonstrating their loyalty; let them offer a pinch of incense in honour of the Emperor, let them swear by his divinity, let them invoke him as "Lord." But the Christians knew that the sense in which the title "Lord" was given to the Emperor was one which connoted his divinity; in this sense they knew but one Lord, Jesus Christ, and to give this title to another was high treason to Christ. All Emperors might not take their divinity so seriously as Domitian did, but the acknowledgment of the Emperor's divinity was a recognized form in which subjects of the Empire must give evidence of their loyalty if so required, and refusal to make this acknowledgment was condemned as criminal contumacy. It is precisely round this point that many of the accounts of Christian martyrdoms under the pagan Empire centre.

Of these one of the best known is the martyrdom of Polycarp, the aged bishop of Smyrna, early in 156. Polycarp was a venerable figure, forming a last link with those who had seen Christ in the flesh, for he had sat at the feet of John, the beloved disciple. A letter written by the Smyrnæan church shortly after his martyrdom tells how, during an outbreak of anti-Christian activity in the province of Asia, the mob raised an outcry for Polycarp. A police squad went to fetch him, and the police captain, probably wishing to spare the old man the indignities which awaited him, said: "Why, what harm is there in saying, 'Cæsar is Lord' and offering incense and saving yourself?" But Polycarp refused to listen to his plea, and went on to the arena, where the proconsul of Asia in person tried to persuade him. "Have respect for your age," he said; "swear by the divinity of Cæsar; repent and say, 'Away with the atheists.' " "Away with the atheists," said Polycarp solemnly, waving his hand towards the pagan crowd. But the proconsul pressed him further: "Take the oath, and I will let you go; revile Christ." Then the old man made his noble confession: "Eighty-six years have I served Him, and He has done me no wrong; how then can I blaspheme my Saviour and King?" Further argument proved equally fruitless, and Polycarp was sent to the stake.

Polycarp's martyrdom seems to have produced a revulsion of feeling for the time being; not only did that outbreak of persecution in Asia cease with his death, but it was probably at this time that the Emperor Antonine sent a rescript to some of his eastern cities, forbidding them (as Hadrian had done) to indulge in riotous attacks on the Christians instead of prosecuting them according to the due processes of law.[1]

The practice of declaring one's loyalty to the state by going through a form of action which is formally if not materially religious has appeared at various times; a well-known example of more recent date may be found in the institution of "Shrine Shinto" upon which such emphasis was placed in the Japanese Empire in the years preceding 1945. The Japanese authorities tried to salve the consciences of their Christian subjects by defining Shrine Shinto as political and not religious in character and placing it in the jurisdiction of the Home Office, by contrast with "Sect Shinto," which was recognized as a state religion and came within the province of the Religious Bureau. But not all Christians were satisfied that this distinction was anything more than verbal.[2] Even in more democratic states difficulties may arise, as

[1] Melito of Sardis, quoted by Eusebius, *Hist. Eccl.*, IV, 26, 10; see Ramsay, *op. cit.*, pp. 331f.; C. J. Cadoux, *Ancient Smyrna* (1938), p. 367.

[2] The parallels between ancient Rome and recent Japan in this respect are brought out interestingly by Professor John Foster in *Then and Now* (1942), pp. 84ff. And there are more subtle forms of state-worship than paying homage at a national shrine or saluting the national flag.

when a certain small but vociferous religious body used to run into trouble in the United States by refusing to salute the American flag. No ordinary American thought of this as a religious ceremony, or regarded the Stars and Stripes as an idol, but these people did, and held that conformity to national practice in this matter would be treason to the Kingdom of God.

The Christians were regarded as incurably perverse for their insane refusal to conform to Roman requirements in this simple manner. Outward conformity was so simple, and (in other people's eyes) it meant very little. The majority of pagans who took part in such ceremonies did so quite unthinkingly. It was the keen religious awareness of the Christians that made them recognize the ceremony as essentially idolatrous, and therefore forbidden to those who worshipped none but God in Christ.

There was no way out of the impasse except by the withdrawal of one side or the other. And when the time for this came, it was the Empire and not the Church that gave way. But before this happened, the Church had to endure several seasons of persecution much fiercer than anything that had befallen her thus far.

CHAPTER XVII

THE FIERY TRIAL

WHAT DID THE CHRISTIANS DO BY WAY OF REACTION to the persecution which befell them from time to time? First and foremost, they maintained their faith and continued to propagate it so successfully that their numbers went on increasing. Some of their number, however, betook themselves to the defence of Christianity, preferring the pen to the sword as their instrument of defence. From the reign of Hadrian down to the end of the second century these writers published a number of works in defence of Christianity, many of which have come down to us. The earliest of these apologists, as they are called, was Quadratus, who addressed his treatise to the Emperor Hadrian. In it he declared that some of the people who had been healed by Jesus actually survived to his own days—that is, probably, to the closing years of the first century.[1] In the middle years of the second century the most notable apologist was Justin, a Greek philosopher from Samaria who had been converted to Christianity and later suffered for his faith at Rome—for which reason he is commonly known as Justin Martyr. He addressed his defence of Christianity to the Emperor Antonine and his two adopted sons, and appended a shorter defence addressed to the people of Rome. The greatest of these works in defence of Christianity was that composed by Tertullian of Carthage in the closing years of the second century and addressed to the Roman governors of his time.

The main arguments of these writings are (1) that the Christians are innocent of the crimes alleged against them, and (2) that Christianity is a reasonable faith. The war is sometimes carried into the enemy's territory and much is made of the fact that the vices of which the Christians are falsely accused are in fact ascribed by the pagans themselves to the very gods whom they worship. The arguments from miracle and the fulfilment of prophecy are developed; and some apologists, like Justin, argue further that Christianity is the true goal of Greek philosophy as well as of Hebrew revelation: the *logos* or divine reason which Greek thinkers revered is the eternal Word of God which John, in the prologue to his Gospel, tells us became incarnate in Christ.

[1] Eusebius, *Hist. Eccl.*, IV, 3 : 2.

One of these apologists, the anonymous writer of a short work called the *Epistle to Diognetus*, about the middle of the second century, sums up the position of Christians in the world as follows:

> Christians are not distinguished from the rest of mankind either in locality or in speech or in customs. They do not live apart in cities of their own, nor do they speak some different language or practise some extraordinary way of life. Nor yet do they possess any invention discovered by the intelligence or study of ingenious men, nor are they masters of any human dogma as some are. They live in cities of Greeks or barbarians as the lot of each is cast, and they follow the local customs in dress and food and the other details of daily life. Yet the constitution of their own polity is remarkable and admittedly paradoxical. They live in their own home-towns, but only as sojourners; they bear their share in all things as citizens, but endure all hardships as foreigners. Every foreign land is home to them, and every home is foreign. . . . Their existence is on earth, but their citizenship is in heaven. . . . They love all, and are persecuted by all. . . .
>
> In a word, what the soul is in the body, Christians are in the world. The soul is spread through all the members of the body, and Christians through the various cities of the world. As the soul has its abode in the body, but is not of the body, so Christians have their abode in the world, but are not of the world. . . . The soul is enclosed in the body, and yet holds the body together; so Christians are kept in the world as in a prison-house, and yet it is they who hold the world together. The soul, immortal itself, dwells in a mortal tabernacle; so Christians sojourn among corruptible things, while they look for the incorruptibility which is in heaven. The soul is improved when it is hardly treated in the matter of food and drink; so Christians, when persecuted, increase the more day by day.[1]

These treatises, however, had little effect, even if they were ever read by those to whom they were addressed. The authorities were not interested in religious arguments, and if the Christians protested that they were unjustly persecuted, it was always open to them to prove their loyalty to the state in the simple and authorized fashion, by offering incense to the Roman gods. Justin himself, for all his eloquence, met his martyrdom in the reign of his fellow-philosopher Marcus Aurelius. Brought with a number of other Christians before Rusticus, prefect of Rome, in the year 165, Justin refused to sacrifice to the gods at his command: "No right-thinking person," he said, "turns away from true belief to false." "Do what you will," said his companions to the prefect, "for we are Christians, and do not sacrifice to idols." So they were led off to execution.

Surprise has often been felt at the anti-Christian sentiments of the Stoic Emperor Marcus Aurelius (161–180), whose *Meditations*

[1] *Epistle to Diognetus*, 5–6.

have throughout the Christian centuries come to rank almost as a standard work of devotion. It is interesting to surmise what further meditation Marcus would have bequeathed to us could he have foreseen the veneration with which so many Christians would in days to come regard his work! Marcus's Stoicism was combined with an old-world piety which looked upon the Christians as dangerous revolutionaries and as a disintegrating ferment in the life of the state. Their very resoluteness in the face of suffering and death, which might in itself have won respect from a Stoic, was explained not as commendable fortitude but as perverse obstinacy. Largely, no doubt, through the influence of his tutor Fronto, Marcus despised what seemed to him the crass superstition of the Christian beliefs, which disqualified them from the respect due to others who maintained their principles at the cost of life itself.

In these years, too, there were troubles within and without which made patriotic Romans particularly sensitive about anything which appeared to diminish the political solidarity of the Empire. The year 166 was an *annus calamitosus*, when havoc was wrought by plague, flood, famine, and barbarian invasion from beyond the Danube frontier. In such circumstances many who despised Christianity as a vulgar superstition betrayed their own brand of superstition by looking around for those whose presence, Jonah-like, was thus bringing down the wrath of heaven upon the whole community, and by finding them in the "atheistic" Christians.

The most notable persecution of Marcus's reign broke out in Gaul, in 177, and affected the churches of Vienne and Lyons in the Rhône valley. The survivors sent a detailed account of the persecution to the churches of Asia Minor, with which they were closely linked.[1] The outbreak, to begin with, was not so much an act of official repression as of mob violence, at which the local magistrates connived. But they might not have connived so readily had they not known that the Emperor was hostile to Christianity. Later, when some of the Christians turned out to be Roman citizens, the Emperor's ruling was sought, and he (to his eternal discredit) replied that those who did not recant should be beheaded, if Roman citizens, and put to death by torture otherwise.

Neither age nor sex was spared in the pogrom; the ninety-year-old bishop of Lyons, Pothinus, was among the victims, together with the fourteen-year-old boy Ponticus. But the outstanding heroine of the occasion was the slave-girl Blandina, for whose constancy in confession others had feared, lest her physical frailty might not be equal to the tortures by which efforts were

[1] Eusebius, *Hist. Eccl.*, V, 1.

made to force them to abjure their Christianity. In the event she showed herself to be such a noble confessor that her example strengthened all the others; her tormentors exhausted themselves in their attempts to make her renounce Christ or admit the evil practices alleged to be rife in Christian meetings: "I am a Christian," was her steadfast reply, "and there is no wickedness among us."

The repression was not always so outrageously brutal as the pogrom in the Rhône valley; we have the account of an examination of some Christians at a place called Scilli in North Africa, on July 17 in the year 180. There the governor of the province showed the Christians every consideration (as he thought), and endeavoured to make them conform not by torture but by persuasion. But even a humane magistrate at last lost his patience at what seemed the incurable obstinacy of these misguided people, and the Scillitan martyrs were sent off to execution.

Tertullian, in his *Defence of Christianity*, tries to make the point that the worst persecutors among the emperors were those like Nero and Domitian, whose memories were generally execrated by their pagan subjects as well; but this argument cannot be squared with historical fact. Marcus Aurelius is regularly included among the good Emperors and his scapegrace son Commodus (180–193) among the bad ones; but Christians had an easier time under Commodus than under his father. This may be due in part to the favour with which Commodus's morganatic wife Marcia regarded the Christians (if she was not actually a Christian herself). However that may be, when Commodus became Emperor several Christians were released from the Sardinian mines, to which they had been condemned in Marcus's reign.

After the fall of Commodus in 193, the Roman world was ruled by a succession of soldier-emperors. The first of these was Septimius Severus (193–211), a name well known in the history of Roman Britain. In 202 Severus issued a decree forbidding people to become either Jews or Christians. This was not the first time that a ban had been put upon Jewish proselytization, but it is the first time, so far as we know, that an imperial edict explicitly forbade conversion to Christianity. The appearance of this decree coincided with outbreaks of persecution in some parts of the empire. There was an outbreak in Egypt at this time so severe that many thought it a sign of the advent of the last Antichrist. It was at this time that Leonidas, father of the philosopher-theologian Origen, met a martyr's death at Alexandria, and Origen, then in his teens, was prevented from going to share his father's fate only by the enterprise of his mother, who hid his clothes. Farther west along the African coast there was persecution at Carthage, where two Christian women's fortitude in confession has been recorded in the *Martyrdom of Perpetua and Felicitas* (a Montanist work). Perpetua was a free-born matron and Felicitas a slave, but when the two young women stood hand in hand in the arena, they bore witness thus not only to the endurance which Christian faith was capable of, but also to the way in which it made class distinctions quite irrelevant.

It was only a few years before this that Tertullian wrote his *Defence of Christianity* in that same province of Africa, fiercely protesting against the treatment meted out to Christians by Roman law.

> The term "conspiracy" should not be applied to us but rather to those who plot to foment hatred against decent and worthy people, those who shout for the blood of the innocent and plead forsooth in justification of their hatred the foolish excuse that the Christians are to blame for every public disaster and every misfortune that befalls the people. If the Tiber rises to the walls, if the Nile fails to rise and flood the fields, if the sky withholds its rain, if there is earthquake or famine or plague, straightway the cry arises: "The Christians to the lions!"[1]

The passing of this wave of repression, however, inaugurated half a century of comparative peace for the Church throughout the world. Some of the Emperors who ruled during these years hailed from the east and were perhaps on that account inclined to be tolerant towards a religion which was itself of eastern origin. Alexander Severus (222–235), whose mother had received some instruction from Origen, included Christ in his pantheon and recognized the Christians as a corporation competent to hold property; some years later the Arabian Emperor Philip (244–249) was reputed to be almost a Christian.

The one exception to the general tolerance which Christianity enjoyed in this period is the brief reign of Maximin the Thracian (235–238). Maximin introduced repressive measures against the church leaders, but in one instance at any rate these measures were providentially overruled for good; by the simultaneous exile in Sardinia of Pontianus, the bishop of Rome, and his rival Hippolytus, bishop of a dissident group in the Roman church, the breach was healed, for the two exiled leaders became reconciled before their death and Hippolytus sent a message to his followers enjoining them to return to the body from which they had separated.

These decades of relative tranquillity brought a great access of membership to the Church. Whatever the official attitude might be, it is plain that many ordinary people found the Christian community extraordinarily attractive. In the absence of opportunities

[1] Tertullian, *Apologeticus*, 40 : 1–2.

for free propaganda, Christianity enjoyed in the lives of its votaries and the fellowship of its communities something which was more effective than any deliberate advertisement. Even in the reign of Septimus Severus, Tertullian could use language which, in spite of its rhetorical hyperbole, must have been intended to be recognized as substantially true:[1]

> We are but of yesterday, and yet we have filled all the places that belong to you—cities, islands, forts, towns, exchanges; the military camps themselves, tribes, town councils, the palace, the senate, the market-place; we have left you nothing but your temples.

It is as well for the Empire, he goes on, that the Christians do not really take up arms against it (they are numerous enough to do it effectively if they were so minded); or depopulate it by packing up and going to a distant corner of the earth. And if they were in truth the incendiaries that some alleged them to be, they could do considerable damage with torches some dark night!

As the middle years of the third century drew on, fresh troubles threatened the Empire. There were barbarian forces on two widely separated frontiers—the Goths on the north and the Persians on the east, under the new and aggressive dynasty of the Sassanids. In these critical times the Christians were suspected of disloyalty. In spite of Tertullian's assertion that the military camps were full of Christians, many of them refused to serve in the army —an attitude which Tertullian himself emphatically approved. Apart from those principles which may be described as Christian pacifism, there were other things which deterred Christians from service in the armies, in particular the idolatrous practices involved in taking the military oath and in several other features of military life. Again, in times of crisis the pagans did not like to hear Christians (particularly, no doubt, those of Montanist persuasion) talking with cheerful expectancy about the signs of the end-time, heralding the collapse of civilization in fire and the ensuing reign of the saints. (Some years ago one charge brought against a group of Protestant pastors who were put on trial in one of the People's Republics of Eastern Europe was that they proclaimed the imminent dissolution of the present order and the cataclysmic advent of the divine kingdom in terms irreconcilable with the Marxian outlook for the future.)

Besides, when trouble threatened from across the Euphrates, it was suspected that Christians in the eastern provinces favoured the Persians; because there were Christians in strength beyond the Euphrates frontier as well as on the Roman side of it, and they received more tolerant treatment from the trans-Euphratean powers than they did in the Roman Empire.

[1] Tertullian, *Apologeticus*, 37 : 4ff.

In this critical time at the mid-century, the Emperor Decius (249–251) adopted as a measure of state security the policy of one Empire and one religion. Since Christianity obviously stood in the way of the success of this policy, Christianity must go. Not merely were Christians to be punished; Christianity itself was to be crushed. The bishops and other leaders were attacked with great ferocity, and every effort was made to make the rank and file apostatize. An edict was published in 250 to the effect that everyone in the Empire must sacrifice to the state gods and get a certificate to say that he had done so. This edict was plainly aimed at the Christians, for the pagan inhabitants of the Empire would sacrifice to the gods as a matter of course, if required. (From 212 onwards all freemen within the Empire were Roman citizens.)

This sudden attack after so many years of peace led to a considerable disorganization of the Church. A large number of Christians—those who had found it easy to join the Church in the recent peaceful times—proved unable to endure the new terror and offered the prescribed sacrifices. Some did so with relatively little pressure; others yielded after severe coercion. There were also those who, in one way or another, managed to secure certificates saying that they had sacrificed when in point of fact they had not done so. These *libellaticii*, as they were called from the certificates or *libelli* which they were able to produce, possibly succeeded in satisfying their own consciences, but such doubtful expedients were naturally not approved by the church authorities. The fact that so many, in one way or another, had conformed to the imperial requirements caused a great deal of trouble, as we shall see,[1] when the question of their readmission to church fellowship arose.

One striking feature of the persecution was that it was carried out by officials of the state without much co-operation from the pagan rank and file. The old hatred with which Christians had been regarded was fast disappearing, together with the old slanders about their practices. The rapid growth in their numbers during the first half of the third century meant that most of the inhabitants of the Empire had Christians in the circle of their friends or acquaintances. They were generally regarded now as decent neighbours, and it was perfectly obvious that they did not indulge in the horrid rites which earlier generations had charged them with. Far from co-operating with the police, the pagan population in several places helped the Christians to escape their attention.

This was evident, for example, in the forcible release of Dionysius, bishop of Alexandria, by a band of peasants, after he had been arrested in his hiding-place by a detachment of soldiers. For,

[1] See pp. 201f., 212f.

like his fellow-bishop Cyprian of Carthage, Dionysius had wisely judged that it was more expedient for his flock that he should continue to direct it from a hidden retreat than that he should court martyrdom by remaining in the city. Fabian, bishop of Rome, on the other hand, was one of the earliest martyrs in this persecution. Another distinguished victim was Origen, the great Biblical scholar, formerly of Alexandria and now of Cæsarea, who was imprisoned and subjected to ill-treatment from which he died soon afterwards.

A few years of peace followed the decline of this persecution. Valerian, who became emperor in 253, appeared favourable to the Christians, for the first few years of his reign. But he changed his policy in 257—partly, no doubt, through panic at a Persian invasion which reached as far west as Syrian Antioch. An edict was published forbidding Christians to hold their ordinary public meetings and banning their access to their cemeteries. In the opinion of a number of scholars, the relics of Peter and Paul were probably removed at this time for safety from the Vatican hill and the Ostian road respectively to find a temporary refuge in the place called *Ad Catacumbas* (i.e. "near the hollows"), where the Church of St. Sebastian now stands on the Appian Way.[1] (Since the underground galleries there were the only early Christian cemeteries known in the Middle Ages, the name "catacombs"— from *Ad Catacumbas*—first used of these cemeteries, was later extended to other early Christian cemeteries which were discovered from the sixteenth century onwards.)

A further edict in 258 codified the penalties for Christianity. The clergy were to suffer the death penalty on conviction; senators and knights were to be degraded from their rank; ladies of rank were to be punished by confiscation and exile; employees of the imperial household were to be sent to forced-labour camps on the imperial estates. Xystus (Sixtus II), bishop of Rome, and Cyprian, bishop of Carthage, were executed in accordance with this edict; Dionysius of Alexandria owed his preservation, as on a former occasion, to some Egyptian peasants who hurried him away to a remote spot.

Valerian was taken prisoner by the Persians during an eastern campaign in 259. The eastern provinces were in dire peril, for the Persians came as far as the Sea of Marmora, while the Goths took advantage of the Romans' preoccupation in the east to launch an invasion across the Danube, and other barbarians raided the empire from across the Rhine. Yet the energy of successive

---

[1] Cf. p. 145; see also J. M. C. Toynbee and J. Ward Perkins, *The Shrine of St. Peter and the Vatican Excavations* (1956), pp. 167ff., and a most valuable article by H. Chadwick, "St. Peter and St. Paul in Rome: The Problem of the Memoria Apostolorum ad Catacumbas," in the *Journal of Theological Studies*, April 1957, pp. 30ff.

emperors succeeded in restoring the frontiers; and settled government returned to the Empire with the accession of Diocletian
in 285.

Although the years following the defeat of Valerian were years
of crisis for the Empire, they were years of tranquillity for the
Church, which now enjoyed a further period of almost unbroken
peace for over forty years. Gallienus, the son and successor of
Valerian, revoked Valerian's anti-Christian edicts, forbade the
molestation of Christians and restored their confiscated burial-
places. The Emperor Aurelian (270–275) planned to fuse all the
religions of the Empire into a monotheistic solar worship derived
from the Syrian city of Palmyra. This would inevitably have led
to a further clash between the Christians and the state, but the
plan came to nothing with Aurelian's death. Aurelian's reign,
however, is noteworthy for the first known Christian appeal for
the intervention of the secular arm in an ecclesiastical dispute.
Paul of Samosata, bishop of Antioch, had in 268 been condemned
as a heretic by a church council and deposed from his see, but
refused to make way for his appointed successor. At this time
Antioch was part of the kingdom of Palmyra, whose ruler Zenobia was Paul's admiring patroness; and Paul could not be ejected.
When Aurelian, in 273, conquered Zenobia and regained Antioch
for the Empire, both parties appealed to him. He ruled that the
church property should be handed over to the party which was
recognized by the bishop of Rome—that is, to the orthodox
party.

During the favourable conditions which Christians enjoyed in
the closing decades of the third century, their numbers increased
more rapidly than ever. It is difficult to estimate the proportion
which their numbers bore to the general population, but they
were certainly a very powerful minority in the Empire as a whole,
while in some parts they were probably in the majority. Their
strength was apparently greatest in the middle classes, although
the highest families in the state were not immune from Christian
influence; Diocletian's wife and daughter were admittedly Christians by faith, if not by baptism. The old, patriotic Roman conservatives, however, still regarded Christianity as an unmitigated
evil for the state.

Diocletian, on acceding to power in an Empire which had
recently been so gravely disrupted by internal strife and foreign
invasion, decided to reorganize it thoroughly to meet the needs
of the contemporary situation. He divided it, for administrative
purposes, into two parts, each ruled by a senior Emperor (bearing
the title Augustus) with a junior colleague (bearing the title
Cæsar). As each junior colleague was put in personal charge of a
separate area, the division of the Empire was practically fourfold.

Diocletian himself took charge of the eastern Empire, with his son-in-law Galerius as junior colleague, while he entrusted the rule of the west to a fellow-Illyrian named Maximian, whose junior colleague was Constantius. The whole administration was rearranged on bureaucratic lines. So long as Diocletian held office, the system worked well, as in fact if not in theory he retained the chief power throughout the Empire; but after his abdication in 305 the division of imperial power between four Emperors led to armed rivalry for the supremacy.

Nearly twenty years of Diocletian's rule had passed before there was any sign of an anti-Christian policy. When the storm broke, as it did suddenly in 303, it was mainly due to the influence of Galerius. The rapid growth of Christianity in the last few decades meant that the opportunity for crushing it would soon be gone. It was now or never. And many influential people, who had the welfare of the state at heart, believed that the time was now. There had been in recent years a resurgence of the old state religion in a new form, expressed in terms of Neoplatonic philosophy, which looked upon Christianity as its deadly rival. There was trouble on the eastern frontier, and the loyalty of the Christians in those parts was suspected, the more so as the kingdom of Armenia, which lay immediately beyond that frontier, was now officially Christian.

The first instalment of the new persecution, in 303, took the form of an edict ordering the destruction of church buildings and of copies of Scripture. This last provision was something new, and reminds us of one of the features of Antiochus Epiphanes's attempt to abolish the Jewish religion in the second century B.C. This edict was quickly followed by outbreaks of fire in the imperial palace. These were attributed to Christian resentment at the edict, although there is some ground for thinking that Galerius was the real fire-raiser, intending thereby to force Diocletian's hand. Diocletian believed that they were caused by the Christians, and he took more repressive action. A second edict was issued, ordering the arrest of the clergy. Next year (304) a further edict ordered that all Christians should offer sacrifice to the state gods, on pain of death. This was a repetition of the edict of Decius of more than half a century before. Even Diocletian's Christian wife and daughter were compelled to offer sacrifice (his daughter was also Galerius's wife).

Not only was there a tendency, as fifty years earlier, for pagans to protect their Christian neighbours; even the officials in charge of the public sacrifices frequently turned a blind eye on refusals to conform. As crowds queued up to file past the altar and throw a pinch of incense on it, the officials might easily fail to notice an odd individual who omitted to perform the rite; if some zealous spirits in the queue thought it their Christian duty to testify aloud against this public idolatry, they might be knocked on the head and hustled along with as much expedition as possible. The severity of the persecution varied with local circumstances. There was comparatively little in the west; in Gaul and Britain, which Constantius ruled as Cæsar, there was hardly any. It was fiercest in Egypt and Palestine: fiercer, indeed, both in intensity and duration, than any previous persecution had been. And in those parts it became even worse after Diocletian's abdication in 305, for Galerius succeeded him as eastern Augustus, with his like-minded nephew Maximin as his Cæsar. The terrors of those years, from 305 to 311, have been described for us in detail by contemporary writers, the matter-of-fact Eusebius and the rhetorical Lactantius. Again, as fifty years before, there were many to begin with who were terrorized into repudiating their faith or consenting to a variety of compromises to avoid punishment.

But, severe as the persecution was, it was locally limited and was not prolonged beyond all endurance. In point of fact, its failure was increasingly evident. Galerius himself issued an edict before his death in 311 rescinding the anti-Christian legislation. His colleague and successor Maximin II attempted for a further two years to promote another kind of anti-Christian activity as part of his aim to establish a catholic church of paganism throughout the realm. He tried to further this plan by means of propaganda calculated to bring Christianity into contempt. Part of his propaganda took the form of the dissemination of a work entitled the *Acts of Pilate*, which represented the origins of Christianity in an unsavoury guise. These *Acts* had to be read and learned by school-children. They were clumsy forgeries, as Eusebius pointed out at the time; among other things, their dating was quite wrong, as they placed the death of Jesus in the seventh year of Tiberius (A.D. 20), whereas our first-century authorities make it plain that Pilate did not become governor of Judæa until Tiberius's twelfth year and that Jesus did not begin His public ministry before Tiberius's fifteenth year.

Maximin's brief reign as Augustus of the East was terminated, however, by his defeat and rout at Adrianople in 313 at the hands of Licinius. Meanwhile, Constantine, son of Constantius, had established his supremacy over his rivals in the west, by his victory at the Milvian Bridge just outside Rome in 312. Constantine immediately restored the confiscated church property to the Christians in his own domain. Next year (313) he and Licinius held a meeting at Milan, and there the two victors agreed upon a new policy of complete toleration for all religions throughout the whole Empire. The way was now open for the banished Christian leaders, in east and west alike, to return from exile. Their property was restored; their demolished church edifices rebuilt. The last round between Christianity and Roman paganism had been the most desperate of all; but it ended with the acknowledgment that Christianity had won.

CHAPTER XVIII

CHRISTIAN LIFE AND WORSHIP

HAVING SKETCHED THE EXTERNAL RELATIONS OF THE Church down to Constantine's accession, we have provided ourselves with a framework which must now be filled in with some account of the Church itself.

Our sources of information for the second half of our period are much more adequate than for the first half. From A.D. 60, where Luke's history fails us, down to 180, we have no continuous account of the progress of Christianity. Eusebius did his best to cover the period when, early in the fourth century, he wrote his *Ecclesiastical History*; but even he was much better informed about the course of events from 180 down to his own day than he was about the century or so preceding 180. For that century we have to piece our information together from a variety of unequal sources. But when the picture becomes clearer, towards the end of the second century, we find not simply a large number of independent Christian communities throughout the civilized world, but the conception of one ecumenical body, the Church Catholic, locally and visibly manifested in the various individual communities. This Church Catholic has certain marks which distinguish it from other groups which might in some way lay claim to the Christian name; chief among these marks must be reckoned the possession of a "rule of faith," a recognized body or canon of sacred literature which forms the standard by which to judge anything that may be taught as a matter of belief or practice. And, as many things were being taught thus in various quarters which were warmly disputed in others, we find the Church Catholic defining with increasing precision the beliefs which it regarded as true. At the end of the second century, then, we can recognize quite clearly the Catholic Church, the Catholic Canon, and the Catholic Faith.

As early as New Testament times, it is clear that one of the chief means of linking the Christian groups planted all over the Eastern Mediterranean world was the practice of mutual aid. Not long after the second Christian community was founded—the largely Gentile-Christian church of Antioch—it seized the opportunity to show its sense of kindly duty towards the completely

Jewish-Christian church of Jerusalem by sending it a donation at a time of great scarcity in Palestine.[1]

The organization of charity, in fact, was a major activity within the individual churches themselves from the start, as is plain from the record of the primitive Jerusalem church, whose wealthier members put their property into a common pool, from which distribution was made to those in need. The first institution of officers in the Jerusalem church, in addition to the apostles who were the natural leaders at the outset, was the appointment of seven almoners to take charge of this distribution.[2]

It was this sense of mutual responsibility between members of the same local church that soon manifested itself as a sense of mutual responsibility between churches. The example of the Antiochene church was followed some years later by Paul, when he organized a large-scale collection, in the churches which he had founded on both sides of the Ægean, to relieve the poverty of the Jerusalem church.[3] The churches were administratively independent, each governed by its own bishops or elders, but this sense of mutual obligation was kept alive and prevented them from forgetting the unity which bound them all together in Christ.

The later documents in the New Testament introduce us to a further charitable organization in the Gentile churches—the order of widows. Widows who had no relatives to support them were an obvious charge upon the charity of the church to which they belonged, and it seemed desirable not only to make provision for these widows, but to employ them as the church's servants in the distribution of charity to others. Being supported by the church, they could be counted upon to practise hospitality and be regular in their attendance at public prayer. The earliest reference to this order of widows is in one of the Pastoral Epistles of the New Testament[4]—the fifth chapter of the First Epistle to Timothy—where their qualifications and duties are set out. It is made plain that a special order of widows is in view, for which not all widows were eligible; the qualifications for enrolment included real destitution (arising from a widow's having no relatives to support her), not being under sixty years of age, having a good reputation already for charity and hospitality, and having been married only once.

A second-century Greek satirist, Lucian by name, a native of Samosata in Syria, satirizes Christian practice in his account of a charlatan named Proteus Peregrinus. Proteus is represented as

---

[1] Acts 11 : 29f.; 12 : 25; see pp. 92f.
[2] Acts 6 : 1ff.; see p. 75.
[3] 1 Cor. 16 : 1ff.; 2 Cor. 8 : 1ff.; Rom. 15 : 25ff.; see pp. 126, 134, 148, 150.
[4] The Pastoral Epistles are those addressed to Timothy and Titus.

having joined the Christians for a time. During that time he was thrown into prison, and the Christians, says Lucian, "left no stone unturned in their endeavour to procure his release. When this proved impossible, they looked after his wants in all other matters with untiring solicitude and devotion. From earliest dawn old women ('widows,' they are called) and orphan children might be seen waiting about the prison-doors; while the officers of the church, by bribing the jailors, were able to spend the night inside with him. Meals were brought in, and they went through their sacred formulas."[1]

This is set down in satire, but it is a very fair picture of Christian practice. It is probable, in fact, that Lucian had more particularly in mind the behaviour of the Christians at the various places where Ignatius of Antioch broke his journey when he was being taken from his Syrian home in 115 to be martyred in the Roman amphitheatre. And the picture can be duplicated many times over from later records showing the care which Christians took of those who were in prison or otherwise suffering for their faith, ignoring the personal risks involved.

Lucian's reference to orphans alongside widows reminds us that orphans were a class similarly in need of support. Not only did the churches look after the orphan children of their own members, as was their natural duty; they also felt a concern for the considerable number of infants who were exposed because they were unwanted by their parents. This was a common practice in the Græco-Roman world and supplies a frequent motif of Greek and Latin drama; for such children were very often picked up by baby-farmers who brought them up to be slaves or courtesans. How little conscience was made of this by decent-minded people is illustrated by a letter written in 1 B.C. by an Egyptian labourer at Alexandria to his wife at Oxyrhynchus, in terms of real affection, instructing her with regard to the baby that she is expecting: "If it is a boy, keep it; if a girl, expose it."[2] The writer of the *Epistle to Diognetus* mentions as something noteworthy about Christians the fact that they do not expose their children.[3]

In this matter of charity the church of the capital constantly showed a worthy example to the others. Ignatius, in the letter which he wrote to the Roman Christians to prepare them for his arrival in their city, hailed them as being pre-eminent in this very regard. More than half a century later Dionysius, bishop of Corinth, praises them for their outstanding devotion to this work. "For this is your practice from the beginning," he writes, "to do

---

[1] Lucian, *Death of Peregrinus*, 12. See G. Bagnani, "Peregrinus Proteus and the Christians," *Historia* iv (1955), pp. 107ff.

[2] Deissmann, *Light from the Ancient East*, pp. 167ff.

[3] See p. 177.

good to all the brethren in various ways, and to send contributions to many churches in every city, thus refreshing the poverty of those in need, and furnishing supplies to the brethren [doing forced labour] in the mines. By these gifts, which you have sent from the beginning, you maintain the ancestral custom of the Romans, true Romans as you are. Your blessed bishop Soter has not only carried on this practice, but has actually extended it, providing great abundance for distribution to the saints, and with his blessed words encouraging the brethren who come from other parts, as a loving father would his children."[1] A church which could receive tributes like this from other churches had no need of any dogmatic basis for its pre-eminence.

The Christian tradition of caring for the sick also goes back to primitive times. When Alexandria was devastated by an outbreak of plague in the middle of the third century, Dionysius, bishop of the church in that city, describes the devotion with which Christians tended the sick, often catching the plague and dying of it themselves in consequence, whereas their pagan neighbours "thrust from them those who showed the symptoms of plague and fled from their nearest and dearest. They would throw them into the streets half dead, or cast out their corpses without burial."[2] When we try to account for the increase in the numbers of Christians in those days, in spite of official hostility, we must give due consideration to the impression that behaviour of this kind would make on the pagan population.

The institution of slavery, so essential a part of the civilized order in classical antiquity, could not but be profoundly modified by Christianity, with its insistence on the nobility and worth of the individual. To the Christian, the slave equally with the freeman was "thy brother, for whom Christ died," by contrast with Roman law, in which he had no personal status, or even with Aristotelian philosophy, in which he was defined as a "living tool." In Christianity, as Paul had insisted, there is neither bond nor free; within the believing community such a distinction disappears, and Paul showed what he meant when he sent Philemon's former slave Onesimus back to his old master, "no longer as a slave, but as a dear brother."

When fierce persecution broke out, slaves showed that they could face the trial and suffer for their faith as courageously as freeborn Romans. The slave-girl Blandina and her mistress alike suffered in the outrageous scenes in the Rhône valley in 177, but it was the slave-girl who was the outstanding heroine of the persecution, impressing friend and foe as a "noble athlete" in the Christian contest. And at Carthage in 202 a deep impression was

[1] Eusebius, *Hist. Eccl.*, IV, 23 : 10.
[2] *Ibid.*, VII, 22 : 10.

made on the spectators by the sight of the freeborn Perpetua standing hand-in-hand in the arena with her slave Felicitas, as both women faced the same death for the same faith. What real difference could there be, to a Christian, between bond and free?

It might very well be that slaves, by reason of their spiritual stature, should be among the recognized leaders of a Christian church, and freeborn members of that church humbly and gratefully submit to their direction and control. Pius, bishop of the Roman church towards the middle of the second century, if not a slave himself, was at any rate the brother of a slave;[1] and Callistus, bishop of the same church in the early part of the third century, was an ex-slave.

Marriages between slaves were not regarded as legal marriages by Roman law, but within the Christian circle marriage between slaves was as sacred and valid as marriage between those of free birth. What was more unnatural still from the viewpoint of Roman law, marriage between freemen and slave-women, and even between freewomen and slaves, was equally recognized in the churches as true Christian marriage.

Some interesting accounts have come down to us of the way in which the church meetings of the early Christians were conducted in various parts of the Empire. We have already seen the information which Pliny elicited in Bithynia on this subject. A document of about the same date (the beginning of the second century) reflects church practice somewhere within the general region of Syria. This document has as its full title *The Teaching of the Lord through the Twelve Apostles to the Gentiles* (the way in which it ignores Paul suggests that it belongs to a Jewish-Christian environment). It is usually referred to more briefly as the *Didaché*, that being the Greek word for "Teaching." After an initial exhortation, setting forth the "way of life" and the "way of death," the *Didaché* goes on to give instructions from which we can gather the general character of church practice in Syria and Palestine about this time.

> Now as regards baptism, baptize as follows. Having recited all that has gone before [i.e. the ethical exhortation on the two ways], baptize them in running water "into the name of the Father and of the Son and of the Holy Spirit." If you have no running water, then baptize them in other water; if you cannot do it in cold water, then do it in warm water. But if you cannot do it in either, then pour water three times on the head "into the name of the Father and of the Son and of the Holy Spirit." But before the baptism let the baptizer and the candidate for baptism fast, together with any others who are able; and you must direct the candidate for baptism to fast a day or two before.

[1] Hermas. See pp. 200f., 204.

There is a spirit of eminent reasonableness here. The meaning
of baptism is much more important than the form. Running
water is best. (Why? Because Jesus was baptized in Jordan?)
But "static water" will do instead; and if there is not enough of
either, affusion is as valid as dipping. Then the mention of pre-
baptismal fasting leads on to the question of fasting in general.

> And you must not fast as the hypocrites do, for they fast on
> Monday and Thursday; you must observe your fast on Wednesday
> and Friday. Neither must you pray as the hypocrites do, but pray
> as the Lord commanded in His Gospel:

and then follows the Lord's Prayer practically as it is given in
Matthew's Gospel, with the liturgical ascription at the end:

> "For Thine is the power and the glory for ever." Three times a
> day you are to pray thus.

The regulation about fasting is amusing in its *naïveté*; Jesus'
injunction to His disciples that they must not imitate the "hypo-
crites" when they fast[1] is interpreted to mean that they must not
fast on the Jewish fast-days, but on two different days.[2] (But, like
the Pharisee in the parable, they might still say: "I fast twice in
the week.") The fact that the Lord's Prayer is quoted, with a
couple of negligible exceptions, in the form which it assumes in
Matthew's Gospel, suggests that this treatise belongs to the same
region as that in which Matthew's Gospel first circulated. And
this is borne out by the fact that the *Didaché* is the earliest extant
writing, apart from Matthew's Gospel itself, to prescribe the
trinitarian formula for baptism. But the *Didaché* deviates from the
Matthæan order when it goes on to prescribe for the eucharistic
service, for there it directs that thanks be given for the cup before
the bread.

> As regards the eucharist, give thanks[3] as follows. First for the
> cup: "We thank Thee, our Father, for the holy vine of David Thy
> servant, which Thou hast made known to us through Thy Servant
> Jesus: Thine is the glory for ever and ever." Then for the breaking
> of the bread: "We thank Thee, our Father, for the life and know-
> ledge which Thou hast made known to us through Thy Servant
> Jesus: Thine is the glory for ever and ever. As this broken bread
> was scattered upon the mountains, and being gathered together
> became one, so may Thy Church be gathered together from the ends
> of the earth into Thy kingdom: for Thine is the glory and the power
> through Jesus Christ for ever and ever." But let no one eat or drink
> of this eucharist, but those who have been baptized into the name
> of the Lord; for indeed this is what our Lord meant when He said:
> "Give not that which is holy to the dogs."

[1] Matthew 6 : 16.   [2] See note on p. 198.
[3] The verb for giving thanks in Greek is *eucharisteô*;) it is for this reason that the
holy supper is called the eucharist (Gk. *eucharistia*), which simply means the
"thanksgiving."

And after you are satisfied, give thanks as follows: "We thank Thee, holy Father, for Thy holy name which Thou hast made to dwell within our hearts, and for the knowledge and faith and immortality which Thou hast made known to us through Thy Servant Jesus: Thine is the glory for ever and ever. Thou, O Lord Almighty, didst create all things for Thy name's sake, and hast given food and drink to men for their enjoyment, that they might return thanks to Thee; but upon us Thou hast bestowed spiritual food and drink, and eternal life through Thy Servant. Before all things we give Thee thanks that Thou art mighty: Thine is the glory for ever and ever. Remember, O Lord, Thy Church, even the Church which Thou hast sanctified, to deliver it from all evil and to perfect it in Thy love; and gather it together from the four winds into Thy kingdom which Thou hast prepared for it; for Thine is the power and the glory for ever and ever. May grace come and this world pass away. Hosanna to the God of David. If any man is holy, let him come; if any man is not, let him repent. *Marana-tha*. Amen."[1]

In this primitive liturgy the unusual order in which thanks are given for the sacred elements is the most striking thing; in fact, there are hints in one or two places in the New Testemant that this order was not unknown in very early days. The emphasis on the eschatological reference of the eucharist is also interesting; we have it both in the prayer "Let grace come and this world pass away" and in the old Aramaic invocation which follows it: *Marana-tha*, "Our Lord, come."[2] The same eschatological reference appears in the Gospel account of the institution of the Lord's Supper, where Jesus anticipates the consummation of the kingdom of God;[3] and in Paul's account of the same occasion, where he adds that, in eating this bread and drinking the cup, Christians "proclaim the Lord's death till He come."[4]

There was, in fact, a recognizable pattern of words and practice in the central acts of the church's worship from the earliest days; and it reappears in widely separated areas. It was not a rigidly fixed form; there was room for extensive local variations, and yet the variations do not obscure the basic pattern, which, indeed, underlies the manifold liturgical usages of the present day, a pattern which represents a true apostolic tradition.[5]

For the order followed in Rome in the middle of the second century we have some detailed information in the First Apology of Justin Martyr; but, as Justin was engaged in defending Chris-

---

[1] These extracts are from *Didaché*, 7 : 1-10 : 6.
[2] Paul uses the same invocation in 1 Corinthians 16 : 22.
[3] See Matthew 26 : 29; Mark 14 : 25 ; Luke 22 : 18 and (especially) 28–30.
[4] 1 Corinthians 11 : 26.
[5] This pattern is based on our Lord's fourfold action at the institution, when He (1) took bread and wine, (2) gave thanks, (3) broke the bread, (4) distributed the bread and wine with an explanation of their significance. One of the most exhaustive treatments of recent years is Dom Gregory Dix's *The Shape of the Liturgy* (1945); not all of Dix's thesis, however, is equally convincing.

tian practice before the imperial authorities, his account has not the precision of a liturgical manual. He describes the baptismal ceremony thus:

> All who are convinced and believe that what we teach and proclaim is true, and undertake to live in accordance with it, are instructed to pray and to entreat God, with fasting, for the remission of past sins; and we pray and fast along with them. Then we bring them to a place where there is water, and they are regenerated in the same way in which we ourselves were regenerated. For they then receive the washing of water in the name of God, the Father and Lord of the universe, and of our Saviour Jesus Christ, and of the Holy Spirit.[1]

Justin then goes on to explain the doctrine of baptism. His language is the language of baptismal regeneration, but as he did not apparently believe in original sin, it is difficult to see how he could have consistently understood by baptismal regeneration what is usually meant by it. Probably for him the expression meant little more than illumination, another term by which he describes the baptismal washing.[2]

Then, after a parenthesis, Justin goes on:

> But after we have thus washed the one who has been convinced by our teaching and has testified his assent to it, we bring him to the place where those who are called brethren are gathered together in order that we may earnestly offer our common prayers both for ourselves and for him who has been "illuminated," as well as for all others in every place, that now that we have learned the truth, we may be accounted worthy by our works also to be found good citizens and keepers of the commandments, so that we may be saved with an everlasting salvation. Having concluded our prayers, we greet one another with a kiss. Then bread, and a cup of wine mixed with water, are brought to the president of the brethren, and he takes them and gives praise and glory to the Father of the universe, in the name of the Son and of the Holy Spirit, and offers thanks at some length because we are accounted worthy to receive these things from Him. And when he has concluded the prayers and thanksgivings, all the people present express their assent by saying "Amen." . . . Then those whom we call deacons give to each of those present a portion of the bread and of the wine mixed with water, for which thanks were given, and they take a portion away for those who are absent.[3]

Justin follows this account with some reflections on the meaning of the eucharist; and then gives a description of the Christians'

---

[1] Justin, *Apol.*, I, 61.
[2] This designation of baptism as "enlightenment" may go back to such New Testament passages as Ephesians 5 : 14 (perhaps a fragment of a primitive baptismal hymn) and Hebrews 6 : 4. See p. 79.
[3] Justin, *Apol.*, I, 65.

weekly worship, in which there is a further, but much briefer, account of the eucharist:

> On the day called Sunday, all who live in cities or in the country gather together in one place, and the memoirs of the apostles or the writings of the prophets are read for so long as time permits. Then, when the reader has ceased, the president instructs us by word of mouth, exhorting us to put these good things into practice. Then we all rise together and pray and, as we have already said, bread, and wine mingled with water, are brought, and the president in like manner offers prayers and thanksgivings according to his ability, and the people assent by saying "Amen." Distribution is then made to each, and they share in that for which thanks have been given, and the deacons take portions to those who are absent. And those who are well off and are willing to do so give as much as each desires, and the money thus collected is deposited with the president, who takes care of the orphans and widows, and those who are in straits through sickness or any other cause, and those in prison, and our visitors from other parts—in short, he looks after all who are in need.[1]

Justin, of course, does his best to use language which would not be too unintelligible to the pagan readers for whom his *Apology* was intended (though we may wonder how much they grasped of the real meaning of Christian worship, even if they troubled to read his work). Fortunately, however, we have an account of the actual words used (as is widely believed nowadays) in the eucharistic service in Rome about the year 215, in the *Apostolic Tradition* now commonly ascribed to Hippolytus. Even if this ascription be doubted, the liturgy here preserved must be practically identical with the liturgy of the Roman and other churches about this time. The service, it will be noted, is conducted by the bishop himself.

> *Bishop.* The Lord be with you.
> *Answer.* And with thy spirit.
> *Bishop.* Lift up your hearts.
> *Answer.* We have them in the presence of the Lord.
> *Bishop.* Let us give thanks unto the Lord.
> *Answer.* It is meet and right so to do.
> *Bishop.* We give Thee thanks, O God, through Thy beloved Servant Jesus Christ, whom in these latter times Thou hast sent to be our Saviour and Redeemer and Messenger of Thy good will; the Logos who went forth from Thee, by whom Thou hast made all things, and in whom Thou art well pleased. Thou didst send Him from heaven into the womb of the Virgin, where He became incarnate and was manifested as Thy Son, born of the Holy Spirit and of the Virgin. Accomplishing Thy good will and acquiring for Thee a holy people, He stretched out His hands in His passion, to

[1] Justin, *Apol.*, I, 67.

deliver from suffering those who have believed in Thee. And when He was about to give Himself up willingly to His passion, to destroy death, to break the chains of the devil, to trample hell under His feet, to give light to the righteous, to set up the boundary stone, and to display the resurrection, He took bread and gave Thee thanks and said: "Take, eat; this is my body, which is broken for you." In like manner He took the cup and said: "This is my blood, which is poured out for you; as often as you do this, you do it as a memorial of me." Remembering therefore His death and His resurrection, we present to Thee the bread and the cup, giving Thee thanks that Thou hast deigned to permit us to stand before Thee and render Thee priestly service. And we beseech Thee, send Thy Holy Spirit upon the oblation of the holy Church; unite them all as one, and grant to all the saints who partake in this communion that they may be filled with the Holy Spirit and strengthened in faith and truth, that we may praise and glorify Thee through Thy Servant Jesus Christ, through whom be glory and honour to Thee in Thy holy Church, now and for ever more. Amen.[1]

About the same time as Hippolytus, Tertullian in North Africa provides us with ample evidence that church services in his part of the world were conducted on the same general lines as in Rome or the East. Here, for example, is a passage where he is at pains to rebut the common slanders that circulated about Christians' behaviour at their meetings:

We are a corporation with a common religious sentiment, a common rule of life, a common bond of hope. We come together for meeting and assembly to approach God in prayer, massing our forces to encompass Him, so to speak. . . . We pray also for the Emperors, for their ministers and those in authority, for the security of the world, for general peace, for the postponement of the end. We meet to read the divine scriptures . . . we also have exhortations, rebukes, divine censure. . . . Our presidents are elders of proved worth, men who have attained this honour not for a price, but by character.

Every man brings some modest coin once a month, or whenever he wishes, and only if he is willing and able; it is a freewill offering. You might call them the trust-funds of piety; they are spent . . . on the support and burial of the poor. . . .

Our meal shows its meaning by its name; it is called by the Greek word for love [agape]. . . . We do not take our places at the table until we have first taken part in prayer to God. Only so much is eaten as satisfies hunger, only so much is drunk as befits people of moderation. They satisfy their appetite like men who remember that even during the night they must worship God; they talk like men who know that their Master is listening. After water for the hands and lights have been brought in, each is invited to sing to God

---

[1] See R. H. Connolly, *The So-called Egyptian Church Order and Derived Documents* (Cambridge, 1916), pp. 175–194; G. Dix, *The Apostolic Tradition of St. Hippolytus of Rome* (London, 1937).

before the rest from what he knows of the holy scriptures or from his own heart. . . . In like manner prayer closes the meal.[1]

This last paragraph does not refer to the eucharist, which, as Tertullian tells us elsewhere,[2] was taken "before daybreak and from the hands of the presidents only." In apostolic times it is fairly clear that the eucharist formed part of the fellowship-meal, or *agape*; but we find a separation between the two as early as the date of Pliny's letter to Trajan,[3] where the Christians' common meal is taken later in the day than their early morning meeting for worship. Indeed, even in apostolic times it might prove necessary, as it did at Corinth, for the two to be separated, lest lack of mutual consideration at the *agape* should prevent the eucharist from being celebrated in a proper spirit.[4] But the *agape* continued to be observed as a separate occasion for long, and even at the present day an *agape* can be an admirable means of fostering church fellowship.

Note to page 193:—The selection of Wednesday and Friday as fast-days was probably dictated by a primitive Christian reckoning which fixed our Lord's arrest and first trial on Wednesday of Holy Week, and His crucifixion on the Friday. See p. 51, n. 1.

[1] Tertullian, *Apologeticus*, xxxix, 1–18. His description of public solo-singing illustrates Paul's reference to "speaking one to another in psalms and hymns and spiritual songs" (Ephesians 5 : 19; cf. Colossians 3 : 16).
[2] *De Corona*, 3.
[3] A.D. 112. See p. 170.
[4] 1 Corinthians 11 : 20ff.

CHAPTER XIX

CHURCH GOVERNMENT

Church Discipline

THE GENERAL STANDARD OF CHRISTIAN CONDUCT IN THOSE early centuries was high enough to make an impression on those pagans who did not allow their judgment to be deflected by baseless scandalmongering. That man of accurate observation, Galen, the second-century physician, regards it as noteworthy that while Christians base their faith on fables, yet they "sometimes act in the same way as genuine philosophers do." He notes in particular their contempt of death and their power of self-control in sexual relations: "there are some who, in ruling and mastering their impulses and in their pursuit of virtue, are not a whit behind real philosophers."[1]

All our evidence goes to show that the ethical requirements of the Christian faith were most earnestly inculcated in new converts, and that for the most part they were accepted and put into practice. Some Gentile converts may have lived very reprehensible lives before they became Christians, but when the Christian message came to them, they embraced it with the assurance that God in Christ had wiped out their past misdeeds.

But what about subsequent failure to maintain the Christian code of behaviour? This question inevitably arose very quickly. Action of a kind that flatly contradicted all that the gospel stood for naturally put the offender outside the Christian community, but even so there remained the hope that expulsion might bring him to his senses and restore him to the community as a penitent. If he remained obdurate, of course, he must remain outside.[2]

A question of this kind, however, could not be settled merely by considerations of practical expediency. The theological position had to be kept in mind. How did God regard such people? That the new convert to Christianity, by repentance and faith, received the full forgiveness of his sins was of the very essence of the gospel. But what of sins committed after baptism? Was there

---

[1] This passage, extant only in an Arabic version of Galen, is quoted in Latin by A. Harnack, *Mission and Expansion of Christianity*, I (1908), pp. 212f.; in English by E. R. Bevan, *Christianity* (1932), pp. 56f. Cf. R. Walzer, *Galen on Jews and Christians* (1949).

[2] Matthew 18 : 17; 1 Corinthians 5 : 5, 13; cf. pp. 120f., 124, above.

any hope that these, too, might come within the scope of God's pardoning grace if they were truly repented of?

There is a statement in the Epistle to the Hebrews which was very commonly interpreted in the early church to mean that there was little hope of forgiveness for post-baptismal sin. "If we sin deliberately," the statement ran, "after receiving the knowledge of the truth, there no longer remains a sacrifice for sins, but a fearful prospect of judgment, and a fury of fire which will consume the adversaries."[1] The writer may well have had in mind a certain irremediable form of apostasy, adopted as a settled policy by one who had once accepted Christianity and later, as deliberately, decided to renounce it. But the writer's intention does not primarily concern us here; what does concern us is the common interpretation of these words and the practical effect of that interpretation. They were taken to mean that there was no hope of forgiveness for sin committed after baptism—certainly not for sin committed with one's eyes open.

To many people this interpretation seemed unduly severe, and early in the second century a Christian writer at Rome, Hermas by name, expressed a milder view. This he did in an allegorical work called *The Shepherd*, which was widely read among the churches in the early centuries as a sort of *Pilgrim's Progress*. The view expressed by Hermas was, briefly, that there might be forgiveness for one sin committed after baptism, but not for more than one.

Now, we shall not properly understand how concerned the early Christians were with this problem unless we realize that the kind of sin which chiefly exercised them was sexual irregularity. For it was here that the ordinary canons of behaviour of Christians and pagans diverged most patently. We may wonder why equal concern was not felt about the other six deadly sins; the fact remains that this was the one which caused the greatest heart-searching in the Christian community. It mattered not that the writer to the Hebrews had not dwelt chiefly on sins of this kind, nor was it sufficiently considered that very often sexual irregularity lacks that element of deliberate policy which that writer condemned most severely. They knew by experience that it was in this field that post-baptismal sin was most likely to appear. And Hermas, knowing in his own heart how prone humanity is to yield to this form of temptation, even if it be confined to the thought-life, and having received the assurance of divine forgiveness himself, formulated his experience in the rule that post-baptismal sin might be forgiven once, but once only. We may think that this curious relaxation in itself shows that Hermas and his contemporaries failed to grasp the real principle at issue.

[1] Hebrews 10 : 26f., R.S.V. Cf. p. 152 above.

Even so, there were many who thought that Hermas was inexcusably lax in making this concession; early in the third century, for example, Tertullian sarcastically brands Hermas's treatise as "the *Shepherd* of the adulterers."

As time went on and further experience was gained, those concerned with the day-to-day guidance of Christian communities worked out certain practical expedients. There were obviously different categories of sins. Some were of such a character that confession and repentance sufficed for the offender's full restoration to Christian fellowship; others, such as murder, adultery, and perjury (the three major sins in Jewish jurisprudence as well), were excommunicable, and to these, of course, must be added apostasy, which was a kind of self-excommunication. But was excommunication irrevocable when one of these offences had been committed? What of those who sincerely repented? On this point opinions differed. Milder and severer answers were given. At Rome itself, in the earlier part of the third century, there was a serious dispute over this very question. Callistus, bishop of Rome from 217 to 222, ruled that sincere penitents might be readmitted to Christian communion even after adultery or fornication. Many, however, disagreed violently. From across the Mediterranean Tertullian sent the shafts of his most biting sarcasm against this "peremptory edict," as he calls it. But there was more serious opposition in Rome itself, where Hippolytus, the greatest scholar of his age in the west, inveighed against Callistus's criminal laxity, as he considered it. Hippolytus, indeed, together with his followers, withdrew from Callistus's communion, and constituted a rival church at Rome, with Hippolytus as rival bishop. Each group considered itself to be the legitimate church of Rome, and the other to be a schismatic sect; Hippolytus refers to the other body as "Callistians." But great scholars are not always good pastors, and there need be little doubt that Callistus more faithfully represented the mind of Christ Himself in this matter. Hippolytus further accused Callistus of maintaining false doctrine. The schism did not last long, however; we have already mentioned that Hippolytus was sent in 235, along with Pontianus, a successor of Callistus, to penal servitude in Sardinia, where the two rival leaders were reconciled before they died. The next bishop of Rome, Anteros, ruled over a reunited church; and Hippolytus has been commemorated, not as a schismatic leader, but as a catholic saint and orthodox theologian.

The problem of how to deal with those who renounced the faith became a live one during the severe Decian persecution in the middle of the third century, and again during the persecution under Diocletian and Galerius at the beginning of the fourth. During the preceding periods of peace the churches' ranks had been swollen by the entry of many recruits who could not withstand the pressure when tribulation came, and under the strong compulsion of terror denied their faith, formally if not really. What was to be done about these "lapsed" brethren? Some Christians of the stricter sort insisted that they should be eternally banished from the Church's pale, regarding them as soldiers who had deserted or shown cowardice in face of the enemy. But more reasonable counsels prevailed among the responsible leaders of churches whose first concern was their pastoral duty. To them it seemed clear that a distinction must be made between those who had taken the initiative in forswearing their Christianity, and those who had broken down under threats or torture. The rigorists overlooked the salutary example of Peter himself, for the prince of the apostles had on one memorable occasion emphatically denied his allegiance to Christ, and yet proved his true worth when the grace of Christ restored him. Dionysius, bishop of Alexandria, might well protest against those who "slander our most compassionate Lord Jesus Christ as unmerciful."[1] Many of the faithful confessors, too, urged that leniency should be shown to those whose strength had proved unequal to the test.

When the bishops in general showed that they were going to take the more lenient line in dealing with the lapsed, the rigorists seceded and formed schismatic bodies. This was the origin of the Novatian schism after the Decian persecution, and of the Melitian and Donatist schisms (in north-east and north-west Africa respectively) after the last pagan persecution.

Church Government and Ministry

But here we must take up the general question of how the churches were governed.

From the first, leaders were appointed in the Christian communities whose functions were largely comparable to those of the "elders" in the Jewish communities of Palestine and other lands. When Paul and Barnabas planted churches in Asia Minor during their first missionary journey, for example, they appointed elders in them all.[2] Paul, writing to the Christians at Philippi, salutes the church in that city together with its "bishops and deacons"—or, to render the Greek terms by words of a different flavour, its "superintendents and ministers."[3] That the language of the New Testament does not allow us to press a distinction between the Greek word translated "bishop" (*episkopos*) and that translated "elder" (*presbyteros*) need not be argued at length. Paul could

---

[1] Eusebius, *Hist. Eccl.*, VII, 8 : 1.
[2] Acts 14 : 23.
[3] Philippians 1 : 1.

address the assembled *elders* of the church of Ephesus as those whom the Holy Spirit had made *bishops*.[1] Later, in the Pastoral Epistles (those to Timothy and Titus), the two terms still appear to be used interchangeably.[2]

But this is not the only form of ministry which we meet in the New Testament. In addition to the settled administrators of the individual churches, there were those whose ministry was of a more prophetic character, not necessarily tied to any one place. Human nature being what it is, situations were bound to arise creating tension between the two kinds of ministry. Perhaps this tension was less likely to lead to serious trouble in apostolic times, when both categories of ministers generally recognized the over-riding authority of the apostles—the more so as the apostolic ministry itself was not tied to any one locality and partook of an inspirational as well as of an administrative and didactic character. Obviously both kinds of gift were united in a man like Paul, as they were later in Ignatius of Antioch. Ignatius, indeed, tried to make the more external and official ministry the expression of the more inward and prophetic. But it became increasingly difficult to find a place for the prophetic ministry within the framework of ordinary church administration. Some of the consequences of this we shall see in due course, but there is a prior question to consider.

Our first-century authorities introduce us to a twofold order of local ministry—the bishops and deacons of the Philippian church and the Pastoral Epistles. The bishops may be called elders, but the difference is one of name only. Generally speaking, the word "elder" has a Jewish background, whereas "bishop" has a Gentile background. But by the time we reach the last quarter of the second century, the local ministry exhibits a threefold order: the local church has one bishop, several elders or presbyters, and several deacons. The transition from the earlier to the later stage is a subject for debate into which we need not enter here to any great extent. Even when one tries to treat it dispassionately as a matter for purely historical research, it is difficult to be sure that unconscious theological or ecclesiastical bias has not affected the conclusion in some degree.

The first unambiguous witness to the emergence of the single bishop is found in the correspondence which Ignatius sent to various quarters in 115 when he was on his way to martyrdom in Rome. Ignatius was himself bishop of Antioch in this sense, and he insisted that the institution of the single bishop was essential in the church and that his authority was paramount. To Ignatius, the bishop or someone delegated by him was the only church official who could conduct a valid baptism or eucharist; even an

[1] Acts 20 : 17, 28.
[2] Compare verse 5 with verse 7 of Titus 1.

agape must not take place without him. "Six out of the seven letters are filled with exaggerated and passionate exaltation of the authority and importance of the bishop's office. . . . To Ignatius the monarchical episcopate is literally an *idée fixe*."[1] The vehemence of Ignatius's protestations, in fact, is the plainest evidence that his view of the indispensable and supremely authoritative character of the office was far from being universally shared. The one letter out of the seven in which Ignatius does not enlarge on the unique dignity of the bishop's office is the letter which he wrote to the Roman church. This church is saluted in the most unqualified terms as pre-eminently worthy, but there is no hint that it enjoys the blessing of a monarchical bishop.

There is other evidence pointing to the same conclusion with regard to the church of Rome at this time. About twenty years before the martyrdom of Ignatius, a letter was sent from that church to the church in Corinth, expostulating with it for certain recent disorders. The writer of this Roman letter is generally identified with Clement, who figures as one of the earlier bishops of Rome in the lists preserved by Irenæus and others; but there is no suggestion that the writer of the letter is acting in any episcopal capacity. The Corinthian church, too, to which the letter is addressed, appears from it to have been governed at the time by a plurality of bishops or presbyters.[2]

If, however, the writer of this letter was indeed Clement (his name does not appear in the letter itself), then there is a reference in *The Shepherd* of Hermas—himself a Roman Christian—which may explain the capacity in which Clement wrote to the Corinthian church. In one of his visions recorded in *The Shepherd*, Hermas is directed by an aged female who represents the Church (like "Mother Kirk" in Professor C. S. Lewis's *Pilgrim's Regress*) to write two little books and send one to Clement, "and Clement shall send it to the foreign cities, for that is his business." And then she goes on, addressing Hermas himself: "But you shall read it to this city along with the elders that preside over the church."[3]

Clement, it appears, was foreign secretary in the Roman church, and wrote to the Corinthians in that capacity. Hermas, although he is said to have been brother to Pius, who appears in the list of Roman bishops later in the second century, knows no governors of the Roman church save the elders who preside over it (as we have just seen) or, as he says elsewhere, "the rulers and those who occupy the chief seats."[4] It looks, then, as if the church of Rome

---

[1] B. H. Streeter, *The Primitive Church* (1929), pp. 164, 173.
[2] Cf. 1 Clement 44 : 1–6.
[3] *Shepherd*, Vision ii, 4, 3.
[4] *Ibid.*, Vision iii, 9, 7.

was governed by a college of bishops or presbyters as late as the time of Ignatius. And this may explain the variation in order of the first bishops of Rome in the lists that have come down to us. Linus, Anencletus, Clement himself, and others, may well have been joint members of this college, conceivably presidents of it, and as such *primi inter pares*. The college would be regarded as being originally of apostolic foundation, just as the presbyter-bishops of Corinth and elsewhere are said to have been in Clement's letter,[1] but the idea that *monarchical* bishops were appointed by apostles appears at a later date than this. Then, "as soon as the habit grew up of including the name of the Apostle-founder as the first of the list rather than as a title at the head of it . . . the use of a single name was dictated by the principle that there could only be one bishop at one time,"[2] and so, as C. H. Turner points out, from Hippolytus onward Peter alone is named at the head of the list of Roman bishops, and not (as previously) Peter and Paul together.

The same situation appears to have existed at Philippi until 115; in Polycarp's letter to the church of that city shortly after the death of Ignatius those in authority are still addressed collectively as presbyters.

No doubt these writings, belonging to the end of the first century and the beginning of the second, reflect the brief period of transition which very soon gave place to the universal institution of the single bishop; but they do suggest that, when Ignatius wrote his letters, the situation was not such as he would have liked to see—hence the vehemence with which he urged his view. But by the middle of the second century we may take it that the Ignatian ideal had prevailed almost everywhere. (The Alexandrian church was governed until the third century by a college of presbyters, which elected one of its members as president or bishop.)

It should be remembered, of course, that the single bishop in the early church was much more like the minister of one of our city parishes than like the diocesan bishop of to-day. Otherwise it would have been impracticable for the bishop to conduct every eucharistic service, as Ignatius urges and the *Apostolic Tradition* prescribes.

But the transition from the college of presbyter-bishops in the first century to the single bishop of the second century demands an explanation, and more than one explanation is offered. A leading scholar of an earlier generation traced the rise in importance of the single bishop to the fact that (as Justin and others tell us) he controlled the church's charitable fund, and found parallels to

[1] 1 Clement 44 : 1.
[2] C. H. Turner *Catholic and Apostolic* (1931), p. 225.

this development in the practice of pagan friendly societies.[1] But there were more important factors than this. One obvious consideration is that the emergence of a single leader was almost inevitable in the circumstances. Committee rule in general is weak unless there is a strong chairman. Quite often the strongest personality will become chairman in any case, and spiritual strength need not be excluded from his qualities. In practice such a man will become *primus inter pares*, and once his position is accepted and perpetuated, before long he will be regarded, in theory as well as in practice, as *primus* pure and simple. An outstanding early example of such a man who plainly acted as *primus inter pares* was James of Jerusalem.

If, on the other hand, the chairman of a committee is not sufficiently strong, someone else will no doubt show himself willing to act with the necessary energy. And here we may consider another New Testament figure, whose status is more enigmatic. This was a leader in one of the churches of Asia who asserted his authority in so high-handed a fashion that he has been characterized for all succeeding generations as "Diotrephes, who loves to have the pre-eminence" (or, as the Revised Standard Version has it, "who likes to put himself first").[2] "It may be (i) that Diotrephes is in fact the first 'monarchical bishop' known to history in the province of Asia.[3] . . . On the other hand, it may be (ii) that Diotrephes is a symptom of the disease which the quasi-apostolic ministry of monarchical bishops was designed to relieve"[4]—the disease in question being the self-assertion of able demagogues. Into whichever category we decide to fit Diotrephes —and heirs of varying ecclesiastical traditions may have preferences one way or the other!—Professor Dodd is no doubt right in thinking that the tendency for ambitious individuals to assume dictatorial powers in local congregations, with the consequent "danger which this state of affairs threatened to the unity and continuity of the Christian Body was one motive in the development of the catholic episcopate during the second century."[5]

A further motive is specially evident in Ignatius's letters. Ignatius was greatly concerned about the inroads of heresy in the churches, especially the heresy called docetism,[6] and he considered the monarchical episcopate to be the best guarantee against it. His insistence that only a bishop or his delegate (who could presumably be trusted to see eye to eye with him) might

[1] E. Hatch, *The Organization of the Early Christian Churches* (Bampton Lectures, 1880), pp. 26ff.
[2] 3 John 9.
[3] This was Harnack's view.
[4] C. H. Dodd, *The Johannine Epistles* (1945), p. 164.
[5] *Ibid.*, Dodd's whole discussion here (pp. 161ff.) is a valuable contribution to this subject.
[6] See pp. 245ff.

conduct a valid baptism or eucharist was calculated to exclude heretics from the holy ordinances.

It is remarkable, indeed, to see what a small part the presbyters of a church played in its acts of worship for several centuries after the emergence of the single bishop. In the *Apostolic Tradition* ascribed to Hippolytus, for example, the bishop is assisted in his liturgical functions not by the presbyters but by the deacons. The presbyters act as his administrative council, but do not share his liturgical ministry.

The question has been asked frequently whether the contemporary mystery religions had any influence on the development of early Christian practice. It would be surprising if they had no influence, but the extent of their influence has often been exaggerated. But, when we bear in mind that the New Testament writings give not the slightest hint that the administration of the sacraments is to be restricted to any special members of the church, it is easily understood that the restriction imposed by Ignatius might lend itself to other interpretations among converts from paganism who did not appreciate Ignatius's real motive. Many of these converts were acquainted with mystery cults in which the due performance and interpretation of the sacred dramas were the province of people called hierophants, specially set aside for this purpose. It may have been at least to some extent under such influences as these that the Christian minister, to quote Professor Angus, "assumed the office of priest as the dispenser of grace-conferring rituals and as the custodian of the kingdom of heaven entrusted with the dread 'power of the keys.' "[1] The well-meant injunction of Ignatius thus chimed in only too well with "the magic fashion of the days when," to quote the same writer, "on the cessation of the primitivep siritual manifestations, the outward rite was correspondingly highly esteemed, and when the idea from the Mysteries had taken permanent root in Christianity that no member of the brotherhood could be saved or benefit by the grace or blessings of the religion except through participation in its rituals of initiation and rebirth."[2] But the question is a complicated one, partly because of our defective knowledge of the mystery religions, partly because the influence may not have been entirely in one direction. Yet certain features of sacramental doctrine which appear in Christian circles in post-apostolic times, and which seem inconsistent with the apostolic teaching itself, may well owe something to mystery influences.

To revert to Ignatius, however, we must observe that with all his insistence on the episcopate he has no thought of an episcopal

[1] S. Angus, *Religious Quests of the Græco-Roman World* (1929), p. 152.
[2] *Op. cit.*, p. 217. See also the same writer's *The Mystery Religions and Christianity* (1925).

succession. That is an idea which arises somewhat later in the second century. And even when it does arise, it does not take the form which the doctrine of apostolic succession commonly assumes nowadays. To-day apostolic succession is commonly taken to mean the tactual transmission of apostolic authority, as bishops are consecrated by other bishops who themselves were consecrated by other bishops and so on right back to the earliest bishops who were set apart for their high office by the laying on of the hands of the apostles themselves. But what was valued when the idea of episcopal succession first came to be stressed— as in the writings of Irenæus, about A.D. 180—was the regular succession of bishops in any one city from the first establishment of Christianity there, especially if Christianity had been established there by an apostle. For that meant that the succession of bishops could be traced back in that place to the apostles themselves. Now, most of the heretical schools (though not all) agreed with the orthodox that the apostles held the true faith. The orthodox argument then ran: in those places where the apostles themselves planted Christianity and appointed bishops, and where the succession of bishops could be traced without intermission from apostolic days, at what point did the error creep in? The bishop, the guardian of the true faith, maintained the same faith as his predecessor had done—and so on back to the apostolic founder of the church in question. The burden of proof lay on those who claimed that the bishops had departed from the original faith, and that they themselves preserved it. What were the credentials of those who made this claim?

The argument was a practical appeal to common sense; there was no emphasis at this stage on episcopal ordination or the transmission of grace. It implied, no doubt, that a bishop in the course of his pastorate was not likely to give up orthodoxy for heresy; but, in fact, bishops have always tended to be orthodox. Even those who have had a reputation for unorthodoxy in their pre-espiscopal days generally exchange it for one that inspires more confidence. If any exception springs to the reader's mind, it is one of those exceptions that prove the rule.

Historically, there seems to be little room for doubt that the single bishop emerged from the ranks of his fellow-presbyters, as the leading figure among the presbyters came increasingly to be regarded as the representative of his church. The necessary impetus was given to this tendency when the situation arose which, in Ignatius's eyes, imperatively demanded the monarchical episcopate to deal with it.

It is freely contended in some quarters, however, that the threefold ministry of bishops, presbyters and deacons from the second century onwards perpetuates the threefold ministry of apostles, presbyter-bishops and deacons in the first century. The primary difficulty in accepting this view is that the apostleship was not a local ministry as the monarchical episcopate is. (Some scholars try to combine the two views, like Dr. Hebert, according to whom, "the office of 'bishop' descends, by succession of Ordination, from that of 'apostle of Jesus,' while gathering up in itself also that of 'chairman of the presbyters.' ")[1] The arguments used in this debate are as much theological as historical, and we are more interested here in the historical evidence. This, it must be said, seems inadequate to justify the view that a truly apostolic ministry can be exercised only in those Christian communities which have preserved the traditional monarchical episcopate. Function, not status, is the really important thing here. A Christian community, however it may be administered, stands in the true apostolic succession if it maintains the apostles' teaching and displays "the signs of an apostle."[2]

[1] A. G. Hebert, quoted in J. W. C. Wand, *The Church: Its Nature, Structure and Function* (1947), p. 82 n.

[2] The debate continues: on the one side the *magnum opus* is the symposium *The Apostolic Ministry*, ed. K. E. Kirk (1946); smaller but not less important works on the other side are D. T. Jenkins, *The Nature of Catholicity* (1942), and T. W. Manson, *The Church's Ministry* (1948). An important and interesting historical approach to the question is provided by A. Ehrhardt in *The Apostolic Succession in the First Two Centuries of the Church* (1953). His attempt to derive the apostolic succession from the supposed new Christian high-priesthood of James and his followers in the church of Jerusalem, however, lacks a sufficiently stable foundation; see R. P. C. Hanson, *Christian Priesthood Examined* (1979), p. 36.

CHAPTER XX

RELATIONS BETWEEN CHURCHES

THE CHURCHES IN THE FIRST THREE CENTURIES A.D. WERE closely linked together in Christian fellowship, but they were not united in any federal organization. There was no idea that the church of one city was subordinate to the church of any other city. The church of Antioch, for example, did not lie within the jurisdiction of the church of Jerusalem, although the mother church naturally enjoyed a special measure of prestige and respect. On the other hand, the church of a city occupied a metropolitan relation to the daughter-churches of the surrounding country-side. Whether this was the relation in New Testament times between the church of Corinth, let us say, and the church of the Corinthian seaport Cenchreæ, is not certain, but it seems to have been the relation between the church of Jerusalem and the other Christian communities in Palestine which resulted from the dispersion of the Jerusalem church in 33 and again in 66. Further, there was in those earlier centuries no suggestion that any one church was subordinate to the aggregate of all the churches.

The relationship between the churches was primarily one of fellowship (*koinonia*) and charity (*agape*). The churches united by this bond came in the second century to be denoted comprehensively as the Catholic Church. The first appearance of the expression, indeed, does not bear this special sense: it comes in one of Ignatius's letters, in the sentence: "Where Jesus Christ is, there is the Catholic Church."[1] There is, however, an easy transition from Ignatius's use of the term to that which it acquired shortly afterwards. The fellowship might be that of an obscure little group of Christians in a remote and insignificant locality, but if Christ was there, there too was the Catholic Church; that little group was the Church Universal in its local manifestation.

Consultation might arise between the churches on a great variety of questions of faith or practice. The earliest consultation of this kind was the consultation in Jerusalem in A.D. 49 between delegates of the Antiochene church and the Jerusalem church on the terms for the admission of Gentiles to church fellowship.[2] A prominent subject for consultation in the second century was the date on which Easter should be observed year by year. There were

---

[1] Ignatius, *Epistle to the Smyrnæans* 8 : 2.   [2] Acts 15 (see pp. 106ff.).

two divergent practices in the second-century churches. In Asia Minor, for the most part, the churches (following, as they claimed, the example of John the Apostle) observed the Christian Passover on the fourteenth day of the month Nisan,[1] reckoning the anniversaries of the death and resurrection of Jesus according to the day of the month and not according to the day of the week. In many other churches, including the Roman church, it seemed more important to commemorate our Lord's resurrection on a Sunday, whatever the day of the month might be.

This divergence of practice was very inconvenient, in an age when Christians travelled about a great deal from one place to another, and about the end of the second century uniformity of practice was brought about. The practice that was ultimately standardized was that of the Roman church—very naturally so, since Rome was the capital and centre of the Empire, the place to which and from which all roads led. But the Quartodecimans (or "Fourteenthers"), as the adherents of the Asian practice were called, did not give up their practice lightly. Indeed, the confidence with which they maintained their case is a strong confirmation of the tradition that they relied in this matter on the authority of a great apostolic figure associated with their province.[2] One of those who claimed to have observed the Quartodeciman Passover in the company of John himself was Polycarp of Smyrna, who paid a visit to Rome when he was at least in his eighty-fifth year (A.D. 154) and discussed the matter with the Roman bishop Anicetus. They failed to agree, but that was not allowed to be a cause of strife; they parted good friends, after Anicetus, out of respect for his venerable fellow-bishop, had allowed him to celebrate the eucharist in his place.

Later in the same century, when the Roman bishop Victor tried to impose uniformity on the Asian churches by the threat of excommunication, this excess of authority was sharply rejected by the Asian bishops, led by Polycrates of Ephesus. And not only they, but Irenæus of Lyons too, while he himself (despite his Asian provenance) followed the Roman and more general practice, remonstrated warmly with Victor and pointed out that the divergence of usage in past decades had not been allowed to lead to a breach of fellowship. And thus, as Eusebius remarks, Irenæus (whose name means "peaceable") showed himself worthy of his name and succeeded in restoring peace.[3] Unity need not imply uniformity.

When such questions had to be discussed, it was natural that the bishops of the churches should consult together. But after consultation each bishop was free to act according to his own

---

[1] This was, of course, the prescribed date of the Jewish Passover. See p. 51.
[2] See pp. 275ff.   [3] Eusebius, *Hist. Eccl.*, V, 24 : 18.

discretion. An instance of this appears when Origen was ex-communicated (or at least deposed from the presbyterate) by the bishop of Alexandria in 231. The bishop, Demetrius, wrote to all the Christian world seeking ratification of his action, and secured the support of the bishop of Rome; but many of the eastern bishops refused to recognize the sentence of Demetrius, and Origen spent the last twenty-three years of his life as a venerated teacher and presbyter in Palestinian Cæsarea.

Further illustration of the independence of the individual church is afforded by the career of the Carthaginian bishop Cyprian. Cyprian maintained what we might call a very "high" doctrine of the bishop's authority and its uniquely priestly character. The episcopal authority, to Cyprian, was identical with apostolic authority. And as Peter was prince of the apostles, so the bishop of Rome, as Peter's successor, occupied a position of peculiar dignity among the bishops. "It was he who first made the Petrine primacy in relation to the Roman Church an integral element of a theory of the episcopate"[1]—possibly, as C. H. Turner suggests, since he became bishop only a few years after his conversion from paganism, he did not realize how recent was the Roman habit of deriving the succession of Roman bishops from Peter alone instead of (as formerly) from Peter and Paul. According to Cyprian, it was to enforce the lesson of unity that Christ conferred the "keys of the kingdom" on one man, Peter, first of all, although later He endowed all the apostles with "an equal share in dignity and authority alike."[2] But, in Cyprian's view, the bishop of Rome could no more dictate to the other bishops than Peter could dictate to the other apostles. No synod of bishops, even, had an authority to compel an individual bishop to act against his own discretion; still less could any individual bishop, even if he were the bishop of Rome himself, act as a bishop of bishops. In fact, Cyprian disagreed on a variety of matters with the Roman bishop Stephen, and especially on the validity of heretical baptism. Cyprian's view was that no baptism performed by heretics or schismatics could be recognized by the Catholic Church; Stephen, on the other hand, held that it could and should; and his view is that which has always prevailed in the Roman communion.

The circumstances of this dispute make Cyprian's point of view all the more significant. We have mentioned the divergent opinions that were held, after the Decian persecution in 251, with regard to the treatment of those weaker brethren who had denied their faith under stress of the terror, but had since repented. The

[1] C. H. Turner, *Catholic and Apostolic*, p. 228.
[2] Cyprian, *On the Unity of the Church*, 4. He refers to John 20 : 21ff. for the conferment of equal authority on all the apostles.

Novatian schism arose out of this divergence of opinion. When the bishop of Rome, in common with Cyprian and most of the other bishops, ruled that after severe penitential probation the lapsed might be restored to Christian communion, the rigorist party, led by the Roman presbyter Novatian, withdrew from his communion and formed a separatist community. Novatian was consecrated as their bishop, and the Novatians, as they were called after him, organized a widespread schism which extended from the vicinity of Rome and Carthage as far west as Spain and as far east as Asia Minor, and did not die out until about the sixth century. They did not call themselves Novatians, but *katharoi* or Puritans, insisting as they did on the supreme importance of a pure communion to which Christians who had fallen into grievous sin could not be readmitted. In doctrine they were strictly orthodox; Novatian himself, indeed, was one of the chief exponents of pure trinitarian theology in the third century.[1] But Cyprian maintained that, however orthodox their doctrine might be, however pure their communion, however correct the wording used at their baptismal ceremonies, the fact that they were out of communion with the Catholic Church made all these other points irrelevant if not meaningless. When the creed recited at a Novatian baptism expressed belief in "the holy church,"[2] that was obviously not the same church as that intended when the same creed was recited at a catholic baptism. And, Cyprian held, only within the Catholic Church was there salvation; only there were there true sacraments. There could be but one true bishop in a city, and the followers of another bishop, whatever body they might belong to, did not belong to the Catholic Church and were therefore excluded from valid sacraments and the salvation which they signified. "No one can have God for his Father who has not the Church for his mother." How then could catholic churchmen recognize schismatic baptism as valid, however formally impeccable in doctrine and practice these schismatics might otherwise appear to be? Stephen, however, insisted on the traditional usage of the Roman church, not to rebaptize returning heretics, and there is no saying to what extremities the dispute might have led. But Stephen died in 257; his successor, Xystus, and Cyprian were both martyred in the following year, and in the end it was the Roman practice that became the standard for the west.

Novatianism, however, was not the only puritan movement to present a challenge to the Catholic Church, and we must now turn our attention to another.

[1] Cf. F. J. Foakes-Jackson's description of them: "The Novatians appear to have been a small and respected party of Puritans, austere in life and not inferior to churchmen in learning. They may be said to bear an analogy with the Plymouth Brethren in England" (*A History of Church History* [1939], pp. 80f.).
[2] See p. 254f.

CHAPTER XXI

PROPHETS AND MONTANISTS

Two OUTSTANDING DEVIATIONS FROM THE CENTRAL STREAM of Christian life in the second century were the movements respectively called Gnosticism and Montanism. The Gnostics concentrated on the intellectual side of Christianity to an exaggerated degree; the Montanists concentrated excessively on what may be called its inspiritional side. The Gnostics will be treated more fully when we come to consider the progressive definition of Christian doctrine during these early centuries; here we may look at the rise and significance of the Montanists. Unlike the Gnostics, the Montanists for the most part did not depart from the apostolic foundation of the Church. To understand their movement we must review the part played by prophets in the early Church.

In apostolic days prophets were recognized figures in church life.[1] They appear in the Acts of the Apostles alongside the churches' teachers; the voice of the Spirit of God uttered through them was accepted as binding. In the Pauline letters, prophets are included in the ministries divinely bestowed upon the Christian communities, and given a place second only to apostles. "God has set in the church first apostles, secondly prophets."[2] The ascended Christ has sent these ministries as gifts to His people: "some to be apostles, some to be prophets, some to be evangelists and some to be pastors and teachers, to equip the saints for their work of service, that the body of Christ may be built up."[3]

In the *Didaché*, about the beginning of the second century, the prophets still occupy an honoured place, but the necessity is felt of making a careful distinction between true and false prophets. The tests proposed are eminently practical. In a previous chapter we have quoted the prescription which this treatise gives for the celebration of the eucharist. That prescription closes with these words:

> But permit the prophets to offer the (eucharistic) thanksgiving as much as they wish.[4]

Then it goes on:

> But concerning the apostles and prophets, you are to act thus,

[1] See p. 92.   [2] 1Corinthians 12 : 28.   [3] Ephesians 4 : 11f.   [4] *Didaché* 10 : 7.

according to the ordinances of the Gospel. Let every apostle, when he comes to you, be received as the Lord; but he shall not remain more than a single day, or (at the most) a second in addition; if he remains three days, he is a false prophet. And when he departs, let the apostle receive nothing but bread, until he finds shelter; but if he asks for money, he is a false prophet.[1]

These tests seem simple enough, but the matter is more complicated than one might think.

But you shall neither test nor judge any prophet who speaks in the Spirit, for every sin will be forgiven but this. Yet not every one who speaks in the Spirit is a prophet, unless he has the ways of the Lord. By their ways, then, the false prophet and the true are to be distinguished. And no prophet, when he orders a table in the Spirit, shall eat of it; otherwise he is a false prophet. And even if a prophet teaches the truth, he is a false prophet if he does not practise what he preaches. And if any prophet who is approved and found true does something as an acted parable with a typical meaning for the church, but does not teach you to do what he does himself, he must not be judged by you; the Lord is his judge, for the prophets of old did the same. If any one says in the Spirit, "Give me money"—or anything else—you are not to listen to him. But if he asks you to give it for others who are in need, let no one judge him.[2]

This seems rather confused, but the general idea is clear enough. A man who obviously trades on his alleged gift of prophecy must not be countenanced. Yet one must be careful in testing those who come as prophets, for to doubt a real prophet is to sin against the Holy Spirit by whose inspiration he speaks. And if a real prophet settles down in a Christian community, they may congratulate themselves. An ordinary Christian traveller should be prepared to earn his living by manual work while he stays with a group of his brethren in any place. But a prophet is worthy of his hire by virtue of his prophetic ministry.

Let everyone who comes in the Lord's name be made welcome; then, when you have tried him you will know him, for you will have understanding on the right hand and on the left. If it is a traveller who comes, give him as much assistance as you can. But he is not to stay with you more than two days or three, in case of necessity. But if he is a craftsman and wishes to settle among you, then let him earn and eat his own bread. If he has no handicraft, then see to it according to your wisdom that he lives a Christian life among you, but not in idleness. If he refuses to do this, he is making merchandise of Christ. Beware of such men.[3]

But every true prophet who wishes to settle among you is worthy of his maintenance. So also a true teacher, like the labourer, deserves

[1] *Didaché* 11 : 3-6. The terms "apostle" and "prophet" seem almost interchangeable here.
[2] *Didaché* 11 : 7-12.
[3] *Didaché* 12 : 1-5.

his maintenance. So you must take every firstfruit of the produce of your wine-vat and threshing-floor, of your oxen and sheep, and give it as a firstfruit to the prophets, for they are your chief priests. If you have no prophet, give it to the poor. If you bake bread, take the firstfruit and give it according to the commandment. Similarly, when you open a jar of wine or oil, take the firstfruit and give it to the prophets; take the firstfruit also of money, clothes, and every possession, as you see fit, and give it according to the commandment.[1]

Here the prophet is to be treated somewhat like the Levite in the book of Deuteronomy,[2] and the community which could persuade a prophet to settle down in its midst might well feel like Micah in the book of Judges, who said: "Now I know that the Lord will do me good, since I have a Levite for my priest."[3]

But a church could not wait on the off-chance of securing the services of a resident prophet; it must have a regular ministry, whether prophetic or not.

Appoint for yourselves therefore bishops and deacons (or superintendents and ministers) worthy of the Lord, men of meekness, not lovers of money, true and approved; for these also perform for you the service of prophets and teachers. So you must not despise them [even if they are not prophets], for they are your honourable men along with the prophets and teachers.[4]

The *Didaché*, in fact, tries to maintain the balance between the authority of local church leaders (the "bishops and deacons") and the authority exercised by those prophets who were not attached to any one local church, and over whom it was not easy to maintain effective control. In any local church there would always be some people who would find the ministry of a visiting prophet wonderfully inspiring by contrast with that of their own more humdrum elders, whom they could hear any Sunday. And if the prophet's injunctions ran counter to the teaching of the local elders, the authority and prestige of the local elders were liable to be undermined. It was easy for the prophets, who had no local responsibility, to tell people the ideal course to follow; but the local rulers had the responsibility of guiding the affairs of their flock and taking the consequences if anything went wrong. Hence it was necessary to make some sort of regulation for the control of prophetic activity, without doing it in such a way as to incur the charge of "quenching the Spirit."[5]

---

[1] *Didaché* 13 : 1–7.
[2] Deuteronomy 18 : 6ff.; 26 : 12ff. Another point of contact between this passage of the *Didaché* and Deuteronomy lies in the directions for testing prophets; in Deuteronomy a man is a false prophet (*a*) if his predictions do not come true (18 : 22); (*b*) if he seduces his hearers from their allegiance to the true God, even though his predictions do come true (13 : 1ff.).
[3] Judges 17 : 13.
[4] *Didaché* 15 : 1–2.
[5] Cf. 1 Thessalonians 5 : 19.

There is, in fact, an inevitable tension between the ordered forms of regular ministry and the more unpredictable and enthusiastic forms. It frequently happens that those who appreciate one form cannot abide the other. When a Salvationist (the story runs) attended divine service once in an Anglican church and heard an evangelical sermon much to his liking, he expressed his pleasure in his accustomed manner by shouting "Praise the Lord!"—only to be approached by the verger and tapped on the shoulder with the quiet admonition: "Excuse me, sir, but that isn't done in this church." More forthright was Bishop Butler's rebuke to John Wesley when the latter invaded the diocese of Bristol: "To pretend to extraordinary revelations from the Holy Ghost is a horrid thing, a very horrid thing." The local rulers are responsible to see that church life goes on "decently and in order," and therefore dislike the disturbances caused by the intrusion of wandering "apostles," especially of the corybantic type, who are here to-day and gone to-morrow. The prophetic visitor, on the other hand, criticizes the bishops' regulations as calculated to quench the Spirit. Either side has its supporters, and the tension may develop into schism, but for the grace of God.

It may very well have been under the influence of such enthusiasts that the trouble broke out in the church of Corinth about the year 95, when some of the presbyter-bishops were actually deposed, and the Roman church wrote by the hand of Clement to expostulate with the Corinthians for their unconstitutional action.

The insistence which Ignatius laid on the supremacy of the single bishop practically excluded the exercise of the prophetic gift. The *Didaché* might allow complete freedom for the prophet to celebrate the eucharist; but Ignatius insisted that its valid celebration be restricted to the bishop or his deputy. That Ignatius should lay down the law thus is the more remarkable, as his own character was strongly tinged with prophetic enthusiasm. But enthusiasm is not confined to the orthodox, and Ignatius was concerned above all for the preservation of orthodoxy. When a prophet is given liberty to deliver his unpremeditated utterances, there is no guarantee that they will not be heretical. A bishop, on the other hand, is the guardian of orthodoxy. The granting of such unrestricted liberty could not be risked. It was all very well for Ignatius himself to cry out "in the Spirit" once when he was visiting the church at Philadelphia, "Do nothing without the bishop!"[1]—but other prophetic utterances could not always be expected to chime in so admirably with Ignatius's settled policy. The effect of paying heed to this prophetic utterance of Ignatius was the restriction of such prophetic utterances in others.

[1] Ignatius, *Epistle to the Philadelphians* 7 : 2.

Something of the true prophetic genius appears about the same time in Hermas's *Shepherd*, and this may help to account for the great popularity of that work, by contrast with the more prosaic writings of other champions of the faith. Hermas, like the *Didaché*, lays down certain tests for prophets, and the very fact that he does so suggests that even in his time, in the early decades of the second century, prophetic utterance had not entirely died out in the Roman church. Hermas's chief test is thoroughly evangelical; a man inspired by the Spirit of God will give proof of that by his life and character. An ambitious, self-assertive, talkative or mercenary spirit betokens inspiration from a very different source.

> When the man who has the divine Spirit comes into a synagogue of righteous men, who have faith in the divine Spirit, and intercession is made to God by the synagogue of those men, then the angel of the prophetic Spirit, who is in contact with him, fills the man, and the man, filled with the Holy Spirit, speaks to the congregation as the Lord pleases.[1]

But the chief manifestation of prophetism in the post-apostolic age was the rise of the Montanist movement, which spread from its home in Phrygia to other parts of the Christian world.

Asia Minor had always been marked by enthusiastic forms of religion, especially in the cult of Cybele, the Great Mother of the Gods. It may therefore have been in part as the result of a local predisposition to this sort of thing that a new variety of Christian life and activity appeared about 156 in the upland parts of Phrygia, which laid particular stress on the prophetic element. The leader of the new movement, Montanus, from whom it derived its name, taught that, as the dispensation of the Father had given place to the dispensation of the Son when Christ came to earth, so now the dispensation of the Son had given place to the dispensation of the Spirit. For (he maintained) Christ's promise of the coming Paraclete had now been fulfilled, and he, Montanus, was the Paraclete's mouthpiece. The coming of the Paraclete was the immediate prelude to the second advent of Christ and the establishment of the New Jerusalem in one of the towns of Phrygia.

If we quote Hort's description of Montanism, we shall recognize manifestations which have recurred time and again in the history of Christianity when the new wine of a spiritual movement has proved too potent to be restrained within the old wineskins of a too rigid organization.

> Briefly, its characteristics were these; first, a strong faith in the Holy Spirit as the promised Paraclete, present as a heavenly power in the Church of the day; secondly, specially a belief that the Holy Spirit was manifesting Himself supernaturally at that day through

[1] Hermas, *Shepherd*, Mandate xi, 9.

entranced prophets and prophetesses; and thirdly, an inculcation of a specially stern and exacting standard of Christian morality and discipline on the strength of certain teachings of these prophets. An increase in the numbers and prosperity of the Church having brought an increase of laxity, it was not unnatural that attempts should be made to stem it by a rigorous system of prohibitions. To these three characteristics of Montanism may be added two others, fourthly, a tendency to set up prophets against bishops, the new episcopal organization being probably favourable to that large inclusiveness of Christian communion in which the Montanists saw only spiritual danger; and fifthly, an eager anticipation of the Lord's Second Coming as near at hand, and a consequent indifference to ordinary human affairs.[1]

The activity of prophetic women, despite precedents in Old and New Testament, has commonly been an embarrassment to settled church officials; they are even more difficult to control than prophetic men. Two women, Prisca and Maximilla, who left their family ties to follow Montanus and act as prophetesses of the new age, were said by the local bishops to be demon-possessed; but the bishops' attempts to exorcize them were frustrated. Among the new revelations which they communicated were some which imposed a strict discipline on their followers, in such matters, for example, as fasting and marriage. It appears that at first there was a tendency to renounce marriage altogether, but later the distinctive Montanist teaching on this subject took the form of a ban on second marriages, not only for ministers of the church but for the rank and file as well. One Montanist feature which combined enthusiasm with rigorism was their tendency to court martyrdom. Anything like the judicious withdrawal of Dionysius and Cyprian when the Decian persecution broke out was alien to the Montanist temper.

Many features of the movement proved attractive farther afield. The confessors in the persecution of Vienne and Lyons in 177 wrote admonishing their brethren in Asia Minor and the bishop of Rome as well not to quench the Spirit by taking too severe action against the Montanists. By the end of the second century the movement had reached the province of Africa, and there it made its most illustrious convert in Tertullian, the jurist-theologian of Carthage. A Dominican scholar once remarked to the writer, in the course of a conversation about Tertullian, that it was amazing that such an intelligent man as he should have been led away by a movement like Montanism. That is one point of view; but it might equally well be said that there must have been something of more solid worth in Montanism than is generally supposed, since it appealed to such an intelligent man as Tertullian. No doubt, when it spread to other lands, it lost some

[1] F. J. A. Hort, *The Ante-Nicene Fathers* (1895), pp. 100f.

of the more extravagant features that were specially characteristic of its Phrygian home. It was probably its stern puritanism that attracted Tertullian; indeed, he shows signs of Montanist influence in his writings for some years before he finally broke with the catholic communion and threw in his lot completely with the "men of the Spirit," as he called them. A Montanist group, called the Tertullianists, appears in North Africa as late as the fifth century. Montanism survived in its Phrygian home until the sixth century, when it was crushed by the Emperor Justinian (527–565).

One interesting by-product of the Montanist movement was the suspicion which it engendered in some people's minds against the Johannine literature of the New Testament, to which the Montanists so confidently appealed. Their doctrine of the second advent was based on a literal interpretation of the millennium mentioned in the book of Revelation,[1] and there were those who found it impossible to reject this Montanist doctrine without at the same time rejecting the book of Revelation. One of those who rejected the book was a Roman presbyter named Gaius, author of a *Dialogue* in which he maintained a debate with Proclus, leader of the Montanists in his day (*c*. 200). Apparently Gaius attributed the book to Cerinthus, a heretic who flourished about the end of the first century. But there is reason to believe that Gaius also rejected the apostolic authority of the Fourth Gospel, from which, of course, the Montanists drew their doctrine of the Paraclete. Our information on this point comes from two later Syriac writers, from whom we gather that Hippolytus defended the apostolic authorship both of the Fourth Gospel and of the book of Revelation in a treatise entitled *Heads against Gaius*. Gaius had no great following in his view of the Fourth Gospel, however; a small group of people who maintained a view similar to his, but (like him) were orthodox in all other respects, are referred to by a fourth-century writer as the *Alogoi*. (This was a convenient nickname because of its double meaning: primarily it meant the people who refused the doctrine of the *Logos* or Divine Word with which the Fourth Gospel opens, but it could also mean the people who are devoid of *logos* in its other sense of "reason.") A number of scholars of recent date have attached much more importance to these people than they deserve; we prefer the opinion of another scholar who says of the *Alogoi*: "I am inclined to think that the best name for them is Gaius and Co."[2]

---

[1] Revelation 20 :1–7.

[2] J. Chapman, *John the Presbyter and the Fourth Gospel* (1911), p. 53. On Gaius see pp. 144, 145, 274; cf. also my *The Epistles of John* (1970), pp. 22, n. 2; 23, n. 10.

CHAPTER XXII

THE NEW TESTAMENT WRITINGS

THE MAN WHO SAYS HE BELIEVES THAT JESUS ROSE FROM the dead because the Church says so, and the man who says he believes it because the New Testament says so, may not appear to see eye to eye on the final seat of authority in religion. But they might both very well express themselves in more concise language and discover that there is, after all, little material difference between them. The first man might say with truth that he believes in the resurrection of Jesus because there is a Church. The second man might say with equal truth that he believes it because there is a New Testament. For, if Jesus had not risen from the dead, there would in fact be no Church and there would in fact be no New Testament. The Church and the New Testament are the joint consequences of His resurrection. The New Testament did not make the Church; there was a Church before there was a New Testament. And "the Church assuredly did not make the New Testament; the two grew up together."[1] Yet when the New Testament came into being, the Church recognized in it her foundation-documents, the title-deeds of her existence and purpose.

It may be thought curious that, when the Christian Church broke loose from Judaism, she did not at the same time break lòose from the Jewish scriptures, the Old Testament. But the fact is, that the Christian Church did not consider the Old Testament to be distinctively Jewish literature. She regarded herself, rather than the Jewish people, as the true heir of the law and the prophets. For, as the Church believed, Christ was the one in whom both law and prophets found their proper fulfilment. And for this belief she had the highest authority. None other than her Lord represented Himself as fulfilling the Old Testament writings. Not only so, but He treated these writings Himself with the highest veneration. They constituted for Him the supreme court of appeal. On them He fed as His necessary food. When He declared in an hour of spiritual crisis that "man doth not live by bread alone, but by every word that proceedeth out of the mouth of God,"[2] He was voicing something that had proved itself true

---

[1] F. J. Foakes-Jackson, *A History of Church History*, p. 21.
[2] Matthew 4 : 4 (Luke 4 : 4), quoting Deuteronomy 8 : 3.

in His own experience, and voicing it in language drawn directly from the Old Testament. For it was the word of God enshrined in those ancient writings that was to Him the true bread of His life. The apostles could do no other than follow their Lord. As He claimed to fulfil the Old Testament writings, so they continued to maintain His claim. "To Him give all the prophets witness, that through His name everyone who believes in Him shall receive forgiveness of sins."[1] And in their writings the appeal is constantly and confidently made to those writings whose authority had been so unambiguously confirmed by their Lord. It is not always realized on what high authority the Church has accepted the Old Testament as holy scripture—an authority even higher, it might seem at first blush, than that on which she has equally accepted the New Testament.

If the Church received the Old Testament pre-eminently on the authority of Christ Himself, it was because His authority was paramount. Of this no Christian had any doubt. The words of Christ were binding upon His followers. Not only was He in the direct succession of those prophets of old time who came to the people of Israel as the spokesmen of God; He was the Messiah Himself, the Lord of the prophets, the Son of God, the Divine Word incarnate. And, since He had commissioned the apostles to be His delegates, to act and speak in His name, they too, when exercising their apostolic authority, shared the authority of the Lord who sent them. The Lord and His apostles, in fact, were invested in the eyes of most early Christians with supreme authority alongside the authority of the law and the prophets, the Lord's authority being direct and the apostles' indirect.

Now, throughout the first Christian century the apostles' witness was conveyed not only by word of mouth but also, on various occasions, in writing. The apostles could give oral teaching when they were present with those whom they taught; but when they were absent and the necessity arose, they could and did impart their teaching by letter. So, for example, when Paul heard at Ephesus of a state of affairs in the church of Corinth which demanded his immediate intervention, he sent his Corinthian converts the letter which we know as the First Epistle to the Corinthians; at a later date, in Corinth itself, when he proposed paying a visit to Rome and wished to prepare the Roman Christians for his arrival, he sent them an outline of the gospel as he understood it, in the document which we know as the Epistle to the Romans. By the sixties of the first century, then, there were several letters from Paul and some other apostles in the possession of various churches and individuals.

The necessity for having a written account of the story of

[1] Acts 10 : 43.

Jesus was not felt to be urgent in the days immediately following the withdrawal of His visible presence from His followers. So long as the personal eyewitnesses of His ministry and triumph were alive to tell the tale, that was satisfactory enough. But the time inevitably drew near, towards the end of the first thirty years from Pentecost, when in the natural course of events the eye-witnesses would no longer be available. The Roman Christians about that time invited Mark, Peter's companion and interpreter, to put on permanent record the account that Peter had so often given in his preaching of the works and passion of Christ. At a somewhat earlier time written collections of the sayings of Christ had begun to take shape. Other individuals and communities cherished their reminiscences, and these were at the disposal of those who wished to have them. So, some time after the appearance of Mark's record of the good news, we find Luke the physician, the travel-companion of Paul, tracing the course of Christian history accurately from the beginning, in accordance with the accounts that he received from eyewitnesses, and setting down an orderly narrative of Christian beginnings in the twofold history which we now know as the Gospel according to Luke and the Acts of the Apostles. Yet another gospel narrative appeared in the Syrian region, embodying some distinctive material which had been preserved in the Jewish-Christian communities of those parts, but laying strong emphasis on the Gentile mission. This is our Gospel according to Matthew. And, towards the end of the century, there appeared at Ephesus yet another account of the Gospel message—the work (according to a contemporary statement appended at the end of the account) of one who figures in the narrative itself as "the disciple whom Jesus loved." We take this figure to be John, the last survivor of the apostolic company, who committed thus to writing his reminiscences of and meditations on the life that was the light of men—"love's memory of Love incarnate," as Dr. Raven has so aptly called this fourth Gospel.[1]

But, so long as the various documents we have mentioned remained scattered, we can hardly speak of a New Testament in the proper sense of the term. No doubt all these documents were accepted as authoritative by those to whom they came. There was no doubt about the authority of the authentic records of the words and deeds of Jesus: these records were simply the apostolic preaching and teaching committed to writing, and they perpetuated in abiding form the unique authority of the Saviour Himself. When Paul wrote, as he did once to the church of Corinth, "If any one of you thinks he is a prophet or under the control of the Spirit, let him recognize that what I am writing to you is the

[1] C. E. Raven, *Jesus and the Gospel of Love* (1931), p. 227.

Lord's commandment,"[1] he expected his words to be taken literally. And in fact they were so taken; although there were some elements in the Corinthian church disinclined at the time to acknowledge Paul's authority, yet in the end they submitted to it. And the very fact that they preserved his correspondence probably indicates that they recognized its distinctive character as containing the instructions of a delegate of Christ. Yet this recognition of the authority of the separate documents is not the same thing as the general recognition of a *canon*, or authoritative list of sacred writings. The early Church did, of course, have such a canon already, in the Old Testament scriptures; but we are now considering the way in which the individual apostolic writings were brought together to form the companion volume which we call the New Testament.

Towards the end of the first century we have signs of a move to collect the literary remains of Paul. These literary remains consisted entirely of correspondence. What gave the impetus for this move we cannot be sure, but one attractive suggestion is that the Acts of the Apostles became more generally known towards the year 90. Probably Luke's twofold history was written in the sixties at Rome, not so much for the church of that or any other city, but for the intelligent reading-public, of which the "most excellent Theophilus," to whom the work was dedicated, was a representative. It has even been suggested that it was deposited as one of the "documents in the case" when Paul was about to appear before the supreme tribunal of the Empire in consequence of his appeal to Cæsar. But at a later date in the first century it began to circulate among the churches and immediately it rekindled a strong interest in the personality and activity of Paul. Church officers began to ransack their church archives for letters or fragments of letters written by Paul, and they wrote to other churches asking for copies of any Pauline correspondence that they might have; and so began the formation of a Pauline *corpus*.

We know, for example, that about the year 95 the cupboard somewhere in Rome which was the Vatican Library of that date contained not only Paul's letter to the Romans (as we should expect in any case) but also copies of his first letter to the Corinthians and (possibly) one or two others. It also contained copies of the Epistle to the Hebrews, which had a close association with Rome, of the First Epistle of Peter, which was written from Rome, and of some Gospel writings, not to mention the Greek version of the Old Testament commonly called the Septuagint. When Clement wrote on behalf of the Roman church in 95, expostulating with the Corinthian church for an outbreak of party spirit, he said:

[1] 1 Corinthians 14 : 37.

Take up the letter of the blessed apostle Paul. What was the first thing he wrote to you in the earliest days of your Christian life? To be sure, he gave you injunctions by inspiration with regard to himself and Cephas [Peter] and Apollos, because even at that time you had formed party-attachments.[1]

Plainly Clement had access to a copy of 1 Corinthians. It is thought, however, that he did not have access at that time to a copy of 2 Corinthians; because, if he had, there are places in his argument where he might have quoted it most aptly. This, of course, cannot be proved; as neither can the further suggestion that it was Clement's appeal to 1 Corinthians that made the church of Corinth search its records for further literary relics of Paul, with the result that they found two or three parts of letters of his which they fitted together to form the document which we now know as the Second Epistle to the Corinthians.

At any rate, the work of collecting Paul's letters was carried out faithfully, and about the end of the first century the churches in general appear to be acquainted not simply with one or two of his letters but with a collection of them, a *corpus Paulinum*, which in the earliest form in which we have certain knowledge of it contained ten of his letters, but was soon afterwards enlarged to include three more—the letters to Timothy and Titus, commonly called the Pastoral Epistles.

It was also about the end of the first century that another collection of Christian writings began to take shape and to circulate among the churches. This was the fourfold Gospel. Mark's Gospel was published at first in the church of Rome, Matthew's in the churches of Syria and Palestine, John's in the church of Ephesus. Luke's presumably had a more widespread circulation as soon as it was released for general publication. But from the second century onwards we find the Catholic Church using all four of these Gospels, and no other. By the time of Irenæus (180), the fourfold character of the Gospel canon had become for orthodox Christians one of the accepted facts of life, as axiomatic as the four cardinal points of the compass. Other individual Gospels might appear and have some currency here or there for a time, but (generally speaking) the four Gospels known to us were accepted to the exclusion of others from the early part of the second century. There is something, indeed, to be said for the view that the gathering together of the fourfold Gospel was accomplished in Ephesus as an almost immediate sequel to the publication of the Gospel according to John.[2]

We know that about 170 an Assyrian Christian named Tatian,

---

[1] 1 Clement 47 : 1–3.
[2] Cf. C. R. Gregory, *Canon and Text of the New Testament* (1907), p. 131; E. J. Goodspeed, *New Chapters in New Testament Study* (1937), pp. 39ff.

H

who had spent some years in Rome as a disciple of Justin Martyr, prepared the first known Harmony of the Gospels, a work usually known by its Greek title, the *Diatessaron*.[1] This was simply the first of very many attempts which have gone on ever since to weave the contents of the four canonical gospels together so as to form one continuous narrative. Some papyrus fragments published by the British Museum in 1935, evidently the remnant of a manual designed to teach people the Gospel story, written in the first half of the second century, equally appear to have been the work of someone who had the fourfold Gospel before him and knew it well.[2] The use which these and other writers made of the fourfold Gospel suggests that it had already become generally established as the uniquely authoritative record of the apostolic witness to Christ; the first appearance of the Gospel-collection, therefore, cannot be dated very much later than the beginning of the second century. It is quite probable, indeed, that when Ignatius of Antioch about 115 refers to "the Gospel" as an authoritative writing, he means by that expression the fourfold Gospel as we know it.[3]

Thus, in the early years of the second century, two Christian collections of authoritative documents were current. One was comprehensively called "The Gospel" (with sub-headings "According to Matthew," "According to Mark," and so on); the other, the Pauline *corpus*, was comprehensively called "The Apostle" (with sub-headings "To the Romans," "First to the Corinthians," and so on).

Now, when the fourfold Gospel-collection took shape, this meant that Part I of Luke's history of Christian origins (our third Gospel) was separated from Part II (our book of Acts). Part I was now incorporated in the fourfold Gospel; Part II had to fend for itself. Perhaps it was at this time that certain textual modifications were introduced at the end of Part I and the beginning of Part II; for example, the words "and He was carried up into heaven" were added in the second-last sentence of Part I, in order to round it off with a reference to the Ascension (which Luke originally narrated in Part II only), and the expression "He was taken up" was consequently added in the first sentence of Part II, referring back to the scope of Part I. But Part II was not neglected after its separation from Part I. In fact, it played a most important part in relating "The Gospel" and "The Apostle" to each other, so that these two did not circulate as entirely independent collections. Part II of Luke's history was related to "The Gospel" as its natural sequel (as well as being by the same author as one of

---

[1] See pp. 285f.
[2] *Fragments of an Unknown Gospel*, ed. H. I. Bell and T. C. Skeat.
Cf. A. Souter, *Text and Canon of the New Testament* (1912), p. 161.

the component parts of that collection), and it was related to "The Apostle" both because it provided the historical background against which that collection could be more readily understood, and because it presented in a convincing manner very real evidence for the validity of the apostolic claims which Paul made for himself in his letters. It brought the two collections together and thus performed a most important service in bringing about a unified New Testament, constituting in fact the pivotal book of the new canon.

The Church was already making progress in the recognition of an authoritative collection of Christian books, worthy to receive the same veneration as that accorded to the Old Testament, when just before the middle of the second century something happened to speed up that progress and give it greater precision than had marked it hitherto.

CHAPTER XXIII

MARCION AND AFTER

ABOUT THE YEAR 140 THE ROMAN CHURCH RECEIVED A VISIT from a man named Marcion, a native of Asia Minor, who had already engaged in doctrinal controversy with some of the church leaders of his native land. He presented his peculiar teaching to the presbyters at Rome, and when it proved utterly unacceptable to them, he seceded from their communion and formed a rival church of his own.

We shall have more to say about Marcion and his teaching later on;[1] suffice it to say here that he repudiated the authority of the Old Testament entirely, together with the authority of all the apostles of Jesus except Paul. The other apostles and their followers, he held, had corrupted the pure teaching of Jesus, by mixing it with their old Jewish beliefs. Actually, he believed, Jesus Himself, far from accepting the authority of the Old Testament, had come to liberate men from the bondage of the God of the Old Testament and reveal to them the superior God of goodness and mercy whom He called the Father. But this had been obscured in the Gospel records by Judaizing corruptions. The writings of Paul, the only apostle who had not apostatized from the pure teaching of Jesus, had also been tampered with by Judaizers, so that they required the discerning scrutiny of Marcion in order to be restored to their true text. Marcion actually produced a canon of holy scripture to supersede the Old Testament canon, which belonged to an order now abolished. This new canon consisted of two parts: one called "The Gospel" (a suitably "purified" edition of Luke's Gospel) and the other called "The Apostle" (a similarly "purified" edition of the first ten Pauline epistles).

The compilation of this canon was a challenge and incentive to the church of Rome and the other churches which held the same doctrine. If these churches denied that Marcion's canon was the true one, then let them show what the true one really was. In consequence, it is from the time of the anti-Marcionite reaction that we find the earliest explicit statements from the side of the Church Catholic defining the Christian canon. But this does not mean that Catholic churchmen did not already recognize a fairly

[1] See pp. 251f.

well-defined canon. In fact, some gnostic bodies were in substantial agreement with them on the limits of the New Testament
canon. Thus, on the testimony of Tertullian,[1] the gnostic leader
Valentinus, who was contemporary with Marcion, apparently
used the complete canon as accepted by the Catholic Church—
evidently a much wider canon than Marcion's. And Tertullian's
testimony is confirmed by the evidence of the recently discovered
Valentinian *Gospel of Truth*. "Round about 140–150 a collection
of writings was known at Rome and accepted as authoritative
which was virtually identical with our New Testament."[2]

In general, the Catholic reaction to Marcion took the form of
saying: We do not reject the Old Testament books; we accept
them because Christ fulfilled them and stamped them with His
authority. The divinely authoritative books of the new age do not
supersede the Old Testament, but stand alongside it. As for these
books, "The Gospel" which we acknowledge contains not only
one Gospel-writing, but four, including the true version of the
one which Marcion has published in a garbled form. "The
Apostle" which we acknowledge contains not ten only of Paul's
epistles, but thirteen; and not Paul's epistles only, but epistles of
other apostles as well. And, linking "The Gospel" and "The
Apostle" together, they laid special emphasis on the second
volume of Luke's history, which Marcion had not included in his
canon. For this document, while it presented (as we have seen)
irrefragable proofs of Paul's real apostleship, presented evidence
for the apostleship of the other apostles as well. Its pivotal function in the Christian canon was appreciated now as it could not
have been before, and that function was emphasized by its being
placed between "The Gospel" and "The Apostle." It was from
this time, too, no doubt, that it came to be called "The Acts of
the Apostles," or even, as one document exaggeratedly calls it in
its anti-Marcionite emphasis, "The Acts of All the Apostles."

The first known mention of the title "The Acts of the Apostles"
comes in a series of prefaces composed for the four Gospels as
part of the anti-Marcionite reaction. These are known as the
Anti-Marcionite Prologues to the Gospels, and their aim was to
establish the reasons for regarding all four as canonical. They
were originally written in Greek, early in the latter half of the
second century. That to Matthew's Gospel has disappeared;
those to Mark and John are extant only in Latin translations;
that to Luke survives in the original Greek text as well as in
Latin.

The Markan prologue is incomplete; what remains of it runs as
follows:

[1] *Prescription*, 38.
[2] W. C. van Unnik, in *The Jung Codex* (ed. F. L. Cross, 1955), p. 124.

So Mark asserted, Mark whom they called "stump-fingered" because his fingers were short in relation to his general bodily proportions. He was Peter's interpreter, and after Peter's departure he committed this Gospel to writing in the parts of Italy.

This account of Mark's Gospel is based on statements by Papias, bishop of Hierapolis in Phrygia in the earlier part of the second century, who compiled a work in five volumes entitled *An Exposition of the Dominical Oracles*.[1] But the information that Mark was called "stump-fingered" has not survived in the extant fragments of Papias.[2] That nickname may be accounted for exactly as the prologue represents; in more recent times the suggestion has been made that the ends of his fingers were sliced off when they got in the way of a sword in the garden of Gethsemane the night that Jesus was arrested there.[3] But possibly the epithet was originally attached not to the evangelist but to his Gospel, because the end of it seems to be mutilated;[4] the epithet in that case was a piece of tradition which the composer of the prologue did not fully understand.

Then comes a lengthy account of Luke:

Luke was a native of Syrian Antioch, a physician by profession, a disciple of the apostles. Later he accompanied Paul until the latter's martyrdom, serving the Lord without distraction, for he had neither wife nor children. He died in Bœotia [a district of Greece] at the age of eighty-four, full of the Holy Spirit. So then, after two Gospels had already been written—Matthew's in Judæa and Mark's in Italy —Luke wrote this Gospel in the region of Achaia, by inspiration of the Holy Spirit. At its outset, he indicated that other Gospels had been written before his own, but that the obligation lay upon him to set forth for the Gentile believers a complete account in the course of his narrative and to do so as accurately as possible. The object of this was that they might not be captivated on the one hand by a love for Jewish fables, nor on the other hand be deceived by heretical and vain imaginations and thus wander from the truth. So, right at the beginning, Luke has handed down to us the story of the birth of John [the Baptist], as a most essential [part of the Gospel-story]; for John marks the beginning of the Gospel, since he was our Lord's forerunner and associate both in the preparation for the Gospel and in the administration of baptism and the fellowship of the Spirit. This ministry [of John's] was foretold by one of the Twelve Prophets.[5] Later on, the same Luke wrote the Acts of the

---

[1] See pp. 274ff.
[2] It is found in Hippolytus, *Heresies*, VII, 18.
[3] See Mark 14 :51f.; cf. J. A. Robertson, *The Hidden Romance of the New Testament* (1920), p. 35. An earlier fancy is that he amputated his thumb to disqualify himself for priestly service!
[4] Our authorities do not carry the original text of Mark beyond 16 : 8 (verses 9–20 are from another source), but whether the Gospel originally ended at 16 : 8 or the end has been lost is disputed.
[5] That is, the "Minor" Prophets; the reference is to Malachi 3 : 1.

Apostles. Later still the apostle John wrote his Apocalypse in the island of Patmos, and then his Gospel in Asia.

The statement that Luke composed his Gospel in Achaia for Greek believers may simply be due to a desire to give the Greek Christians one of the synoptic Gospels, seeing that the other two had been allocated to those of Judæa and Italy respectively. The anti-Marcionite emphasis of this prologue is obvious when we reflect that Marcion cut out (among other things) the whole account of the birth and ministry of John the Baptist from his edition of Luke's Gospel, since that account linked the story of Jesus all too closely with the Old Testament order which Marcion repudiated. The reference to "The Acts of the Apostles"— the first recorded occurrence of this title—reminds us of Marcion's omission of this work from his canon and of the importance which the Catholic Church attached to its inclusion. As for the final reference to the apostle John, that is amplified in the anti-Marcionite prologue to John's Gospel, which in some ways is the most intriguing of all:

> The Gospel of John was published and given to the churches by John when he was still in the body, as Papias of Hierapolis, John's dear disciple, has related in his five exegetical books. He wrote down the Gospel accurately at John's dictation. But the heretic Marcion was rejected by John, after earning his disapproval for his contrary views. Marcion had carried writings or letters to him from the brethren in Pontus.

Now here is a whole nest of the most fascinating problems. The Latin text, in which alone this prologue has survived, is corrupt in more places than one; one of these corruptions we have tacitly emended in the phrase rendered "his five exegetical books." But there the source of the corruption is obvious and the emendation is equally so; the reference is to Papias's above-mentioned *Exposition of the Dominical Oracles* in five volumes. Was Papias a disciple of John, as the prologue says? Irenæus, who knew Papias's work in its complete form (as we do not), and used it, says he was; Eusebius has to admit it too, although he had no high opinion of Papias's intelligence and disliked his eschatological views. As Papias was contemporary with Polycarp, and lived *c.* 70–150, there is no chronological improbability in this statement, and we should probably accept it. Did Papias act as John's amanuensis? This is also quite possible, but it is more likely that the prologue here is based on a misreading of a statement of Papias, which actually said that "they" (i.e. John's circle of disciples) wrote down the Gospel at John's dictation, and not that Papias himself did so. But what of the reference to Marcion? Can he have been contemporary with John? Even if we distinguish two Johns at Ephesus around this time, John the apostle and John the elder, and suppose that the latter is intended in this prologue (which he almost certainly is not),[1] can Marcion's activity as a heretic be dated even in the lifetime of John the elder? It is unlikely. More probably this statement of the prologue is due to a further misreading of Papias, and we should infer that it was not John but Papias himself who ejected Marcion when the heresiarch arrived at Hierapolis from his native province of Pontus. (We are told elsewhere[2] that when Marcion asked Polycarp of Smyrna to recognize him, Polycarp retorted: "I recognize —the first-born of Satan!") We conclude that either the writer or one of the transcribers of our prologue was a somewhat unintelligent man, but it is much easier to see behind the mistakes of unintelligent men than to envisage the original form of a statement which has been "corrected" by an intelligent man to conform to what he believes to be the truth. Certainly, no efforts were spared to show how thoroughly Marcion and all his works had been repudiated by all reputable authorities!

Another product of the anti-Marcionite reaction, though not so outspokenly anti-Marcionite as these gospel prologues, is a list of New Testament books which probably represents the canon accepted at Rome towards the end of the second century. This list was discovered in 1740 by the antiquarian L. A. Muratori, and is consequently called the Muratorian canon. It is a Latin text, but the original composition was in Greek. It is mutilated at the beginning, but as the extant part starts off by calling Luke the third Gospel, it is not unduly rash to assume that Matthew and Mark were originally named as first and second. Here is a translation of the part that remains:

> . . . but he was present at (some of) them and has set them down thus. The third book of the Gospel, that according to Luke, was written in due order by Luke the physician in his own name after the ascension of Christ, when Paul had taken him along with him as a disciple and fellow-traveller: he himself never saw our Lord in the flesh. Luke, then, as far as he could trace the course of events, begins his narrative thus from the birth of John [the Baptist]. The fourth of the Gospels is by John, one of the disciples. When his fellow-disciples and bishops urged him, he said: "Fast along with me for three days, beginning to-day, and whatever shall be revealed to any one, let us relate it to each other." The same night it was revealed to Andrew, one of the apostles, that John should commit the whole story to writing and that they should all revise it. And so, even if the various books of the Gospel have had different beginnings handed down for them, yet these make no difference to the faith of believers, since by one controlling Spirit there is set forth in them all the whole

[1] The anti-Marcionite prologue to Luke explicitly identifies John the evangelist and John the apostle. See pp. 231, 275ff.
[2] Irenæus, *Against Heresies*, III, 3 : 4.

story of the [Lord's] birth, His passion, His resurrection, His conversation with the disciples, and His twofold advent—the first in
lowliness and without honour, His first coming; the second in
kingly power and glory, His coming again. What wonder, then, that
John in his epistles as well should lay such bold claim to the following experiences, one by one, saying of himself: "What we have seen
with our eyes and heard with our ears and our hands have handled,
this is what we write to you."[1] For in these words he not only
claims to be a spectator and hearer, but also a writer of all the
Lord's wondrous works in order.

Then the Acts of all the apostles were written in one book. Luke
tells the "most excellent Theophilus" that the various incidents took
place in his presence, and indeed he makes this quite clear by omitting the passion of Peter, as well as the journey of Paul when he set
out from Rome to Spain.

Now the epistles of Paul themselves tell their own story to those
who wish to know what they are and whence they were sent and
why. First of all to the Corinthians he forbids schisms and heresies,
then to the Galatians he forbids circumcision, but to the Romans he
wrote at greater length concerning the sequence of the scriptures,
pointing out in addition that Christ was their prime subject. It is
not necessary for us to examine the various details, since the blessed
apostle Paul himself, following the plan of John who was an apostle
before him, wrote by name to seven churches only, in the following
order: (1) to the Corinthians, (2) to the Ephesians, (3) to the Philippians, (4) to the Colossians, (5) to the Galatians, (6) to the Thessalonians, (7) to the Romans. (To the Corinthians and Thessalonians,
indeed, he wrote two apiece, if only by way of rebuke.) And yet the
Church dispersed throughout the world is recognized to be one. For
also John in his Apocalypse, even if he writes to seven churches, yet
speaks thereby to all the churches.

Besides, one epistle [of Paul] was written to Philemon, one to
Titus and two to Timothy, out of good will and friendship, for the
honour of the Church Catholic, for the arrangement of ecclesiastical
procedure. There is also an alleged epistle to the Laodiceans, and
one to the Alexandrines—both forged in Paul's name in conformity
with Marcion's heresy; and several others which cannot be admitted
into the Catholic Church, since it is not fitting that poison should
be mingled with honey.

An epistle of Jude and two by the aforementioned John are
included in the catholic list, and *Wisdom*, written by Solomon's
friends in his honour.[2] We receive only the Apocalypse of John and

---

[1] 1 John 1 : 1ff.

[2] It is surprising to find the book of Wisdom, from the Old Testament Apocrypha,
mentioned here; although, so far as its date goes, it belongs to the New Testament
period rather than the Old Testament period. Th. Zahn thought the original wording of the list at this point was: "the *Wisdom of Solomon*, written in his honour by
Philo" [the Jewish philosopher of Alexandria, *c.* 20 B.C.–A.D. 50]. The twelfth-
century commentator Hugh of St. Victor knew of some people who ascribed this
book to Philo. In our own day Mgr. R. A. Knox tells us that he has at times toyed
with the idea of writing a thesis to prove that it was written by Paul before his
conversion!

that of Peter, but some of our people refuse to have the latter read in church.

As for the *Shepherd*, that was composed recently, in our own times, in the city of Rome, by Hermas, while his brother Pius occupied the episcopal see of the city of Rome. And therefore it should be read, indeed, but it cannot be published to the people in church either along with the prophets, whose number is complete, or with the apostles of these last days. But the writings of the Arsinoite Valentinus and his associates we do not admit at all; they have also written a new book of psalms for Marcion along with Basilides and the Asian founder of the Phrygian sect.[1]

The miscellaneous information proffered in this list about the origin of individual books of the New Testament is almost entirely worthless; its statements about the writing of the Gospels, for instance, are much less deserving of consideration than those in the anti-Marcionite prologues. The value of this list is that it clearly indicates the books which were recognized as canonical in the Roman church towards the end of the second century—the four Gospels and Acts, the thirteen Pauline epistles, together with the epistle of Jude, two epistles of John (but possibly John's second and third epistles were reckoned together as one), and John's Apocalypse (our book of Revelation). But a second Apocalypse is included—that ascribed to Peter. We know this work; other Christian writers tell us that it was read in some churches, and its lurid pictures of the torments of the damned underlie much mediæval imagery on this subject, including that of Dante's *Inferno*. But it is surprising to find no mention of Peter's first epistle in a Roman canon. Zahn thought that the reference to the Apocalypse of Peter was really a corruption of a reference to Peter's two epistles; he suggested that the words italicized had fallen out, as follows: ". . . John's Apocalypse and Peter's *epistle. There is also another epistle of Peter,* which some of our people refuse to have read in church."[2] But here at any rate the text of the fragment needs no emendation (however much it may need elsewhere), and it is more likely that 1 Peter has been omitted by a scribal accident. The *Shepherd* of Hermas we have mentioned already;[3] its reading was recommended for purposes of devotion and edification, but it was not included among the properly canonical writings—those of the prophets and apostles. (There may be an implication, however, that if the list of prophetic writings had not been closed, the *Shepherd* would be better suited for inclusion in them than among the apostolic writings.) The Marcionite and Gnostic scriptures are banned altogether.

---

[1] On the Valentinian scriptures, see pp. 229, 249. The Phrygian sect is that of the Montanists.
[2] Th. Zahn, *Geschichte des neutestamentlichen Kanons*, II (1890), p. 142.
[3] See pp. 200f., 204, 218.

In short, we have the recognition of practically the same New Testament canon as our own. The omission of the Epistle to the Hebrews is noteworthy, especially as it was known to Clement of Rome nearly a century before; probably the Roman church still knew for a fact at the end of the second century that it was not the work of an apostle. James and 2 Peter are also missing.

Irenæus, whose writings are contemporary with the Muratorian list, presents the same picture. And Irenæus's evidence is the more important because of his world-wide contacts: he spent his earlier life in Asia Minor and his later life in Gaul, and was in close touch with Rome. In addition to his regarding the fourfold Gospel-canon as axiomatic (as we have already seen), he attests the canonical character of Acts, of all the Pauline epistles (except Philemon, which he had no occasion to mention), of 1 Peter, 1 John, and Revelation. He refers to the *Shepherd* of Hermas as "scripture," but does not include it in the list of apostolic writings.

Origen of Alexandria, and later of Cæsarea, writing about 230, lists these same books (including Philemon) as of undisputed canonicity, and adds that Hebrews, 2 Peter, 2 and 3 John, James and Jude, with the *Epistle of Barnabas*, Hermas's *Shepherd*, the *Didaché*, and the *Gospel according to the Hebrews* were disputed by some. (The *Epistle of Barnabas* was a tract written between 70 and 135 to prove that the Jews had mistaken the real import of the Old Testament ceremonial law when they interpreted it literally; the *Gospel according to the Hebrews* seems to have been a variant edition of Matthew's Gospel used by some Jewish-Christian groups.)[1] Plainly by Origen's time there was general agreement about the great majority of the New Testament books; there was a margin of doubt about a few, and of these some finally had their canonicity stabilized while others failed to win general acceptance.

At the beginning of the fourth century, Eusebius of Cæsarea mentions all the books of our New Testament as universally acknowledged in the churches, except five (James, Jude, 2 Peter, 2 and 3 John) which, while recognized by the majority, were disputed by some (probably the Syriac-speaking churches). Later in the fourth century we find our list of twenty-seven books enumerated by Athanasius in Alexandria (367) and by Jerome and Augustine in the west.

It should be clear by now that our New Testament of twenty-seven books does not represent the more or less arbitrary selection of some ecclesiastical synod or other, which sat round a table with a pile of Christian documents on it, and said: "Now, let us decide which of these are to be set apart as having divine authority." It was not until the twenty-seven books had been generally accepted by Christians throughout the known world that they

[1] See p. 280.

were first made the subject of a decree by an ecclesiastical council
—the North African Synod of Hippo[1] in 393 (whose findings
were confirmed at the Synod of Carthage four years later). And
when at last a church council gave a ruling on the matter, all that
it did was to ratify the general consensus of Christians, who (we
may well believe) had been guided in this respect by a wisdom
higher than their own.

Canonicity implies supreme authority in matters of faith. By
including a document in the canon, the early Christians meant
that it might be confidently appealed to in the establishment of
matters of doctrine, whether in debates within the Catholic
Church itself or in disputes with heretics. But they included these
writings in the canon because they already recognized their
authority; the writings did not acquire authority by being included in the canon. One of the chief criteria (though not the
only one) in recognizing the authority and canonical quality of a
work was apostolic authorship. So much was this so, that individuals or groups wishing to invest their own line of teaching
with special authority liked to set it forth in the form of a "Gospel," a book of "Acts," an "Epistle," or even an "Apocalypse,"
bearing the name of an apostle. Thus we have a work called the
Gospel of Peter setting forth Docetic views,[2] which was being read
in all innocence in a Syrian church about the end of the second
century, until the bishop of Antioch, Serapion, came to hear
about it and forbade its further use.

It is evident that several books were commonly read in church
without being formally canonized. After all, copies were not
available in large quantities, and if the book was for edification
the most convenient time to edify the faithful with it was at a
church meeting where they were all together. We may compare
what the Muratorian fragment says about Hermas's *Shepherd*.
Some of the most important manuscripts of the Greek Bible include at the end a few of those books suitable for church reading;
the Sinaitic Codex has the *Epistle of Barnabas* and part of the
Shepherd, and the Alexandrine Codex has the letter of Clement of
Rome and an ancient homily commonly but erroneously called
the Second Epistle of Clement.[3]

An influential heretical book of "Acts" was one called the *Acts
of John*, produced in the middle of the second century by a writer
named Leukios, which presents the apostle John as a Gnostic
teacher, and incidentally has a number of curious anecdotes about
him, and a most interesting Gnostic hymn in which Jesus accom-

---

[1] The church of which Augustine became bishop in 395 (see p. 334).
[2] See p. 245.
[3] Originally it also contained the collection of Jewish hymns from the first
century B.C. known as the *Psalms of Solomon*. See pp. 29f.

panies His followers, performing a solemn dance the while. This hymn (which has been set to music by Gustav Holst) contains the following perfectly orthodox quatrain, very much in the manner of the canonical Gospel of John:

> To you who gaze, a lamp am I;
> A mirror, to you who know;
> To you who knock, a door am I;
> The way, to you who go.

Another book of apocryphal "Acts" was not so much a heretical composition as a work of historical fiction, the *Acts of Paul*, composed by a presbyter of Asia who was taken to task for it by his less imaginative brethren, to whom "a novel was a lie." He pleaded that he had written it "for love of Paul," which was no doubt true, but he was deposed from the presbyter's office none the less. Fictional as the work is, it contains many interesting sidelights on Christianity in Asia Minor in the second century, and preserves a pen-portrait of Paul which, because of its unconventional vigour, has been thought to represent a good local tradition of the apostle's appearance.

Another problem with regard to the distinction between canonical and other literature arose in the last imperial persecution. As we have seen, during this persecution the Christians' sacred books were sought out for destruction. Now, it went without saying that, when the police arrived at a church and demanded that the scriptures should be handed over, this was something that a Christian must not do. A good Christian should defend the sacred writings with his life. But a church might well possess other books which were not part of their sacred scriptures —Hermas's *Shepherd*, for example, or a treatise on church order. The police would not be experts on the New Testament canon, and would probably go away satisfied with any Christian literature that was given to them. Might it not therefore be permissible to fob them off with something that was less than canonical and thus save the sacred books? One can envisage the arguments between the stricter and the more accommodating elements in the churches as this nice point of conscience was debated. Of course this question did not help to fix the canonical limits, as by this time (303) these limits were already determined to all intents and purposes. But the canonical limits perhaps became more generally known as a result of this new practical issue.

CHAPTER XXIV

THE EARLIEST CHRISTIAN CREED

The Baptismal Confession

IN THE EIGHTH CHAPTER OF THE ACTS OF THE APOSTLES THE story is told of an interview which Philip the evangelist had in the vicinity of Gaza with an Ethiopian official who was returning home from a pilgrim-visit to Jerusalem. The Ethiopian was beguiling the hours of travel by reading a scroll of the prophet Isaiah, and Philip explained the Isaianic prophecy of the obedient and suffering Servant to him so effectively in terms of its fulfilment by Jesus, that (as the narrative goes):

> As they went along the road, they came to a place where there was water, and the chamberlain said, See, here is water; what prevents me from being baptized? And he ordered his chariot to halt, and both of them went down into the water, Philip and the chamberlain, and he baptized him.[1]

So runs the original narrative. But readers of the English Authorized Version will remember that in it the story is amplified. When the Ethiopian asked to be baptized, says the Authorized Version:

> Philip said, If thou believest with all thine heart, thou mayest. And he answered and said, I believe that Jesus Christ is the Son of God.[2]

And not till then, according to this amplified form of the text, did Philip consent to baptize him. This longer reading, found in the bulk of our later manuscripts, is not part of the original narrative, to be sure, but it probably goes back to the earlier part of the second century and certainly reflects early Christian practice.

When a convert was formally admitted to the early Christian community by baptism, he made a public confession of his new faith, probably in response to a definite question.[3] When he had made this confession of Jesus as Lord, he was forthwith baptized "into the name of the Lord Jesus"[4] and henceforth was publicly known as a member of the Christian community.

[1] Acts 8 : 36–38 (cf. R.V. and R.S.V.).
[2] Acts 8 : 37 (A.V.).
[3] Acts 22 : 16; 1 Peter 3 : 21.
[4] Acts 8 : 16; 19 : 5; cf. also Acts 2 : 38; 10 : 48.

It is evident from the New Testament that the earliest Christian creed, or profession of belief, was one of few words: "Jesus is Lord." But the simplicity and brevity of the statement need not imply a "simple" Christology. When the earliest Christians gave Jesus the title "Lord," they used it as a divine title. The Greek word *kyrios* (which is translated thus) was used in the Septuagint, the pre-Christian Greek version of the Old Testament, as the rendering of Yahweh (Jehovah), the Hebrew name of the God of Israel; and more than once in the New Testament we find strict monotheists like Paul and Peter quoting Septuagint passages where the word *kyrios* is employed in this unique sense, and applying them to Jesus of Nazareth.[1]

If, again, the alternative title "Son of God" was used of Jesus, that also had a special significance. The words of Psalm 2 : 7, in which the God of Israel addresses His anointed one (His Messiah) with the words "Thou art my son," were applied to Jesus by the Heavenly Voice which addressed Him at His baptism.[2] But to Him the title "Son of God" was no merely official messianic designation; it expressed His own awareness of the unique filial relationship which He constantly enjoyed with His Father. This awareness finds supreme expression in the oracle of Matthew 11 : 27 and Luke 10 : 22:

> All is delivered to me from the Father,
> And none knows the Son but the Father;
> Nor does any know the Father but the Son,
> And he to whom the Son would reveal Him.[3]

This oracle, which is ascribed on critical grounds to a very early collection of sayings of Jesus, expresses a very high doctrine of the Person of Christ, and is sufficient proof that a high Christology is not a late development in the history of Christian doctrine. The resurrection and exaltation of Christ were regarded as a demonstration of this Divine Sonship,[4] confirming the truth of the baptismal allocution and of the claim to unique relationship with God which Jesus made for Himself. When the early Christians talked about Jesus being now enthroned at God's right hand, they knew as well as we do that the expression was not to be understood in any literal sense, but that it meant that Jesus, by His passion and triumph, has attained the position of predominant supremacy in the universe. "He ascended far above all the heavens, in order that He might pervade the whole universe": that is how Paul puts it.[5]

[1] Cf. Philippians 2 : 10 with Isaiah 45 : 23; 1 Peter 3 : 15 with Isaiah 8 : 13.
[2] See p. 37.
[3] See p. 80.
[4] Cf. Acts 2 : 36; Romans 1 : 4.
[5] Ephesians 4 : 10.

Christ crucified was, as Paul said, a stumbling-block to Jews. The claim that the crucified Jesus was the Lord's Anointed was so preposterous that it cried out for explanation; and the explanation given was couched in terms of the prophecy of the suffering Servant of Isaiah 53. In giving this explanation, of course, the early Christians were following Jesus Himself. When He said, "The Son of man did not come to be served but to be a servant, and to give His life a ransom for many,"[1] or again at the Last Supper, "This is my covenant-blood, which is shed for many,"[2] He was deliberately accepting this prophecy as the programme of His own messianic work. And in His acceptance of this prophecy as a true account of His own sacrifice, we have the basis of the whole doctrine of the atonement. This doctrine, however, was not much developed after apostolic times until the early Middle Ages. The Latins were more interested in it than the Greeks, although the Latins, from Tertullian onward, tended to treat it as a mainly legal transaction. The doctrine of the work of Christ was never formulated in an ecumenical creed, as the doctrine of His Person was. The Greeks were not so interested in the rationale of the atonement; indeed, some of their accounts of it (even in the works of such a master as Origen) show amazing crudity of thought and expression. A crucified Messiah may have been foolishness to the Greeks,[3] but once they accepted Jesus as a divine being, the fact that He suffered death at the instance of the Jewish hierarchy presented no such difficulty to them as it did to orthodox Jews. The Greeks were much more interested in the metaphysical problems of His Person.

The first Christians were Jews by birth and upbringing, or else they were Gentiles who had imbibed much of the Jewish belief in one living and true God. When Jesus was accepted as Messiah and Lord by people whose existing beliefs about God were based on the Old Testament revelation, a simple confession of faith in Jesus as "Lord" or "Son of God" at their baptism was enough to admit them to the Christian community. But the situation was different when the Gospel was carried to complete pagans. Not only had they to learn about Jesus as Saviour and Lord, but they must learn to begin with that God is one, and that He is the Creator and righteous Judge of all. Therefore, when they wished to receive baptism, they were required to give a more detailed

---

[1] Mark 10 : 45.

[2] Mark 14 : 24.

[3] A rudely scratched *graffito* on a wall on the Palatine Hill in Rome represents a young man doing reverence to a crucified figure with an ass's head; it is accompanied by an illiterate Greek inscription: "Alexamenos worships his god." On a more literary plane is Lucian's poking fun at the Christians for worshipping a "crucified sophist" (*Death of Peregrinus*, 13), though he elsewhere couples them with the Epicureans as being too wary to be taken in by religious quackery (*Alexander*, 25, 38).

confession of faith than believing Jews or God-fearers. This condition of affairs is provided for in the words of Jesus in Matthew 28 : 19, where He commissions His apostles to "make disciples of all the nations [not merely of Jews and God-fearers], baptizing them into the name of the Father and of the Son and of the Holy Spirit" [not simply into the name of the Lord Jesus]. This injunction to baptize converts into the Threefold Name is repeated, as we have seen, in the *Didaché* about the beginning of the second century.[1]

Thus the question addressed to the candidate for baptism was no longer simply "Do you believe in Jesus as Lord?" or "Do you believe in the Son of God?"[2] but something to this effect:

> Do you believe in God the Father?
> And in Jesus Christ, His only Son, our Lord?
> And in the Holy Spirit?

The answer would be, accordingly:

> I believe in God the Father;
> And in Jesus Christ, His only Son, our Lord;
> And in the Holy Spirit.

The catechumen was thus baptized into the Threefold Name which he confessed. And in this threefold confession we plainly have the skeleton of the later more developed credal affirmations; the skeleton is an affirmation of faith in the Triune God.

Now, all this is not the speculative theorizing of theologians; it is the expression of the threefold way in which Christians had received the divine revelation and experienced the divine grace. They knew God as Father, in His creative power and loving providence, for Jesus had taught them to know Him so. They had come to know God in Christ, in His redeeming and reconciling love, and the hymn of praise which (according to Pliny) they sang to Christ as God was their spontaneous response to this revelation. And they had also come to know the Holy Spirit of God as He manifested His unseen presence in their meetings and made His will known through prophetic utterances, and as He supplied the spiritual grace and sanctifying power in their personal lives which enabled them to live as Christians ought.

The question was how they were to formulate this threefold experience which they had of the one God—an experience which resulted from the threefold way in which the one God had revealed Himself. Paul, wishing to invoke the fullest divine blessing on his friends at Corinth, did so in words which have become a recognized benediction in the Church: "The grace of the Lord Jesus Christ, and the love of God, and the fellowship

[1] Cf. G. F. Moore, *Judaism*, I (1927), pp. 188f.
[2] Cf. John 9 : 35.

of the Holy Spirit be with you all."[1] But sooner or later someone was bound to ask what the precise relationship between these Three was. And what was the proper term by which any one of the Three was to be designated? Christians of Jewish antecedents were not so greatly troubled about such questions, but those with a Greek background and a consequent metaphysical turn of mind were intensely interested in just such questions as these.

The first element in this complex question concerned the precise relation of Christ, the Son of God, to the Father. And then, in what sense could one who was evidently a real man be also divine? The first two clauses in the threefold creed were therefore elaborated before the third clause. The doctrine of the Holy Spirit was not tackled until the doctrine of the Person of Christ was adequately formulated. And of the first two clauses the second was the one which was given the most elaborate expansion, in view of the special problems attending the definition of Christ's Person and His relation to the Father. Therefore, in those historic formularies which we commonly (if inaccurately) call the Apostles' Creed and the Nicene Creed, it is the clause "And (I believe) in Jesus Christ, His only Son, our Lord" that is chiefly elaborated. And, to be sure, this is as it should be, when we consider how central Christ is to Christianity. As John Newton put it:

> You cannot be right in the rest,
> Unless you think rightly of Him.

Hebrew and Greek Thought

Since the Christians who paid most attention to these questions in those days were Greeks by upbringing, it is necessary to say something about the difference between Hebrew and Greek thought, and to note some modifications which Greek modes of thinking and expression introduced into the original presentation of the Christian message.

The relation of Christ to God is conveyed in the New Testament by two principal terms: He is the *Son* of God; He is the *Word* of God. Both these terms have a definite Biblical (and therefore Hebraic) connotation, but when they were taken over by Greek thinkers in the Church and used in the definition of Christian doctrine they underwent a subtle change.

The word "son," in addition to its literal sense, has in Hebrew the sense of moral kinship. Thus Paul can assert that all who believe God as Abraham did are the true sons of Abraham, whether they are his physical descendants or not. We find the same idea in the words of Jesus, "Blessed are the peacemakers,

[1] 2 Corinthians 13 : 14 (13 : 13 in Greek).

for they shall be called sons of God"; that is to say, they will reproduce the character of God, who is the God of peace. True, when He spoke of Himself as the Son of God, He used the term in a unique sense, but the same general idea is there: the Son of God, as the Epistle to the Hebrews puts it, "reflects the glory of God and bears the very stamp of His nature."[1]

But the sense that Greek thinkers tended to give the word "son" when it was used in another than its literal sense was metaphysical rather than moral; to them it denoted derivation of being. In what sense, then, they would ask, did Jesus derive His being from God? And this question did not relate primarily to His coming into the world as a man, but to His eternal being, for the New Testament writers had already asserted that He existed before His incarnation—that He was, in fact, the one through whom God had created the universe.

Or take the other term "word." In Hebrew thought "the word of God" is a way of denoting the divine activity; to say that Christ is the Word of God is to say that in Him God is uniquely and self-revealingly active, whether in creation or in redemption. But the Greek word by which this concept was rendered, the word *logos*, had already been current in Greek circles in a somewhat different sense, to denote the divine principle of reason or order immanent in the universe. The Hebrew and Greek ideas, though distinct, had a sufficient superficial similarity to make the transition from one to the other easy. So, when a Christian like Justin Martyr, brought up in the Greek philosophical schools, read the opening words of St. John's gospel, "In the beginning was the *logos*," the sense in which he understood them was not exactly that which the evangelist intended. Justin thought at once of *logos* in the sense of "reason" and concluded that the *logos* which became incarnate in Christ was the *logos* which had governed the thought and action of men like Socrates and Heraclitus and the Stoics. These men, because they lived in conformity with reason (Greek *meta logou*, "with [the] *logos*"), were really, if unconsciously, guided by the pre-incarnate Christ; they might therefore be quite properly regarded as Christians before Christ came, in much the same way as the holy men of Israel in Old Testament times.[2]

H. G. Wells introduced one of his novels, *The Soul of a Bishop*, with a drawing-room scene where a bishop is suddenly asked the question: "Why, Bishop, was the Spermaticos Logos[3] identified with the Second and not the Third Person of the Trinity?" The answer, of course, is not the indiscreet one which the bishop gave

---

[1] Hebrews 1 : 3 (R.S.V.).

[2] Justin, *Apology*, I, 5, 46; II, 8.

[3] The *spermatikoi logoi* (plural) of the Stoics were the "germinal principles" or laws of generation contained in matter.

("Ah, that indeed *is* the unfortunate aspect of the whole affair"),
but simply that in the Fourth Gospel the term *logos* had already
been used of Christ and not of the Holy Spirit, although not in
the sense which it had in Greek philosophy. The term did indeed
form a bridge between Hebrew and Greek thought, but the fact
that the term was common to both vocabularies concealed the
fact that its sense was not exactly the same in both. And nothing
can be more misleading than when two parties use the same term
in differing senses (as when the nations on either side of the "iron
curtain" use terms like "peace" and "democracy" and mean quite
different things by them).

There were other features of Greek thought which exercised an
influence on the formulation of Christian belief at this time.
There was, for example, the widespread idea (actually oriental in
origin) that matter was inherently evil while spirit was inherently
pure, so that God was remote from the material world and could
not come into direct relation with it. When this idea was allowed
to bulk too largely in the thinking of Christians, it led to an inevitable modifying of the doctrines of creation and incarnation.
In the Hebrew-Christian scheme, the material creation as it came
from its Maker was very good, and no ultimate obstacle in the
nature of things made it impossible for the Divine Word to
become flesh. But in this other view the supreme God could not
come so closely into contact with the world as to be its Creator,
and an intermediary being was therefore brought in to take over
this function, one commonly called the demiurge or "architect."

A further corollary of this view of matter was that the body
was regarded as the prison-house of the soul. This idea came into
Greek thought from the Asiatic body of ideas called Orphism, but
through the schools of Pythagoras and Plato it exercised a profound influence on Greek thinking, and entered largely into
Christian thought. The measure of its influence may be appreciated if we consider how current Christian ideas of immortality
bear a closer resemblance to Platonism than to the Biblical doctrine of resurrection. In Biblical thought the body—whether it
be the natural body of the present life or the spiritual body of the
resurrection life—is more essential to wholeness of being than is
often realized.

CHAPTER XXV

EARLY CHRISTIAN HERESIES

Docetism

BEFORE THE END OF THE FIRST CENTURY THE EFFECTS OF the belief that matter was inherently evil manifested themselves in Christian thinking, especially in some quarters of Asia Minor. The Johannine writings of the New Testament make several allusions to a school of thought which denied that the Son of God really became a man and died. The fourth Gospel aims at putting this school out of court as emphatically as possible; for example, in the uncompromising affirmation that the Divine Word *"became flesh"*[1]—not simply *assumed* a bodily form. And just as the incarnation of the Divine Word was real, says John, so also was His death. When he describes the piercing of Jesus' side on the cross by a soldier's lance, he says: "And immediately blood and water came out. It is one who actually saw this for himself who has testified to it—his testimony is true, and God above knows that he is speaking the truth—in order that you also [my readers] may believe."[2]

John's emphatic language here is due to the fact that he is opposing a doctrine called Docetism (from the Greek verb *dokein*, which means "to seem"), which taught that the incarnation of Christ was not real but only an appearance. One Docetic school (represented by Cerinthus, a contemporary of John) held that the Christ-spirit came upon the man Jesus at the baptism and left Him again at the crucifixion. This, according to the Docetic *Gospel of Peter*,[3] was the cause of Jesus' cry of dereliction, which it renders in the form: "My power, my power, why hast thou forsaken me?" Another variety of Docetism represented Jesus' humanity as being of a completely phantom nature, so that those who crucified Him were deceived; an alternative suggestion was that it was really Simon of Cyrene who was crucified, while Jesus looked on from a place of safety.[4]

The reason why John in his first two epistles similarly de-

---

[1] John 1 : 14.
[2] John 19 : 34f.
[3] See p. 236.
[4] One or other of these ideas seems to lie behind the statement in the Koran (4 : 157) that the Jews "did not kill him nor did they crucify him, but it was made ambiguous (or a semblance) to them."

nounces as deadly error the view that "Jesus Christ has not come
in the flesh"[1] is his realization that this view is destructive of
everything that is distinctively Christian. This is the reason, too,
why he insists in his first epistle that Jesus "came by water and
blood—not by the water only, but by the water *and* the blood";[2]
that is to say, Jesus was manifested as Messiah and Son of God
not at His baptism only, but on the cross as well; the one who
died was as truly the Incarnate Word as the one who was baptized.

A decade or so after John wrote, Ignatius of Antioch makes the
same point in his letter to the Smyrnæan church, where he quotes
Jesus as saying (in words taken from a writing now lost): "I am
not a bodiless spirit."[3]

Another idea, closely allied to Docetism, was calculated to safeguard the doctrine that God has no passions or emotions, that He
is (to use a technical term) impassible. This properly means that
God always takes the initiative, that He always acts and is not
subjected to or conditioned by the activity of others. This is what
is meant in the first of the Thirty-nine Articles when it says that
God is "without body, parts, *or passions*." But the docetism or
near-docetism of those early centuries added to this Biblical
emphasis the Greek conception of God as being without emotions and incapable of feeling in any such sense as we do. This
conception is far removed from the Biblical revelation of God;
the God of the Bible is dynamic enough, but He is by no means
devoid of feelings!

Gnosticism

Then, the lands of the eastern Mediterranean were fascinated at
that time by a conception of the universe which had very much
assumed the dimensions of a "New Learning." This conception
of the universe is roughly what we call the Ptolemaic theory,
although in its main features it is much older than the second-
century astronomer and geographer after whom we so call it. It
envisaged the earth as a sphere surrounded by a number of other
spheres—hollow, crystal-clear and crystal-hard—in each of which
one of the planetary bodies moved. Beyond these was the sphere
of the fixed stars, and beyond these . . . ? Each of the planetary
bodies, moreover, was a spirit-ruler, governing his particular
sphere.

All this, of course, is to us outmoded nonsense, pre-Copernican,
the fallacious premises from which the conclusions of astrology

---

[1] 1 John 4 : 2f. (cf. 2 : 22f.); 2 John 7.
[2] 1 John 5 : 6.
[3] Ignatius, *Letter to Smyrnæans* 3 : 2, quoting possibly from a work called *The Teaching of Peter*; cf. Luke 24 : 39.

are drawn. True, but at one time it represented a great advance on an earlier and more naïve outlook which thought of the earth as the floor of a tent, the tent itself being the vault of the sky, the tent-roof spangled with heavenly luminaries.

Now, this new learning was embodied by many in a theological system which regarded the lords of the planetary spheres as intermediaries between the supreme God (whose dwelling lay beyond the outer sphere of the fixed stars) and men upon the earth. This system also was admirably adapted to the belief that the supreme God could have no direct contact with this earth; if He used the lords of the planetary spheres as His intermediaries, that was a means of avoiding such contact.

The general name given to the new learning was *gnosis*. This is simply the Greek word for "knowledge," but it tended to be used in a superior sense, much in the way that more recently the Latin word for "knowledge," *scientia* or science, has come to be spelt with a capital letter and used almost personally as the subject of sentences. "Science tells us" that such and such is the case; that was very much the way in which people in those days spoke of *gnosis*. When Christianity made headway in the Greek world, it soon came into collision with *gnosis*, or with the possessors of *gnosis*, who were known as Gnostics (the people who possess real knowledge). The result was an attempt to restate Christianity in terms of *gnosis*, to fit it into the current cosmology. And henceforth it is this restatement of Christianity that we shall have in mind when we speak of Gnosticism. The proponents of this Gnosticism allowed that the ordinary orthodox Christianity was good enough for the rank and file, but for the intellectual *élite*, the Gnostics, a higher and truer account was available.

Gnostics and Docetics shared many basic presuppositions. But the distinctive feature of the Gnostics was the emphasis that they laid on Christianity as *gnosis*, a way of knowledge, and on this *gnosis* as a means of salvation. The Christian *gnosis* was expounded in a bewildering variety of forms, but in general it identified Jesus with the divine being who, according to much Gnostic teaching, descended into this lower world of ours to release the divine element that had become imprisoned in flesh, and to lead it back to its true home. The Biblical fall of man became transmuted in Gnosticism into the fall of the divine element into the material realm—a fall which was perpetuated by the ordinary propagation of the race, because that meant that more and more particles of the divine element were imprisoned in more and more bodies of flesh. The lower material realm was the workmanship of the demiurge, not of the supreme God, and this demiurge was commonly identified in Gnosticism with the God of Israel.

Like Docetism, the attempt to restate Christianity in terms of the current cosmological speculation also manifests itself as early as New Testament times, and again in Asia Minor. For it is plain from the letter which Paul wrote about A.D. 60 to the church at Colossæ in the Lycus valley that a kind of incipient Gnosticism had affected the thinking of some of its members. Paul in that letter attacks the belief that the divine fullness—the *pleroma*, to use the Greek term—was distributed throughout a hierarchy of planetary and other mediators intervening between the supreme God and the world of men. No, he says, the fullness of deity is absolutely embodied in Christ, and in Him alone can you attain perfection. Besides, by His passion and triumph Christ has inflicted an irremediable defeat on those cosmic rulers to whom you are disposed to pay some meed of divine homage. An appreciation of what Christianity really means, he insists, will show how inadequate and unnecessary this new theosophy is.

But the new theosophy was very attractive, and throughout the second century it made considerable headway among the more intellectual Christians of the Græco-Roman world. While it was pre-Christian in origin, deriving elements from Jewish as well as from pagan thought, and absorbing a good deal of sheer magic in the process, it developed a variety of definitely Christianized forms. The surviving documents of Christianized Gnosticism have a bewildering nightmare character in our twentieth-century eyes, but (to quote F. C. Burkitt)

> A very slight acquaintance with our Gnostic writings is enough to show that they all have the same general aim, and that is to present the role of Jesus in a new way. The presentations are most diverse, and some of them are to our taste childish, but in the opinion of their authors they were something satisfactory, more satisfactory than the common account. In other words, they are not developments of Religion in general, but explanations of the particular mystery presented by Christianity.[1]

One of the chief schools of Gnosticism was that called after Valentinus, whose system was embodied in a myth which told of the fall and deliverance of Sophia, Divine Wisdom, in terms of the characteristic Gnostic cosmology. One of Valentinus's pupils, Heracleon, has the distinction of being the first known commentator on the fourth Gospel. (The confidence with which this Gospel was invoked by Gnostics and their orthodox opponents alike indicates that its authority was already so widely recognized that neither side could hope to refute the other's arguments by repudiating it.) Basilides, another Gnostic who quotes this Gospel (*c.* 130), developed a Gnostic system for which he claimed apostolic authority, representing himself as a pupil of one Glaucias, an alleged disciple of Peter.

[1] *Church and Gnosis* (1932), p. 40.

Most of the Gnostic writings which have come down to us consist of translations into the Coptic language of Egypt. One of these, entitled *Pistis Sophia* ("Faith Wisdom"), tells how Jesus continued to teach His principal disciples for twelve years after His resurrection, and professes to record the last revelation which He gave them before He withdrew for the last time to the upper realm of light.

The Coptic manuscript of *Pistis Sophia* was acquired towards the end of the eighteenth century. But the greatest find of Gnostic works was made in 1945, when thirteen papyrus codices were discovered, buried in a jar, at Nag Hammadi, about sixty miles north of Luxor. These codices contain some forty-eight Gnostic treatises, mostly translated from Greek into a Coptic dialect. Many of them were already known by name. One has now been edited and published[1]—that is the *Gospel of Truth*, which belonged to the school of Valentinus, and may well have been written by Valentinus himself, towards the middle of the second century.

But whatever forms this Christianized Gnosticism took, the attempt to explain the central mystery of Christianity by the mythologizing of a cosmological philosophy, drawn from such various sources, too often succeeded only in obscuring or losing the central truth of Christianity.

In its practical consequences for daily life, Gnosticism was usually associated with a strict asceticism. This tendency appears as early as the incipient Gnosticism attacked in the Epistle to the Colossians, where the tendency of this teaching is summarized in the words, "Touch not, taste not, handle not."[2] There is some evidence, indeed, for a Gnosticism which drew directly opposite corollaries from the doctrine of the inherent worthlessness of matter; the body, it was argued, is material and therefore morally indifferent, and its desires may be indulged at will without any harmful consequences to the true life of the spirit. But this outlook was not characteristic of the main Gnostic schools.

The various Gnostic schools are usually reckoned among the earliest Christian heresies. This word, heresy, is derived from the Greek word *hairesis*, which properly means "choice." From that it came to mean the party or school of a man's choice. In the New Testament, for example, this word is used of the parties of the Pharisees and the Sadducees, and also of the party of the Nazarenes.[3] But before the end of the New Testament period the word begins to take on its distinctively Christian sense, of a line of thought or practice which deviates from the main stream of

---

[1] *Evangelium Veritatis*, edited and translated by M. Malinine, H. C. Puech and G. Quispel (Zürich, 1956).
[2] Colossians 2 : 21.
[3] Acts 5 : 17; 15 : 5; 24 : 5, 14; 26 : 5; 28 : 22.

Christianity. The Gnostics were therefore called heretics, because they were out of the main stream of Christianity in the second century. If they replied that that did not necessarily mean that they were wrong, the opposing party argued that the main stream was that which stemmed directly from the apostles, who as the accredited delegates of Christ could be trusted to know what Christ's own teaching was. The churches which had been founded by these apostles and were ruled by men in the direct line of succession from those whom the apostles had appointed as bishops —these were the churches in which the purest Christian teaching might be sought, and their teaching might safely be taken as representing the norm. If anyone doubted this, it was open to them to compare the current teaching of these churches with the apostolic writings themselves, which were available as the rule of faith, the standard by which all Christian teaching might be judged. This argument was specially insisted on by Irenæus. Irenæus has left as his chief work a treatise in five books *Against Heresies*. Other opponents of Gnosticism were Irenæus's contemporary Clement of Alexandria, and, in the following generation, Hippolytus of Rome. It was, in fact, these writers' attacks on Gnosticism that formed our main sources of information about the various Gnostic schools, until the discovery within recent years of large collections of Gnostic writings in Egypt.

The influence of Gnosticism on the Church was partly good and partly bad. It was good in so far as it stimulated intellectual activity in the Church and made the orthodox leaders, like the writers already mentioned, present reasoned statements of their faith. Clement of Alexandria went so far as to present what he called the true Christian *gnosis* by contrast with the false; one might be an orthodox Gnostic, he held, by contrast with the heretical Gnostics. Clement's teaching profoundly influenced the catechetical school of Alexandria, the Church's first theological college; and whereas Clement's writings present his teaching in unsystematized form, the head of the school in the next generation, Origen, has (in addition to his many other writings) left us in his treatise *On First Principles* the first Christian attempt at a systematic theology.[1]

The influence of Gnosticism was less desirable, however, in that it led to the excessive intellectualizing of Christian faith. Faith henceforth comes to denote intellectual orthodoxy rather than personal commitment to Christ. Intellectual orthodoxy is good, of course, if it be not blindly accepted from tradition but

---

[1] This work is extant only in fragments so far as the Greek original is concerned; it is available in its entirety in the Latin translation by the fourth-century writer Rufinus, but Rufinus unfortunately thought it his duty to improve Origen's orthodoxy in accordance with the accepted standards of the fourth century. See pp. 259f.

reached intelligently from first principles; but it is no substitute for love to Christ and life in Christ.

Marcionism

One of the most important figures in the history of second-century Christian thought was deeply influenced by Docetic and Gnostic ideas, but the doctrines which he taught were so distinctive that the school of thought which he founded is called Marcionism, after his own name, Marcion. We have already had something to say about Marcion's importance for the history of the New Testament canon,[1] but we must also consider his relevance for the subject we are now discussing.

In his insistence on the evil character of the material order, in his consequent asceticism and refusal of marriage for himself and his followers, in his doctrine of a demiurge who made the world (since the supreme God could obviously not incur the contamination which must attach to such contact with matter), Marcion had much in common with the Docetics and Gnostics. The distinctive feature of his teaching, however, was his profound reverence for Paul. He was, as has been said, the only man in the post-apostolic age who understood Paul—and even he misunderstood him! In particular, he interpreted Paul's teaching about the supersession of the Law by the Gospel to mean that the Old Testament had no authority for Christians. And this was a further line of cleavage between Marcion and the Church. For the Church in general, as we have seen, took the Old Testament over from Israel as Holy Scripture, on the authority of Jesus and His apostles. The Christian retention of the Old Testament, indeed, is not only justified by Christ's own example, but also by the fact that Christianity grows integrally out of Israel; and it preserved in the Church that historical outlook which prevented Christianity from becoming just another mystery religion—the kind of mythology of which the Emperor Julian could say: "These things never happened, and yet they are eternally true."

How Marcion's "theological anti-Semitism" appears in the formation of his canon and the editing of its contents we have already seen. His Docetism comes out in the opening words of his Gospel. Luke's nativity narratives are left out, together with all mention of John the Baptist and of the genealogy of Jesus given in Luke 3 : 23–38. By combining Luke 3 : 1 with 4 : 31 Marcion's Gospel plunges *in medias res* thus: "In the fifteenth year of Tiberius Cæsar, Jesus came down to Capernaum" (down from heaven, his readers must suppose).

But it was not mainly in the Docetic interest that Marcion's

[1] See pp. 228ff. above.

editorial work was done. Everything which seemed to acknowledge the authority of the Old Testament must go. For Marcion
was the first man, so far as we know, to elaborate the notion that
the God of the Old Testament and the God of the New Testament are two distinct deities. The severely righteous God of the
Old Testament, the Creator or Demiurge of the world, the
Jehovah of Israel, has a real existence, but He is different from
and inferior to the good and kind Redeemer-God of the New
Testament, the God whom Jesus knew and revealed as Father.
Plainly so, Marcion thought, for why otherwise should the worshippers of the righteous God have procured the death of the
Revealer of the good God? And he enlarged on the differences
between the two in a work called the *Antitheses*, which appears
to have had an authority almost as high as Marcion's New Testament canon in the eyes of his followers.

Marcionism, in spite of the fact that its ascetic principles and
prohibition of marriage meant that it could not perpetuate itself
by the ordinary means of family life, did show a surprising vitality
and endured as a sort of rival Church for many generations. The
basic principle of Marcionism, the repudiation of the Old Testament and the God of the Old Testament, has of course manifested
itself time and again in the course of Christian history. But the
chief importance of Marcionism in the second century lies in the
reaction which it provoked among the leaders of the apostolic
churches. Just as Marcion's canon stimulated the more precise
defining of the New Testament canon by the Catholic Church,
not to supersede but to supplement the canon of the Old Testament; so, more generally, Marcion's teaching led the Catholic
Church to define its faith more carefully, in terms calculated to
exclude a Marcionite interpretation.

CHAPTER XXVI

DEFINING THE FAITH

THE CHURCH'S REACTION TO MARCION'S TEACHING MAY BE seen, among other things, in the new way in which the threefold baptismal creed was formulated. Marcion and his followers might say, "I believe in God the Father," meaning the God whom Jesus proclaimed as Father; but they could not add "Maker of heaven and earth," as we do, for that is an explicit identification of the God of the New Testament with the God of the Old Testament, and such an identification Marcion rejected with all his might. It was very probably, therefore, in order to exclude Marcion's doctrine that such a phrase as this was added to the first clause of the baptismal creed. Irenæus, for example, about the year 180, states the Church's belief in these terms:

> [The Church believes] in one God, the Father Almighty, Maker of heaven and earth, and the sea, and all things that are in them;
> And in one Christ Jesus, the Son of God, who became incarnate for our salvation;
> And in the Holy Spirit, who proclaimed by the prophets the (divine) dispensations and the coming of Christ, His birth from a virgin, His passion, His rising from the dead, and the bodily ascension into heaven of our beloved Lord Jesus Christ, and His manifestation from heaven in the glory of the Father to sum up all things in one and to raise up again all flesh of the whole human race. . . .[1]

Here it is made plain that the God and Father of our Lord Jesus Christ is also the Creator of the world, and that the Christian dispensation is vitally related to that which went before, since it was proclaimed by the Holy Spirit through the Old Testament prophets. Such a threefold confession of faith was in general use among the churches; it was variously amplified by them, but always in much the same sense.

The *Apostolic Tradition*, usually ascribed to Hippolytus nowadays, contains a baptismal liturgy in which an ancient interrogative form of the creed is preserved. The catechumen is baptized three times, each time after giving an affirmative answer to one of the three parts of the interrogative creed. The threefold interrogation runs thus:

[1] *Against Heresies*, I, 10 : 1.

Do you believe in God, the Father Almighty?

Do you believe in Christ Jesus, the Son of God, who was born of the Virgin Mary by the operation of the Holy Spirit, was crucified under Pontius Pilate, died and was buried, rose again the third day, alive from among the dead, ascended into heaven, and sat down at the right hand of the Father, from whence He shall come to judge the living and the dead?

Do you believe in the Holy Spirit, and in the holy Church, and in the resurrection of the flesh?

The formulary which we commonly call the Apostles' Creed appears to have developed from the early baptismal confession used in the Roman church. It may properly be called the Apostles' Creed in the sense that its statements are based on apostolic authority, but there is no substance in the tradition once widely held that the apostles had anything to do with its composition. In its earliest extant form this Roman creed ran as follows:

I believe in God (the Father) Almighty;

And in Jesus Christ, His only Son, our Lord, who was born of the Holy Spirit and the Virgin Mary, who was crucified under Pontius Pilate and was buried, and the third day rose from the dead, who ascended into heaven, and sits on the right hand of the Father, whence He is coming to judge the living and the dead;

And in the Holy Spirit, the holy Church, the forgiveness of sins, the resurrection of the flesh (and the life everlasting).

We see that these credal affirmations expand the second clause more than the first and third; the simple statement of faith in Jesus Christ as Son of God is, in fact, amplified to a summary of the early apostolic witness concerning Him. And this was wise; it was good that people should know exactly who this Person was whom they acknowledged as Lord, and what was implied by their so acknowledging Him. Besides, Christian doctrine rests on historic facts, and should never be divorced from them. "Councils, we admit, and Creeds, cannot go behind, but must wholly rest upon the history of our Lord Jesus Christ."[1]

But even when the churches variously amplified their baptismal creeds in such a way as to exclude Marcion's teaching and other varieties of Docetism and Gnosticism, much remained to be defined in regard to the threefold revelation of God to which their creeds bore witness. What was the exact nature of this threefold revelation? Did its threefold character belong only to the circumstances of the revelation, or did it also belong to the Divine Essence so revealed? What was the relation of the Father and the Son and the Holy Spirit to each other? More particularly (at this earlier stage), what was the precise relation of the Son to the Father? And, later, what was the relation of Christ's divine Sonship (a

[1] R. C. Moberly, in *Lux Mundi* (1890), p. 243.

truth of revelation which found a response in Christian experience) to His manhood (which was a patent fact of history)?

An explanation of the threefold revelation of God which commended itself to many thinkers in the third century is that which is summed up under the general description of Monarchianism. This explanation was particularly aimed at excluding the idea that Christians worshipped more Gods than one. It might appear at first blush that they did, for they acknowledged the God of Israel, and at the same time paid divine honours to Jesus of Nazareth. The Monarchians of various kinds maintained that the Son and the Holy Spirit were but emanations from God the Father, or else that they were different forms in which the Father chose to manifest Himself from time to time.

One of these Monarchian schools goes by the name of Dynamism, from the Greek word *dynamis*, "power" or "faculty." Christ, said the thinkers of this school, was a faculty of God, or (otherwise expressed) an emanation of deity, like a stream flowing from a fountain or rays from the sun. The outstanding proponent of Dynamism was Paul of Samosata, bishop of Antioch,[1] who is, incidentally, noteworthy as being the first man to use the Greek adjective *homoousios* ("of the same substance") to denote the Son's relation to the Father in the Godhead. The Son, that is to say, was "of the same substance" as the Father in the way in which a stream is "of the same substance" as the fountain from which it flows. It is remarkable that this very adjective, used by Paul of Samosata in a sense judged to be heretical, later became the hallmark of orthodoxy when used in a rather different sense by Athanasius in his struggle against the Arian heresy.

Dynamism was commonly coupled with the view called "Adoptionism," according to which the man Jesus was promoted to be Son of God as a reward for His perfect obedience to God— whether this promotion took place at His baptism or after His death and resurrection. This doctrine has found classic expression in English literature in words which Milton puts into the mouth of the Divine Father:

> This perfect Man, by merit call'd my Son.[2]

Actually, it is an older doctrine than Dynamism; it was held, for example, by some people of Jewish race known to Justin Martyr, who accepted Jesus as the Messiah while regarding Him as "a man born from men";[3] these are probably to be identified with the Jewish Christian groups called Ebionites, whose views of Christ's relation to the Father were generally of this Adoptionist character.

---

[1] See p. 184.
[2] *Paradise Regained*, I, 166.
[3] *Dialogue with Trypho*, 48. See pp. 277ff.

There is, however, another Monarchian school which has proved more attractive from one generation to another than Dynamism. This school is called Sabellianism, after Sabellius, its most distinguished proponent. According to this school, Father and Son and Holy Spirit are simply descriptions given to three *rôles* filled by the one God, three *modes* of His self-manifestation. For this reason the Sabellian doctrine is also known as Modalism. The trinitarian language of the creed, that is to say, referred only to the way in which God had revealed Himself, but bore no relation to His inner being.

Another name given to the Sabellians was "Patripassians," from Latin *pater* ("father") and *passio* ("suffering"), because their practical identification of the Father and the Son led to the conclusion that the Father suffered on the cross. Patripassianism was denounced as a heresy in the third century, but more recent times have seen its revival in a new form among some of the more popular writers and preachers who speak of the Father as suffering in the Son. Leading exponents of this way of thinking at the beginning of the third century were Noetus and Praxeas, the latter of whom, according to Tertullian, "drove out prophecy and brought in heresy, expelled the Paraclete and crucified the Father."[1] The charge of driving out prophecy and expelling the Paraclete (the Holy Spirit) has reference to Praxeas's opposition to Montanism. It has been suggested that Praxeas, of whom we hear nothing outside Tertullian's treatise *Against Praxeas*, was actually a nickname (meaning something like "busybody") for some well-known figure in the Church, possibly Callistus, who became bishop of Rome a few years later.[2] But this is quite doubtful.

The publication of these Monarchian views was beneficial in that it stimulated a closer consideration of the whole subject and an attempt to state the doctrine of God in terms which did more justice to the Biblical revelation, Christian experience, and historical fact. It was realized that even Sabellius's doctrine, while less unsatisfactory than some other forms of Monarchianism, was quite inadequate to accommodate the Christian doctrine of the Incarnation, nor did it agree well with the New Testament language which described the Father as sending the Son, the Father and the Son as sending the Holy Spirit, the Son as obeying the Father and praying to Him, and so forth.

Tertullian played a notable part in this debate, using his powerful gifts of advocacy in the defence and exposition of the Biblical faith and in the refutation of the inadequate formulations of

---

[1] *Against Praxeas*, 1.
[2] Cf. E. Evans, *Tertullian's Treatise Against Praxeas* (1948), p. 10; he refers to P. de Labriolle as author of this suggestion.

Monarchianism. Hippolytus also brought his learning into play in defence of the same cause, and launched an attack upon the Roman bishops, Zephyrinus (202–217) and Callistus (217–222), for what he regarded as their guilty complicity in the spread of the heresy of Sabellius (although Callistus ultimately excommunicated Sabellius himself). But Tertullian's importance in this matter is the greater in that he provided the terms which since his time have been regarded as the orthodox expression of the doctrine of the Godhead in western Christendom; it is to him that we owe the word "Trinity" (Latin *trinitas*), and also the definition of the Godhead as being "one substance (Latin *substantia*) in three persons (Latin *personæ*)."

In the legal circles in which Tertullian had been trained the Latin word *persona* (which had previously meant a part played by someone on the stage) denoted one who played a part or performed a particular function in society. Tertullian adapted this word to a theological setting and spoke of three *personæ* in the Godhead. The term was readily intelligible at the time. It has survived in our theological vocabulary to the present day, but since in ordinary parlance the word "person" has come to mean much more than the Latin *persona* ever did, its theological use is misleading to people who have had no theological training. When people hear of three persons in the Godhead, they naturally tend to think of three personalities in such a way as to give colour to the charge that trinitarianism is actually tritheism, a belief in three distinct Gods.

As a matter of fact, of course, Christianity starts off with as firm a belief in one God as Judaism. That God is one is axiomatic in the New Testament, in the teaching of Christ and His apostles. Whatever further statements Christians may make about the being of God, the absolutely basic statement is that He is one. If they proceed to make further statements about the being of this one God, about the nature of His unity, these do not affect the basic fact. Christians can join with Jews in reciting *ex animo* that article in the Creed of Maimonides which affirms "that the Creator, blessed be His name, is a unity, and that there is no unity in any manner like unto His, and that He alone is our God, who was, and is, and will be." But the unity of God is not necessarily a monolithic unity. And we must insist again that, when these early Christian thinkers undertook to find words which might give adequate expression to their belief about God, they were not philosophizing idly, or deliberately trying to make the Christian faith difficult; they were endeavouring to do justice to the data of revelation and experience. God had revealed Himself, and they had experienced Him, as Father and Son and Holy Spirit. When they spoke of Jesus as the Son of God, they did not simply mean that

God had waited until He found a man of such character that He could make Himself known through him—which is what Adoptionism implies. No, the love of God had done more than this; God had taken the initiative and sent His Son, sent Him as one who was altogether man, none the less. Nor did the data of revelation and experience allow them to be content with the Sabellian view that Father and Son and Holy Spirit were no more than aspects which God assumed and laid down alternately. On the other hand, any tendency to regard Father and Son and Holy Spirit as three Gods was ruled out by the fundamental principle that there is but one God.

Our conception of God must fall far short of His real being, and our language about Him must fall short of our conception. But the terms that Tertullian employed commended themselves as much less inadequate than those of the schools which he opposed. Tertullian's terms did justice to the facts of revelation and experience, and yet they did not err in either of the extremes—modalism or tritheism. There were three "persons," he said (using that word in something like the legal sense which it bore at that time), but only one "substance." And here again we have a word which has changed its meaning in general use. When philosophers speak of "substance," they still mean by it something like what Tertullian meant; but when physical scientists use it, they mean something quite different, and it is this latter sense in which the word is commonly understood now, with an inseparable connotation of materiality. (The same occasion of misunderstanding attaches to the mediæval term "transubstantiation," but that is outside our present province.) In the sense in which the Latin word *substantia* was used by Tertullian, it was the equivalent of the Greek word *ousia*, which means the "essence" or "being" of anything. To Tertullian and other third-century theologians, God is one Being, eternally existing in the threefold relationship of Father and Son and Holy Spirit; each of these Three is "the one God, thinking, willing and acting, in one of His three eternal spheres of thought, volition and activity . . .the indivisible Godhead subsisting and operating in one of the essential relations of His Tripersonal Life."[1]

Tertullian's discussions of this subject, in which he takes to task the earlier expressions of Modalism and formulates a more satisfactory statement of the true Christian belief, are scattered throughout a number of his works. But so penetrating and masterly was his treatment, that later writers on the subject followed the main line of his arguments to a very considerable degree. Some decades later, the conclusions of Tertullian's discussians were brought together and set out in logical sequence by Novatian of Rome, who published a work *On the Trinity* which

[1] H. B. Swete, *The Holy Spirit in the Ancient Church* (1912), p. 376.

is the first extant treatise dealing explicitly with this subject, as well as the first extant Latin work produced by a member of the Roman church. (Up to the time of Hippolytus, Roman Christians wrote in Greek.) Novatian dealt not only with the relation between the Father and the Son, round which the debate with the Modalists had chiefly centred, but went on to give a brief but independent exposition of the doctrine of the Holy Spirit.

Where Latin theologians spoke of God as existing in one *substantia*, Greek theologians, using the corresponding Greek term, spoke of Him as existing in one *ousia*. But they did not use the Greek term that corresponds most closely to the Latin *persona*. That Greek term is *prosōpon*, which literally means "face" and was also used of a part played in a drama. But Greek theologians avoided the use of this term to denote the Persons in the Godhead, perhaps because it lent itself too readily to a modalist interpretation (and in fact it was used in this way by later Sabellians). The word which ultimately prevailed in Greek as most adequately denoting each of the Three Persons was *hypostasis*—a word which theologians still use at times as a technical term to avoid the present-day ambiguity of referring to the *Persons* of the Godhead. But what needs to be remembered and emphasized again and again is this: these terms were devised to give formal expression to something real—the threefold revelation of the Divine Being as Christians had experienced it. The problem was (and still is) to find words which give adequate and unambiguous expression to this reality.

But greater still than Tertullian and Novatian was the Alexandrian theologian Origen, the greatest scholar and thinker of the Church in the first three centuries. He too grappled with the doctrine of the Triune Godhead. Thoroughly trained in Greek philosophy as well as in the Scriptures, he was the first Christian thinker (as we have seen) to produce a carefully constructed system of theology, his main work in this field being his treatise *On First Principles*.[1] It was not Origen's fault if his theology was in certain points judged heretical in the light of standards of orthodoxy formulated at a later time. The main fault which subsequent thinkers found with his system was that in his reaction to Monarchianism he went too far towards the other extreme. He envisaged the Father and the Son and the Holy Spirit as occupying a hierarchical relation in the unity of the Godhead, the Son being subordinate to the Father and the Spirit to the Son. He goes so far, indeed, as to call the Son a creature, though only in the sense that His being is derived from the Father's and subject to His will. He was far from accepting the view later maintained by Arius, that the Son was created in time; on the contrary, it

[1] See p. 250.

was Origen who first formulated the doctrine of the eternal generation of the Son, which has found a secure place for itself in catholic theology. (Other distinctive features of Origen's thought have been left on one side, such as his belief in the pre-existence of human souls, his identification of original sin with sin committed in a pre-existent state, and his hope for the ultimate reconciliation of all rational creatures—not only men, but demons, and the devil himself.)

The third century, however, saw no finality in the debate on the doctrine of God; a full and detailed statement which would conserve all the values of the Biblical revelation of the Son's relation to the Father was not attained until the great Christological controversy of the early fourth century made a settlement imperative.

CHAPTER XXVII

THE JEWS AFTER A.D. 70

Reconstituted Judaism

WHEN THE CITY AND TEMPLE OF JERUSALEM FELL IN A.D. 70, the religious life of Israel demanded a thorough reorganization if it was to survive. So long as men could remember, the temple and the priesthood had been the centre of the national life. Now both were swept away. Providentially, however, it was not necessary to improvise a new foundation for the life of the people. The new foundation was already there. An alternative organization had been growing up quietly for several generations, and was now ready to occupy the central place formerly taken by the temple order—an order which had in any case outlived its usefulness.

This alternative organization was the synagogue. The synagogue, as a meeting-place where members of Jewish communities might come together for the reading and exposition of the law and for common prayer, may have had its beginnings as early as the years of the Babylonian exile; and its original intention possibly was to provide the Jews of the dispersion with a partial substitute for the temple worship. But by the first century A.D., as is abundantly clear from the New Testament, the synagogue was as important an institution in Palestine itself, and even in Jerusalem, as it was in the lands outside. The synagogue was the means through which the rabbis or acknowledged teachers of the law exercised their deep influence on the people, and most of these rabbis belonged to the party of the Pharisees. And it was precisely this party, because of its relative detachment from the temple order, that proved its capacity to survive the catastrophe and reorganize the life of Israel.

With the suppression of the revolt of A.D. 66–70, the Zealots, who had formed its spearhead, were crushed. The Essenes, with their quietist outlook, exercised little or no influence on public life. The Sadducees, who had supported the interests of the chief priestly families, disappeared as a party with the end of the old order. But the Pharisees were in a position to grasp the opportunity to replace that order by a new one which fitted the changed situation.

One result of all this is that Judaism after A.D. 70 presents much more of the appearance of a one-party state than it did before that date. We must constantly bear in mind that the Judaism of the period with which the New Testament mostly deals was a much more variegated religion than it later became. For this reason, it is always precarious to make dogmatic inferences from Jewish literature of the period after A.D. 70 with regard to the era preceding that date, and to conclude that, where the New Testament and the Mishnah disagree, the New Testament must be wrong. The Mishnah, in the main, reflects the period after A.D. 70; the New Testament, in the main, reflects the period before that year and is, in fact, one of our basic sources of information about Judaism in the first six or seven decades of the first century.

The survival of the Jewish polity after the destruction of Jerusalem was due in large measure to Yohanan the son of Zakkai, who amid the disaster received Roman permission to set up a school of rabbinical study at Jamnia in western Palestine. Here the Sanhedrin was reconstituted on a purely spiritual basis. The old Sanhedrin, consisting of the chief priests and elders of the people, had come to an end. The new Sanhedrin, established at Jamnia, consisted, like the old one, of seventy-one members, but these elders were all doctors of the law, and their president was regularly one of the most distinguished rabbis of the day. As time went on, and people became accustomed to this new Sanhedrin, there arose a tendency to suppose that the Sanhedrin had always had a leading rabbi as president; and later rabbinical literature represents rabbis like Hillel and Gamaliel the Elder as acting in this capacity. It is clear, however, from the New Testament and the writings of Josephus, that this is simply a projection back into these earlier times of the state of affairs that obtained later.[1]

The main function of the new Sanhedrin was to act as a supreme court for the organization of religious law. By its constitution a preliminary step was taken towards the codifying of the "Tradition of the Elders," as the long accumulation of oral law is called in the Gospels. The area of disagreement among the rabbis in their interpretation of the law was no longer so extensive as it had been when the schools of Shammai and Hillel were at the height of their rivalry. The school of Hillel had now established its supremacy; and here is a further point that must be borne in mind when we are told that the Gospel picture of the rabbis is inconsistent with the picture given in the rabbinical sources, for the Pharisaism attacked by Jesus seems to have been largely Shammaite Pharisaism.

A further step forward was taken at the beginning of the second century when Rabbi Akiba began to arrange the codified tradition

1 See pp. 53f.

according to subject-matter. After his death in 135, his work was carried on and revised by his disciple Rabbi Meir. The work of codification was completed about the end of the second century by Rabbi Judah, President of the Sanhedrin, and when it was completed it was reduced to writing. Previously it had been preserved and transmitted by word of mouth alone. It is this work, first committed to writing about the year 200, that we know by the name of the Mishnah. Primarily it is a code of religious jurisprudence.[1]

Jews and Christians in Palestine

What was the relation between Christian and non-Christian Jews in Palestine and the neighbouring territories in the years following A.D. 70? This is a fascinating question which requires more intensive research than it has hitherto received.[2] Some, at any rate, of the members of the Jerusalem church who had taken refuge in Transjordan in A.D. 66 returned to Palestine after the war, and continued to regard themselves as the church of Jerusalem. Simeon the son of Clopas appears to have been their acknowledged leader for a long time after the Jewish War, as James the brother of Jesus had been for the two decades preceding A.D. 61. Simeon is said to have suffered a martyr's death at a very advanced age about the year 107, in Trajan's reign; and from that time to 135 Eusebius (following a list compiled a century or more before his own time) enumerates thirteen further leaders of the Church of Jerusalem. Eusebius, in accordance with the custom of his own day, calls them bishops; but in their Jewish Christian community they would certainly have been called elders. Eusebius also regards them as consecutive, and infers that they must have been unusually short-lived; but we may conclude either that they were really colleagues (members of a Nazarene Sanhedrin), the oldest survivor of whom was regularly promoted to be president, or else (less probably) that they were contemporary leaders of a number of decentralized groups of the scattered Church of Jerusalem.

There is ample evidence in the rabbinical writings and else-

[1] A good elementary introduction to this whole subject is *The Earlier Rabbinic Tradition*, by my friend and former pupil R. A. Stewart (I.V.F., 1949, 47 pp.). This completed Mishnah itself became an object of study and exposition, and a body of commentary grew up around it in the rabbinical schools of Palestine and Babylonia. These commentaries or Gemaras formed a supplement to the Mishnah, and Mishnah plus Gemara equals Talmud. The Palestinian Talmud, consisting of the Mishnah plus the accumulated Gemara of the Palestinian schools, reached its present form in the fourth century; the larger and more authoritative Babylonian Talmud continued to grow after that time and was finally completed and reduced to writing about the year 500.

[2] See, for example, M. Simon, *Verus Israel* (Paris, 1948), and H. J. Schoeps, *Theologie und Geschichte des Judenchristentums* (Tübingen, 1949).

where of the energy with which these Nazarenes and their fellow-Jews engaged in theological debate. The destruction of the temple must have provided the Nazarenes with a powerful apologetic. They could refer to the prediction of Jesus—now so literally fulfilled—that one stone would not be left standing upon another of that magnificent building. They could appeal to the disappearance of the priestly order as proof that they had been right in recognizing Jesus as the Messiah, divinely commissioned to inaugurate the new order. And they freely invoked the prophetic scriptures, which both sides alike accepted as supremely authoritative, in support of their arguments.

We may be certain that some of these Jewish Christians of Palestine are included among the *minim* or heretics mentioned in the rabbinical tradition. This tradition contains several reminiscences of the debates which went on between the orthodox leaders of Judaism and these *minim*. The *minim*, we gather, were much given to arguing their case from the Old Testament Scriptures and doing so very cogently. It may have been partly in consequence of this that the rabbis about this time set themselves seriously to consider the canonicity, text and interpretation of their sacred writings.

The limits of the Old Testament canon, or list of divinely authoritative books, had been fixed for all practical purposes before the close of the pre-Christian era, but in the discussions of the learned schools the question was now reopened. Some participants took advantage of the reopening of the question to suggest the addition of other writings, such as the book of Ecclesiasticus (*alias* the Wisdom of Jesus the son of Sira, a sage in Israel who flourished about 200 B.C.), and even of works called *gilyonim*, in which we must recognize some sort of Gospel composition. These *gilyonim* were not the canonical Gospels which we are familiar with, but documents in Hebrew or Aramaic, probably bearing some kind of relation to our Gospel of Matthew or to a work later in vogue among Jewish Christians and known as the *Gospel according to the Hebrews*.[1] The upshot of all these discussions, however, was the definite fixing of the same canonical limits as had previously enjoyed general recognition. If no book hitherto recognized was ousted from the canon (although some were subjected to strict scrutiny), it is also true that no book was now admitted which had not been part of the canon before. Least of all was there any chance of recognizing the Nazarene documents: "the Gospels and the books of the *minim*," it was laid down, "are not sacred scripture." Some of the leading rabbis, like Yohanan and Meir, made unfriendly puns on the word "gospel," known among them in its Greek form *euangelion*; they changed

[1] See p. 235.

some of the vowels and called it *awen-gilyon*, which is Hebrew for "iniquity of the writing-tablet" or something like that. "The vehemence with which the leading rabbis of the first generation of the second century express their hostility to the gospel and other books of the heretics, and to their conventicles, is the best evidence that they were growing in numbers and influence; some even among the teachers of the Law were suspected of leanings toward the new doctrine."[1]

The assiduity with which the Nazarenes appealed to the Old Testament writings, in both their Hebrew and Greek forms, led to a consideration of the various forms in which the text of the Old Testament was current at the time. Under Rabbi Akiba, about the beginning of the second century, a standard form of the consonantal Hebrew text of the Old Testament was fixed[2]—and fixed, so far as we can judge, on remarkably sound principles. Then not only the text, but its interpretation also, had to be fixed, in order especially that an authoritative explanation might be provided of those scriptures which Christians were continually invoking to support their claim that Jesus was the Messiah and Son of God. In some cases interpretations which had previously been perfectly admissible were now banned because they lent themselves too readily to Christian propaganda. A recent writer[3] has drawn our attention to an interesting discussion on the significance of the plural noun "thrones" in Daniel 7 : 13. The passage describes a vision of the Day of Judgment. "I looked," says Daniel, "until thrones were placed, and one who was Ancient of Days took His seat. . . . Thousands upon thousands ministered to Him, and myriads upon myriads stood before Him: the judgment was set and the books were opened. . . . And see, with the clouds of heaven there came one like a son of man; he drew near to the Ancient of Days and was brought right before Him. He was given the kingdom and the power and the glory, that all peoples and nations and languages should serve him; his dominion is an eternal dominion, never to pass away, and his kingdom is imperishable."[4]

Now the question arose: if *thrones* were placed, for whom were they intended? One for the Ancient of Days, of course; that is the throne described as being like fiery flame, with wheels like burning fire. But what of the others? The true answer probably is that they were intended for the assessors of the Ancient of Days.[5]

---

[1] G. F. Moore, *Judaism*, I (1927), p. 244.

[2] The Hebrew script originally expressed consonant-sounds only; the later system of vowel signs belongs to the eighth and ninth centuries A.D.

[3] J. Jocz, *The Jewish People and Jesus Christ* (1949), p. 186.

[4] Daniel 7 : 9–14.

[5] Compare Revelation 20 : 4, "I saw thrones, and they sat upon them, and judgment was given unto them," with Daniel 7 : 22, where the vision of the one

But we have traces of a school of thought among the earlier rabbis which held that the plural "thrones" was used because there was a second throne set for the "one like a son of man."

Now this was the scripture to which Jesus referred in His reply to the high priest at His trial, when He acknowledged that He was the Messiah and added: "And you will see the Son of man sitting at the right hand of the Power, and coming with the clouds of heaven."[1] If this was held to imply that He claimed a throne, set specially for Himself, alongside that occupied by the Almighty, we can understand the immediate unanimity with which His words were construed as blasphemous.

The Talmud preserves the account of a discussion on this very point. Various explanations of the plurality of the thrones were offered, and Rabbi Akiba suggested that one throne was placed for the Ancient of Days Himself "and one for David"—meaning by "David" the Messiah, "great David's greater Son." This was no doubt an ancient and respectable interpretation. But, because it was an interpretation which would obviously have commended itself to Christians as a confirmation of their belief, it had become unacceptable, and even blasphemous, to the Jewish doctors in general. Hence a vigorous protest was made when Akiba aired it: "How long will you profane the divine glory, Akiba?"

Among the Greek-speaking Jews the Septuagint, as we call the older Greek version of the Old Testament, fell into disfavour for the same reason. Many of the expressions in the Greek of the Septuagint might almost have been providentially framed with a view to Christian propaganda, for sometimes they suited the Christians' arguments better than the original Hebrew itself. As a result, the Septuagint, which had originally been produced by Jews for Jews, was entirely abandoned to the Christians. For Greek-speaking Jews a new Greek translation was commissioned, which should represent as closely as possible the text and interpretation of the Hebrew scriptures established by Akiba and his colleagues. The man who made this new Greek version bore the name Aquila; he was a native of Pontus and a proselyte to the Jewish community. His version is so excessively literal that the words only are Greek; the construction is thoroughly Hebraic. But at any rate it proved a barrier to Christian interpretations. Christians, for example, might quote the Septuagint form of Isaiah 7 : 14, "See, a virgin (Gk. *parthenos*) will conceive and give birth to a son and call his name Immanuel" (as is done in Matthew 1 : 23), and press it upon their Jewish acquaintances as a clear prediction of the virginal conception of Jesus; but now the

like a son of man is interpreted thus: "judgment was given to the saints of the Most High; and . . . the saints possessed the kingdom."
[1] Mark 14: 62. See pp. 52f.

Greek-speaking Jew could retort that the Greek version which *he* recognized as authoritative made no mention of a virgin (Gk. *parthenos*) but simply of a young woman (Gk. *neanis*).

But this was not all. These heretics were such a nuisance in synagogue services, where they insisted on their Nazarene interpretations, that drastic means were adopted to exclude them. Then (as now) the Jewish liturgy contained a prayer known as the Eighteen Benedictions, because each section of the prayer concludes with an ascription of blessing to God. About the year 90 this prayer was expanded by the inclusion of an extra section: "For the apostates let there be no hope, and may the arrogant kingdom be uprooted speedily in our days, and may the Nazarenes and the heretics (*minim*) perish as in a moment and be blotted out of the book of life, and not be inscribed with the righteous. Blessed art thou, O Lord, who humblest the arrogant."[1] The idea was that Christians would not be able to take part in a service which involved the invocation of a curse upon themselves.

But some Christians might have done their work so well that, even if they themselves were absent from synagogue services, their influence could be felt. Some scriptures were so constantly used by Christians that whenever they were read, in synagogue or anywhere else, people were reminded of the Christian interpretation of them. It is a distinguished orthodox Jewish scholar[2] who tells us that the reason why the prophecy of the Suffering Servant (Isaiah 52 : 13–53 : 12) is not included in the synagogue lectionary, although the passages immediately preceding and following it are found there, is the Christian application of that prophecy to Jesus.

Jews and Romans after A.D. 70

The Jews throughout the Roman Empire were not greatly affected by the outcome of the Jewish War so far as their position at law was concerned. Their general unpopularity increased, naturally, and the war was attended by anti-Jewish riots in Alexandria, Cæsarea and Antioch. At Rome, too, the feeling against Jews was strong enough to make Titus, when crown prince, give up his plan to marry Berenice, sister of Herod Agrippa the Younger, although both she and her brother had shown themselves ardent supporters of the Flavian dynasty in the recent war and subsequently.

[1] In the modern Jewish liturgy this "Benediction against the heretics" survives in a modified form: "And for slanderers let there be no hope, and let all wickedness perish as in a moment; let all thine enemies be speedily cut off, and the dominion of arrogance do thou uproot and crush, cast down and humble speedily in our days. Blessed art thou, O Lord, who breakest the enemies and humblest the arrogant" (cf. S. Singer, *Authorised Daily Prayer Book*, p. 48).

[2] The late Herbert Loewe, in *A Rabbinic Anthology*, by C. G. Montefiore and H. Loewe (1938), p. 544.

What legal changes there were were mainly financial in character. Formerly every male Jew over the age of twenty had been obliged to contribute half a shekel (roughly one shilling and sixpence) each year to the maintenance of the Jerusalem temple and priesthood. The temple was now in ruins, and its priesthood no longer functioned; but imperial law, which had formerly lent its authority to the exacting of this contribution, continued to exact it—no longer for the worship of Jehovah, but for the upkeep of the temple of Jupiter on the Capitoline hill at Rome. This exaction was offensive to Jewish religious sentiment, but it was enforced by the three Flavian emperors, Vespasian and his two sons. Domitian enforced it with special rigour; he exacted it not only from those who were Jews by birth or proselytization, but even from Gentile "God-fearers" who had a looser association with Judaism, and also (it appears) from all circumcised persons, no matter what the reason for their circumcision might be.[1] This unwarranted extension of the tax to non-Jews was repealed by the Emperor Nerva when he succeeded Domitian in 96, and a coin was struck to mark the occasion, bearing the legend, FISCI IVDAICI CALVMNIA SVBLATA ("the offence of the Jewish tax removed"), surrounding a large and handsome date-palm (a regular symbol of Judæa on Roman coins). Whether Nerva also relaxed the offensiveness of the tax in relation to Jews (as is sometimes said) is not so clear. The tax itself continued to be exacted in the second century.

Domitian initiated other legislation with an anti-Jewish tendency, including even more severe restrictions than those which were already in force on the proselytization of Roman citizens. It appears, too, that fear of another Jewish rising made him suspicious of any who might conceivably serve as a focus of disaffection, including in particular those who claimed descent from the old royal line. It is probably this that underlies the story of his interview with members of the family of Jesus.[2] As for the "Judaism" for which he took severe measures against some members of his own family, we have already considered what this might mean.[3]

But anti-Jewish feeling was not confined to the Emperor himself during Domitian's reign; there was enough of it about for Josephus, who now lived at Rome as a pensioner of the imperial family, to take up his pen to rebut it. This he did in two works: a short treatise in two books, entitled *Against Apion*,[4] and his full-

---

[1] See E. M. Smallwood, "Domitian's Attitude towards the Jews and Judaism," *Classical Philology*, 51 (1956), pp. 1-14.
[2] See pp. 167f.
[3] See pp. 162ff.
[4] Apion was an Alexandrian schoolmaster who took the lead in publishing the stock anti-Jewish calumnies.

length work on *Jewish Antiquities*, in twenty books, written to show that for antiquity, culture and general prowess the Jewish nation could compare favourably with any other.

Twenty years earlier Josephus had written his *History of the Jewish War*, in which he had not minimized his own importance as an insurgent leader. But now, to have taken a prominent part in a rebellion against Rome was too dangerous a reputation to have, and when he wrote his *Autobiography* under Domitian, he represented himself as playing a very minor part in the revolt. At the time when he wrote the *History of the Jewish War*, however, he did Rome a useful service, by showing how hopeless it was to take up arms against her; and a preliminary edition of that work, in the Aramaic language, was sent to the Jews of Mesopotamia in order to impress that lesson upon them.

For some fiery spirits who had escaped the destruction of A.D. 70 were attempting to stir up their fellow-Jews elsewhere to disaffection. Some fugitives from Judæa attempted this in Alexandria, but without success. The Alexandrian Jews were in no mood to court disaster.

Elsewhere in Egypt the war had a further repercussion when Vespasian ordered the closing of the Jewish temple at Leontopolis. When the high priesthood at Jerusalem was taken away from the old high-priestly line in the middle of the second century B.C., a member of that older line, Onias IV, left Palestine for Egypt, where he obtained permission from the reigning Ptolemy to build a temple at Leontopolis. There a similar ritual was carried out to that in Jerusalem. Now that the mother-temple had been destroyed, Vespasian did not wish the daughter to be a fresh centre of disaffection, and so its services were brought to an end as well, after they had been carried on for over two centuries.

A papyrus document discovered some years ago gives us some information of a quarrel between the Jewish and Gentile inhabitants of Alexandria in 110, which was settled by the Emperor Trajan in favour of the Jews.[1] The exact nature of the quarrel is uncertain, as the papyrus is incomplete. It is clear, however, that the Roman authorities had no thought of discriminating against Jews; in fact, Jews appear to have enjoyed considerable favour at court at this time, for Trajan's wife Plotina was pro-Jewish.

All the same, when Trajan set out a few years later on an expedition against the Parthians east of the Euphrates, a concerted Jewish revolt broke out in Libya, Cyrene and Egypt. The insurgents apparently aimed at setting up a Jewish state in north-east Africa, for they appointed one Lykyas as their king. Similar risings broke out in Cyprus and Mesopotamia. (The rising in Mesopo-

[1] See H. I. Bell, *Juden und Griechen im römischen Alexandreia* (1926), pp. 34ff.; H. A. Musurillo, *Acts of the Pagan Martyrs* (1954), pp. 44ff., 161ff.

tamia was probably undertaken in collusion with the Parthians, with whom the Jews had many ties.) There were extensive massacres and counter-massacres in all those places before the revolts were crushed.

Much more serious was the revolt which broke out in Palestine itself in the reign of Trajan's successor Hadrian. Hadrian took a great interest in strengthening the frontiers of the Empire; in our own island we have an abiding memorial of that interest in Hadrian's Wall. But the eastern frontier was in more urgent need of strengthening than the north-western, and as part of his general eastern policy Hadrian decided to build a new city on the derelict site of Jerusalem. On the temple site a new shrine would rise, dedicated not to the God of Israel but to the patron deity of Rome, Jupiter Capitolinus. This proposed desecration of the sacred place made the Jews feel as if Antiochus Epiphanes had come again.

And that was not the only measure of Hadrian which made them think thus. Hadrian, who attached great importance to what he considered Rome's civilizing mission, promulgated an edict which was aimed at humanizing some of the outlying peoples of his Empire, and at putting a stop to certain barbaric practices. These practices included various forms of mutilation, and it happened that circumcision came within the scope of the ban. There is no evidence that Hadrian wished to offend Jewish religious sentiment or that the Jews were in any way a special target of this edict. But obviously the prohibition of the distinctive external mark of Jewish religious and national solidarity, the sign of God's covenant with Abraham, was no more to be tolerated at Hadrian's hands than at those of Antiochus.

And, as if all this were not enough to start a conflagration, there arose at this moment a messianic claimant, a man named Simon. Simon might not have made much headway but for the fact that his messianic claims were warmly supported by Akiba, the leading rabbi of the day. In vain did some of Akiba's more cautious colleagues remonstrate with him ("Akiba," said one, "grass will grow out of your jaws before the son of David comes"); Akiba was sure that Simon was the Messiah, and hailed him as the "star out of Jacob" celebrated in Balaam's prophecy long centuries before.[1] For this reason Simon became known by the surname of Bar-kokhba, which is Aramaic for "son of the star."

The suddenness of the rising (132) took the Romans unawares. Judæa, since the late war, had been governed not by a procurator but by an imperial legate of independent status, with a stronger

[1] Numbers 24 : 17. This was a favourite messianic proof-text among the Qumran covenanters (see p. 30). The original reference was probably to King David.

military force on the spot than Gessius Florus had in 66. Even so, it proved inadequate; Bar-kokhba was soon master of Judæa. To mark the regaining of national independence a new coinage was struck, bearing such legends as "Simon Prince of Israel"[1]; "For the Freedom of Jerusalem"; "Year 1 of the Redemption of Israel"; "Year 2 of the Freedom of Israel." The warfare was guerrilla in character, as it had been in the days of the Maccabees, and it took the Romans a long time to put it down. Three and a half years' severe fighting followed before the Roman general Julius Severus succeeded in crushing the revolt.

The losses on both sides were heavy. When Hadrian made his report to the senate, announcing the termination of hostilities, he is said to have omitted the customary formula, "I and the army are well."

Bar-kokhba was put to death with the other instigators of the revolt, including the intrepid Akiba himself. Later tradition loved to tell how he died at the time of the evening oblation, reciting the Jewish creed, "Hear, O Israel, the Lord our God, the Lord is one," and prolonging the last word "one" (Heb. *echad*) as long as his breath remained in him. And he laughed amid his torments, they said, for as he fortified himself with the words, "Thou shalt love the Lord thy God with all thy heart, and with all thy soul, and with all thy might," he understood as never before how it was possible to love God with all his soul, in the very moment of breathing it out.

And now Jerusalem was rebuilt as a Roman colony and the temple duly consecrated to Jupiter Capitolinus—an order which was to endure until the time of Constantine, nearly two hundred years later. The city was renamed Aelia Capitolina—Aelia after the Emperor's family name (his full style was Publius *Aelius* Hadrianus), and Capitolina after the Roman Jupiter to whom the new temple was dedicated. It was a completely Gentile city; no Jew was permitted to come near it.

So fierce were the reprisals taken against the Judæans that the rabbinic succession was kept up with difficulty, and the rabbis granted their followers a dispensation from all breaches of the law except idolatry and fornication. But the reprisals came to an end with the death of Hadrian in 138. The ban on circumcision was relaxed by his successor Antonine. The history of the Jews did not come to an end in Hadrian's time; but, interesting as their subsequent history is, we cannot trace it further here.

---

[1] Cf. his self-designation, "Simon Ben-kosebah, Prince of Israel," in a letter found in a cave in the Wadi Murabba'at (see my *Second Thoughts on the Dead Sea Scrolls*, p. 54). Ben-kosebah was evidently his proper patronymic.

CHAPTER XXVIII

JEWS AND CHRISTIANS IN WESTERN ASIA

The Migration to Asia

WHEN THE EMPEROR HADRIAN REFOUNDED JERUSALEM as a Roman city in 135 and forbade Jews to approach it, his prohibition applied to Jewish Christians as well as to non-Christian Jews. Shortly after 135 we find a church in Jerusalem once again, but now it is a purely Gentile church, quite distinct from the purely Jewish-Christian church of Jerusalem in earlier times. This complete breach of continuity in the history of Jerusalem Christianity is one among several reasons for the uncertainty attaching to the identification of sacred sites in that city. The new Gentile church of Jerusalem had no communal memory, no local traditions among its members, which might preserve the identity of the holy places. In this respect there is a wide difference between Jerusalem and Rome, for in Rome there is an unbroken continuity of Christian tradition going back to the first century.

The year 135 also marks the final breach between the Jewish Christians and their fellow-Jews. The Nazarenes had refused to take part in the Bar-kokhba rising, because they could not by any means recognize his messianic claims. For them there could be no other Messiah than Jesus. Because of their refusal to join what seemed the patriotic cause, they suffered considerable persecution. From that time onwards, then, the distinctively Jewish Christian communities went their own way, isolated in religion from their fellow-Jews, and to a large extent isolated also from the main stream of catholic Christianity. As the Gentile Christians in the following centuries formulated their faith in ever more explicit terms—terms, too, largely drawn from the vocabulary of Greek philosophy—the Jewish-Christian groups, with their more primitive and more Semitic ways of expressing their faith, found themselves increasingly regarded as heretical by the generality of catholic Christians. Some Jewish Christians of Palestine and Syria did, indeed, join the ranks of catholic orthodoxy and were merged in the mainly Gentile-Christian churches of Jerusalem, Cæsarea, Antioch and other cities of those countries. There was an Aramaic-speaking church of orthodox Jewish Christians or Nazarenes at Aleppo in Syria as late as the closing years of the fourth century. And a few Jewish Christians made contributions to the Church's literature in the early centuries, even after 135. There was, for example, Hegesippus (a name which is evidently a Greek disguise for Joseph), who flourished in the middle of the second century; he was a convert from Palestinian Judaism, and one of the first Christians to conceive the idea that the true faith could be identified by ascertaining the consensus of belief in all the apostolic churches. In pursuit of this quest he travelled from Palestine to Rome, questioning the churches which he visited on the way about the beliefs that they held, and recording his findings in five books of *Memoirs*. His conclusion was that "in each [episcopal] succession and in each city the faith is just as the law and the prophets and the Lord proclaim it."[1] His *Memoirs*, long since, unfortunately, lost, contained many interesting items of ecclesiastical tradition from Jerusalem and the other churches with which he became acquainted; he was, in fact, one of the first Christian writers of the post-apostolic age who tried to support his theological belief on a basis of history, and his work was a valuable source-book for Eusebius. Probably many succession-lists of bishops of various churches were first established and recorded by him.

The orthodox Jewish Christians, however, lost their identity almost completely in the mainly Gentile churches; those Jewish Christians who preserved their identity belonged for the most part to the Ebionite communities which survived for centuries in Syria and Transjordan. But before we say something more about them, we must mention an interesting extension of first-century Palestinian Christianity.

Palestinian Christianity had sent out missionaries to all parts in the decades preceding the Jewish War of 66–70, and it did not cease to do so after that war. But the most noteworthy extension of Palestinian Christianity in the second half of the first century is the migration of some of its leading figures to Asia Minor. These emigrants appear to have represented the less Judaistic element in the Palestinian church, by contrast with those who perpetuated the more legalist tradition in Transjordan and elsewhere.

The Christians of the province of Asia valued very highly the memory of those Palestinian Christians who came to spend the remainder of their days among them. When Victor, bishop of Rome, tried to enforce the Roman observance of Easter on the Asian churches about 190, Polycrates, bishop of Ephesus, wrote to him and quoted the precedent of those early Christians from Palestine whose example in this matter was followed by the Christians of Asia:

[1] Eusebius, *Hist. Eccl.*, IV, 22 : 3.

For great luminaries sleep in Asia, to rise again at the last day, the day of our Lord's advent, when He comes from heaven with glory to seek out all His saints—Philip, one of the twelve apostles, who sleeps at Hierapolis, with his two daughters who grew old as virgins and another daughter who lived in the Holy Spirit and now rests in Ephesus; and also John, who leaned on the Lord's breast, who was a priest wearing the *petalon* and a martyr and teacher withal —he too sleeps at Ephesus.[1]

Although Polycrates identifies the Philip who came from Palestine to Phrygia with Philip the apostle, Eusebius, who has preserved his letter for us, obviously understood him to mean Philip the almoner and evangelist, whose four prophesying daughters are mentioned by Luke in Acts 21 : 9; and Eusebius is probably right. Polycrates is not the only writer to mention their residence and burial in Asia Minor. About the same time, Proclus, a leader of the Montanists, refers to them in the *Dialogue* which he sustained with the Roman presbyter Gaius:

The four daughters of Philip, who were prophetesses, were in Hierapolis in Asia. Their grave is there, and so is their father's.[2]

And Papias, who was bishop of that very city of Hierapolis in the earlier part of the second century, knew the ladies personally in their old age. As old ladies will, they loved telling stories of the personalities and events of their younger days, and Papias found them useful informants on the early days of Christianity in Palestine. Among the remarkable stories they told was one about Justus, otherwise called Barsabbas, the man who had been nominated along with Matthias for the vacancy in the apostolate caused by the defection of Judas Iscariot.[3] This story related how Justus on one occasion drank poison but suffered no harmful consequences.[4]

Papias appreciated reminiscences like these very much. He was engaged on his *Exposition of the Dominical Oracles,* and he much preferred to get what information he could about those early days from "a living and abiding voice"[5] instead of relying on what others had written. Incidentally, in the course of his *Exposition* he gives us the earliest external evidence we possess about the origins of some of the Gospels. He tells us, for example, how "Matthew compiled the [Lord's] oracles in the Hebrew speech and everyone translated them as best he could," and how "Mark, who was Peter's interpreter, wrote down accurately all that Peter recorded

---

[1] Eusebius, *Hist. Eccl.*, III, 31 : 3. The *petalon* was the gold plate, inscribed "Holy to the LORD," which the high priest of Israel wore on his turban. Compare the ascription of high-priestly privileges to James the Just (p. 151, n. 3).

[2] Eusebius, *Hist. Eccl.*, III, 31 : 4. See pp. 145, 220.

[3] Eusebius, *Hist. Eccl.*, III, 39 : 9; cf. Acts 1 : 23ff.

[4] Cf. Mark 16 : 18.

[5] Eusebius, *Hist. Eccl.*, III, 39 : 4.

of the words and deeds of the Lord, though not in strict order."[1] The information about Mark he says he got from a person called "The Elder," whose identity is one of the most fascinating problems connected with the Palestinian emigrants to Asia Minor.

Papias's references are not the only ones to a respected leader in Asia Minor who was known as "The Elder." The author of the two tiny letters in the New Testament which we call the Second and Third Epistles of John introduces himself by this title. Now we know from Irenæus that the disciples of the apostles were known to later generations as "the elders"; but when, at the close of the first century, a writer describes himself as "The Elder" *sans phrase*, it is more probable that he is using the designation which others were in the habit of giving him because of his great age. If, as seems certain, the author of these two short letters was also the author of the First Epistle of John, then he was one who had known Jesus personally in the days before His passion.[2]

Now, in our quotation from Polycrates we are told that one of the Palestinian Christians who had settled in Asia Minor was John, the disciple who leaned back on Jesus' breast at the Last Supper.[3] What exactly Polycrates means by saying that John was "a priest wearing the *petalon*," (that is to say, the plate of gold in front of the high-priestly mitre), is a question to which no certain answer can be given. In spite of attempts to prove that this John was a member of a high-priestly family of Jerusalem (such as the John of Acts 4 : 6), Polycrates may simply be speaking metaphorically of the veneration in which this Ephesian John was held.

Nor is Polycrates the only writer to refer to this John. We have further references to him in the works of Irenæus. Irenæus's references are particularly interesting, because he was a disciple of Polycarp, the bishop of Smyrna who met a martyr's death in 156, and he makes it plain that Polycarp in his turn was a disciple of John. Here is Irenæus writing to Florinus, a companion of his boyhood with whom he sat at Polycarp's feet:

> When I was still a boy I knew you in Lower Asia, in Polycarp's house, when you were a person of note in the royal court and endeavouring to stand high in his estimation. I remember the events of those days more clearly than those which have taken place recently, for what we learn as boys grows up with our lives and becomes united to them, so that I can tell you the very place where the blessed Polycarp sat and held discourse, how he came in and went out, his manner of life and bodily appearance, the discourses which he used to deliver to the people, and how he used to tell of

---

[1] Eusebius, *Hist. Eccl.*, III, 39 : 15f.
[2] This seems to be the natural implication of 1 John 1 : 1-4. C. H. Dodd's arguments to the contrary in *The Johannine Epistles*, pp. 9ff., lack his usual cogency.
[3] Cf. John 13 : 23, 25.

his intercourse with John and with the others who had seen the Lord, how he remembered their words, and what he had heard from them concerning the Lord, and about their mighty works and their teaching; and how Polycarp reported everything in harmony with the Scriptures, as he had received it from eyewitnesses of the Word of life.[1]

Again, in his letter of remonstrance with Victor of Rome, when the latter was minded to force his view of the proper observance of Easter on the Asian churches, Irenæus reminded him how Polycarp had always observed Easter in the same manner as "John, the disciple of our Lord, and the rest of the apostles with whom he associated."[2] Nor are we surprised when Irenæus identifies this John with the author of the Fourth Gospel: "John, the disciple of the Lord," he says, "the one who had reclined upon His breast, himself also published his Gospel when he was resident at Ephesus in Asia."[3] For, as we have remarked before, the presence in Asia of someone with extraordinary prestige is required to account for the persistence of the Quartodeciman practice in that area; and the Quartodeciman practice reflects the chronology and theology of the Fourth Gospel, which views the passion of Christ as the true passover sacrifice and the culminating manifestation of the divine glory which was revealed in Him.

Papias as well as Polycarp is said by Irenæus to have been one of John's disciples. And if this is true, then it is tempting to suppose that John was "The Elder" who supplied Papias with some of his information, nor is it excessively rash to go on and identify him further with "The Elder" who wrote the Johannine epistles of the New Testament. But here we may turn back to Papias himself, and look at another fragment of his work which Eusebius has preserved. In pursuance of his policy to rely as far as possible on first-hand testimony, Papias says:

> If ever any one came who had kept company with the elders, I would inquire into the words of the elders—what Andrew or Peter, or Philip or Thomas or James, or John or Matthew or any of the Lord's other disciples, had said—and the things that Aristion and the elder John, the Lord's disciples, were saying.[4]

Now here is a much disputed question. Does Papias in this passage refer to one John or two? The authorities for either view are very evenly divided, in point of numbers, scholarship and orthodoxy (or heterodoxy). Papias expresses himself quite ambiguously, and as we have only fragments from his work, we cannot look up other passages at will to find out what he really

[1] Eusebius, *Hist. Eccl.*, V, 20 : 5f.
[2] Eusebius, *Hist. Eccl.*, V, 24 : 16.
[3] Irenæus, *Against Heresies*, III, 1 : 1; cf. Eusebius, *Hist. Eccl.*, V, 8 : 4.
[4] Eusebius, *Hist. Eccl.*, III, 39 : 4.

means. (It is possible that a manuscript of Papias's work may still be lying, uncatalogued, in some monastery library or the like. A copy is known to have been extant at Nîmes as late as 1341.[1] If ever a copy does turn up, it is a solemn thought to contemplate what a weight of more recent literature will at once become obsolete.)

Eusebius, to whom we owe this last-quoted fragment of Papias, thought that it indicated two Johns; but Eusebius was not unbiased in this matter. He did not appreciate the Book of the Revelation, and would feel happier in his mind if he could believe that it was not written by an apostle. So he concluded that, of the two Johns whom he discerned in the passage from Papias, one, the apostle (referred to by Papias in the past tense), was the author of the Johannine Gospel and Epistles, and the other, the elder (referred to by Papias in the present tense), was the author of the Book of the Revelation. He was supported in this conclusion by a discussion on the authorship of these works by Dionysius of Alexandria in the previous century, in which Dionysius argued acutely on grounds of literary criticism that Revelation was the work of another author than the Fourth Evangelist. Dionysius also mentioned a report that two places were pointed out in Ephesus as the tomb of John.[2]

Whether Eusebius was right in his inference must remain uncertain. It is equally permissible to infer from Papias's language that he refers, however awkwardly, to one John only, and that this John was the last survivor of the original apostles, who, after many vicissitudes, had settled in Ephesus, where because of his great age he was known to his friends as "The Elder." In Ephesus, according to Clement of Alexandria and Irenæus, he lived on into the reign of Trajan.

The Dialogue with Trypho

In this city of Ephesus, shortly after the Jewish revolt in Palestine was crushed in 135, an interesting meeting took place between a Jew who had escaped from that disaster and the Christian philosopher Justin. Justin himself was a Palestinian by birth, belonging to a pagan family of the city of Gitta in Samaria, but after receiving a thorough training in Greek philosophy, he found an answer in Christianity to the problems which Greek philosophy raised but to which it provided no satisfying solution. An account of the discussion between the two men, entitled the Dialogue with Trypho the Jew, has been preserved among Justin's writings. Possibly it has been edited for publication, but even so it remains

[1] E. J. Goodspeed, History of Early Christian Literature (1942), p. 164.
[2] Eusebius, Hist. Eccl., VII, 24f.

a most illuminating and attractive account of the way in which cultured Jews and Christians could debate the points at issue between them. There is a good deal of hard hitting on either side, but the debate is conducted with great courtesy.

Justin tells how he was converted to Christianity after pursuing Greek philosophy, and Trypho smilingly suggests that it would have been better to stick to Plato than to desert him for the opinions of men of no repute. But if Justin really wants to do the right thing, says Trypho, let him become a Jewish proselyte. For even if Messiah is now alive, he is unknown—to himself as much as to others—and will remain unknown and devoid of all authority until Elijah comes to anoint him and make him manifest to all.

Justin is quick to defend his faith, and asks Trypho whether his objections to Christianity are based on vulgar report of unseemly behaviour among Christians, or simply on his own disapproval of Christian teaching. Trypho assures him that he has no time for the slanders of the rank and file, and adds: "I know that the commands given you in what you call the Gospel are so wonderful and great that I suspect no one can keep them. For I have taken the trouble to read them."[1] But he criticizes the Christian refusal to conform to the Jewish ritual of circumcision and food-laws and sabbaths and festivals and so on, and for resting their hopes on a man who had been crucified.

Then the argument really gets going, and both men appeal confidently to the Old Testament writings—Justin to support his thesis that Jesus is indeed the Messiah, and that the ceremonial Jewish law has been abrogated by Him; Trypho to refute Justin's arguments. The *Dialogue* illustrates the contemporary tendency to press the Scriptures into service with little regard to context. Some of Justin's points fail to come home to Trypho, because they are based on a form of the Septuagint (the Greek version of the Old Testament) which Trypho does not recognize. A famous instance of this is Justin's quotation of Psalm 96 : 10 in the form, "Say among the nations, The Lord reigned *from the tree*," which he uses to prove that the crucified one was Israel's God and King. Trypho protests, as well he might, against this unwarrantable addition to the Biblical text. (It was probably a Christian gloss introduced from a collection of "Testimonies.")[2] But Justin assures him that the Jewish rabbis have mutilated the text in order to remove the clear prediction of Messiah's cross. Trypho replies (mildly enough, under the circumstances): "Whether the rulers of our people have erased any portion of the Scriptures, as you allege, God knows; but it seems incredible."[3]

Trypho even comes to the point of conceding that Justin is

[1] *Dialogue*, 10.   [2] See pp. 76f.   [3] *Dialogue*, 73.

right in saying that, according to the Scriptures, the Messiah must suffer; but that (he insists) does not prove Jesus to be the Messiah, and in any case it is monstrous blasphemy to say that the crucified one is identical with Him who spoke to Moses in the burning bush.

Mention is made of some people of Jewish race who acknowledge Jesus as the Messiah, while they hold Him to have been "a man born of men" and continue to observe the ceremonial law. Justin refers to them critically, but Trypho says that he can appreciate their point of view much more than that of Justin and his like, who worship the crucified one as God. "Those who say that he was a man, chosen and anointed by God, and thus made Messiah, seem to me to speak more convincingly than those who hold the opinions which you express."[1]

After a two days' debate, neither has succeeded in convincing the other, but Trypho says: "I confess I am delighted with our discussion. . . . We have found more than we expected; more, indeed, than we possibly could have expected, and if we could do this more frequently we should be greatly helped in searching the Scriptures themselves. But since you are on the eve of departure, and expect to sail any day, please remember us as friends when you are gone." And as he and his friends wish Justin *bon voyage*, Justin prays for them and says: "I can wish nothing better for you than this, gentlemen, that you may come to the same opinion as ourselves and believe that Jesus is the Son of God."[2]

It is a pity that relations between Christians and Jews did not always manifest this friendly spirit. We get a different picture in the attitude of the Jews of the province of Asia during the anti-Christian outburst there in 156 which culminated in the martyrdom of Polycarp; and a still more unpleasing one in the Christian attitude to Jews throughout the centuries that followed the triumph of the Church in the reign of Constantine.

The Ebionites

Justin's reference to those people of Jewish birth who, while believing in Jesus as the Messiah, held an Adoptionist view of His person and continued to observe the Jewish law is very interesting. These are no doubt the people whom later Christian writers call Ebionites. This word simply means "the poor" (Hebrew *ha-ebyonim*) and was probably used by Jewish Christians as a self-description, just as they were called Nazarenes by other Jews. But there is a tendency to specialize the use of these two terms, and reserve "Nazarenes" for those Jewish Christians who adhered in general to catholic orthodoxy, while describing as

[1] *Dialogue*, 48.   [2] *Dialogue*, 142.

Ebionites those who deviated from it in doctrine or practice. It is evident that Christian writers who mention the Ebionites (in this latter sense) do not know what the name really means; Tertullian, for example, derives it from a hypothetical founder of the party called Ebion.

In addition to observing a great part of the Jewish law and holding an Adoptionist view of Christ's divinity, those who are called Ebionites in the restricted sense also refused to believe in the virginal conception of Jesus and repudiated the apostolic claims of Paul. To them James the Just was the great figure among the disciples; they are said to have reckoned him as the twelfth apostle. Peter was also a venerated name among them. Ebionite views are very apparent in a remarkable body of literature attributed to Clement of Rome, but actually dating from the third century, in which (among other things) James is addressed as "bishop of bishops" and Peter is described as going about from place to place on his missionary tours, only to find his steps dogged by the arch-heretic Simon Magus, who seems in this literature to be a thin disguise for Paul!

This literature in its extant form consists of two works called the *Clementine Recognitions* and the *Clementine Homilies*. These appear to be derived from a work called *The Ascents of James*[1] and another called *The Travels of Peter*. This latter work was known to Origen in the earlier part of the third century, and goes back to earlier sources, notably a second-century treatise called *The Preachings of Peter*, which may in its turn have drawn upon an Ebionite counterblast to the Lukan *Acts of the Apostles*.[2]

They used a Gospel which they called the Gospel according to Matthew; church writers call it the *Gospel according to the Hebrews*. This Gospel bore some relation to the canonical Gospel of Matthew, but was a shorter work, edited in the Ebionite interest. The *Gospel according to the Hebrews* was current in Transjordan and Egypt, and was known to the Alexandrian Fathers, Clement and Origen, who give us some quotations from it. One of these quotations is a curious variant of one of the temptation incidents; in this version Jesus Himself is made to say:

> But now my mother the Holy Spirit took me by one of my hairs and carried me away to the great mountain Tabor.[3]

Another passage in this Gospel gave details of our Lord's appearance to James after His resurrection:

> But when the Lord had given His linen cloth to the high priest's servant, He went to James and appeared to him. For James had

[1] Hegesippus probably depended on this work for his description of the death of James (see pp. 150f.).

[2] See H. J. Schoeps, *Theologie und Geschichte des Judenchristentums* (1949), p. 1ff.

[3] Origen, *Commentary on John* 2 : 6; *Homily on Jeremiah* 15 : 4.

sworn that he would eat no bread from that hour in which he had drunk the cup of the Lord, until he saw Him rise from the dead. And again, after a little, the Lord said, "Bring a table and bread"; and immediately it adds: He took bread and blessed and broke it, and thereafter He gave it to James the Just and said to him: "My brother, eat thy bread, because the Son of man has risen from among them that sleep."[1]

Later Christian writers, however (Jerome in particular) seem to have confused this Ebionite *Gospel according to the Hebrews* with another Jewish-Christian Gospel, called the *Gospel of the Nazarenes*. This was simply an Aramaic translation or "targum" of the canonical Gospel of Matthew, used by the more orthodox Jewish Christians of Syria and the lands farther east. When Jerome first came upon a copy of this Nazarene Gospel in Syria, he not only identified it with the *Gospel according to the Hebrews* of which he had read in Clement and Origen, but also imagined that it was the Aramaic original of the canonical Matthew, and proceeded to translate it into Greek and Latin.[2]

To the Ebionites, Jesus came to fulfil the law and the prophets in the rôle of a new Moses—not only in the sense that He was the Deuteronomic Prophet like unto Moses, but also in that He acted as the Reformer of the Law. He removed from the Law falsifications and accretions which had been introduced after the time of Moses, such as the sacrificial system, but laid fresh emphasis on the demands of the true Law. Hence the Ebionites stressed the laws of purification as well as insisting on the virtues of poverty, vegetarianism and asceticism of other kinds. In these respects they remind us of the Essenes, and it may well be, as Hort held, that the form of Ebionitism with which we are best acquainted owed some of its special features to Essene influence.[3] Also, if we may judge by their written remains, the Ebionites do not seem to have remained quite free from Gnostic influences.

The Ebionites may not have been so weak numerically as is often supposed. They maintained their organization and propaganda for centuries. One of their best-known men, Symmachus (after whom they were occasionally called Symmachians), produced a revised version of the Greek Old Testament towards the end of the second century.[4] They considered themselves to be the heirs of the primitive church of Jerusalem, even after Jerusalem itself had been rebuilt as a pagan city and was the seat of a Gentile-Christian church. They thought of themselves as forming a bridge between catholic Christianity and Jewish orthodoxy, combining

---

[1] Jerome, *On Illustrious Men*, 2.
[2] A. Schmidtke, *Judenchristliche Evangelien* (1911), pp. 246ff.; B. W. Bacon, *Studies in Matthew* (1931), pp. 478ff.; also my *Jesus and Christian Origins* (1974), pp. 99f.
[3] F. J. A. Hort, *Judaistic Christianity* (1894), pp. 201f. Cf. my *Second Thoughts on the Dead Sea Scrolls*, pp. 123f.   [4] Eusebius *Hist. Eccl.*, VI, 17.

and conserving all that was of value in both, while rejecting the errors of both. If they hoped to be able one day to reconcile these two on an Ebionite basis, they were disappointed. The orthodox Jews disowned them as apostates; the orthodox Christians disowned them as heretics. They lingered on in Transjordan and Egypt until the seventh century, and those who were not absorbed by Jewish or Christian orthodoxy lost their identity in the overflowing tide of Islam.

It is to be regretted that Jewish Christianity was not more completely integrated in the Catholic Church; the valuable contributions that it could have made to the life and thought of Christendom would have been a healthy corrective to certain tendencies, as the contribution of Jewish Christianity in more recent times has been.

CHAPTER XXIX

CHRISTIANITY FARTHER EAST

MOST OF OUR AUTHORITIES FOR THE HISTORY OF EARLY Christianity tell us of its expansion within the Roman Empire. For example, Luke, our earliest historian of the Christian movement, is mainly concerned to trace its rise in Palestine and then its extension along the road from Jerusalem to Rome. Only now and then in his pages have we any hint of the progress of Christianity in other directions as well. He tells us, for instance, of the Ethiopian or Nubian official who was converted on his southward journey as Philip explained to him the Old Testament prophecy of the Suffering Servant in terms of the story of Jesus.[1] He tells us, again, that on the first Christian Pentecost, in the year 30, there were found among Peter's hearers not only visitors from the west, from as far off as Rome, but also "Parthians and Medes and Elamites, and the dwellers in Mesopotamia";[2] that is to say, people who lived east of the Euphrates, across the frontier of the Roman Empire, in territory which at that time formed part of the Parthian Empire, and which after 226 belonged to the new Persian Empire. The Jews in those lands, like many of their Gentile neighbours, spoke Aramaic.

We cannot be sure whether any of those easterners who were present in Jerusalem at Pentecost carried the gospel back home with them. Nor can we be sure whether any of those parts was evangelized by any of the apostles. It is remarkable, indeed, how little we know about the later career of most of the twelve apostles. James, the son of Zebedee, we know, was executed in Jerusalem under Herod Agrippa I in 44; we can trace the movements of his brother John from time to time, and we can reconstruct the outline of Peter's later life with considerable probability.[3] But what do we know of Andrew and Thomas and Matthew, Philip and Bartholomew, James the son of Alphæus and Judas the son of James, Simon the Zealot and Matthias, the successor of Judas Iscariot? Legend is lavish in its willingness to tell us what became of them, but we have amazingly little historical knowledge.[4] They do not appear to have remained in

---

[1] Acts 8 : 26ff.; see p. 99.   [2] Acts 2 : 9.   [3] See pp.139ff.
[4] See B. H. Streeter, *The Primitive Church*, pp. 3ff. (This work opens with the question: "What became of the Twelve Apostles?")

Jerusalem after the middle of the first century. Some of them may have evangelized parts of Asia Minor; others are said to have gone farther east, Thomas and Bartholomew in particular, whom tradition associates with "India." But what is meant by "India" in this connexion is not so clear; any land bordering the Indian Ocean or Persian Gulf might be so described. Eusebius tells us that when Pantænus, head of the catechetical school of Alexandria, went on a mission to "India" about 180, he found a Christian community, converted by the preaching of the apostle Bartholomew and possessing "Matthew's writing in the script of the Hebrews" (probably an Aramaic "targum" of the Greek Matthew, like the *Gospel of the Nazarenes*).[1] There was, at any rate, a trade-route between Alexandria and the mouth of the Indus.[2]

But there was a large mission-field for the apostles in the Jewish population of the lands across the Euphrates, and some of them probably found their way there. For the introduction and expansion of Christianity in those lands we are indebted to a work called the *Chronicle of Arbela*, which was compiled late enough, to be sure—in the sixth century—but which rests upon good local tradition, and has been recognized by a number of historical students (including Harnack) as possessing real worth. Arbela lies north-east of the Tigris, and was the capital of the kingdom of Adiabene. The evidence of the *Chronicle of Arbela* points to the conclusion that Christianity had been introduced to Adiabene before the end of the first century.

Now, this is specially interesting, because the royal family of Adiabene was converted to Judaism about A.D. 40 and remained faithful to that religion for thirty years at least. (Two members of the royal house fought on the Jewish side in the war of 66–70.) There was a large Jewish population in that area, as we may judge from the fact that about the year 75 Josephus produced the first edition of his *History of the Jewish War* in Aramaic for their benefit—no doubt to impress them with the power of Rome and the hopelessness of revolt.

The Jewish propaganda which was so successful in those parts around the middle of the first century may well have paved the way for the Christian mission which followed later in the century. Certainly the Christian mission enjoyed astonishing success in Upper Mesopotamia and the adjoining regions. About the middle of the second century the city of Edessa (modern Urfa), east of the upper Euphrates, emerges as the chief centre of Christianity in that area. Edessa was sacked by the Romans during Trajan's

---

[1] Eusebius, *Hist. Eccl.*, V, 10 (and cf. p. 281).
[2] See J. N. Farquhar, "The Apostle Thomas in North India," *Bulletin of the John Rylands Library*, X (1926), pp. 80–111; "The Apostle Thomas in South India," *ibid.* XI (1927), pp. 20–50.

Parthian campaign in 116, and Christianity had probably been planted in the city before that, although not at such an early date as local tradition pretended. For it is to this local tradition that we must assign the apocryphal correspondence between Jesus and Abgar V, king of Edessa from A.D. 13 to 50, which attempts to date the Edessene mission as early as the lifetime of Jesus Himself. This curiosity of apocryphal literature has been preserved by Eusebius in the first book of his *Ecclesiastical History*, where he reports how Abgar, suffering from an apparently incurable disease, heard of the healing ministry of Jesus and sent Him a letter asking Him to come and cure him. Jesus replied in a letter to the effect that He could not come just then, but that he would shortly send one of His disciples to heal his disease and bring life and salvation to himself and his people.[1]

Then Eusebius, continuing to translate from the Syriac narrative which recorded this friendly correspondence, goes on to tell how one of the apostles, "Judas Thomas" (that is, Judas the twin), sent Thaddæus, one of the seventy disciples of Luke 10, to Edessa after the ascension of Jesus, and how Thaddæus healed Abgar and other Edessenes who were in trouble, and evangelized the land.

This legend is a later and garbled antedating of a Christian forward movement in Edessa in the reign of a later Abgar— Abgar IX (179–216). This Abgar was actually converted to Christianity, so that the kingdom of Edessa was the first to have a Christian dynasty; but he was overthrown by the Roman Emperor Caracalla, who embarked upon an aggressive policy in the east and penetrated as far as Media. The name Thaddæus (Syriac *Thaddai*) in the legend is an error for Addai, who is listed as the first bishop of Edessa. After the death of Addai's successor Aggai, there seems to be a break in the episcopal succession; the next bishop, Palut, is said to have been ordained by Serapion, bishop of Antioch from 190 to 203.

The Christians of Upper Mesopotamia had considerable parts of the Bible in their Syriac tongue at a very early date. The Syriac translation of the Old Testament had probably been carried out during the Jewish forward movement in Adiabene in the first century A.D. and revised by the Christian missionaries some time later; in the course of the second century the Gospels and the book of Acts were also available in a Syriac version. (How much more of the New Testament was available in Syriac at this time we do not know.) In fact, the Gospels were available in two forms; for not only did they have versions of the four separate Gospels, but they also had a harmony of the Gospels, a compilation in which the four Gospels were woven together so as to

[1] Eusebius, *Hist. Eccl.*, I, 13.

yield one continuous narrative. This, the first of many such harmonies, was the work of a Mesopotamian Christian named Tatian who, after spending some years in Rome, where he was the pupil of Justin Martyr, returned to his native land and presented his people with the fourfold Gospel in this novel form. Tatian's *Diatessaron*,[1] as it is called, became very popular among the Syriac-speaking Christians and almost displaced the "separate Gospels" altogether. When a revision of these "separate Gospels" and of most of the other New Testament books (the Peshitta, as we call it) was introduced among the Syriac churches by episcopal authority early in the fifth century, it was not without a struggle that they were induced to give up the use of the *Diatessaron*.

As the Syriac churches pressed their evangelizing mission north and east, other Biblical translations appeared—in Armenia and Georgia, for example. The missionary work carried on by the Syriac Christians at this time was a prelude to the greater missionary enterprise upon which they embarked in later centuries and which carried the Gospel into the heart of China. Even within the period we are dealing with here, they carried the Gospel to Bactria and India. One monument of Syriac Christianity, called the *Acts of Thomas*, written about the middle of the third century, describing a visit of the apostle Thomas to India, is full of legend indeed, but it certainly indicates that Christianity had been carried to India by a Syriac mission before the time when this work was written. And, as we know, Syriac Christianity has survived in India to the present day.

Like Christianity farther west, Syriac Christianity was not untroubled by heresy. Tatian himself was not quite orthodox; he founded an ascetic and vegetarian sect called the Encratites (or "continent people") and even seems to have introduced some of his peculiar notions into the text of the *Diatessaron*. John the Baptist, for example, was made to turn near-vegetarian, and to live on *milk* and honey instead of *locusts* and honey!

But a more interesting form of heresy than Tatian's was that with which Bardaisan was charged. Bardaisan (or Bardesanes, to give him the Greek form of his name) was a man of exceptional ability, and was the founder of Christian Syriac literature. Eusebius tells us that he wrote against Marcionism, and that his writings against this and other heresies were translated into Greek.[2] But when the character of his teaching was reported to Serapion, bishop of Antioch, Serapion recognized it as deeply tinged with Gnosticism. A great number of the Edessene Christians, however, adhered to Bardaisan in spite of his conviction

---

[1] Greek *dia tessaron*, literally "through four," used in music to denote a harmony of four parts. Cf. p. 226.

[2] Eusebius, *Hist. Eccl.*, IV, 30.

for heresy; and it was probably for this reason that Serapion, in the interests of orthodoxy, inaugurated a new episcopal succession at Edessa by consecrating Palut as bishop (*c.* 200). Some of Bardaisan's literary work has survived, both in prose and in poetry; the most outstanding being his *Hymn of the Pearl*—about the soul that went down to Egypt for the sake of the one pearl. This hymn, which owes its preservation to its being incorporated in the Syriac *Acts of Thomas*, is thoroughly Gnostic in outlook, but of such high quality that F. C. Burkitt could call it "the most noble poem of Christian Antiquity," adding that "it is worth while to learn Syriac, so as to be able to read it in the original."[1]

The small community of Mandæans, surviving to the present day in Iraq, have preserved a variety of Gnosticism which in several important features appears to have been derived from the teaching of Bardaisan, although it has drawn upon other sources as well, such as Marcionism and Manichæism.[2]

Of Manichæism we shall speak in a moment, but a word should be said first about the Phrygian bishop Avircius Marcellus, who about the year 190, at the age of seventy-two, paid a visit to Rome and returned via Syria and Mesopotamia. His own epitaph (consisting of twenty-two Greek hexameters) gives us an account of his tour in figurative language; he went to see "the imperial majesty and to behold the queen robed and shod in gold" (the city of Rome); he found there "the people with the shining seal" (the Church), and found them, too, throughout Syria and the territory of the upper Euphrates, for he visited those lands, having Paul as his fellow-traveller in the carriage with him (that is, having a copy of Paul's epistles as his book of devotion). Wherever he went, he found the same catholic faith and the same eucharistic meal, serving as the bond of unity for all Christians in east and west. His description of the eucharistic meal is particularly remarkable in its metaphors: it is the "fish from the spring, gigantic, pure, caught by the Holy Virgin," the "food which Faith set before him in all places." But these metaphors have their close counterpart in the Christian art of the catacombs at this period. Avircius's journey took him as far afield as Nisibis, some distance east of Edessa.

In 231 this city of Nisibis was the scene of an action which marked a new epoch in those lands. The Parthian kingdom had just fallen to pieces through internal weakness, but a vigorous successor was on the spot. This was the new Sassanid dynasty of Persia, the rise of which coincided with a revival of Persian

---

[1] F. C. Burkitt, *Early Christianity outside the Roman Empire* (1899), p. 61.
[2] F. C. Burkitt, *Church and Gnosis* (1932), pp. 100ff. The Mandæans are so called from the phrase *manda de-chayye*, which in their dialect of Syriac means "knowledge of salvation," *manda* being the equivalent of Greek *gnosis*.

national spirit and of the Zoroastrian religion. The new dynasty conceived its mission to be the restoration of the old Persian Empire which had been overthrown by Alexander the Great, and Ardashir, founder of the new dynasty, began his campaign with the siege of Nisibis. This brought him into conflict with Rome, and a long period of strife ensued between the two Empires.

It was in the early years of the Sassanid dynasty that a new religion was introduced in Persia which was to exercise an influence far beyond the Persian frontiers. This was the Manichæan religion, so called after its founder Mani (c. 216–276). Mani's idea was to found a universal religion, combining features of Zoroastrianism, Buddhism and Christianity. He called himself "the apostle of Jesus Christ" and identified himself with the Paraclete promised by Jesus on the eve of His departure. (The same self-identification was made subsequently by Muhammad and, much more recently, by the founder of Bahaism.) The Christianity which Mani knew, however, was a Gnosticized form, and his basic ideas owe much to Marcion and Bardaisan. As we might expect from its origin, Manichæism is strongly marked by dualism. It spread to China in the east and to Gaul and Spain in the west, and both Asia and Europe saw a revival of it in the Middle Ages. In earlier times its most notable convert in the west was Augustine, who was a Manichæan for some years of his life before he became a Christian.

It was subjected to constant persecution, in east and west alike. In the Roman Empire, Diocletian proscribed it in 296, and his anti-Christian policy which manifested itself a few years later may have been (so far as his personal attitude is concerned) an extension of his anti-Manichæan policy. But while the Persian authorities were equally hostile to Manichæism (Mani himself was crucified by a Persian king at the instance of the Zoroastrian leaders), they do not appear at this time to have been so hostile to Christianity; at any rate, during the last imperial persecutions, many eastern Christians were glad to flee for refuge from Roman to Persian territory.

The first state to become officially Christian (if we except the kingdom of Edessa, which lost its independence almost immediately after it adopted Christianity) was the kingdom of Armenia, which lay as a buffer-state between the Roman and Persian Empires. There King Tiridates and the royal family were baptized about the year 300. Both inside and outside the Roman Empire the beginning of the fourth century marks a new stage in the progress of Christianity.

Christianity was organized for catastrophe. Jesus never tried to conceal from His followers the fact that they would have to

face trouble and persecution if they persisted in following Him—
trouble and persecution which would appear to be sheer disaster.
But if they held out to the end, triumph would be theirs. So it
proved in His personal experience. Christianity could be faced by
no greater disaster than what seemed to be the irretrievable disaster of the cross. But the apparent disaster turned out to be actual
victory. And His followers, He insisted, would find true victory
in exactly the same way. "He who conquers, I will grant him to
sit with me on my throne, as I myself conquered and sat down
with my Father on his throne."[1]

The story of the Christian Church of the first three centuries is
largely a commentary on this. In the fiercest of tribulations Christianity proved its capacity for survival, and not for mere survival,
but for actual victory. And the victory was won by spiritual
weapons alone. Behind the imperial persecutors, Christians saw
the prince of darkness himself, putting forth all his might to overthrow them; "and they overcame him by the blood of the Lamb,
and by the word of their testimony; and they loved not their lives
unto the death."[2] Whatever failures may be marked here and
there, they disappear in the light of "the patience and the faith of
the saints."[3] We review the history of Christianity up to the year
313 with no sense of shame, but with a sense that here is something to evoke gratitude and inspire courage. The qualities that
triumphed then are the qualities which still transmute disaster
into victory.

But what of the new era which began in 313? Could the distinctive qualities of Christianity triumph over imperial patronage
as signally as they had triumphed over imperial hostility? There
are some who would go so far as to say that the prince of darkness, having found the earlier weapon so ineffective, changed his
tactics in the fourth century and found the second weapon much
better adapted to his purpose. Disaster, however, did not vanish
finally from the Church's horizon in 313, and the days were to
come, both sooner and later, which gave fresh opportunity in
abundance to show that Christianity was still organized for
catastrophe. But in 313 we can pause, and take note that the
Servant of the Lord who triumphed by suffering single-handed
in the year 30, now triumphed by suffering again, in His people.

[1] Revelation 3 : 21, R.S.V.   [2] Revelation 12 : 11.   [3] Revelation 13 : 10.

PART III

LIGHT IN THE WEST

The Progress of Christianity from the Accession of Constantine to the Conversion of the English, A.D. 313–800

CHAPTER XXX

CONSTANTINE AND CHRISTIANITY

SOME ASPECTS OF THE DEVELOPMENT OF CHRISTIANITY IN THE Roman world from the time of Constantine onwards are none too pleasant. Time and again in the review of these years we have to record an unhappy precedent. The evident patronage extended to Christianity by the ruling power made Christianity popular in an undesirable sense. Christian leaders were tempted to exploit the influential favour they enjoyed, even when it meant subordinating the cause of justice to the apparent interests of their religion. On the other hand, they were inclined to allow the secular power too much control in church affairs, even if it was by way of gratitude for the imperial good will. Where church leaders were able to exercise political as well as spiritual authority, they did not enjoy any marked immunity from the universally corrupting tendency of power—a tendency which presents an even more displeasing spectacle in Christians than it does in other people, because it clashes so with the first principles of Christianity. We see in those centuries the emergence of worldly ecclesiastics on the one hand, balanced by the inordinate extremities of asceticism on the other. We see nationalist animosities interfering with the proper exercise of Christian duty, to the point where national groups professing Christianity wage fierce warfare upon each other. We see the ugly spirit of intolerance not only directed against non-Christians but also against Christians of divergent beliefs or practices; we even see some Christians invoking against others the aid of the imperial state which but lately had persecuted all Christians alike. We see an unreasonable insistence on uniformity in non-essential matters, such as the fixing of the date of Easter and even more unimportant things than that. We see spiritual liberty hampered by a steady increase of centralized control and organization.

What, we may ask, has all this to do with the mission of the Servant of the Lord, handed on by Jesus to His followers? How could Christians carry out the task which He bequeathed to them and bring the true light to the nations if they disgraced in this way the message which they ought to proclaim? Fortunately, as we shall see, there is another side to the picture; and it is in this other side that the progress of real Christianity appears. But we may as well recognize the fact that its progress to this day has been seriously retarded by the presence of stumbling-blocks—scandals, to use the word of Greek origin—which were first placed in position in the fourth century and which we have not yet entirely succeeded in removing. Nor can any Christian or group of Christians contract out of some share of responsibility for these scandals; un-Christian behaviour on the part of any Christian is a disgrace to all Christians.

When Constantine overthrew his rival Maxentius at the Milvian Bridge in 312 and thus became master of the western empire, the change which this portended in the fortunes of the church was such that it came to be looked upon as practically a Christian victory. Constantine had hitherto been a worshipper of the "Unconquered Sun," whom he regarded as his patron deity. But he ascribed his victory at the Milvian Bridge to the direct intervention of the Christians' God. Before he marched into Italy against Maxentius, he had (according to Eusebius's account, based on Constantine's own later testimony) seen a vision of the cross in the sky,[1] and in a dream the night before the battle at the Milvian Bridge he was commanded to mark his soldiers' shields with the monogram of Christ, a monogram formed of the two initial letters of the Greek name of Christ—X (*ch*) and P (*r*)—and to use the same monogram combined with the cross as his standard or *labarum*. The accounts of the vision and the dream were naturally embellished in later legend, but Constantine did from that time forth consider himself to be in a special sense under the tutelage of the God of Christianity.

This claiming of the sanction of Christianity for warfare was, of course, a new departure, and proved none too happy a precedent. It seemed strangely inconsonant to invoke in armed conflict the name of Christ who had said, "All who take the sword will perish by the sword."[2]

The settlement of Milan, announced by Constantine and his eastern colleague Licinius after the victory, was one of toleration and restitution—toleration for all religious cults and the restitution of all Christian property confiscated in the recent persecutions. The recognition of the right of conscience, which the Milan policy implied, was something much in advance of the times, and it soon ceased to be implemented. The Milan settlement did not establish Christianity as the religion of the empire, as is frequently supposed, nor did it involve a public confession

[1] "What Constantine probably saw was a rare, but well-attested, form of the 'halo-phenomenon,'" says A. H. M. Jones, *Constantine and the Conversion of Europe* (1948), p. 96, on the authority of Professor E. N. da C. Andrade (*op. cit.*, p. xiv).
[2] Matthew 26 : 52.

of Christianity by Constantine—still less by Licinius. Constantine retained the title Pontifex Maximus, as head of the old Roman state religion, and his successors continued to bear it for several decades after him.

For twelve years after the victory at the Milvian Bridge, Licinius remained emperor of the east, and in spite of the Milan agreement the earlier and later parts of this period were marked by conflict between himself and Constantine, in the course of which Constantine's authority extended steadily eastward. Towards the end of the period Licinius indulged in further persecution of Christianity in the east, for the Christians in his realm were suspected (not unnaturally) of favouring the western emperor and desiring his success. Two land victories in 324—at Adrianople and Scutari—and a naval victory in the Dardanelles gave Constantine the command of the whole Roman world. He marked this expansion of his power by a fresh proclamation of toleration throughout the whole empire.

Most of the consequences of Constantine's religious policy were highly beneficial for Christianity. But some were, inevitably perhaps, more doubtful. The church had won out in her struggle with the empire; she had fought throughout with spiritual weapons only, and justice, long denied, had at last been granted her. The liberty now gained had been abundantly earned by the blood of martyrs and confessors. If before long she began to deny to others the freedom of conscience that she herself had contended for and ultimately won, that is a sad commentary on human nature. Religious toleration, even more than any other kind of toleration, is a plant of late and tender growth. Even when it has been secured, it does not survive automatically; it must be most assiduously fostered. The price of religious liberty as of all liberty is eternal vigilance. And it is the adherents of a revealed religion who need to be most specially on their guard against religious intolerance.

Constantine, however, did not merely tolerate Christianity. He acknowledged his indebtedness to the God of Christianity, and long before he finally committed himself to the Christian faith he showed clearly in a variety of ways that Christians enjoyed his special favour. Christianity thus became fashionable, which was not really a good thing. It meant a considerable ingress of Christianized pagans into the church—pagans who had learned the rudiments of Christian doctrine and had been baptized, but who remained largely pagan in their thoughts and ways. The mob in such great cities as Rome and Antioch and Alexandria became Christian in name, but in fact it remained the unruly mob. There was a great temptation for ambitious ecclesiastical statesmen to use the mob for their own ends—a temptation well illustrated in Kingsley's *Hypatia*. For it was the "Christian" mob of Alexandria that tore Hypatia to pieces in 415, and although the complicity of the bishop (Cyril of Alexandria) is not established, yet the outrage suited his book well enough. The election of Damasus as bishop of Rome in 366 was preceded by much unseemly mob-rivalry in the city streets. Doctrinal controversies which should have been confined to the calm consideration of synod and lecture-room were bandied about in the market-place and became the playthings of popular turbulence.

On the other side we have to place the undoubted effect which Christian humanitarianism began to have upon imperial legislation. The doctrine of man as the image of God led to the restriction of branding; it must not be performed on the face. An attempt was made to discourage the practice of exposing unwanted children by making family allowances from the imperial treasury—and by the less Christian device of legalizing the sale of children by their parents. The idea was that parents would be less disposed to expose unwanted children if they could get a price for them. Laws were passed to safeguard the sanctity of marriage, and a greater measure of protection was extended to slaves and animals.

The imperial patronage of Christianity was the cause of another momentous and unfortunate precedent. The Christian leaders were so grateful to Constantine for his favour that they allowed him to have more say in internal church affairs than was his due. By this course they unwittingly but effectively mortgaged the future of Christian liberty. How this worked out in practice in Constantine's reign appears in his intervention in the Donatist dispute, and still more in the part he played at the Council of Nicaea. (The story of this council is told in our next chapter.)

When Constantine enacted that property should be restored to the churches and largesse distributed to them, he found two bodies claiming to represent the Catholic Church[1] in North Africa, and therefore to be the lawful recipients of the restored property and compensation for damage. The emperor had to investigate which party was entitled to have its claim recognized. Hosius, bishop of Cordova, Constantine's spiritual adviser, counselled him to entrust his benefactions in Africa to Caecilian, bishop of Carthage. But this procedure was opposed by the party called the Donatists.

The Donatists took a line after the persecutions under Diocletian similar to that taken by the Novatians half a century before,

---

[1] We may recall here that the Catholic Church comprised the churches founded by apostles, together with the churches in communion with these, which maintained the Catholic faith, based on the apostolic teaching. See pp. 188, 210.

and that in the same province of Africa.[1] They opposed anything like leniency towards those who had weakened in the persecution, especially by surrendering copies of the Scriptures to the police. They objected to the consecration of Caecilian as bishop of Carthage in 312, partly because the bishop who consecrated him was believed to have been one of those *traditores* who handed over sacred literature for destruction. Next year they appealed to Constantine against the appointment, and he commissioned three Gaulish bishops, with the bishop of Rome as chairman, to investigate the matter. (Fifteen Italian bishops were co-opted by the chairman.) The Donatists received no satisfaction from this commission, and in response to a further appeal from them Constantine convoked a council at Arles (in Gaul) in August, A.D. 314. This was a meeting of twenty-three western bishops, and is noteworthy among other reasons because it was attended by three bishops from Britain.[2] It acquitted Caecilian of the charges brought against him by the Donatists.

The Donatists consequently seceded from Caecilian's communion and in 315 they consecrated their leader Donatus as schismatical bishop of Carthage—an office which he retained for about forty years. They held that they were the true Catholic Church, and excommunicated not Caecilian only, but all who maintained communion with him—that is to say, all the rest of Christendom, west and east alike. When, in 316, in reply to a further Donatist appeal, Constantine formally declared Caecilian innocent, his declaration was followed by sanctions against those who refused it; but attempts to repress them only increased the Donatists' resistance. There was, in fact, a strong nationalist element in their resistance—African nationalism against Roman imperialism. They referred to the Catholic Church as the "transmarine" church, and regarded the Catholic bishops as agents of imperial policy. Their resistance continued with various fluctuations for about a hundred years, and from 318 to 411 they even maintained a bishop in Rome to rule the tiny group of their adherents there. Disappointed by the result of their appeal to the emperor, they claimed to stand for spiritual liberty. Their watchword, *Quid imperatori cum ecclesia?*—"What has the emperor to do with the Church?"—was a fine one; it was, however, somewhat inappropriate in the mouth of people who had originally invoked imperial support for their claims. Associated with them were bodies of militant nationalists called *circumcelliones* who went round the countryside armed with clubs, terrorizing adherents of the Catholic party. We must remember, to be sure, that most of our information about them comes from their opponents. But such disturbances of public order naturally called for the intervention

[1] See pp. 212ff. [2] See p. 353 below.

of the civil power, and much of the persecution which the Donatists said they suffered for conscience' sake was really police action against the fomenters of public disorder.

Constantine was convinced of his indebtedness to the God of the Christians, and believed that the maintenance of unity in the Church was of supreme importance to Him. He therefore exerted himself especially when this unity seemed to be threatened, and his desire to mend the breach was usually much greater than his understanding of what caused it.

The new relation between the church and the imperial power was made specially evident at the Council of Nicaea in 325, when Constantine, unbaptized as he was, presided over the deliberations as a "bishop of bishops," so to speak. ("You are bishops of those within," he once told another assembly; "I am appointed by God as bishop of those without.") The eastern conception of the emperor as a sacred personage, vested with spiritual authority, not only survived until the fall of the eastern empire in 1453, but enjoyed a new and lengthy lease of life in Tsarist Russia down to 1917. It can be traced directly back to the veneration paid to the Roman emperors from Constantine onwards.

There is no reason to doubt the genuineness of Constantine's acceptance of Christianity, in spite of his barbaric outbursts which deface the record of his reign from time to time. He compares not unfavourably with another princely Defender of the Faith of later times, the English Henry VIII.

Various economic concessions were made to the Christian clergy; their lands were made exempt from taxation in 315, for example, and they themselves were relieved of certain onerous municipal obligations. But, lest some citizens should attempt to gain this coveted relief by seeking ordination, those of the higher ranks requisite for these honorary offices were debarred from becoming clerics. The numbers of the clergy were limited by statute, and it was provided that they should be recruited from the poorer classes; the rich had their duty to the state. The church calmly submitted to these decrees. She had withstood the secular power when it was hostile and invoked all the sanctions of direct persecution against her. Now, no doubt through boundless gratitude to Constantine, she was less willing to resist the dictates of the civil power when these were accompanied by such generous concessions.

Among these concessions was the right now given to the church to receive legacies. Slaves might be emancipated with legal effect in the presence of a cleric. Civil suits might be transferred to the jurisdiction of a bishop. Sunday was declared a public holiday in 321; as the weekly commemoration of Christ's resurrection it had, of course, been recognized by the Christians as a day specially suitable for divine worship since the first century (although Constantine may also have thought of it as the day of the "Unconquered Sun"). The copying of the Scriptures and the building of church edifices were encouraged; Constantine himself granted large sums for these purposes. From this time copies of the Scriptures are more elaborately and carefully finished, like the great Sinaitic and Vatican codices of the Greek Bible in London and Rome respectively, which belong to the later part of the same fourth century.

Among the church buildings erected by Constantine special mention must be made of the basilica[1] of St. Peter in Rome, on the Vatican hill on the right bank of the Tiber, and the Church of the Holy Sepulchre in Jerusalem. St. Peter's was built on the site where, a hundred and twenty years before, the Roman presbyter Gaius said he could point out the apostle's "trophy";[2] the side of the Vatican hill was excavated at immense trouble and expense to accommodate the foundation. Owing to the complete breach of continuity in Jerusalem Christianity before and after 135, the traditional sacred sites in and around that city are not so certain as those in Rome. However, Macarius, bishop of Jerusalem, identified to the best of his ability the site of the crucifixion and burial of Jesus, and on that site Constantine had the Church of the Holy Sepulchre founded in 327. Its dedication in 335 was a magnificent occasion, attended by bishops from every province, says Eusebius, and by Persian bishops from outside the empire. Basilicas were also erected, largely through the efforts of Constantine's mother Helena and other ladies of the imperial family, to mark the reputed sites of the nativity and ascension of Jesus, and the tombs of the patriarchs of Israel at Hebron. Jerusalem, now under Christian control, was purified of pagan traces and received special honour as a holy city.

In 326 Constantine paid his last visit to Rome. It was marred by quarrels within his own family. His son Crispus was put to death on suspicion of disloyalty; then the Empress Fausta was executed (possibly at the instigation of Helena) for having roused these suspicions. This outbreak of savagery appears to have been followed by some quickening of conscience on Constantine's part. When he left Rome for good after this trouble, he handed over Fausta's palace of the Lateran to Silvester, bishop of Rome, to be his official residence. (This donation was magnified four and a half centuries later into the Emperor's alleged bestowal on the Pope of the sovereignty of all Italy and the west. By this legend, which was widely believed in the Middle Ages—by Dante among

[1] The basilica was the regular Roman form of church meeting-place; it followed the general plan of the Roman dwelling-house.
[2] See pp. 145f.

others—until it was refuted in the fifteenth century by Lorenzo Valla, a canon of St. John Lateran, and the German scholar Nicholas of Cusa, apparent foundation was given to the papal claim to temporal as well as spiritual supremacy.)

The years from 330 to 334 were devoted to the building of a new Rome in the east, on the site of the ancient city of Byzantium, which was henceforth to be the capital of the empire. The new foundation was called Constantinople ("Constantine's city"), and is still widely known by that name, although the Turks call it Istanbul.[1] Rome was henceforth to be of secondary political importance in the empire. When the emperor no longer resided at Rome, the bishop of Rome tended increasingly to be regarded as the most important citizen of that city, and indeed the most important personage in Western Europe. There was really no need of a legendary "donation" to underline the importance of the papacy.

But even when he took up residence permanently in the east, Constantine found trouble and disappointment in plenty. His ambition to restore unity in the Church saw no hope of being realized. Both the Donatist controversy and the more serious dispute which led to the convocation at Nicaea went on giving trouble long after Constantine's death.

Constantine received Christian baptism in 337 and continued thereafter to wear the white robes of a neophyte until his death, which fell later in that year. In the east he was canonized with the title *isapostolos*, "peer of the apostles." The west did not canonize him, but venerated his memory as the founder of the temporal power of the papacy. Though he was not this in the manner which legend imagined, yet he was so in the long run, by virtue of his ecclesiastical policy and his removal of the imperial capital from Rome, with the consequent enhancement of its religious prestige.

But when we try to estimate the real value of his impact upon the Church, it is not easy to strike a balance between its good and evil effects. The blessings which Christianity derived from his policy are obvious enough. On the other hand we have to place the undesirable results of his intervention in affairs of which he had no real understanding and in which he should not have been permitted to play the part he did. Not that he is to be blamed for that; he desired peace and concord within his realm, and especially among churchmen, for whom he had a very real respect. But a desire for concord does not always carry with it the capacity to distinguish between what is true and what is false, and may result

---

[1] Istanbul is a corruption of Greek *eis ten polin*, "into the city." The Greek-speaking population of the eastern empire knew Constantinople as *he polis*, "the city" *par excellence*.

in action which is nothing more than a papering over of cracks. The behaviour of those churchmen who permitted him to have his way with no attempt at protest may be understood well enough, but must be deplored none the less. In the event this course of action proved to be to the disadvantage of state and church alike. "It was a fatal mistake," says a French Roman Catholic historian, "and the two powers were destined to suffer long from its unfortunate consequences. Thus the Church was scarcely freed from the oppression of its persecutors when it had to encounter a trial more terrible perhaps than that of hostility: the embarrassing and onerous protection of the State."[1]

[1] J. R. Palanque, *The Church in the Christian Roman Empire* (1949), p. 69. On Constantine's life and work see (in addition to the work by A. H. M. Jones quoted on p. 294, n. 1) N. H. Baynes, *Constantine the Great and the Christian Church* (1929), A. Alföldi, *The Conversion of Constantine and Pagan Rome* (1948), and J. Burckhardt, *The Age of Constantine the Great* (1949; first published in German, 1853).

CHAPTER XXXI

THE COUNCIL OF NICAEA

MORE IMPORTANT EVEN THAN CONSTANTINE'S PART IN THE Donatist dispute, however, is the part he played in the Council of Nicaea and the events which preceded and followed it. To get the background of this Council we must recall the third-century debates on Christian doctrine, especially where the being of God and—more particularly—the person of Christ were concerned.[1] People like Paul of Samosata and Sabellius, on the one hand, we remember, thought of the Son of God as an emanation from the Father, or as one of the *rôles* assumed by the Father in manifesting Himself and His ways to men. Tertullian and Novatian and Origen, on the other hand, defined the relation between God the Father and Christ the Son in terms which did more justice to the facts of Biblical revelation and Christian experience. No definitive ruling, however, had been given which the churches in general could regard as binding. All parties, generally speaking, accepted the statements in the current baptismal creeds, but differed on their interpretation. The debate came to a head in the fourth century.

In 318 a dispute broke out at Alexandria between the bishop, Alexander, and one of his presbyters named Arius. Arius had been trained at Antioch by a distinguished scholar named Lucian, head of the theological school in that city, who met a martyr's death in 312; and Lucian in turn had been a disciple of Paul of Samosata. The schools of Antioch and Alexandria differed widely in their theological outlook and emphasis, and each suspected heretical tendencies in the other's emphasis. This might well be so; we remember a remark of Dr. Emil Brunner, that a heresy is a truth carried to its logical conclusion! At any rate, Arius saw fit to charge his bishop with Sabellianism, because of the terms in which he insisted on the unity of the Godhead in one of his episcopal charges. No doubt the bishop's language, whatever his intentions were, did suggest that he regarded the Son and the Spirit of God as little more than "modes" of the divine activity. Arius's views, however, were equally open to criticism in the other direction. To use the terminology of the later canticle popularly called the Athanasian Creed,[2] if Alexander seemed

[1] See pp. 254ff.   [2] See p. 308.

guilty of "confounding the persons," Arius was certainly guilty of "dividing the substance." That is to say, Arius taught that there was a real difference in essence between the deity of the Father and the deity of the Son.

But the real defect of Arius's teaching lies in the fact that it starts off with the Greek doctrine of a remote God. God (to this way of thinking) is too far removed from men, too wholly other, to come into direct relation with them. Christ, the Mediator between God and man, was for Arius neither God nor man, but something betwixt and between. The catholic doctrine, on the other hand, maintains that the incarnate Son is at one and the same time altogether God and altogether man. The catholic doctrine is, in fact, bound up closely (more closely, perhaps, than many of the early Fathers realized) with the Biblical statement that man was made in the image of God. It is because of this creative fact that it is possible for the Mediator to be simultaneously both.

> He deigns in flesh to appear,
>   Widest extremes to join,
> To bring our vileness near
>   And make us all divine;
> And we the life of God shall know,
> Since God is manifest below.

Arius, however, provided a statement of the divine relationship to man which was as congenial to the common man of that day as it is unattractive to us. Origen, indeed, had taught that the Son was subordinate to the Father, in person and office at any rate if not in essence; and had gone so far as to call the Son a creature, in the sense at least that His being was dependent on the Father's will. But he safeguarded the Biblical presentation by emphasizing that Christ was the Son of God from all eternity, by what he called an "eternal generation." Arius also taught the subordination of the Son to the Father, but went on to speak of the Son as a created being in a much more literal sense than Origen allowed. Whereas Origen held that the Son existed as the Son from all eternity, Arius denied this, expressing his view in the sentence, "There was (a time) when He was not." The Son, according to Arius, was created by the Father out of nothing, as the first of all created beings. The time at which the Son came into being might belong to the infinitely remote past, but it was theoretically possible to conceive of a time before He began to exist. Far from thinking that such abstruse questions as these should be confined to theological study circles, he set them forth in doggerel verses which were sung to popular tunes by the rank and file of Alexandrian Christians.

Many Arians were in practice excellent and energetic Christians.

Their missionary activity among the Goths is something specially to be remembered to their credit.[1] But Arianism was none the less a menace to Christianity. There is considerable truth in the cynical remark of the historian Bury that the triumph of Arianism would have meant the "premature" disappearance of Christianity, although opinions will differ about the aptness of the adjective. For Arianism reflected a temporary phase of thought, and by conceiving of Christ as neither God nor man, but something in between, it deprived Him of any real mediatorship or saving power.

At length the bishop convened a council at Alexandria (321), and Arius was deposed from the presbyter's office. But he had a considerable following in Alexandria itself, and he knew that many Christian leaders of the east were, like himself, adherents of the school of Antioch and more particularly disciples of Lucian, so that he could count on widespread and influential sympathy. The dispute spread beyond the boundaries of Egypt, and it looked as if a schism might result in eastern Christendom. When Constantine became master of the east in 324, he was concerned by this threat of a cleavage, a threat more serious than that presented by the Donatists in the west, and he offered his good offices in an attempt to restore peace between the two parties. First he sent letters to Alexander and Arius, and expressed his readiness to act as mediator between them. He had yet to learn how hopeless it is for a well-intentioned layman to try to reconcile theologians of contrary views! When these efforts proved fruitless, he called a general council of representatives of all Christendom—possibly at the suggestion of Hosius, bishop of Cordova in Spain, in whom he placed great confidence.

The council, which met at Nicaea in north-west Asia Minor on May 20, 325, was the first ecumenical council of the Church; that is to say, the first to which representatives were called from churches all over the known world (Greek *oikoumene*, "inhabited earth.") It was attended by nearly three hundred bishops. Representatives were even present from eastern churches beyond the limits of the Roman Empire, from such lands as Persia and Scythia. The west, however, was sparsely represented. The bishop of Rome, Silvester, did not attend, but sent two presbyters to represent him; Caecilian (the Donatists' pet aversion) came from Carthage, and Hosius from Cordova, the emperor's right-hand man in ecclesiastical affairs. One bishop came from Gaul.

The Arian side was supported at the Council by Arius himself and a number of his sympathizers, prominent among whom was his old fellow-student, the bishop of Nicomedia, not far from Nicaea. On the other side, Alexander was strongly supported by

[1] See pp. 321f.

some of his fellow-bishops, but above all by his own deacon Athanasius. This young man had already made his mark as a theologian with his treatise *On the Incarnation of the Divine Word*— one of the great classics of Christian theology. A mediating position was taken by Eusebius, bishop of Palestinian Cæsarea, the great church historian. He put forward the baptismal confession of his own church of Cæsarea as a basis of agreement:

> We believe in one God the Father Almighty, the Maker of all things visible and invisible;
>
> And in one Lord Jesus Christ, the Word of God, God of God, Light of Light, Life of Life, Son only-begotten, Firstborn of all creation, begotten of God the Father before all the ages, through whom also all things were made; who became flesh for our salvation and lived among men, who suffered, and rose again the third day, and ascended to the Father, and will come again in glory to judge the living and dead;
>
> We believe also in one Holy Spirit.[1]

This confession, conforming to the regular tripartite pattern, was perfectly orthodox, but it did not give an explicit answer to the questions which the council was considering. The council therefore, did not adopt it as it stood, but revised it in an anti-Arian sense and promulgated the revised version as the Creed of Nicaea.[2] It ran as follows:

> We believe in one God the Father almighty, Maker of all things visible and invisible;
>
> And in one Lord Jesus Christ, the Son of God, begotten of the Father, only-begotten, *that is to say of the essence of the Father*, God of God, Light of Light, *true God of true God, begotten, not made, of the same essence as the Father:* through whom all things were made, *things in heaven and things on earth:* who *for us men and* for our salvation *came down and* became flesh and lived among men, who suffered and on the third day rose again, ascended into heaven, is coming to judge the living and dead;
>
> And in the Holy Spirit.
>
> *But those who say, "There was a time when He was not," and "Before He was begotten He did not exist," and "He came into being from that which is non-existent," or those who maintain that the Son of God is "of another substance or essence," or "created," or "capable of change," or "subject to alteration"—those the holy catholic and apostolic Church pronounces accursed.*

The italicized words, both those inserted in the confession itself and those added at the end, were intended to make the council's rejection of Arianism explicit. The phrases anathematized in the appendix give a fair idea of the characteristic Arian positions.

[1] The repetition of the numeral "one" in the successive clauses of this and other Eastern Creeds (by contrast with the Roman Creed) is probably due to the influence of 1 Corinthians 8 : 6 and Ephesians 4 : 4–6.

[2] See note on p. 308.

This practice of including anathemas in credal statements was a further unhappy precedent of the Constantinian age. Unlike previous credal statements, the Creed of Nicaea was not a baptismal confession but an expression of ecclesiastical doctrine.

Agreement on a formula can often mask fundamental disagreement, as other councils than ecclesiastical ones have learned to their cost. The Creed of Nicaea was no exception; it was accepted for the time being by many who sympathized with Arius, in the hope that they might suceed in interpreting its wording in a less anti-Arian sense. Only two bishops refused to sign it; they were forthwith excommunicated, along with Arius himself.

The phrase "of the same essence (Greek *homoousios*) as the Father" caused some heart-searching. Not only was it absent from the Bible; it had actually been used by the heretic Paul of Samosata in the previous century to express his conception of Christ as an emanation from God.[1] Many questioned the wisdom of including it in the Creed of Nicaea. It was, however (according to Eusebius), suggested by Constantine himself; and when the Arians showed their dismay at it, the anti-Arian party took it up and insisted that it was indispensable, as no other term could so explicitly exclude Arianism. The Arians and their sympathizers would have agreed to describe Christ as "like (Greek *homoios*) the Father," or "of a like essence (Greek *homoiousios*) with the Father;" but these terms were naturally judged inadequate to safeguard the catholic belief. It is silly to speak ironically (as some do) of all the trouble that arose over the presence or absence of the letter *i* (as between *homoousios* and *homoiousios*), or to belittle the "battle of the diphthongs;" there are many words where the presence or absence of a single letter makes a mighty difference to the sense. And to say that the deity of the Son is similar to, but not identical with, the deity of the Father, is in effect to say that there are two Gods. But the glory of God which shines in the face of Jesus Christ is the glory of the only living and true God: "for in him all the fullness of God was pleased to dwell."[2]

When the bishops came together at Nicaea, it proved convenient to deal with other matters of general interest. One of these was the Melitian schism in Egypt. This schism was called after its leader Melitius, a south Egyptian bishop who assumed the episcopal function in Alexandria during the late persecution in the absence of the canonical bishop. Like the Donatist schism farther west, it was a product of that persecution. Here too the schismatics were those who considered that they alone had maintained true fidelity in the face of martyrdom. The council, however, did not succeed in settling the dispute, and it continued for some

[1] See p. 255.   [2] Colossians 1 : 19.

time to complicate the life of the Egyptian churches, as it constituted a second cleavage in their ranks which crossed the doctrinal one.

Other matters which were settled at Nicaea were various questions of church discipline, the procedure for provincial church councils and the consecration and precedence of bishops. Rome, Antioch and Alexandria were acknowledged as the three leading sees, in accordance with "ancient custom"; their bishops were accorded the title "patriarch."[1]

The date of Easter was another subject discussed on the same occasion. The Nicene councillors confirmed the majority practice —that which had been followed in Rome since the early second century—and the quartodeciman observance was discontinued, except in one or two remote communities.[2] The Alexandrian church was commissioned to fix the date of Easter year by year according to the appropriate lunar calculations, and to announce it in advance to the Christian world. Thus each year the bishop of Alexandria sent out a circular "Festal Letter" to his fellow-bishops announcing the date of Easter in that year. When Athanasius was bishop of Alexandria (he succeeded Alexander in 328 and held the see, apart from intervals of banishment, for forty-five years), he used the opportunity offered by these Festal Letters to discuss some topic of ecumenical interest. Most interesting is his Festal Letter of 367, in which he dealt with the canon of Scripture. He arranges the canonical books of the Old Testament so as to yield a total of twenty-two, but these twenty-two correspond to the thirty-nine in our Protestant Bible,[3] except that Esther is left out and that Jeremiah has appended to it not only Lamentations but also Baruch and the "Epistle of Jeremiah." Then he adds: "There are also other books outside this list which are non-canonical but have been handed down with approval from our fathers to be read to new converts . . . the Wisdom of Solomon, the Wisdom of Sirach, Esther, Judith, Tobias."[4] His New Testament list is noteworthy because it is the first known to us which enumerates exactly the twenty-seven books which have come down to us as forming the second part of the Biblical canon.[5]

The rules or "canons" drawn up by the council of Nicaea were

[1] Soon after the foundation of Constantinople as the new imperial capital (334) the bishop of that city acquired patriarchal rank, and eventually took precedence over those of Antioch and Alexandria. The Bishop of Jerusalem was accorded patriarchal status in 451.

[2] See pp. 210ff., 276.

[3] The number twenty-two was thought to correspond to the number of letters in the Hebrew alphabet. Josephus, in the first century A.D., also reckoned the Hebrew canon to contain twenty-two books (*Against Apion*, I, 8). This number was attained by counting the double books as one each, by counting the Twelve (Minor) Prophets as one, and so forth.

[4] See my *The Books and the Parchments* (1950), pp. 94ff., 156ff.

[5] See p. 235.

generally accepted in the churches, and provided a nucleus for the subsequent development of canon law.

Note:—The Creed of Nicaea, quoted on p. 305, is of course not the formulary which we commonly call the Nicene Creed, although it expresses the same distinctive teaching. Our so-called Nicene Creed was sanctioned at the Council of Chalcedon (the fourth general council) in 451. There its composition was mistakenly assigned to the Council of Constantinople held in 381 (the second ecumenical council), and for that reason it has sometimes been wrongly called the Constantinopolitan Creed. In actual fact, it may have been based on the baptismal confession used about that time in the Church of Jerusalem. After 451 it was used alongside the Creed of Nicaea. In 553 the Second Council of Constantinople (the fifth ecumenical council) treated it as if it were a revised edition of the Creed of Nicaea. It was popular because of its fuller statement of the doctrine of the Holy Spirit, a doctrine which was not fully discussed and defined until the post-Nicene period.

What is traditionally called the Athanasian Creed is not really a creed at all, and is not the work of Athanasius. It is a theological exposition in the form of a canticle, composed in the west towards the end of the fourth century. It is more accurately referred to by its opening words *Quicunque Vult* ("Whosoever will . . .").

Only in the sixth century did the custom arise of general recitation of the creed apart from its use as a confession by those about to be baptized. The eastward-facing position in reciting the creed does not seem to be earlier than the seventeenth century. In the early Christian centuries catechumens at their baptism turned west to renounce the devil and east to confess Christ.

J. N. D. Kelly's *Early Christian Creeds* (1950) is one of the most authoritative works on the subject indicated by its title.

CHAPTER XXXII

FROM NICAEA TO CHALCEDON

THE DISPUTE BETWEEN THE ARIANS AND THE ATHANASIANS did not come to an end with the Council of Nicaea. Although the council explicitly condemned Arianism, imperial patronage in the following decades veered from one party to the other. Arius, who was excommunicated at the end of the council, was reconciled to the emperor two years later, on satisfying him that he really accepted the orthodox faith. But Athanasius, who became bishop of Alexandria in 328, was not so easily satisfied as Constantine, and would not have Arius back in Alexandria at any price. Constantine, out of his depth, blamed now one, now the other, for being the real obstacle in the way of Christian unity. Athanasius in particular he found exasperatingly unbending in this regard. Athanasius stood for principle at any price; Constantine for concord at any price. Athanasius had many enemies; Melitians, Arians and semi-Arians were leagued against him. His election to the see was not unanimous, and a succession of serious charges was levelled against him—illegal consecration, venality, rapacity, sacrilege, assault, and murder. Most of these broke down on investigation. But it seemed plain to Constantine that there would be no peace in the church so long as Athanasius remained in Alexandria, and when, towards the end of 335, it was reported to him that Athanasius had threatened to interrupt the supply of grain from Egypt to Constantinople, he peremptorily exiled him to Trier (Trèves) in the Rhineland. He did not deprive him of his see, however, and the Egyptian bishops and people in general remained loyal to their exiled metropolitan.[1] Even when Athanasius was away, they refused to readmit Arius to communion. Arius returned to Constantinople, where he died soon after. And Athanasius returned from exile soon after the emperor's death in 337.

After Constantine's death his son Constantius (337–361) tried to hold a mediating, "semi-Arian" position, with unfortunate results. The next emperor, Julian the Apostate (361–363), was

---

[1] A metropolitan is a bishop who presides over the other bishops in a province. He was so called because originally he was the bishop of the capital city or metropolis of the province. The term is practically, but not completely, synonymous with "archbishop."

interested in promoting division so as to weaken Christendom in general and the catholic faith in particular. Athanasius was exiled from his see in Alexandria four times more after his restoration on the morrow of Constantine's death.[1] In 381, however, at the second ecumenical council, held at Constantinople, the Creed of Nicaea was declared to be the sole legal religion in the empire. Theodosius, who was then eastern emperor, did not share Constantine's preference for toleration, and those who did not conform might henceforth look for trouble from the secular arm over and above ecclesiastical discipline.

This Council of Constantinople also condemned the doctrine known as Apollinarianism. This doctrine was concerned not so much with the relation between the Son and the Father as with the relation between the divine and human sides of Christ's own person. Granted that He was God and man, how, they asked, did God and man combine in Him? Apollinarius, bishop of Laodicea in Syria, reading the opening words of St. John's Gospel, concluded that the Divine Word too a human body into union with Himself and that in this new Man the Divine Word Himself took the place that in other men is taken by a rational mind or spirit. While Arius regarded Christ as being rather less than God but rather more than man, Apollinarius admitted that He was altogether God, but not man in the full sense—*like* man but not *a* man. This was rightly held to deny the reality of the incarnation. Any doctrine which fails to recognize unambiguously the true and complete manhood of the historical Christ is a menace to the Christian gospel. Apollinarianism was in a sense a revival of the old docetic heresy. It had been condemned at several provincial synods of the church—at Alexandria in 362, at Rome in 377, and at Antioch in 379—before it received (or seemed to receive) its quietus at Constantinople. But it did not really die out; it has reappeared many times since, and to this day it is the heresy to which many Christians who think themselves orthodox are specially, though unconsciously, prone.[2]

The Council of Constantinople did not deal only with the doctrine of the person of Christ; it had something to say about the Holy Spirit as well, affirming Him to be a "person"—an *hypostasis*[3]—equal within the unity of the Godhead to the Father and the Son, "proceeding from the Father."[4] This concern with the true doctrine of the Holy Spirit reflects serious theological thinking that had gone on during the preceding half-century, especially on the part of three Christian leaders usually called "the Cappa-

---

[1] See pp. 317ff. for the period 337-381.

[2] See C. E. Raven, *Apollinarianism* (1923).

[3] See p. 259. The term *hypostasis* occurs in the Greek New Testament in Hebrews 1 : 3, of the Father's "person" (A.V.), "substance" (R.V.), "nature" (R.S.V.).

[4] A Biblical expression; cf. John 15 : 26.

docians"—Basil, bishop of Cappadocian Cæsarea (329–379), his younger brother Gregory, bishop of Nyssa in the same province (c. 335–395), and another Gregory (329–389), commonly known as Gregory of Nazianzus after the Cappadocian city where he spent much of his life.[1] These three theologians maintained Nicene orthodoxy, but were also keen students of the works of Origen. They were able to remove the difficulties which many Christians of Asia Minor felt in accepting the term *homoousios* with its implications, and greatly clarified Greek theological terminology by the careful distinction which they drew between the one essence (Greek *ousia*) of the Godhead and the three *hypostases* in which the one essence subsisted. This distinction did for Greek theological terminology a similar service to that which Tertullian did for Latin-speaking Christians over a hundred and fifty years earlier when he spoke of the Godhead as one *substantia* in three *personae*.[1] Those who feared that the term *homoousios* made way for a Sabellian conception of God were now relieved; the Cappadocians' formulation of the Nicene doctrine excluded a Sabellian interpretation. A form of words was now available in which the simple Nicene declaration of belief "in the Holy Spirit" could be expanded in the direction of greater precision—although, remarkably enough, the Cappadocian fathers themselves were suspected of not being completely orthodox in respect of this branch of Christian doctrine.

Fifty years after the Council of Constantinople the third ecumenical council was held, at Ephesus. Two further heresies came up for condemnation here. In fact, from Nicaea onward, it was mainly by way of reaction to heresy that the Catholic Church went on to formulate her belief more and more explicitly. On the one side and on the other attempts were made to accommodate the Christian faith to current modes of thought, but these accommodations usually proved, on scrutiny, to be basically inconsistent with the substance of the faith itself. And this was just as well, for the current modes of thought to which people tried to accommodate the faith sooner or later went the way of most modes of thought; and had one of these accommodations been established as "Christianity rightly so called," it would have accompanied them into the limbo of creeds outworn.

The two heresies dealt with by the Council of Ephesus in 431 were called after two outstanding leaders of thought, Pelagius and Nestorius, the former from the west, the latter from the east. Pelagianism was not concerned with the doctrine of God but

[1] They should be distinguished from an earlier Gregory, whose traditions they imbibed—Gregory Thaumaturgus (the "Wonder-worker"), one of Origen's most illustrious and devoted pupils (died A.D. 268).

[2] See p. 257.

with the doctrine of man, and something will be said about it in a later chapter.[1] Nestorianism was a development of the distinctive emphasis of the Antioch school of theology.[2] The Antiochians stressed the real manhood of Christ, and very necessarily so, for the tendency of the age was to make it unreal. But Nestorius (who became bishop of Constantinople in 428) and his followers stressed it to a point where Christ appeared to be a dual personality—a divine personality and a human personality within one living consciousness. The test by which Nestorius's theological soundness was examined was not a very happy one: it was his willingness or unwillingness to give our Lord's mother the title *theotokos*, a Greek compound noun which means the "God-bearer"—or, more diffusely but more exactly, "she who gave birth to the Child who is God." Nestorius, making the distinction he did between two personalities in Christ, refused to accept that as a proper appellation of Mary: Mary, he held, was the mother of the human personality but not of the divine personality. To be sure, many Christians who are far from holding Nestorius's Christology prefer not to speak of Mary as *theotokos*, especially as popularly but loosely rendered "Mother of God;" she is not usually given this title, for example, among orthodox Protestants. But Nestorius's reason for refusing her the title was a formally heretical one. He was opposed by Cyril, bishop of Alexandria, and by the Roman bishop Caelestine. Cyril's opposition was as much political as theological; he was only too glad to seize an opportunity to discredit the Constantinopolitan patriarch to increase the influence of his own see. After the condemnation of Nestorianism at Ephesus, a large part of Syrian Christendom continued to espouse it, and it was the Nestorian Christians who in the following centuries carried out the great missionary enterprise in Central Asia which in the early Middle Ages brought them right into China itself.

The opposite heresy to Nestorianism was associated with the name of one Eutyches, a monk of Constantinople. Far from emphasizing the distinction between the divine and human natures in Christ to the point of making Him a double personality, this school of thought blurred the distinction altogether, maintaining that His humanity had been deified by being united with His divinity. As Nestorianism was an exaggeration of the characteristic emphasis of Antioch, this "Monophysite" doctrine, as it was called (i.e. the doctrine of the single nature), was an exaggeration of the characteristic emphasis of Alexandria—although the ablest Monophysite theologian, Severus, was an Antiochian. Cyril of Alexandria, although not a Monophysite himself, had a good deal

[1] See pp. 335ff.
[2] See J. F. Bethune-Baker, *Nestorius and his Teaching* (1908).

of sympathy with their leader Eutyches. Through the influence of Dioscorus, successor of Cyril (who had died in 444), Eutyches was acquitted of heresy at a provincial synod held at Ephesus in 449—a synod which Leo the Great, bishop of Rome, described indignantly and scornfully as a gang of robbers. The question came up for further discussion at the fourth ecumenical council, held in 451 at Chalcedon, on the Asiatic side of the Bosporus. Here Leo's influence prevailed; he sent five legates to represent him, and they presided at the council. The terms in which the Chalcedon councillors formulated their findings were based on a letter sent by Leo of Rome two years before to Flavian of Constantinople and now submitted to the council. These terms constitute a definition of the doctrine of Christ's Person which has since been accepted as authoritative by all the main streams of Christian tradition. Here it is:

> Therefore, following the holy fathers, we all with one accord teach men to acknowledge one and the same Son, our Lord Jesus Christ, at once perfect in Godhead and perfect in Manhood, truly God and truly Man, consisting also of a rational soul and body; of the same substance as the Father in respect of His Godhead, and at the same time of the same substance as ourselves in respect of His Manhood, like us in all respects apart from sin; in respect of His Godhead begotten of the Father before the ages, but yet in respect of His Manhood begotten of Mary, the Virgin who gave birth to Him who is God, for us men and for our salvation; one and the same Christ, Son, Lord, only-begotten; recognized in two natures, without confusion, without change, without division, without separation; the distinction of natures being in no wise annulled by their union, but rather the properties of both natures being preserved and coming together to form one person and *hypostasis*, not as divided or separated into two persons, but one and the same Son and only-begotten God the Word, the Lord Jesus Christ; even as the prophets from earliest times spoke of Him, and our Lord Jesus Christ Himself taught us, and the belief of the fathers has handed it down to us.

The technical terminology of this definition sounds strange and remote in the ears of men to-day, apart from those who have had a special training in historical theology. Its vocabulary is largely drawn from that of Greek metaphysics, and inevitably so under the circumstances. It would be an interesting exercise to try to express the same essential teaching in language more readily intelligible to reasonably educated men and women of our own day. The ordinary Christian, now as then, worships God through Christ and is not troubled about exact definitions; but intellectual honesty demands that those who are able to do so should give a reasoned statement both to themselves and to others of what they really believe about Christ.

We shall not understand the formulation of the Chalcedonian statement, or of the promulgations of any of those early councils, unless we grasp what were the particular deviations which were deliberately excluded by their careful choice of words. And those deviations were *intellectually* unsound apart from anything else. Had any one of them been finally approved as the ecumenical faith, the survival power of Christianity would have been seriously weakened. Bury might have said of any of these deviations what he said of Arianism, that its triumph would have caused the "premature" disappearance of Christianity.

Historically it may be true, as Foakes Jackson puts it, that "the Chalcedonian definition was a Roman formula forced on the Oriental Church by imperial authority"[1]—referring to the parts played by Pope Leo and by the Emperor Marcian, who was present at the council and was determined to exalt the prestige of the see of Constantinople at the expense of that of Alexandria. We know that, in spite of the council's decision, Monophysite views remained strong in the Egyptian Church, which was ultimately lost to orthodox Christendom (the Coptic Church, with the Ethiopic, being Monophysite to the present day). But so sound and penetrating a theological thinker as B. B. Warfield had reason for his claim that the Chalcedonian settlement well deserves to remain "the authoritative statement of the elements of the doctrine of the Person of Christ." "For," he goes on, "this 'settlement' does justice at once to the data of Scripture, to the implicates of an Incarnation, to the needs of Redemption, to the demands of the religious emotions, and to the logic of a tenable doctrine of our Lord's Person."[2]

The various heresies that sprang up in the earliest Christian centuries are by no means out of date. They reappear regularly in one form or another from generation to generation; as Miss Dorothy Sayers has emphasized, they are "largely the expression of opinion of the untutored average man, trying to grapple with the problems of the universe at the point where they begin to interfere with his daily life and thought."[3] We have in our day a vocabulary for expressing the various concepts and problems associated with personality which was not available in the fifth century. It may be that the fundamental Christian belief should be restated in terms which will be seen to exclude the classical heresies in their modern expression, as the Chalcedonian statement plainly excluded them in their ancient expression; and that the restatement should be seen to have a meaning which (to quote

[1] F. J. Foakes Jackson, *History of the Christian Church* (1914), p. 474.
[2] B. B. Warfield, *The Person and Work of Christ* (1950 edn.), p. 189.
[3] D. L. Sayers, *Creed or Chaos?* (1947), p. 35. The whole context of this quotation shows how necessary and relevant is the whole question of right and wrong thinking on this subject.

Miss Sayers) is "clear to the ordinary uninstructed heathen to whom technical theological language has become a dead letter."[1] But if they are so restated, it will be surprising if the restatement does not turn out to be but the translation of the Chalcedonian definition from fifth-century Greek into the living idioms of to-day.

We need not pursue the ecumenical councils further. There are three others recognized by the whole historic Church of east and west—the Second and Third Councils of Constantinople (553 and 680) and the Second Council of Nicaea (787). But for our present survey of the progressive definition of Christian doctrine, Chalcedon provides a suitable terminus.[2]

[1] *Op. cit.*, p. 37.
[2] See R. V. Sellers, *The Council of Chalcedon* (1953).

CHAPTER XXXIII

IMPERIAL DECLINE

To MANY READERS OF TO-DAY THE HISTORY OF CREEDS AND councils appears singularly uninspiring, although the precise nature of the divine-human union in the Second Person of the Holy Trinity was debated with animation by the men in the streets of Constantinople and Alexandria in those centuries. But there are features of the church history of the time which are more uninspiring by far, and justify Dr. Inge's remark that "a great deal of what passes for church history . . . is really a rather unedifying branch of secular history."[1] And much of this chapter must be devoted to largely uninspiring and unedifying material, which is necessary to our purpose because it provides the background to our main theme and serves as a link between the Christianizing of the Roman Empire as a whole (which we have considered hitherto) and the Christianizing of the British Isles in particular (to which we are coming in the second half of this part).

But we must bear in mind that against this background the real work of Christianity was going on all the time, outside the imperial frontiers as well as inside them. Let Dr. Foakes Jackson summarize the situation for us:

> The growth of the Church beyond the imperial frontiers was perhaps more rapid in the sixth than in the fifth century, when we find large Christian communities in southern Arabia, traces of missionary work far inland in northern Africa, churches established among the Nubians and Blemmyes by the energy of the Egyptian Christians. In addition to this were the vast operations of the Nestorians, those undaunted missionaries who journeyed across Asia preaching the word and establishing churches even in China. It appears that scant justice has been done to the expansive powers of the Christianity of the fifth and sixth centuries, and to the enormous efforts then made to evangelize the world. Nor must the influence of the monks and hermits be overlooked, whose austerities and blameless lives exercised so potent an influence on the barbarian tribes of the desert. We are apt to forget, whilst studying the often barren and profitless controversies of the age, the astonishing vitality of the Church in every part of the world. If missionary zeal is a proof of

[1] W. R. Inge, *Things New and Old* (1933), p. 58; see the whole passage quoted on p. 161.

life, the Christian Church was never more alive than at the close of our period.

By A.D. 461 there were strong and vigorous churches in Armenia, Iberia, Mesopotamia, Persia, and Ethiopia. The gospel was being preached in the Sahara . . . Ireland, which had never been incorporated in the Empire, was a province of the Roman Church; and Christianity had overstepped the wall of Hadrian, which the Romans had had such difficulty in defending. Britain was over-run by heathen invaders who were powerless to eradicate what must have appeared to be but a feeble branch of the Christian Church. By means unknown to us, by missionaries whose names will never be revealed, every invader of Gaul and Italy, Spain and Africa, had heard of Christ. Rome had fallen into the hands of barbarians, but those barbarians were Christian. Already the Syriac, Ethiopian, Armenian, Gothic and Coptic languages had been pressed into the service of Christ; and the Gospels were translated into tongues whose very alphabet it had been necessary for missionaries to compose. At Nicaea, at Ephesus, at Chalcedon, the delegates of churches over which the Emperor had no authority appeared, to shew that Christ claimed not the Roman but the human race.[1]

All the Roman emperors after Constantine were Christians by formal profession, if in no other sense, with the exception of Julian the Apostate. They continued Constantine's policy of playing a dominant rôle in church affairs, and the consequences were unhappier than they had been in Constantine's time. The struggle between Athanasians and Arians went on until 381, and now one party, now the other, prevailed in accordance with the sympathies of the imperial power.[2]

Constantine's realm was divided at his death between three of his sons. But it was reunited in 353 when the survivor of the three, Constantius, ruled the Roman world as sole emperor. Constantius, thinking doubtless that truth is sure to lie about half-way between two extremes (which is very seldom so), took up a position in the Arian controversy which is usually described as semi-Arian. From this mediating position he appeared to favour now one, now the other, of the contesting parties. Probably his idea was to recognize whichever side seemed at any particular time to command the majority verdict in the Church, thinking that this was the best way to promote unity within the Church and concord between the Church and the Empire. "Balanced on this imperceptible centre between truth and error," says Cardinal Newman, "he alternately banished every party in the controversy, not even sparing his own; and had recourse in turn to every creed

[1] F. J. Foakes Jackson, *History of the Christian Church to A.D.* 461 (1914), pp. 564f. For a fuller account of the missionary enterprise of this period see K. S. Latourette, *History of the Expansion of Christianity*, I (1938), pp. 171ff., II (1939), pp. 1ff.
[2] See S. L. Greenslade, *Church and State from Constantine to Theodosius* (1954).

for relief, except that in which the truth was really to be found"[1] (and by that, of course, Newman meant the Creed of Nicaea).

Few of the leading churchmen of the time, whichever side they took in the controversy, could approve the emperor's policy, and least of all did Athanasius approve it. The word compromise was foreign to Athanasius's vocabulary, and he would not countenance any deviation from the position he had maintained at Nicaea. But Athanasius was uncompromising in other respects as well, and was consequently, as we have said, the sort of man who has many enemies. His personal enemies and ecclesiastical opponents were not slow to exploit his opposition to Constantius's policy. The result was that, soon after returning from his first exile at the end of Constantine's reign, he had to go into exile again. He spent a period of exile in the west from 339 to 346, while Constantius was emperor in the east only; and after ten years' restoration to his Alexandrian see he had to seek refuge in the deserts of Upper Egypt in 356, and stayed there until after the death of Constantius. For a time (356-361) his see was occupied by a usurping Arian bishop, the unprincipled pork-contractor, George of Cappadocia, in whom the historian Gibbon thought he had discovered the original of England's patron saint.[2]

Not all the leaders in the Church were as resolute as Athanasius. Athanasius may have been a spiritual autocrat, but he was a man to whom principle was the one thing that mattered. He knew where he stood, and determined to stand there, even if it was a case of "Athanasius against the world." Hilary, bishop of Poitiers, one of the chief defenders of Nicene orthodoxy in the west, was also exiled from his see in 356 and had to spend some years in banishment in Phrygia. The bishop of Rome, Liberius, was similarly banished the following year. But others—including Hosius of Cordova, Constantine's adviser, now nearly a hundred years old—were compelled by *force majeure* to do violence to their Nicene convictions and sign on the semi-Arian line. Nor were there lacking other leading churchmen who availed themselves of the opportunity afforded by the changes of imperial favour to acquire more power for themselves and injure those with whom they disagreed. One council followed another until 359, when the western bishops at Rimini (Ariminum), in North Italy, and the eastern bishops at Seleucia, in Cilicia, agreed to a mediating formula which had the emperor's approval. From the Athanasian point of view, the formula gave the orthodox case away by omitting the term *homoousios* and by using language capable of an

---

[1] J. H. Newman, *The Arians in the Fourth Century* (3rd edn., 1871), p. 297.
[2] E. Gibbon, *Decline and Fall of the Roman Empire* (1774-94), chapter 23. St. George of England is probably to be identified with a native of Lydda in Palestine who was martyred in Diocletian's persecution (303).

Arian interpretation. "The whole world groaned," as Jerome said later, writing of the council at Rimini, "and marvelled to find itself Arian."[1]

The middle half of the fourth century presents a squalid enough story; Christianity, we may say, proved its living power by showing itself able to survive the disgraceful behaviour of some of its chief official agents in those years. "Odious" is the adjective that a recent writer applies to the period; "the fourth century", he says, "is a bleak and terrible one on which to work." And he adds, aptly: "The reader who has grown up alongside of the League of Nations, U.N.O., and the Security Council will find the technique of General Councils, Peace Manifestos, and the exile of deviationists all dismally familiar."[2]

Constantius died in 361 and was succeeded by his younger cousin Julian, whom he had appointed to command the imperial forces in the west, with the rank of Cæsar. Julian proved himself an able commander and had actually been persuaded by his Gallo-Roman followers to assume the supreme imperial authority in the west a short time before Constantius died. When Constantius died, the whole empire without a dissentient voice accepted Julian as his successor.

Julian had been brought up as a Christian at the court of Constantine, but now that he had attained sovereign power he renounced Christianity and proclaimed himself an adherent and champion of the old classical paganism, interpreted in a generally Neoplatonic sense. For this he has gone down in history with the strictly accurate epithet, "the Apostate." But it must be confessed that the so-called Christianity which Julian saw at the imperial court, professed by those who had removed so many of his nearest kinsfolk to strengthen their own hold on the imperial succession, did not make any appeal to one of his thoughtful and cultured turn of mind. His attempt to revive paganism, however, was foredoomed to failure; it was an attempt to resuscitate a corpse.

Under Julian, Christians lost many of the privileges which they had acquired during the preceding fifty years, and they were subjected to various forms of petty vexation. He maintained complete impartiality towards the conflicting parties in the Church, hoping to play one off against another and so to weaken both. Athanasius was allowed to return to Alexandria, but as he proved to be just as resolute and independent under Julian as he had been under Julian's predecessors, he soon had to go into exile again. Christian teachers were forbidden to give instruction in the

[1] Jerome, *Against the Followers of Lucifer*, 19.
[2] G. R. Dunstan, *Theology*, Nov. 1950, pp. 438f., in a review of *The Church in the Christian Roman Empire*, I (1949), by J. R. Palanque and others.

Greek and Latin classics, on the pretext that it was inconsistent for them to expound literature in whose basic religious presuppositions they disbelieved—as if pagan teachers at this time of day believed in them any more than Christians did! One eminent professor of rhetoric who was thus deprived of his chair was the African-born Marius Victorinus, whose eminence as a teacher at Rome was such that in 353 he was honoured by the erection of a statue of himself in the forum.[1] A year or two after this honour, when he was now fifty-five, he was converted to Christianity. The story of his conversion, when related to Augustine many years later, made a deep impression on him shortly before his own conversion; Augustine's interest in Victorinus would be all the greater because it was in the Latin translations made by Victorinus that he first made the acquaintance of the Neoplatonic philosophers Plotinus and Porphyry. Augustine has preserved the story of Victorinus's conversion as it was told to him, in the eighth book of his *Confessions*.[2]

Julian's reign was short, however. In 363 he met his death on the eastern frontiers of the empire, fighting against the Persians. There is no evidence that his last words were "You have won, Galilæan!" (as the traditional account has it); but the Galilæan (Julian's usual description of Jesus) had indeed won, though not perhaps in the sense that Julian would have meant if he had used those words.

His successor, an old soldier named Jovian, patched up a makeshift peace with the Persians (which enabled them to extend their territory considerably) and died almost immediately after. The army then chose as emperor another soldier named Valentinian (364–375). Valentinian saw that it was no longer possible for one man to rule the whole empire, and appointed his brother Valens to rule the east (364–378), while he himself governed the west. Valentinian's relations with the Church were characterized by impartiality, although he himself professed the orthodox faith of Nicaea. Valens, however, was a much weaker character and allowed himself to be used by the Arian party as their tool. In his reign Athanasius had to endure his fifth and last spell of exile. But this lasted only for four months; he was then allowed to return, and spent the remaining seven years of his life in undisturbed possession of his see, until he died in 373.

Meanwhile the Danube frontier was gravely menaced. The Huns,[3] one of the nomadic peoples from the steppe-lands of Asia which have periodically invaded Europe in the course of recorded

---

[1] See my paper on "Marius Victorinus and his Works" in *The Evangelical Quarterly*, April 1946, pp. 132ff.
[2] Augustine, *Confessions*, VIII, 2 : 3.
[3] See E. A. Thompson, *Attila and the Huns* (1948); F. Altheim, *Attila und die Hunnen* (1951).

history, were pressing hard on the Germanic tribes and driving them west and south towards the Rhine and Danube. One body of Germans, the Gothic confederation, which dominated the area between the Baltic and the Danube, was officially allied with the Roman state. But so desperate was their case that they appealed to Valens for help, and he allowed them to cross the Danube and settle on territory which he allotted them for this purpose.

These were not the first Goths to settle south of the Danube. An earlier settlement is associated with the name of Ulfilas, the apostle of the Goths.

Ulfilas belonged to a Christian family of Cappadocia which had been taken captive in the course of a Gothic raid in Asia Minor in 267. He himself was born in 311, and brought up among the Goths. His very name is Gothic, and means "little wolf." In 332 he took part in an embassy to Constantinople and remained there for nine years. In 341 he was consecrated bishop of the Goths north of the Danube. This suggests that there were already Christians among the Goths, as bishops were not normally appointed until there was a Christian community for them to supervise. In point of fact one of the signatories to the Creed of Nicaea in 325 was one Theophilus, bishop among the Goths; but we know little more about him and our knowledge of the beginnings of Gothic Christianity is very slight. Ulfilas may have been a disciple of this Theophilus, but if so he did not maintain his teacher's Nicene orthodoxy, for he came to hold the Arian position.

From 341 to 348 he carried on active missionary work among the Goths in Dacia (modern Romania), and great numbers of them became Christians under his preaching. But to other Goths it seemed that the Christian mission was simply a form of Roman propaganda, calculated to bring the Gothic people under the domination not only of the imperial religion but of the imperial state as well. Such persecution was consequently brought to bear on the Gothic Christians that in 348 Ulfilas sought and obtained permission for himself and his converts to settle south of the Danube, in the province of Moesia (modern Bulgaria). Here he continued to act as their bishop until his death in 383.

Ulfilas's greatest monument is his Gothic translation of the Bible—the oldest literary work in any Germanic language. To carry this out he had first to reduce the language to writing, using for this purpose Greek uncial (capital) letters, with Latin letters and Gothic runes added where necessary. The Arian church historian Philostorgius,[1] who was about fifteen years old when Ulfilas died, tells us that Ulfilas did not include the books of Samuel and Kings in his translation, because the Goths were war-

[1] Philostorgius, *Hist. Eccl.*, II, 5.

like enough already without having their military appetite whetted
by these books. It is much more likely that Ulfilas died before his
translation was complete, and that he had left to the last those
parts of Scripture which he judged least important for inculcating
the Christian graces in his flock.

But now so huge was the influx of Goths south of the Danube
when Valens gave them leave to settle there that trouble was
bound to arise. Fighting broke out between them and the imperial
forces, and a disastrous battle was fought at Adrianople in 378, in
which they wiped out the Roman army and killed Valens himself.

Meanwhile the western empire had its own frontier problems.
Valentinian did his best to keep back other Germanic groups, the
Franks and the Alemanni, who were trying to make their way
across the Rhine owing to the pressure of the Huns in their rear.
He was still engaged in this task when he died in 375, leaving the
empire to his elder son Gratian (who associated with himself in
the imperial dignity the four-year-old Valentinian II, son of
Valentinian by his second wife Justina).

Gratian was the first Christian emperor to renounce the dignity
of Pontifex Maximus which all his predecessors—pagan and
Christian alike—held as official heads of the ancient Roman religion. There was no formal continuity between this title as held by
the emperors and the same title as given to the bishops of Rome.
Naturally, after Gratian discarded it, it could be assumed by the
Roman bishops without ambiguity as a convenient indication of
their claim to supremacy over other bishops. But the earliest
known attribution of the title to a bishop of Rome is in a work of
Tertullian, *On Chastity*, written, about 218, which opens with an
attack on a "peremptory edict" issued by Pope Callistus, whom
he describes sarcastically as "supreme pontiff forsooth—in other
words, bishop of bishops."[1]

Gratian received an urgent call for help from Valens when the
Gothic war broke out in the Balkans, but was unable to respond
at once because he himself was closely engaged with the Alemanni. By the time he had crushed them, Valens had been defeated
and killed at Adrianople. Gratian showed his wisdom by selecting
as emperor in the east Theodosius, son of a former military commander in Britain. This is the Theodosius in whose reign, as we
have seen, the Council of Constantinople was held; it was he, too,
who made Christianity—and Christianity understood in a Nicene
sense—the established religion of the Roman state. No more was
heard henceforth of the Milan policy of equal toleration for all
religions.

Theodosius quickly tackled the Gothic problem in the Balkans,
and settled it by diplomacy instead of warfare. He established a

[1] See p. 201.

reasonably enduring peace, and provided an outlet for the military ardour of the Goths by arranging for their recruitment into the imperial army. But hardly had he accomplished this when he had to take action in the western empire.

In 383 the army in Britain renounced its allegiance to Gratian and proclaimed as emperor its own commander, Magnus Maximus, a Spaniard by origin. Maximus crossed into Gaul with his army to establish his imperial title there, and Gratian, who was then in residence at Paris, had to flee to Lyons, where he was assassinated. Maximus sent a message to Theodosius, disclaiming all responsibility for Gratian's murder, but justifying his assumption of the imperial title and inviting Theodosius to grant him recognition. Theodosius deemed it politic to do so, stipulating that the infant Valentinian II should continue to be recognized as emperor in Italy and Africa. (Valentinian's mother Justina acted as regent for him, using Milan as her capital.)

For four years, then, Maximus reigned as emperor in the west. The most notable event from the Christian point of view which marked his reign was the suppression of the Priscillianists. These were the followers of a Spanish Christian named Priscillian, the leader of a sort of fourth-century Society of Friends, calling themselves the "people of Christ." Priscillian was consecrated bishop of Avila shortly before 380. Charges of Manichaeism[1] and sorcery were made against him and his followers, but the discovery of genuine Priscillianist writings in 1886 provided a more trustworthy picture of their true beliefs. "Whatever the origin and precise views of the Priscillianists, there can be no doubt that they were a devoted and ascetic group of intellectual people—a little intelligentsia,"[2] with outstanding poetical and literary gifts. The western church in fact would have done well to pay respectful heed to the distinctive witness of the Priscillianists, which was characterized by the perennially wholesome principle of "reformation according to the word of God." But other Spanish bishops stirred up opposition to them, and procured their condemnation for heresy and magic at the synod of Bordeaux in 383. Priscillian appealed to Maximus, who heard the case at his capital of Trier in the Rhineland in 385. But Maximus was anxious to strengthen

[1] See p. 288.
[2] Nora K. Chadwick, *Poetry and Letters in Early Christian Gaul* (1955), p. 45. An illuminating account of the Priscillianists is supplied for the English reader in E. H. Broadbent, *The Pilgrim Church* (1931), pp. 36ff. In German two indispensable works are: G. Schepss, *Priscillian: ein neuaufgefundener lateinischer Schriftsteller des vierten Jahrhunderts* (Würzburg, 1886), and F. Paret, *Priscillianus: ein Reformator des vierten Jahrhunderts* (Würzburg, 1891). It is an ironical commentary on the charge that Priscillian denied the doctrine of the Trinity that he is apparently our earliest authority for the words interpolated in the text of 1 John 5 : 7, "There are three who bear witness in heaven, the Father, the Word, and the Holy Spirit; and these three are one." See also H. Chadwick, *Priscillian of Avila* (1977).

his position by posing as the champion of catholic orthodoxy, especially as the empress-mother Justina in Milan was an Arian, and the appeal was rejected. Priscillian and several of his followers were executed, and thus begins the sorry tale of executions carried out technically by the secular arm, but really at the instance of a dominant ecclesiastical party in order to suppress religious "deviationism." This shameful proceeding did not go unchallenged; Martin of Tours and Ambrose of Milan, in particular, the two foremost western churchmen of the day, protested against the execution and voiced the general horror which it aroused.

Among those executed were a mother and her daughter, Euchrotia and Procula, who belonged to a distinguished Gaulish family. Euchrotia was the widow of Delphidius, a famous orator and poet of Bordeaux. His father, Attius Patera, was a professor of rhetoric in what one may call the University of Bordeaux, and *his* father, Phoebicius, had been priest in the temple of Belenus, the Gaulish Apollo, in the same city, and belonged to a well-known druidical family of Bayeux in Britanny. But the druidical business was falling off by the time of Phoebicius's old age, and he obtained a lectureship at Bordeaux, thanks to the good offices of his professorial son. Another lady who belonged to the same family towards the end of the fourth century was Hedibia, whose learning is manifest in the correspondence which passed between her and Jerome. "A few generations could hardly show more startling changes of faith and of intellectual and spiritual activity on the part of both men and women."[1]

Maximus tried to enlarge his realm by invading Italy in 387. Justina threw herself on Theodosius's protection; he acted promptly, overthrew Maximus and killed him, and restored young Valentinian II to his western sovereignty. When Valentinian met his death in 392, Theodosius nominated his own son Honorius as emperor of the west, designating the eastern rule for his other son Arcadius, who acceded to the throne at Constantinople on his father's death in 395.

But the imperial power was rapidly declining. The pagans blamed the Christians for the increasing disasters and held that the old gods were displeased at the favour shown to this upstart cult. Christians, on the other hand, were inclined to put the blame on the continued practice of paganism and on general sin. The armies on the imperial frontiers, long since unable to draw the manpower they required from the ranks of Roman citizens, were being increasingly manned by barbarians from across the frontiers, and these were not the best men for keeping their own kinsfolk at bay. And inside the frontiers, the overgrown bureaucracy which was the consequence of Diocletian's administrative

[1] N. K. Chadwick, *op. cit.*, p. 35.

reforms must be credited with some of the responsibility for the decline. There is considerable truth in Gwatkin's observation that "the Empire fell at last, largely because it had succeeded in convincing its subjects that the outrages of barbarians could not be more intolerable than the oppressions of civilized government."[1]

The years following the death of Theodosius were marked by fresh waves of barbarian invasion. It was during the reign of Honorius that Rome was sacked by the Goths under Alaric (410). For some decades now Rome had ceased to be the headquarters of the western imperial court; Justina, and after her Theodosius, had made Milan their capital, and Honorius moved for greater safety to Ravenna. But the sack of the imperial city—its first sack at the hands of a non-Roman army for eight hundred years—sent a wave of awed horror round the Roman world. Jerome heard of it at Bethlehem; "my tongue," he wrote, "cleaves to the roof of my mouth and my voice is choked with sobs, to think that that city is captive which led captive the whole world."[2] Even so, all was not lost: "the Roman world is falling, but we hold up our heads instead of bowing them down."[3] How Augustine in North Africa responded to the news which reached him from across the Mediterranean we shall see in our next chapter. What moved him to take his pen to write *The City of God* was mainly the charge that the disaster had fallen because the Roman people had forsaken their old religion for this new-fangled one from the Middle East. But in fact it was thanks to Christianity that everything of permanent value in the old classical civilization was preserved. The Goths had been sufficiently Christianized to respect such basic decencies as the sanctuary of church-buildings; pagans and Christians alike who sought refuge there could be sure of having their lives spared. Even the Vandals, who overran other tracts of the western empire and crossed into Africa, and who have given their name to the wanton destruction which they perpetrated, might have been more destructive still but for the very thin veneer of Arian Christianity which they had acquired. For a century they maintained themselves as a pirate state in North Africa, building a navy which made them the strongest maritime power in the western Mediterranean, and even enabled them to raid and sack Rome in 455. An even greater threat to Roman civilization was offered by the Huns, who penetrated Italy in 452 in the wake of the Germanic invaders, but turned back after a short spell of looting and destruction and were dispersed two years later when

[1] H. M. Gwatkin, *Early Church History*, II (1909), p. 327. A good summary and evaluation of suggested causes of the imperial decline may be found in M. Cary. *History of Rome* (1935), pp. 771ff.
[2] Jerome, *Epistle* 127.
[3] Jerome, *Epistle* 60.

their Germanic vassals turned on them and wiped them out as a military force.

During those years the throne of the western empire at Ravenna was filled by a succession of puppet figures who were mere tools of the Germanic military leaders, but maintained a face-saving fiction according to which these leaders were regarded as friends and allies. This fiction was extended over the greater part of the western empire. In Italy and Illyria (Yugoslavia) one branch of the Goths, the Ostrogoths, were dominant; in Spain and south-west Gaul other branch, the Visigoths, established themselves; another Germanic group, the Burgundians, dominated the upper Rhône valley, and northern Gaul was dominated by yet another, the Franks, from whom the whole land of France received its new name in due course.

The last of these imperial puppets in the west, by the irony of history, bore the name of Romulus Augustulus. Romulus was the legendary founder and first king of Rome in the eighth century B.C.; Augustus was the founder of the Roman Empire towards the end of the first century B.C. But this latter-day Romulus bore as his surname not Augustus but the diminutive Augustulus, "little Augustus." In 476 he was deposed by Odoacer, commander of the Germanic forces in Italy. Odoacer thenceforth ruled as king in Italy—independently in fact, but in theory as viceroy of the Emperor Zeno at Constantinople, to whom the western imperial insignia were sent, on the ground that they were no longer required in Italy. The deposition of Romulus is usually referred to as the fall of the western empire. In theory, however, the sovereignty reverted to Zeno, who (equally in theory) now ruled a reunited empire; but it was only in theory that Romulus and his immediate predecessors had ruled the west, so that the incident of 476 was of very small importance.

The theory that the emperor in Constantinople was ruler of the west as well as of the east was partially translated into fact in the reign of Justinian (527–565).[1] His generals Belisarius and Narses regained Italy from the Ostrogoths, southern Spain from the Visigoths and—most important of all—North Africa from the Vandals. A good part of the European reconquests was soon lost again, but North Africa was reunited to the empire until the Muslim conquest a century later.

The closing years of the fourth century, however, saw the end of political unity in western Europe. But a more fundamental unity survived. Rome was no longer the political centre of the empire, but Rome was the spiritual and ecclesiastical capital of western Christendom. The imperial prestige of the city died hard, and when there was no longer an emperor in Rome to serve as

[1] See P. N. Ure, *Justinian and his age* (Pelican Books, 1951).

the focus of imperial loyalty, there was always a bishop of Rome. As Rome's political importance waned, its ecclesiastical importance grew. We may remember here Thomas Hobbes's description of the papacy as "the ghost of the deceased Roman Empire, sitting crowned upon the grave thereof"[1]—although "ghost" is not the best word for so lively an institution.

The Franks of northern Gaul were still pagans when they established their régime there, but the acceptance of Christianity in 496 by their king, Clovis, heralded the conversion of the whole nation. Gradually the provinces of the western empire were being reunited in a new kind of allegiance to Rome. A Frankish link with the royal house of Kent towards the end of the sixth century facilitated the evangelization of Saxon England. The Frankish kings regarded themselves as militant champions of catholic orthodoxy against heretics and unbelievers alike. By crushing the Arian Visigoths in 507, Clovis extended his realm southwards. "It grieves me to see these Arians hold part of Gaul," he said. "Let us attack them with God's aid, and having conquered them, subjugate their land." And by doing so, he subjected southern France to the spiritual dominance of Rome as well as the northern part. It was a later Frankish ruler, Charles Martel, who turned back the Muslim invasion of France by his victory near Poitiers in 732. It was Charles Martel's son, Pepin III, who established the temporal power of the papacy in 753 and 756 when he forced the Lombards (German invaders of North Italy) to cede to the Pope territory which they had taken from the imperial domains. The Frankish kingdom indeed made itself so increasingly indispensable to the papacy that their special relationship must be appropriately marked, as it was on Christmas Day in the year 800, when Pepin's son, Charlemagne, was crowned emperor by Pope Leo III in St. Peter's at Rome. And so began the millennial career of the Holy Roman Empire.

The imperial crown added no real power to Charlemagne, who had built up his predominant strength during the thirty-two years that he had already ruled as king of the Franks. Ecclesiastics farther afield than the Pope of Rome knew a real emperor when they saw one. Even before Charlemagne's imperial coronation the Patriarch of Jerusalem had sent him the keys of the holy places, indicating in this way that he put more faith in his protection than in that of the eastern emperor.

For the legitimate heirs of the Roman Emperors still reigned in Constantinople, and continued to do so, over a gradually shrinking realm, until their imperial city itself fell to the Turks in 1453. But they continued to be prayed for in the western Church; the Roman missal for Good Friday still contains the petition: "Let

[1] T. Hobbes, *Leviathan* (1651), Part 4, chapter 47.

us pray also for our most Christian emperor, that our God and Lord may make all the barbarian nations subject to him."

But we have gone beyond our chronological goal, and must now return to consider some more specifically Christian interests in the closing decades of the western empire.

CHAPTER XXXIV

FIVE LEADING CHURCHMEN

SOME OF THE MAIN FEATURES OF CHRISTIAN LIFE AND THOUGHT in the second half of the fourth century and first half of the fifth may best be grasped by looking at the careers of certain outstanding Christian leaders of that period, in east and west.

Chrysostom (347–407)

In the east there is none to match John of Constantinople, better known as Chrysostom because of the eloquence of his preaching—*chrysostomos*, "golden-mouthed," men called him. He belonged at first to the church of Antioch, in which he was a presbyter, but his chief fame came in his later years, after he became bishop of Constantinople in 397, at the age of fifty.

He acquired very great influence in Antioch during a period of great public strain and fearful expectation of severe punishment which followed a mad and riotous outbreak among the citizens, in which the statues of the Emperor Theodosius and his family were mutilated. That Theodosius would avenge the insult was certain, but the bishop of Antioch set out for the imperial court in order to beseech his moderation. In the meantime, during the weeks of Lent in the year 387, Chrysostom preached twenty-one sermons in which he constrained the people to consider the error of their ways. In the event, Theodosius's vengeance was not so severe as might have been expected from his fiery nature, but it was long before the awesome impression of Chrysostom's sermons faded from the minds of the Antiochians. Many pagans in the city population were converted to Christianity in consequence of them.

When Chrysostom was preferred to the see of Constantinople, he proved a strict disciplinarian, and won the dislike of his clergy as a result. Over and above that, he fell into disfavour at court. This was largely because of the influential hostility of Theophilus, bishop of Alexandria, who had opposed Chrysostom's preferment to Constantinople. But his position was made still more uncomfortable when he won the hatred of the Empress Eudoxia, wife of Arcadius. This hatred is not quite incomprehensible; it would have required a very saintly empress to overlook a sermon which began: "Again Herodias rages; again she is confounded; again she dances; again she demands the head of John on a charger"—and Eudoxia was not as saintly as all that. At last Chrysostom was banished from Constantinople for a short time in 403, and banished again the following year to Armenia, where he died in 407.

Chrysostom was a great expositor of Scripture as well as a great preacher; the most valuable of his works are his *Homilies* on various books of the Bible, where he displays much sound exegetical insight.

But his career illustrates the domination of the Church by the secular power in the eastern empire. In the east (unlike the west) there were several great sees nearly equal in prestige, and these tended to be rivals for supremacy. The emperor could play one off against another, as when the Alexandrian bishop's opposition to Chrysostom made it easier for Arcadius to take coercive measures against the latter. Ever since the fourth century, in fact, there has, for one reason and another, been a stable tradition of the secular power's supremacy over the Church throughout eastern Christendom; the forms assumed by the tradition may change, as indeed they have changed in a radical fashion in our own day, but the tradition itself lives on in dominant vigour.

In the west, on the other hand, the see of Rome dominated all others both in prestige and in actual authority; from the fourth century onwards its primacy was unquestioned, and the disappearance of the great North African churches in the sixth and seventh centuries helped to accentuate its lone eminence. Christianity in the west has always tended to be more independent of state control than in the east. Nor was this tendency manifest only in Rome at the time with which we are dealing; it appears in very marked fashion at Milan during the episcopate of Ambrose.

Ambrose (339–397)

"I have known no bishop but Ambrose," said the Emperor Theodosius, so impressed was he by the authority which Ambrose displayed in his ecclesiastical office. As Milan was the western capital at the time, the two were brought into fairly close contact.

The circumstances in which Ambrose became bishop of Milan are curious. Ambrose was a civil servant in North Italy, who found himself charged with the preservation of public order during the election of a new bishop of Milan in 373. There was considerable strife about the election, and an agreed decision seemed impossible, when suddenly, during an election meeting, a child's voice sang out: "Ambrose for bishop!" Straightway the Christian populace took this as a token of divine guidance ("Out of the mouths of babes and sucklings . . ."), and insisted that Ambrose should consent to occupy the see. Ambrose, although the son of Christian parents, was not even baptized at this time (he was now thirty-four years old), but he yielded to popular pressure and in breath-taking succession was baptized, ordained to the Christian ministry, and consecrated bishop.

In spite of the unusual circumstances of his appointment, he served his people excellently as their chief pastor. He has left us a number of Latin commentaries in which he introduced to the west the allegorizing methods of Alexandrian exegesis, but his chief claim to literary fame lies in his being one of the founders of Latin hymnody, even if we can no longer regard him as the author of the *Te Deum*.

But his relations with the imperial power illustrate the greater independence of western bishops. Perhaps the noblest, and certainly the most impressive, display of this independence was his excommunication of Theodosius for a period of eight months in consequence of his massacre of seven thousand inhabitants of Thessalonica. The emperor at last submitted to Ambrose's spiritual authority and did public penance for his sin on Christmas Day, 390.

Some other instances of Ambrose's dictation to the secular power, however, do not so readily command our admiration. When some monks in the Euphrates district burned down a Jewish synagogue, Theodosius, as was but just, ordered that restitution should be made. But Ambrose, when he heard of the affair, forbade the emperor to do any such thing. Civil justice must give way to religious interest! And so we recognize another of these unhappy precedents so plentiful in the history of fourth-century Christianity.

The religious strife which was resolved by Ambrose's election as bishop of Milan arose from conflicting Arian and Athanasian interests in the church of the city. The Arians welcomed Ambrose's election because they judged that he, a man of the world and no ecclesiastic, would be neutral in theological disputes. But they had mistaken their man. The high sense of duty which Ambrose had previously shown in public service was now transferred to his ecclesiastical career, and he took seriously his episcopal duty to resist heresy. As he embraced the Athanasian position, heresy to him meant Arianism. Ten years after he became bishop, Milan fell into the power of the Arian Empress Justina, regent for her infant son Valentinian II. Justina claimed that one church at Milan should be reserved for Arian worship, but Ambrose withstood her claim. This was a courageous thing to do, for Justina had Arian Gothic soldiery to support her, and the consequences might have been serious for Ambrose. In the end, however, he gained his point. To be sure, circumstances co-operated with him. The usurping emperor in the lands farther west, Magnus Maximus,[1] would have been only too glad of the chance to strengthen his position by posing as the imperial pro-tector of the catholic faith against the patrons of heresy. Justina could not afford to give him the chance. The upshot was a victory for Ambrose's view that the Catholic Church should not only be independent in her own sphere, but should also be able to count upon imperial championship against heresy and other hostile forces.

Jerome (347–420)

No survey of the great Christians of this period would be com-plete without a reference to Jerome, although his great work did not bring him into contact with public affairs as some of the others were brought. His abiding contribution lies in the new Latin version of the Bible which he produced, much more ade-quate than those that had formerly been in use, and approved to this day as the authoritative Biblical version of Latin Christendom.

The earliest Latin translations of the Bible were apparently produced in North Africa rather than in Europe. Down to the middle of the third century the Roman church and other churches of Western Europe were Greek speaking rather than Latin speak-ing. When a Latin version of the Bible did appear in Europe, it exhibited considerable divergence from that which was used in Africa. In fact, by the end of the fourth century a number of Latin translations were current, belonging in the main to two distinct types, African and European. But there was no one "authorized" Latin Bible. How these earlier Latin translations came into being is described thus by Augustine: "When a Greek manuscript [of part of the Bible] came into anyone's hands in the earliest days of the faith and he thought he possessed a little faci-lity in both Greek and Latin, he ventured to make a translation."[2] If that was so, we are not surprised at a statement of Jerome: "If we are to rely on the Latin versions, then let us be told which of these we are to rely on, for there are almost as many distinct versions as there are copies of Scripture."[3]

Jerome, a native of Dalmatia, was educated at Rome, and spent much of his life in the east, where he improved his knowledge of Greek and seized the opportunity to learn Hebrew. In this latter acquisition he stands almost alone among the Latin Fathers. In 382 he returned to Rome and was charged by Damasus, bishop

---

[1] See pp. 323f.
[2] Augustine, *On Christian Doctrine*, II, 11.
[3] Jerome, *Letter to Damasus*, prefaced to Jerome's version of Matthew.

of Rome, with the task of revising the Latin New Testament. He obeyed with some reluctance, for he knew that many Bible readers would not thank him for changing their favourite texts, even in the interests of accuracy. ("I think the original must be wrong," said one such of more recent date, when told that his favourite interpretation of a passage of Scripture was put out of court by the original text.) His revision of the Latin Gospels appeared in 384, and the rest of the New Testament soon followed. Then he proceeded to revise the Old Testament. This, he soon found, was a much more formidable undertaking. Up to this time all Latin versions of the Old Testament had been based, not on the original Hebrew text, but on the Greek translation of the Old Testament commonly called the Septuagint, produced at Alexandria in Egypt in the last three centuries B.C. Their general quality was very unsatisfactory, and Jerome found it a hopeless task to revise them. So he cut loose from all existing Latin translations of the Old Testament, and in 405 he completed a version direct from the Hebrew. Such an innovation evoked a great deal of furious opposition, and Jerome's letters to his friends express somewhat unsaintly impatience with his critics—"two-legged donkeys," he calls them, those people "who think that ignorance is holiness!" By sheer intrinsic worth, however, his version held the field, and became known as the "vulgate" or common version, the version which the Council of Trent in 1546 declared to be the one authoritative Latin text of Scripture, to which appeal must be made in all controversy.

Jerome spent the last thirty-five years of his life in monastic retirement at Bethlehem, devoting himself to the cause of Biblical learning. It was here that he worked on his translation of the Old Testament. He had hoped to succeed Damasus as bishop of Rome, but when Damasus died in 384 Jerome was not elected, and the new bishop was no friend of his. At Bethlehem, however, he had an admiring circle of disciples, mainly noble Roman ladies who had devoted themselves to the celibate life in Palestine and organized themselves in three conventual houses.[1]

Augustine (354–431)

Seven years younger than Jerome was Augustine, "the greatest Christian since New Testament times," to quote one eminent patristic scholar lately deceased, and "assuredly the greatest man that ever wrote Latin."[2] "The greatest psychologist and political thinker since Aristotle, Augustine was also no mean metaphy-

[1] See pp. 346ff.
[2] A. Souter, *The Earliest Latin Commentaries on the Epistles of St. Paul* (1927), p. 139.

sician"—such is the verdict of one of our leading contemporary church historians.[1]

The steps of Augustine's spiritual pilgrimage until his conversion to Christianity at the age of thirty-two have been traced for us in his immortal *Confessions*. He came under the influence of Ambrose when he was appointed to a professorship of rhetoric at Milan in 384, and it was there two years later that he became a convinced Christian while reading part of Paul's Epistle to the Romans. The following Easter he was baptized by Ambrose and in 388 he returned to his native Africa. In 395 he was consecrated bishop of the African see of Hippo (modern Bona), and occupied that position for the remaining thirty-five years of his life, making contributions to theological literature unparalleled in extent and importance among patristic writings in any language.

The spiritual and intellectual stature of Augustine may be gauged from the fact that all the main streams of western Christianity draw upon him—Roman, Lutheran, Genevan and Anglican. There is a frequently repeated epigram to the effect that the Reformation of the sixteenth century, on its theological side, represented the revolt of Augustine's doctrine of grace against Augustine's doctrine of the Church. Whatever the accuracy of this statement may be, it will serve for the moment as a text for our consideration of some of Augustine's main contributions to Christian thinking.

It has often been remarked that the Biblical doctrine of divine grace, God's unmerited favour shown to sinful humanity, so clearly (as we might think) expounded in the teaching of Christ[2] and the writings of Paul, seems almost to go underground in the post-apostolic age, to reappear only with Augustine. Certainly the majority of Christian writers who flourished between the apostles and Augustine do not seem to have grasped what Paul was really getting at in his contention that God's forgiveness and salvation are bestowed entirely as a free gift, by His unconditioned grace, to be received in the spirit in which they are given; and that Christian behaviour is rooted in a lifelong response of thanksgiving for the divine gift.[3] (In the New Testament, another epigrammatist has said, theology is grace, and ethics is gratitude.) Marcion has been called the only one of these writers who understood Paul, and even he misunderstood him. We do get some appreciation of the Pauline doctrine of grace in the charming second-century essay called the *Epistle to Diognetus*,[4] and again in Tertullian; but not until we come to Augustine do we find an

[1] S. L. Greenslade, *Chambers's Encyclopaedia* (1950), Vol. I, p. 775.
[2] Compare our Lord's parable of the two debtors and their creditor: "when they had nothing to pay, he frankly forgave them both" (Luke 7 : 42, A.V.).
[3] Cf. T. F. Torrance, *The Doctrine of Grace in the Apostolic Fathers* (1948).
[4] Cf. p. 177.

adequate and sympathetic comprehension of what it really is. Paul and Augustine were both of the "twice-born" type, to use the terminology of Francis Newman and William James.[1] Both experienced a revolutionary conversion in their early thirties, which altered their whole manner of life. Although Paul's manner of life before conversion was vastly different from Augustine's, both were deeply conscious of their sin and deeply conscious of the divine favour that had been shown them so freely. As Augustine read Paul, he had no difficulty in understanding what Paul meant by grace; Paul's unfolding of this theme spoke directly to Augustine's condition.

Augustine's development of the doctrine of grace, however, was not only bound up with his own spiritual experience but also with his reaction to the teaching of Pelagius. The teaching of Pelagius, it may be recalled, receives dishonourable mention in the Thirty-Nine Articles. "Original sin" (runs Article IX) "standeth not in the following of Adam (as the Pelagians do vainly talk); but it is the fault and corruption of the nature of every man, that naturally is engendered of the offspring of Adam . . ."

Who then was this Pelagius, who gave his name to these Pelagians?[2] He was a native of the British Isles—the first one to make any contribution to literature, and this he did in Latin commentaries on the thirteen epistles of Paul. Whether he was a Briton or an Irishman is not clear; Augustine calls him a Briton and Jerome an Irishman (*Scotus*), so perhaps he was an Irishman settled in Britain. (There were considerable Irish settlements in Wales in the latter part of the fourth century.)

However that may be, Pelagius came to Rome in 384 and was shocked at what he considered the low moral standard of the city. He himself was a man of high moral character, and unlike Paul and Augustine he probably belonged to the "once-born" category. He rejected the doctrine of original sin. In his view this doctrine, which attributed the universal human proneness to go wrong to a vitiated nature inherited from the first man, encouraged people to acquiesce in their sinful ways instead of pulling themselves together and mastering the power of evil. Adam's descendants, Pelagius held, are born as innocent as Adam was before his fall; in so far as they are sinners it is not because they have inherited a sinful tendency from him but because they have followed in his footsteps of their own free choice. It follows that there is no need of divine grace to enable a man to do the will of

[1] It must be remembered that "twice-born" and "once-born" in this special sense are not exact equivalents respectively of "regenerate" and "unregenerate" in the New Testament sense.

[2] See John Ferguson, *Pelagius: An Historical and Theological Study* (1956).

God—what he needs is simply to make up his mind to do it; doing does it. He disapproved strongly of Augustine's epigrammatic prayer: "Give what Thou commandest, and command what Thou wilt." Infants are baptized, he held, not (as Augustine taught) to purge them from the original guilt inherited from Adam but to impart to them a higher sanctification through union with Christ. On this last point Pelagius's view has come to be accepted by many who otherwise are generally Augustinian in their outlook. But Pelagius was probably not greatly interested in the theology of baptism; on his premises it was not really necessary, but as it was essential for membership in the visible church, he and his followers conceded it, with the proviso that, since there was no such thing as original sin, baptism could not take it away.

To all this Augustine felt bound to give a vigorous rejoinder, especially when Pelagius, with his compatriot Caelestius, left Rome for North Africa in 409. Pelagius went on from there to Palestine (where he met Jerome), but Caelestius remained at Carthage and sought ordination to the Christian ministry. His Pelagian views, however, gave rise to disputes, and a number of them were condemned at a synod held at Carthage in 412. We are not concerned here with the series of further synods in various centres which examined and condemned the Pelagian doctrines; we are more concerned with Augustine's reaction to them.

Augustine's whole experience emphasized those elements in Christian faith which Pelagius denied, and rejected as false many points on which Pelagius insisted. His two chief anti-Pelagian treatises are *On the Spirit and the Letter* and *On Nature and Grace*. In Christian reflection on the interaction between the divine act and man's response in salvation, there is inevitable tension between those who insist chiefly on the divine initiative and man's inability to please God without it (which are undoubtably Biblical teachings), and those on the other hand who insist chiefly on the freedom of the will and man's responsibility to say "Yes" to the divine command (which again are undoubtedly Biblical teachings). The difficulty in holding the proper balance lies largely in the fact that theology is not divorced from religious experience—nor indeed should it be. Those who share Augustine's experience will emphasize the former elements; those to whose consciousness the divine act has not manifested itself as "irresistible grace" will emphasize the latter. Pelagius, indeed, so far as his formal teaching goes, seems to have denied the need of divine grace at all, and thus in theory put himself off Christian ground altogether. But, although he lived before the English settlement of southern Britain, he is the spiritual father of all those who profess the popular English creed of justification by decency. A recent writer finds in Pelagius's "rational or philosophical approach to questions of human behaviour" a recrudescence of the characteristic attitude of classical philosophers. "We are in the world of accepted Greek ethical thinking. It is natural and proper to treat the question of sin and freewill by the method of argumentation from self-evident moral axioms." This classical treatment "carries with it a strong impression of common sense, which commends Pelagianism to the English and may serve to warn us how easily European common sense merges into a Greek ethic."[1]

On the other hand one may so emphasize the divine initiative and the "irresistibility" of divine grace as to rob the concepts of man's moral choice and responsibility of all real meaning. If some of Augustine's treatment seems to err in this direction, yet Professor Greenslade says rightly that "its realistic judgment of human nature, if not the whole truth, is a bulwark against facile optimism; and its insistence upon the divine initiative and the prevenience of grace protects Christianity against confidence in man without God."[2] Happy are those who have learned that the truth in this matter lies, as Charles Simeon said, "not in the middle, and not in one extreme, but in both extremes."[3]

If it was Pelagianism that stimulated Augustine to formulate his doctrine of grace, it was the Donatist schism that stimulated him to formulate his doctrine of the Church. The Donatists, as we have seen,[4] seceded from the catholic communion early in Constantine's reign and caused considerable trouble in North Africa, not least in Augustine's own diocese. Ultimately they were suppressed by military force, following a conference at Carthage in 411, where an imperial commissioner heard both sides, the Catholics and the Donatists, and pronounced in favour of the former. For a long time before that, Augustine had reasoned with the Donatists, and in reply to their doctrine of a pure communion, from which all whom they regarded as apostates and similar offenders must be excluded, developed his inclusive theory of the Church. He pointed out that in our Lord's parable the wheat and the darnel were to grow together in the field until the harvest, which was interpreted as being the end of the age, not the time of Donatus. (The Donatists might have replied that the field was interpreted as being the world, not the Church.) Augustine also adduced the Old Testament picture of Noah's ark, long since regarded as a sort of prophetic allegory of the Church. In

[1] J. Barr, "The Pelagian Controversy," *The Evangelical Quarterly*, October 1949, pp. 253ff.

[2] S. L. Greenslade, *s.v.* "Augustine," *Chambers's Encyclopaedia*, Vol. I, p. 774.

[3] H. C. G. Moule, *Charles Simeon* (1948 edn.), p. 77. Simeon's words had primary reference to the Calvinist-Arminian controversy, the form which this perennial debate took within the Reformation tradition.

[4] See pp. 296ff above; and G. G. Willis, *Saint Augustine and the Donatist Controversy* (1950); W. H. C. Frend, *The Donatist Church* (1952).

the ark were animals of all kinds, clean and unclean alike. There was hope of salvation for the unclean creatures inside the ark, and none for the clean creatures outside it. So it is with the Church, within which the means of grace are available for sinners, whereas there is no salvation for the most upright of men outside it. But Augustine's reasoning did not convince all the Donatists; it is, in fact, very difficult for inclusive and exclusive churchmen to come to agreement, because (like Sydney Smith's two women slanging each other across the street) they are arguing from opposite premises. To the Donatist type the "garden walled around" is a much more apt picture of the true Church than Noah's ark is— at least, in the use that Augustine made of it.

When the threat of force was introduced against the Donatists, Augustine at first opposed it, holding that persuasion alone should be employed; but later he acquiesced in it, considering that the peace of the Church was an end worthy enough to justify such means. He even found New Testament authority for his change of attitude in the words of the Gospel parable, "Compel them to come in"[1]—and thereby set a bad example to clerics of later days. Yet he continued to prefer the method of persuasion, and by such means did much to mend the century-old breach in North African Christianity. He made it as easy as possible for Donatists to return to catholic communion; their sacraments were regarded by him as quite valid, though irregular so long as they persisted in schism. Thus returning Donatists were not to be rebaptized, nor were their ministers to be reordained. Returning Donatist bishops remained bishops, and some Catholic bishoprics were divided to make room for them.

A further stimulus was given to Augustine's development of church doctrine by the sack of Rome in 410. This disaster, said those who maintained the old pagan faiths, was the result of the empire's abandonment of the old gods. Augustine took up this challenge and responded in his monumental treatise, *The City of God*. This work "contains the Christian answer to the reproaches levelled in the name of classical culture against the new faith and life, the answer to the higher perennial paganism no less than to its lower and temporary forms. It reveals, as no doubt it helped to sustain, the spirit which enabled the Church to survive the Empire and to maintain faith and hope in a darkening age."[2] Standing as it does between the two worlds of classical antiquity and mediæval Christendom, setting forth the thought of one who inherited the traditions of the former and paved the way for the latter, *The City of God* has a special message for people who feel that they are living at the end of an era, or even the downfall of a

---

[1] Luke 14 : 23.
[2] J. H. S. Burleigh, *The City of God* (1949), p. v.

civilization. The city of this world, secular civilization, is transient and must pass away; the city of God endures for ever. Augustine does not make the simple identification of the city of God with the Catholic Church, although his language suggests this at times. Rather, as Professor Burleigh has pointed out, the Church is the "pilgrim" part of the Eternal City, "the part which sojourns on earth, a captive and a stranger in the earthly city, subject to the temptations and vicissitudes of earthly existence . . . Moreover present membership in the Church is no security for final citizenship in the Eternal City."[1]

In spite of all his emphasis on sacraments as vehicles of the divine grace, Augustine does not promise final salvation to all members of the Church as it is seen at present: "it is only the Church predestined and elect before the world's foundation, the Church of which it is said, 'The Lord knows those who belong to Him',[2] that shall never be led astray."[3] It is quite true that much of Augustine's doctrine of the Church leads on to the mediæval identification of the kingdom of God with the visible ecclesiastical organization (with the corollary of papal supremacy over secular governors, in view of the supremacy of the city of God over the earthly city). But there is a deeper level of thought in Augustine which anticipates the Reformation doctrine of the invisible over against the visible Church—and, be it added, the more recent and perhaps as yet unofficial Roman Catholic distinction between the soul of the Church and the body of the Church. Thus the epigram that the Reformation represents the revolt of Augustine's doctrine of grace against his doctrine of the Church must be modified. To some extent his formulation of the doctrine of grace, especially where he deals with the problem of predestination, fails to break completely away from the framework of classical thinking and become wholly Biblical; while, on the other hand, his doctrine of the Church contains germs which fructified at the Reformation.

Leo the Great (c. 390–461)

This last Christian leader whom we shall look at in this sketchy survey is Leo the Great, who was bishop of Rome from 440 to 461.[4] Leo marks an advance in the doctrine of papal supremacy. The church at Rome had from a very early period in Christian history enjoyed an honorary precedence among the churches. No doubt the central position of Rome as the imperial capital lent

---

[1] *Op. cit.*, p. 178.
[2] 2 Timothy 2 : 19.
[3] Augustine, *City of God*, XX, 8.
[4] See T. G. Jalland, *Life of St. Leo the Great* (1941); *The Church and the Papacy* (1944).

some prestige to the church of that city, and after the capital was moved from Rome to Constantinople the prestige of the bishop of Rome, far from being diminished, actually increased through the absence of the imperial court. But there were much more important reasons than that. Rome, as we have seen, was the only church in the west which could claim apostolic foundation, and western churches at any rate accorded her special veneration on that account, the more so as her character and influence were such as befitted an apostolic see. In purity of doctrine and in practical Christianity the church of Rome had consistently exhibited to the Church at large an example worthy of emulation.

This recognition of the Roman church as the model church led to the custom of consulting the bishop of Rome on various questions of procedure and discipline. This was done especially by the bishops of Gaul and the western provinces. When an unprecedented situation arose in one of the western churches, it became the usual practice to inquire what Rome did in such a case, and the Roman bishop's replies to these questions were called decretals. The earliest decretals preserved belong to the episcopate of Damasus (366–384). They had no necessarily binding force; they were simply answers to questions; but the western bishops normally acted in accordance with them so as to preserve uniformity of ecclesiastical practice, and they were gradually invested with increasing moral authority.

The Council of Nicaea in 325 recognized the Roman church, along with those of Antioch and Alexandria, as one of the three leading sees of Christendom, whose bishops were entitled to the title "patriarch." The Council of Constantinople in 381, by ruling that the bishop of Constantinople should have precedence of honour next to the bishop of Rome, gave formal if indirect recognition to the precedence already granted by general consent to the bishop of Rome. Damasus, who was then Pope, soon afterwards extended his authority by securing appellate jurisdiction over other metropolitan bishops throughout an indefinite area. A later bishop of Rome, Caelestine I (422–432), receives a title to something more than a merely honorary precedence in a large contemporary mosaic in the Church of St. Sabina at Rome, bearing the Latin inscription:

> Culmen apostolicum cum Caelestinus haberet,
> Primus et in toto fulgeret episcopus orbe—

which may be rendered: "When Caelestine occupied the summit of apostolic authority and shone as first bishop throughout the whole world."

The emperor himself recognized the precedence of the Roman church when he accorded the Roman delegates the right to preside at the Council of Chalcedon in 451 and gave the Roman bishop the title of *princeps episcopalis coronae*, "chief wearer of the episcopal crown."

But Leo sought a theological foundation for this precedence and found it in the words of our Lord to Peter, recorded in Matthew 16 : 18f., "You are Peter, and on this rock I will build my church . . . I will give you the keys of the kingdom of heaven, and whatever you bind on earth shall be bound in heaven, and whatever you loose on earth shall be loosed in heaven."[1] Leo argued that, since Peter was the founder of the Roman church, the Roman bishop inherited his authority, including the dominion of the keys.

This position represents a definite advance on Cyprian's.[2] When Cyprian invoked these words of Christ he did so in order to emphasize that the Church's unity was expressed in the episcopate —the whole episcopate—and that this had sprung from a single apostolic root. But, in Cyprian's eyes, as Peter's precedence did not give him jurisdiction over the other apostles, so neither did the Roman bishop's precedence give him jurisdiction over other bishops. Leo, however, attempted to bring the whole of western Christendom under unified control by a network of metropolitan bishops, to whom other bishops would be subject, and who in turn were to acknowledge the supremacy of the bishop of Rome. In particular, he procured a rescript from the emperor giving him authority over the bishops of Gaul.

Leo made his mark in theology as well as in ecclesiastical policy, and has been enrolled among the doctors of the Church. He firmly suppressed heresy within the territory which he could control himself, and his *Tome* or thesis on the Person of Christ, which was first composed for the Council of Ephesus (449) as a reply to the Monophysite heresy of Eutyches, was accepted by the Council of Chalcedon two years later. Leo in turn accepted the Council's findings.[3]

There was another field in which Leo had an opportunity to show what stuff he was made of; in 452 he proved his courage when he went as imperial envoy along with Avienus, leader of the Roman senate, to meet Attila the Hun in North Italy, and so helped to avert the threatened Hun attack on Rome. He was not able to avert the Vandal sack of Rome in 455, but his intervention did something to mitigate its horrors.

[1] Revised Standard Version. The reference to the keys designates Peter as chief steward in Christ's household (cf. Isaiah 22 : 22); the terms "binding" and "loosing" are used in rabbinic idiom to denote authoritative prohibition and permission. Cf. Matthew 18 : 18, where this authority is conferred on all the apostles.

[2] See p. 212.

[3] See pp. 313ff.

CHAPTER XXXV

THE MONASTIC LIFE

IN MANY RELIGIOUS MOVEMENTS THERE HAVE BEEN MEN AND women who sought to achieve their religious aims more effectively by withdrawing for longer or shorter periods from the company of their fellows and abstaining from the common comforts of life. In the pre-Christian era Buddhism is the outstanding example of ascetic religion. Gautama himself, the founder of Buddhism (c. 560–480 B.C.), practised the most rigorous form of asceticism at one stage of his religious experience. When the Indian king Asoka (whose wheel appears on India's new flag) became a Buddhist about 260 B.C., he exhibited the zeal of a new convert by sending missionaries to the courts of other rulers; although we must treat with caution statements to the effect that his missionaries visited Antiochus II of Syria, Ptolemy II of Egypt, and the kings of Cyrene and Epirus (modern Albania), or that the saffron garb of the Buddhist monk was a common sight in Alexandria at that time. There is no evidence of a direct connexion between Buddhist influences and the appearance of ascetic movements in the Middle East around the beginning of the Christian era.

Among the Jews, in the closing decades B.C. and the early decades A.D., we find a number of ascetic communities arising. Unlike Buddhism, Judaism does not inculcate asceticism as an ideal; and the emergence of ascetic groups within Judaism at this time has by some been put down to influences from farther east. But it is not necessary to suppose that this was the cause of their emergence. A time when external conditions—political, economic or religious—appear specially hopeless is particularly favourable to movements which turn their back upon the world; and the closing decades B.C. and early decades A.D. suggested to many Jews that the hope of Israel was not likely to be realized by any of the prevalent trends of public life. Among the Jewish ascetic communities the best known are the Essenes, living in the Dead Sea region, of whom Josephus and other first-century writers give us vivid accounts.[1] Even so, we do not know as much about them as we should like; but our knowledge has been considerably

---

[1] Josephus, *Jewish War*, II, 8 : 2–13; *Antiquities*, XVIII, 1 : 5. See my *Second Thoughts on the Dead Sea Scrolls* (1956), pp. 112ff. *et passim*.

increased by the discovery of the scrolls and fragments at Qumran, north-west of the Dead Sea. For it appears that these scrolls were deposited in the caves where they were found by a group of Essenes or a similar community, whose headquarters have been excavated at Khirbet Qumran.

Not only do we find these ascetic communities in Judaism at this period; we also find some people leading largely solitary lives for religious ends, like the hermit Banus, to whom Josephus at one stage in his career went for instruction,[1] and John the Baptist, who emerged from his solitude to call Israel to the baptism of repentance.

Jesus, on the other hand, was not an ascetic in the ordinary sense of the word; His contemporaries contrasted him in this respect with John the Baptist and His opponents called Him a glutton and a winebibber.[2] Even the Pharisees, who were far from being ascetic rigorists, criticized the followers of Jesus for not fasting on the appointed days as they did.[3] But Jesus did warn people against covetousness and absorption with material interests; He spoke of some who refrained from marriage "for the sake of the kingdom of heaven";[4] He declared that it was "easier for a camel to go through the eye of a needle than for a rich man to enter the kingdom of God."[5] The practical outcome of His teaching, therefore, was a considerable independence of temporal amenities.

Much asceticism, both pre-Christian and later, however, was bound up with the idea of the inherent evil—or else the complete unreality—of the material order in general and the body in particular. This idea, which runs counter to both Jewish and Christian teaching, is markedly present in Indian thought, and (as we have seen)[6] made its way into Greek thought in the pre-Christian era. In the early centuries of the Christian era it persists in certain Greek schools of thought (the Neoplatonic philosophy in particular) and appears also in Gnosticism of various kinds and in Manichaeism. But the Christian varieties of asceticism do not appear to have been directly indebted to any of these sources.

In Christianity asceticism for the most part took the form of monasticism. Christian monasticism, properly so called, makes its appearance about the middle of the third century A.D. It may be said to take its beginning with Antony, a native of Upper Egypt. He was born into a Christian family about 251, and as a youth of eighteen he made up his mind to distribute his property among the poor and lead an ascetic life. Some years later he went into the western desert and for about twenty years lived a completely solitary life. His example spurred numbers of other

[1] Josephus, *Life*, 2. [2] Matthew 11 : 19; Luke 7 : 34. [3] Mark 2 : 18ff.
[4] Matthew 19 : 12. [5] Mark 10 : 25. [6] See pp. 244ff.

Christians to do the same, and although he did not organize a community he directed a number of hermits living in scattered cells in the area. ("Hermits" and "anchorites" are terms used for people who live in individual solitude, and "monks"—from Greek *monachoi*—originally meant the same thing, "people who live alone." The word "monasticism," therefore, if used with strict regard for its etymology, should be confined to the solitary life and not be used of ascetic communities. The earliest monks were hermits or solitaries; the fashion of living in ascetic communities—practising the "coenobitic" life, to use the strictly correct term—came later. A monastery in the ordinary sense of the word is etymologically a contradiction in terms. But since the meaning of words depends on their use and not on their etymology, we shall follow the common practice, and use the terms "monk," "monastic," and so forth in reference not exclusively to solitaries but to ascetic communities as well.)

To return to Antony: it is he who is credited with the observation that "a monk out of his cell is like a fish out of water." Readers of Chaucer's *Canterbury Tales* may remember his "monk, a fair for the maistrye," of whom it is recorded:

> He yaf nat of that text a pullèd hen,
> That seith, that hunters been nat holy men;
> Ne that a monk, whan he is cloisterlees,
> Is lykned til a fish that is waterlees;
> This is to seyn, a monk out of his cloistre,
> But thilke text held he nat worth an oistre.[1]

In later life Antony took more interest in general church affairs; he strongly supported the Nicene faith, and won an ardent admirer in Athanasius, to whom a *Life of Antony* is ascribed.

But solitary life is unhealthy for most people. Since the Creator Himself declared at the beginning of human history, "It is not good that man should be alone," we need not be surprised that people who decide otherwise run into disadvantages that they never expected. In one sense the solitary life did prove exceedingly healthy for Antony. If a reporter had come to him in his old age and asked, "And to what do you attribute your extraordinary longevity, St. Antony?" he would no doubt have answered: "To living alone, and on the plainest fare imaginable"—and it would be difficult to say he was wrong, for he lived to be a hundred and five. But in another way he experienced the unhealthiness of the solitary life, although he put it down, not to his unnatural way of living, but to the temptations of the devil. For he had frequent visitations of a kind calculated to turn his thoughts clean away from religious contemplation—so much so that the temptations

[1] G. Chaucer, *Canterbury Tales*, Prologue, 165, 177–182.

of St. Antony have proved an attractive subject for painting and fiction—and while he believed that he was being treated as a special target by the Evil One because of his aspirations after holiness, a modern psychologist would no doubt explain the matter much more simply.

A new phase in the development of monasticism is associated with the name of Pachomius. Pachomius was an ex-soldier who adopted the solitary life in the earlier days of his retirement from military service. But he soon came to envisage a more excellent way than a hermit's career, and gathered other hermits around him to establish a corporate monastery, at Tabennisi on the Nile. To those who entered into this community life with him he gave a "rule" or code of discipline, which had some influence on similar rules imposed by later founders of monastic orders. The sister of Pachomius followed his example and founded the first known Christian nunnery.

Monasticism, of both the solitary and the community forms, flourished particularly in Egypt, no doubt because the desert was specially congenial for its development. But it was widely practised in western Asia as well, having spread there from Egypt. Hilarion, a youth in his teens, after meeting Antony in Egypt, introduced monasticism into Palestine about 315. Later in the fourth century Epiphanius, bishop of Constantia (Salamis) in Cyprus, visited Palestine and gave a rule to a monastic community there. From Palestine the tendency in both its forms spread over Syria. It was in Syria that the fantastic cult of pillar-sanctity arose. The first and most eminent of those "stylites"— hermits who attained the desired solitude by living on the top of lofty pillars—was Simeon (390–459), who kept on increasing the height of his pillar-cell until it was seventy-two feet high. Simeon and his fellow-stylites varied the prolonged contemplation which they enjoyed on this higher plane by preaching to the crowds of visitors who were attracted by the fame of their manner of life.

The most important figure in the monastic history of western Asia, however, is Basil of Cappadocia, whose place in the history of Christian dogma we have already mentioned.[1] Basil made a careful study of Egyptian monasticism and adapted it to the conditions of Cappadocia. He encouraged the growth of communities, the observance of corporate discipline, and the pursuit of such useful activities as prayer, Bible study, agriculture and nursing. This innovation—a welcome contrast to anything so ineffectual as the pillar-cult—formed a happy precedent for monastic life throughout western Asia and Europe in the days that lay ahead.

Basil's own interests may be gathered from the account of the

[1] See p. 311.

beautiful retreat on the banks of the Iris in Pontus, where he lived with his friend Gregory of Nazianzus, tending their vegetable garden and compiling an anthology from the writings of their favourite author Origen. When Basil became bishop of Cappadocian Cæsarea in 370, he used the services of his monks in staffing the great hospital founded in connexion with his see. The rule which he gave his monks remains the basic rule for eastern monasticism to this day; the Basilian order is still the sole monastic order of the Greek Orthodox Church.

The relations between monastic establishments and the diocesan authorities were uncertain at first. Where the ruler of the monastery was himself a bishop, as Basil latterly was, the situation was comparatively simple; but that happened but rarely. Otherwise the monks often proved unruly and were a source of anxiety to bishops, to whom they even tried to dictate. The independence of the monks made them to some extent the counterpart of the earlier prophets, who also had difficulty in submitting to episcopal authority. The Emperor Theodosius I tried to deal with the situation by forbidding monks to live in towns. But the matter came to a head at the "robber-synod" of Ephesus in 449, when monks handled Bishop Flavian of Constantinople so roughly that he is said to have died as a direct result of the treatment. When the Council of Chalcedon was convened two years later, all monks were expelled from the neighbourhood as a precautionary measure before the councillors met. When they did meet, they dealt with the trouble decisively by ordaining that monks should be subject to the authority of the bishops of their respective dioceses.

It was the great Athanasius of Alexandria who introduced monasticism to western Europe. He took a great interest in Egyptian monasticism, and was a warm admirer of Antony. When he visited Rome in 340, during his second exile from Alexandria, he told the Roman Christians about the Egyptian monks; and some of them were impelled to follow the Egyptian example.

Of Roman monks the most illustrious was Jerome. He was already a cultivator of the ascetic life when in 373 he went to Syria and spent four years there as a hermit, passing the time in penitential exercises and Bible study (including the study of Hebrew). Later he returned to Rome to become the secretary of Damasus, and undertake the revision of the Latin Bible at his master's direction; but after the death of Damasus he went back to the east. Along with a number of Roman ladies of good family, who had similarly devoted themselves to the celibate life, he visited sacred sites and monastic establishments in Palestine and Egypt, and then settled at Bethlehem. Here Paula, one of the

Roman ladies, founded four monastic houses, three for women and one for men; and here Jerome lived in his cell for the rest of his life, conforming to monastic routine, continuing his great work of Bible study and translation, and maintaining a voluminous correspondence with churchmen and (more especially) churchwomen over the whole Roman world.

Much of Jerome's correspondence shows the high and indeed exaggerated value which he placed upon ascetic ideals, and especially upon celibacy and virginity. The increasing tendency in the early Christian centuries to regard celibacy as superior to the married life is remarkable, when we remember how little there is in the Bible to justify such an attitude. In the Old Testament to marry and bring up children is assumed throughout to be the proper thing to do. And while the New Testament teaches (as Jesus Himself said) that celibacy is a special vocation for some, it also regards marriage and family life as the normal sphere in which Christians should please God. Paul himself may be celibate, but he knows that Peter and the other apostles and the Lord's brothers are married and take their wives about with them on their pastoral and missionary journeys, and he regards this as a perfectly proper state of affairs.[1]

It was largely the laxity of sexual relations among the pagan Greeks and Romans—so different from the healthy outlook and practice of the Jews—that led so many Gentile Christians, by way of reaction, to regard all such relations, even the normal relations of married life, as inherently undesirable. The idea that the material part of man (like the material world in general) was the seat of evil, by contrast with the soul, fostered the same tendency. Something of this kind underlay the questions on marriage which the Corinthian Christians sent to Paul, as may be inferred from the answers which he gave them, preserved in 1 Corinthians 7.[2]

Monasticism naturally implied celibacy—although at a later stage of monastic development in the British Isles we shall see that this implication was not universally accepted; there is good evidence that some Celtic monks were married.[3] The Montanist disapproval of second marriages[4] was soon echoed in the Catholic Church, so far as the marriage of clerics was concerned. For this, indeed, there seemed to be Scriptural authority in the passages in the Pastoral Epistles which prescribe that a bishop or a deacon must be "the husband of one wife," although that expression might originally have meant something else.[5] At the Council of Elvira, in Spain (c. 306), celibacy was recognized as the ideal

---

[1] 1 Corinthians, 9 : 5.   [2] See pp. 124f.
[3] See p. 394, n. 4.   [4] See p. 219.
[5] The New English Bible translates "faithful to his one wife," but the expression might well have been intended to mean "undivorced."

state of life for clerics. And by 325 it seems to have been a general rule that clerics should not marry after ordination.

But at the Council of Nicaea in that year an attempt was made to impose an even more drastic restriction on clerical marriage; it was proposed that clerics should, on ordination, withdraw from the society of their wives. This motion was defeated through the energetic opposition of an Egyptian bishop named Paphnutius. Paphnutius must be listened to with respect; he was a rigorous ascetic, and the late persecution had left its mark on him in a lamed leg and an eyeless socket. He urged that marriage was an honourable estate, and that the proposed separation would be too great a strain on the parties—especially on the wives. He carried the council with him, and it contented itself with reaffirming the old rule forbidding marriage after ordination.

Jerome in his correspondence never wearies of emphasizing the superiority of celibacy and disparaging matrimony. It is quite evident that he considers marriage to be, at best, a concession to human weakness; he thinks it a good institution for people who are afraid of things that go bump in the night! It was all very well to write in this way to his admiring disciples; but when other men took him to task for his views and exposed their unreasonableness and unscripturalness he betrayed the weakness of his case by the violence of his vituperation. "Argument weak here; shout!" is said to have been seen as a pencilled note in the margin of some preacher's sermon manuscript; Jerome knew the worth of this principle, and when he shouted he became scurrilous. This is evident particularly in his controversies with two men who opposed him in this matter, Jovinian, a monk of Rome, and Vigilantius, another monk from the Pyrenees. Vigilantius has frequently been described as an early Protestant;[1] in his debate with Jerome he criticized not only the excessive veneration of celibacy, but also such increasingly popular practices as the honouring of the relics of the martyrs, the invocation of saints and so on. Jerome retorted in a treatise *Against Vigilantius*, written in the course of a single night, in which he describes Vigilantius's arguments as so blasphemous that they need no reasoned refutation but simply the indignant outcry of outraged piety. "This is certainly the treatise in which Jerome felt most sure that he was in the right, and it is the only one in which he was wholly in the wrong."[2]

In one revealing passage Jerome attacks Vigilantius for deprecating the solitary and celibate life as contrasted with a life lived

---

[1] Cf. an article, "Vigilantius: An Early Gallic Protestant," by J. T. Hornsby in *The Evangelical Quarterly*, July 1945, pp. 182ff.

[2] W. H. Fremantle, in *Dictionary of Christian Biography*, ed. W. Smith and H. Wace, III (1882), p. 44.

in the society of one's fellows. Jerome was a presbyter, but had never agreed to undertake pastoral duties. "If all were to shut themselves up and live like hermits." said Vigilantius, "who will serve the churches? Who will win the men of the world? Who will exhort sinners to righteousness?" Jerome resented this pointed question. There is no fear, he says, that all will embrace celibacy; it is a very rare virtue, and not widely coveted. Vigilantius may ask why he chooses a hermit's career instead of staying in the world and fighting evil. Vigilantius may stay and fight if he pleases; Jerome knows that safety for him lies in flight. "You, who fight, may either conquer or be conquered. I, who run away, shall not be conquered, since I flee from the enemy; and the reason why I flee is that I may not be conquered."

Jerome perhaps gives away more than he intends in these significant words; they may well be perfectly true so far as he is concerned, and this will go far to explain the unrestrained violence of his language when he is criticized on this score. His critics have touched a sore place.

The most significant name in the early days of western monasticism is that of Martin of Tours (c. 316–397). Martin was the son of an army officer and was obliged by law to follow his father's profession. Accordingly he became a cavalry officer. But Martin could not be a conventional military man. Though his parents were pagan, he himself became a Christian at the age of ten, and even before he entered his teens he looked upon a hermit's life as the most desirable. The Roman army was not the most promising environment for the practice of Christian charity, but Martin did his best. The most famous incident of his military career is the story of his cutting his officer's cloak in two and giving half to a beggar whom he met when he was in winter quarters at Amiens. As he slept that night, he thought he saw Christ Himself wearing the half-cloak which he had given to the beggar, and heard Him say to the attendant angels, "Martin, though as yet he is only a catechumen, has clothed me with this garment."

Martin submitted to baptism forthwith, and when his term of military office was over, he left the army and went to Poitiers, to place himself under the spiritual direction of Hilary, bishop of that city, who was renowned for his saintly life and orthodox theology. Later he went home to his native province of Pannonia (modern Austria and Western Hungary) to try to win his parents for the Christian faith. He succeeded in winning his mother; but his father, who was sadly disappointed by Martin's abandonment of a promising military career, would have nothing to do with the religion which had prevented the realization of his ambitions for his son.

After spending some time in a number of temporary retreats, Martin returned to Poitiers about 360 and received from Hilary a site at the neighbouring village of Ligugé, where he founded a monastery. The rule which he gave the monks who joined him there was similar to the rule of Pachomius, but laid less emphasis on the importance of manual labour. During the next ten years Martin's fame spread far and wide throughout Gaul. He was a noted exorcist and many tales were told of his success in expelling demons. As for personal interviews with the prince of the demons himself, he was subjected to these as frequently as a later Martin was. But Martin of Tours and Martin Luther both proved themselves more than a match for the enemy of God and man, when he tried to make them despair of pardon either for their own sins or for the sins of their friends. He assured Martin of Tours that there was no forgiveness for mortal sins committed after baptism (the devil can be a moral rigorist when he pleases), and that some of his monks were therefore doomed. "On the contrary," said Martin; "even if you yourself were to give up tormenting men and repent of your wickedness at this late date, when your day of judgment is nearly upon you, I would confidently and fearlessly promise you compassion in the name of Christ." Thus Martin made a place for himself in a remarkable succession which includes such diverse spirits as Origen and Robert Burns!

These and other details of Martin's life are preserved in the biography which was written by his contemporary and admirer, Sulpicius Severus. The fact that an almost contemporary biography contains so much miraculous and legendary detail may serve as an object-lesson to people who think that a record which narrates supernatural incidents must be considerably later than the events with which it deals. But there is nothing necessarily legendary in the account of the apparitions which Martin saw in his cell; some of them Sulpicius heard from Martin's own lips.

What with his exorcizing, healing, and missionary activity, Martin showed that he belonged to the true evangelical succession. As his fame spread, it was inevitable that one day a Christian community should covet him as its chief pastor. When the bishop of Tours died about 371, the Christian populace of the city demanded that Martin should be chosen to succeed him; and the local clergy and neighbouring bishops were compelled to accede to the popular will, despite their dislike of Martin's unkempt asceticism. It is said that only by a ruse could Martin be enticed from Ligugé to Tours to be installed in the episcopal seat.

Tours was more accessible than Ligugé had been, and the fame of Martin brought crowds of visitors to Tours to see him. At last, to gain the privacy which he longed for, he established a new monastery near Tours. The new retreat was called the "Greater

Monastery" (probably to distinguish it from Ligugé) and it is from this name (Latin *maius monasterium*) that the modern place-name Marmoutier is derived. But Martin did not use his monastic preferences as a pretext for complete withdrawal from the world. On the contrary, he made Tours the centre of an intensive campaign for the evangelization of the heathen Gauls, as a result of which the frontiers of his bishopric were greatly extended.

When Magnus Maximus, commander of the legions in Britain, was acclaimed as emperor by his troops in 383, and crossed into Gaul, he regarded the support of the leading churchmen of Gaul as highly desirable, and was specially eager to win the good will of so revered and influential a bishop as Martin. Martin at first declined to accept Maximus's invitation to be his guest at Trier (Trèves), where he set up his court; later, however, he relented, and was treated with great veneration by Maximus, and with even greater by the very religious empress, who esteemed it a high honour to prepare and serve Martin's food with her own hands. Sulpicius Severus comments on this remarkable proceeding —only what seems so remarkable to him is not the imperial lady's humility but the fact that Martin permitted a lady to come so near him!

But Martin was too genuinely humble himself to be spoiled by such attention in high quarters. His gentleness of character was such that it was difficult not to love him; even the heathen regarded him with affection. He made scarcely any enemies; the exceptions, his biographer remarks, were almost all bishops! Yet when righteousness required to be maintained and wickedness denounced, Martin did not hesitate. He saw to it that Maximus knew just what he thought of the murder of the Emperor Gratian, which happened so opportunely for the usurper; and, like Ambrose, he condemned the iniquitous execution of Priscillian and his followers.

The impression made by his holiness of life and missionary enterprise was immense; his fame spread widely throughout western Europe, and not least in the British Isles. In the year of his death (397), a church bearing his name was erected at Whithorn in the south of Scotland; another was erected not long afterwards in Canterbury. His feast—November 11 (possibly the anniversary of his funeral)—still marks the beginning of the winter term in Scotland, where it is called Martinmas; a spell of good weather about this time is called St. Martin's summer in his honour.

The impetus which he gave indirectly to the evangelization of the British Isles will be considered in our following chapters. He may be regarded as the real founder of western monasticism and one of the three great figures associated with its development.

Early in the following century John Cassian (*c.* 360–435), abbot of the monastery of St. Victor near Marseilles, introduced among his monks a system of life founded on the eastern rule instituted by Basil.[1] But it was Benedict of Cassino (*c.* 480–547), over a hundred years later, who composed the rule which has since remained as normative for western monasticism as Basil's has for the eastern variety. The Benedictine rule, while strict, did not impose unreasonable austerities. It made corporate life the normal practice, instead of the hermit life. The latter was slow in disappearing, as we shall see, especially on the western fringe of European civilization; but it was the Benedictine rule that gave character to mediæval monasticism at its best.[2]

[1] See O Chadwick, *John Cassian: A Study in Primitive Monasticism* (1950).
[2] See F. R. Hoare (ed.), *The Western Fathers* (1954).

CHAPTER XXXVI

EARLY BRITISH CHRISTIANITY

THE EARLIEST CERTAIN DATE IN THE HISTORY OF BRITISH Christianity is August 1, A.D. 314. On that day the Synod of Arles met, a council of western bishops summoned by the Emperor Constantine to consider the Donatist claim to represent the true Catholic Church in North Africa. Among the bishops who came to Arles for the synod three came from Britain. They were Eborius of York, Restitutus of London, and Adelphius, probably of Lincoln.

That such an episcopal delegation could be sent by the British church to the synod suggests that by this time Christianity had spread over a good part of the province. But of the beginnings and early growth of the British church we know almost nothing. Later legend is very willing to fill up the gaps in our knowledge with stories about Joseph of Arimathæa and other eminent representatives of the first generation of Christians; but real evidence is extremely slight.

It has been frequently suggested that Christianity was introduced to Britain by the Roman army of occupation. But all the evidence at our disposal is against this. The army of occupation seems to have been wholly uninfluenced by Christianity during the first three centuries A.D. True, there is the probability that Christianity made its way into the family of Aulus Plautius, who conquered Britain for the empire in A.D. 43, when Claudius was emperor, and governed it as an imperial province for four years; but this has nothing at all to do with Christianity in Britain.[1]

In fact, if there was one eastern religion more than another cultivated by the Roman army in Britain (as elsewhere), it was Mithraism and not Christianity. Mithra was the god of light and truth in Iranian mythology; his cult was introduced to the Romans towards the middle of the first century B.C. and by the middle of the third century A.D. it had spread so widely that an impartial observer might have concluded that Mithraism and not Christianity would become the dominant religion throughout the empire. It envisaged the world as a battleground between light

[1] See pp. 137f.

and darkness; worshippers of Mithra must take part in this warfare in order to attain union with him. Those who did attain it were purified by mystic rites in which he was believed to escort them through the seven planetary spheres to the highest heaven, where they might expect to live in eternal light. Mithraism made a special appeal to serious-minded men, and particularly to soldiers, as is perhaps natural when we consider the military language in which its principles were expressed. Three temples on Hadrian's Wall, and Mithraic inscriptions and symbols there and at York and other places in the north of England indicate that it had its votaries in the Roman army in Britain.[1] No such evidence exists for the knowledge of Christianity there, even in the fourth century.

It is much more likely that Christianity was carried to Britain by ordinary people—traders from Gaul and other parts, it may be. Or Britons who had occasion to visit other parts of the empire may have come in contact with the new faith and carried it home. We must remember how unrestricted travel was throughout the Roman world; a man might go from Carlisle to Babylon without crossing an international frontier. The free interchange of populations has been illustrated on the one hand by an Aramaic inscription on Hadrian's Wall (now in the museum at South Shields), set up by a Syrian trader in memory of his British wife, and on the other hand by an inscription attesting the presence of a British auxiliary cavalry regiment (normally stationed on the Danube frontier) at Amasia in Cappadocia on its way to or from the Emperor Trajan's Mesopotamian expedition in A.D. 115.

There were thus many opportunities for the new faith to be brought to Britain. At a later time the evangelization of various parts of the British Isles is associated with a few outstanding names, as those of Ninian, Patrick, Columba and Augustine, of whom we shall have more to say anon. But no great name has been handed down in connexion with the earliest evangelization of Britain. We must remember that much more missionary work was done by ordinary Christians in the course of their daily business and intercourse than is often realized.

If, however, we take account of the probabilities of the situation, we may suppose that it was from Gaul that Christianity first spread into Britain. Gaul began to be evangelized at quite an early time. There is a possible reference to a Gaulish mission in the New Testament itself; in the statement towards the end of the

---

[1] The only Mithraic temple thus far known in the civilian area of Roman Britain is the one at Walbrook, London (near the Mansion House), discovered in 1954, and even here the name of a legionary veteran appears among those of rich merchant-worshippers.

Second Epistle to Timothy, "Crescens has gone to Galatia,"[1] Galatia may mean Gaul (indeed, "Gaul" is actually the reading here in some early authorities for the text). At any rate, the south-eastern part of Gaul was evangelized quite early, and apparently from Asia Minor. The churches of Vienne and Lyons in the Rhône valley, which were the victims of a savage outbreak of mob violence in 177, had close links with Asia Minor, and it was from there that they received their bishop, Irenæus, who took the place of the aged bishop who met his death in the persecution.[2] Irenæus, while bishop of Lyons, had oversight over all the churches of Gaul;[3] and while Greek was his own language, as it was that of the churches of Vienne and Lyons, he found it necessary to learn the Celtic vernacular of Gaul in order to carry out his duties properly. By the middle of the third century, however, there were several bishops in Gaul, by 325 there were twenty-eight, and fifty years later there were fifty-four. These figures give some idea of the rapid development of church organization in Gaul during those centuries;[4] and the progressive Christianization of Gaul must have influenced the province on the other side of the English Channel.

Tertullian at the end of the second century, and Origen a few decades later, both mention that Christianity had by their time penetrated Britain; and some time before the Synod of Arles Britain had its first recorded Christian martyr, whether the martyrdom of St. Alban at Verulam (later called St. Albans after him) is to be referred, with Bede,[5] to the persecution of Diocletian's reign, or to the earlier Decian persecution. In Britain, as in Gaul, the persecution under Diocletian was mild, as Constantius Cæsar, who administered that part of the empire, contented himself with carrying out the minimum requirements only of his superiors' policy. And one of the most notable events in British provincial history was the proclamation of Constantine as emperor by the army at York on July 25, 306, on the death of his father Constantius.

The recorded Christian history of Britain, in fact, begins with Constantine. And throughout the fourth century, together with the increasing weakness of Roman military strength in the province, we trace the steady growth and expansion of Christianity, and the coincidence of these two tendencies is not merely haphazard.

---

[1] 2 Timothy 4 : 10.
[2] See pp. 178f.
[3] The Cardinal Archbishop of Lyons still bears the title "Primate of the Gauls."
[4] See T. S. Holmes, *The Origin and Development of the Christian Church in Gaul* (1911).
[5] Bede, *Hist. Eccl.*, I, 7.

After the Synod of Arles, the next recorded convention of the kind to be attended by British delegates was the Council of Rimini in 359,[1] where again several British bishops were present. It is recorded of these that all but three of them were among the minority of the bishops present who claimed the privilege of paying their own expenses instead of travelling at the cost of the imperial treasury. The three exceptions could not afford to do this, and thought it better to draw upon the emperor's bounty than upon the charity of their brethren.

In Britain itself the earliest material monument of Christianity has been found in recent years in a Roman villa at Lullingstone, Kent. About 350 or soon after, a group of upper rooms in this building (a chapel, antechamber and vestibule) were apparently set apart for Christian worship, to judge from their wall paintings, which include the monogram of X and P (the initial letters of Christ's name)[2] and *orante* figures—i.e., figures with their arms outstretched in an early Christian attitude of prayer.[3] There is also a tiny church edifice of basilica form at Silchester, which may date from about this time; and there are remains of what may be another at Caerwent. Also from about the same period we have the following inscription on a fragment of wall-plaster from a Roman house at Cirencester:

R O T A S

O P E R A

T E N E T

A R E P O

S A T O R

This "magic square" in an identical or similar form has been found in a number of places throughout the Roman world, the earliest example being at Pompeii (to be dated necessarily before the destruction of that city in A.D. 79) and the most easterly examples being four discovered at Dura on the Euphrates.[4] Various explanations of the formula have been offered, but a very attractive one finds in it an early secret Christian anagram, to be resolved thus:

---

[1] See pp. 318f.
[2] See p. 294.
[3] See G. W. Meates, *Lullingstone Roman Villa* (1955), pp. 126–155.

[4] See D. Atkinson, "The Sator-Formula and the Beginnings of Christianity" in *Rylands Library Bulletin*, XXII (1938), pp. 419ff. and "The Origin and Date of the 'Sator' Word-Square" in *Journal of Ecclesiastical History*, II (1951), pp. 1–18; J. Carcopino, "Le christianisme secret du 'carré magique'" in *Museum Helveticum*, V (1948), pp. 167f.; H. Last, "The Rotas-Sator Square: Present Position and Future Prospects," *Journal of Theological Studies*, N. S., III (1952), pp. 92ff.

```
            A

            P
            A
            T
            E
            R
A  PATERNOSTER  O
            O
            S
            T
            E
            R

            O
```

If this solution is right—and in the nature of the case this cannot be demonstrated but must remain a matter of inherent probability one way or the other—then the "magic square" represents the opening words of the Lord's Prayer in its Matthæan form, *Pater noster* ("Our Father"),[1] written twice in such an arrangement that the letter N is used once only, and accompanied by the twofold writing of A and O, the Latin letters corresponding to the Greek *alpha* and *omega*.[2]

The second half of the fourth century in Britain was a time of increasing aggression by peoples outside the empire, while calls of one kind and another were made upon the Roman army there which diverted its strength to the continent. We have already mentioned, for example, the bid for power made by Magnus Maximus in 383, and what he did on the continent. But here it is important to note that in native British tradition Maximus is a great hero; he figures in Welsh legend as Maxen Wledig ("Maximus the commander-in-chief"), and his wife is said to have been a British princess, Helena. (It may be by confusion with this lady that Constantine's mother, whose name also was Helena, is traditionally represented as a native of Britain, but she was really the daughter of an Illyrian taverner.) M. P. Charlesworth has pointed out that "no people will thus take a ruler to its heart unless he has done some great and memorable thing for it"; and he makes the very attractive suggestion that when Maximus left Britain to consolidate his position in Gaul, he made arrangements for the protection of the province in the absence of his troops by making a treaty of alliance with two British tribes who lived north of

---

[1] Matthew 6 : 9. In Luke 11 : 2 the opening word is simply "Father." This interpretation of the word-square thus involves a problem of New Testament criticism.
[2] Revelation 1 : 8; 21 : 6; 22 : 13.

Hadrian's Wall and had for a long time enjoyed friendly relations with the Roman citizens south of the wall. "Henceforth, in the north, British tribes, trained in Roman ways of fighting and in the use of Roman weapons, were quite capable of defending their own country." Maximus, on this interpretation, enjoys his legendary prestige because he was the Roman governor who "first recognized the two tribes in North Britain as allies, first gave a chieftain Roman insignia, and first entered into a marriage-alliance with a British royal line. If you like it—the history of an organized Welsh people begins with an act of recognition by this Spanish-born governor, Magnus Maximus."[1]

Some such arrangement as this is certainly demanded by the events that followed the final withdrawal of centrally controlled Roman forces from Britain. This withdrawal, which took place about 407, was not followed by immediate collapse and barbarization, as older school histories suggested. For several decades before this date, Roman Britain had been attacked not only by Irish from the west and Picts from the north, but also by the first raiding Saxons from the continent, so much so that the south-east coast of England was called the Saxon Shore, and was put in charge of a separate military commander, the Count of the Saxon Shore. (The remaining military forces were commanded at this time by the *dux Britanniarum*, "General of the Britains," whose headquarters were at York.) But the withdrawal of the imperial forces in 407 was followed by a more vigorous defence of Britain by native forces in the north of the province, who carried the war into the invaders' territory and pushed the frontier of Romano-British influence up to the Clyde, while others marched south into Wales and expelled or subjugated the Irish invaders there.

For the withdrawal of the imperial armies was not the withdrawal of the Romans. The Roman population of Britain remained. This population did not consist of colonists from Rome or any other part of the continent; it consisted of freeborn Britons who were Roman citizens, as all freeborn provincials had been since 211. Roman civilization had penetrated through Britain in varying degrees, being most evident in the cities and country-estates or villas. When we look at Roman remains in Britain, such as the Roman baths at Bath, we must think not that these amenities were installed for the benefit of Roman officers and their memsahibs; the Romans who enjoyed the baths in Bath and lived lives of leisured culture in the villas of Britain were Britons as well as Romans—Romano-Britons. And when the centrally controlled armies left Britain, because there were more desperate demands on their services in other parts of the empire, the Romano-Britons mobilized their own forces in defence of

M. P. Charlesworth, *The Lost Province* (1949), pp. 28ff.

Roman civilization, and for several decades they did so very effectively. Nor were they content to rely on arms alone; the evangelization of Scotland and Ireland, as we shall see, was undertaken by Romano-Britons and was closely bound up with Romano-British defence policy.

Although Pelagius was a native of the British Isles, his personal propagation of Pelagianism does not strictly belong to the story of British church history, for he was far from his native land when he first made his name as a heretic. But if (as seems probable) he was an Irishman born in Britain, we may best regard him as a native of one of the settlements which invading Irishmen formed in South Wales and other westerly parts of Britain during the fourth century, and we must further conclude that by 370 (the approximate year of Pelagius's birth) some of these Irish colonies had been evangelized by their British neighbours.

And though Pelagius himself did not propagate his heresy in Britain, Pelagianism made its way to Britain in due course, especially after its proscription by successive provincial councils between 412 and 418 and Pelagius's banishment from Rome in the latter year. In fact, it made such headway in the British Church that serious alarm was felt by Christian leaders on the continent. It may be, indeed, that one section of British opinion, from nationalist motives, welcomed Pelagianism the more readily because it had been condemned at Rome.

However that may be, in 429 a council of Gaulish bishops met in response to a request from the anti-Pelagian party in the British Church, and sent two of their number, Germanus of Auxerre and Lupus of Troyes, to deal with the situation in Britain. Of these two, Germanus was the leading figure, and his mission was authorized by Cælestine, who was bishop of Rome at the time. Germanus was assisted by a deacon named Palladius, of whom we shall hear more. The mission was successful; Germanus and his companions went up and down the country preaching the true faith, confirming the orthodox and restoring the heretics. Pelagianism was checked—for the time being, at any rate.

But Pelagianism was not the only enemy that Germanus had the opportunity of checking. While he was still in Britain, during the season of Lent in 430, a concerted attack upon the northern frontiers and shores was launched by Picts and Saxons. Germanus not only gave the British defenders such spiritual encouragement as a chaplain-general might; he showed no mean military prowess. For, before he became a cleric, he had been a soldier, general officer commanding the Roman army in Aquitaine, and he proved in the present emergency that his hand had not lost its cunning. He himself took charge of the defence, and routed the invaders. In the form which the story ultimately took, the rout was caused by the cries of Alleluia repeated by the defending forces who awaited the enemy's approach in a narrow valley; as the shout echoed through the defile the enemy panicked, and "faith, not force, won a bloodless victory."[1]

A recrudescence of Pelagianism some years later brought Germanus to Britain again, accompanied this time by Severus, bishop of Trier.[2] But the political situation was worse this time and it would have taken more than Germanus's strategy to repel the fresh assaults of the invaders. In 446, the year before Germanus's second visit, a desperate message had been sent by the British leaders to Aëtius, the Roman general in Gaul. "The barbarians drive us into the sea, and the sea throws us back on the barbarians; our only choice lies between two kinds of death—massacre or drowning."[3]

We know of no response to this appeal for help, and it was followed very quickly by a new scheme, that of playing off the invading groups one against the other. A British king conceived the idea of enlisting the aid of the Saxons against the Picts, and for a time this policy seemed to work well. The king who adopted it was Vortigern, leader of the nationalist party in Britain and probably also champion of Pelagianism, which he favoured as a counteraction to "transmarine" influences. This last point is a fair inference from the hostility which tradition represents as existing between him and Germanus, when the latter visited Britain the second time.

Vortigern's Saxon alliance intensified the settlement of Saxons on the east coast of our island. But the alliance did not last long; Vortigern was accused of bad faith and the Saxons turned on their temporary British confederates and wrought tremendous damage to the cities in eastern Britain, overthrowing much of the surviving Roman culture. After this wave of fury died down, however, the initiative passed again to the Britons—not, however, to the nationalists but to the party that was still consciously Roman, which was led about 460 by Ambrosius Aurelianus. Ambrosius, assuming a command similar to that formerly held by the *dux Britanniarum*, rallied the Britons in a revival which checked the westward flooding of the barbarians from the continent and the southward incursions of those north of the border. In the following generation his work was apparently carried on by another Romano-Briton named Artorius, whose name has been preserved in the Arthurian legend, fertile in reminiscences of King Arthur and his knights along the whole line which the

---

[1] Bede, *Hist. Eccl.*, I, 20, following Germanus's biographer Constantius.
[2] Mrs. Chadwick believes that Germanus's second visit to Britain has no historic basis (*Poetry and Letters in Early Christian Gaul*, pp. 255ff.).
[3] Gildas, *Ruin and Complaint of Britain*, 20.

Britons for a shorter or longer period succeeded in establishing as their eastern frontier—from Edinburgh and Camelon in Scotland southward through Cumberland, Wales, Cornwall and Brittany. This Romano-British revival culminated in a decisive defeat inflicted upon the invaders about the beginning of the sixth century at Mount Badon, near Swindon in Wiltshire. The Saxons fell back on their settlements in the east of the country, and British Christianity enjoyed a respite of half a century.

But indeed it was more than a respite that British Christianity enjoyed; during this half-century and even during the preceding decades of Romano-British revival it enjoyed a revival that was religious and not political—a revival associated with the names of two Welsh saints, Illtyd and the national patron, David. Both those names are associated with a monastic revival which spread from Gaul to the British Isles in those years. Illtyd (who flourished in the latter half of the fifth century) was a native of Brittany, a great-nephew of Germanus. After serving his monastic apprenticeship at St. Honorat and Auxerre, he came to Britain and founded the monastery at Llantwit Major in Glamorganshire. (Llantwit Major preserves its founder's name in a corrupt form; the older Welsh form of the place-name is Llanilltyd Fawr, "the great church of Illtyd.") The Welsh also credit him with introducing an improved method of ploughing. David belonged to one of the chief royal families of Britain, and studied under Illtyd at Llantwit Major as well as under one or two other Christian scholars of the day. He founded a monastery at Glyn Rhosyn in Pembrokeshire, the site of the cathedral of St. Davids. Much that is told about him in our sources is legend and not history, but he was certainly the most influential leader of British Christianity in the sixth century. Another prominent Christian figure about this time was Cadoc, David's cousin, founder and first abbot of Llancarvan in Glamorganshire, which became a renowned centre of sacred and secular learning. Cadoc maintained close and friendly relations with the Irish Church. Among his pupils at Llancarvan the most illustrious was the learned Gildas, whose Latin treatise *On the Ruin and Complaint of Britain*, written shortly before 550, is a primary authority for the century 450–550, although it is a homiletic denunciation of the vices of his fellow-countrymen rather than a history. The fellow-countrymen denounced by Gildas belong mainly to the nationalist and consciously Celticizing party; he himself was one of the last of the Romano-Britons, well versed in the Latin classics as well as in the Bible, still referring to Latin as "our language."[1]

Soon after Gildas wrote, the pressure from the eastern invaders was resumed, and this time it suffered no major check as it had

[1] Gildas, *op. cit.*, 23; cf. Charlesworth, *op. cit.*, p. 74.

done at Mount Badon. Probably the resumption of their pressure
was made easier because of the "yellow plague" which attacked
the Britons about 546. This plague started in Persia in 542, and
spread slowly westward over the Middle East and Europe. In
Britain it hastened the collapse of the remnants of Romano-
British civilization and left the land an easy prey to the barbarians,
who somehow seem not to have suffered from the plague as much
as the Britons did.

During the half-century which followed 550 the invaders
steadily consolidated their hold on the greater part of England.
In the extreme south-east, where contact with the continent was
easiest, the Jutes were in control. The Saxons spread over the rest
of southern England, south of the Suffolk Stour and the upper
Thames, ultimately reaching the Cornish border. Three Saxon
kingdoms took shape—in Essex, Sussex and Wessex. The Angles
occupied the rest of the country as far north as the Forth. They
ultimately grouped themselves into three kingdoms—East Anglia
(Norfolk and Suffolk), Mercia (the Midlands) and Northumbria
(from the Humber to the Forth, comprising what were, to begin
with, the two separate kingdoms of Bernicia in the north and
Deira in the south, whose common frontier was the Tees).

The Celtic states were pushed steadily back. We must not
imagine, of course, that all the former inhabitants of England
were simply wiped out if they did not flee to Wales; it is certain
that many, if not most, of them remained, but they lost their
national identity and were for the greater part reduced to servitude
under the newcomers.[1] At last the independent British territory
was reduced to a few areas cut off from each other by sea—
Strathclyde and Cumbria, Wales, Cornwall, and Brittany, which
had its name from the settlements of Britons there which date
from the fifth century onwards. Apart from these areas, the last
Celtic territory to hold out against the English was the kingdom
of Elmet in the West Riding of Yorkshire, with its capital at
Loidis (Leeds). Edwin, king of Northumbria, annexed this state
about 620 and expelled Cerdic, its last king. A completely new
pattern of civilization thus imposed itself over almost the whole
of England, in which nothing but the merest fragments of
Romano-British civilization could be discerned. But, more important still from our point of view, Christianity suffered a major
setback, being confined to the territory north and west, and cut
off from the continent by English paganism. Such a state of
affairs could not be allowed to go on.[2]

[1] Shepherds in the Yorkshire Dales and the Lake District continued to count
their sheep in "Welsh" within living memory: I do not know if the practice still
survives anywhere in those parts.
[2] For the general background of this period, see H. M. Chadwick and others,
Studies in Early British History (1954).

CHAPTER XXXVII

BEYOND THE ROMAN WALL

BUT WHAT OF THE TERRITORY WHICH LAY NORTH OF THE provincial frontier? The country which we now call Scotland had no such name in Roman imperial days. At that time the people called Scots lived in Ireland; it was not until the fifth century that the first Scots settled in the land which was later to be named after them. For the sake of convenience we shall refer to the country as Scotland, but let it be remembered that, for the period we are dealing with, this is strictly an anachronism.

Scotland was not completely unknown territory to the Romans. One Roman governor of Britain, Julius Agricola,[1] waged a number of campaigns in the north between 79 and 83, from his advance base at Inchtuthil on the Tay; and in the latter year fought a pitched battle with the Caledonians under their leader Calgacus at a place which Tacitus calls Mons Graupius. The exact location of this site is uncertain; it may have been near Stonehaven, where the mountain-range commonly called the Grampians comes down to the North Sea coast;[2] it was possibly even farther north, at one of the natural gateways from the province of Mar to the province of Moray.[3] Agricola did not attempt, however, to bring all Scotland into the Roman provincial system; having broken the Highland resistance, he built a chain of forts between the Forth and Clyde to serve as a protective barrier north of the province. This barrier does not seem to have been very effective, for it was decided in A.D. 120, during the Emperor Hadrian's visit to the province, that the line from the Solway to the Tyne offered the best defence, and here Hadrian's Wall was built. Nineteen years later, however, the governor Lollius Urbicus marched north again as far as the Forth-Clyde line and there he built a wall which he called Antonine's Wall, after the reigning emperor. This wall can still be traced in parts from Bridgeness on the Forth to Old Kilpatrick on the Clyde. For some forty years this wall was held, until it was overrun and wrecked by Caledonians in 182. After this irruption it was apparently recovered and repaired, but three

[1] See A. R. Burn, *Agricola and Roman Britain* (1954).
[2] O. G. S. Crawford, *Topography of Roman Scotland* (1949), pp. 130–33.
[3] I. A. Richmond, "Gnaeus Iulius Agricola," *Journal of Roman Studies*, XXXIV (1944), pp. 34ff.; M. P. Charlesworth, *The Lost Province* (1949), pp. 10f.

years later it was deliberately abandoned because of a change of policy.[1]

Hadrian's Wall now became the definitive northern frontier of the province. It was subjected to attacks from the north, and was completely overrun in a mass invasion of the province about 200. In 207 the Emperor Septimius Severus decided to teach the northerners a lesson once and for all. So he led his legions in person not only as far as the line of Antonine's Wall, but still farther north—"to the limit of the island," says the historian[2] (probably to the Moray Firth)—in order to strike the terror of Rome into Caledonian hearts.

From remains of Roman camps we can trace a Roman line of penetration beyond the Forth, as far north as Aberdeenshire. From Cramond, north-west of Edinburgh, the line runs westward, crossing the Roman wall south of Camelon (near Falkirk), where there was a Roman fort; then, turning north, it follows roughly the (former L.M.S.) railway line from Stirling via Perth to Stonehaven. Then it turns in a north-westerly direction, and can be traced by the remains of temporary camps (accommodating from ten to fifteen thousand men) at Peterculter, Kintore, and Ythanwells, on to the Pass of Grange, the natural gateway to the Moray Firth.[3] Whether the northern limits of this line of penetration go back only to Severus, or still farther to Agricola, is a matter of doubt; though such evidence as there is points to Agricola. But the importance of the line for our purpose will appear in due course.

It may not be without significance that it is round about the time of Severus, or shortly after, that we find the earliest references to the spread of Christianity in Britain, even beyond the provincial frontier. Tertullian refers to "districts of Britain not penetrated by the Romans, which yet have been brought under the sway of Christ;"[4] and Origen writes: "The power of our Lord and Saviour is found even among these people who are separated from the Roman world in Britain."[5] Even if these statements (especially Tertullian's) have some element of rhetorical exaggeration, it is clear that parts of Scotland were influenced by the Roman civilization of the province. There is ample archæological evidence of this, and in any case it is what we should expect. In more peaceful times there must have been much commercial intercourse across the border; in less peaceful times prisoners of war were taken on both sides. Fugitive slaves passed from south to north; mercenary soldiers were enlisted north of the border.

---

[1] See Sir George Macdonald, *The Roman Wall in Scotland* (1934), pp. 12f., 477ff.
[2] Dio Cassius, *Epitome*, LXXVII, 13.
[3] See J. K. St. Joseph, "Air Reconnaissance of North Britain," *Journal of Roman Studies*, XLI (1951), pp. 52ff.
[4] Tertullian, *Against the Jews*, 7.   [5] Origen, *Homily*, VI, on Luke 1.

Roman coins have been found in Celtic sites as far north as the shore of the Moray Firth; Roman coinage, indeed, may well have come to be used as the staple British currency outside as much as inside the province. Perhaps some Latin was known, as it was in South Britain before the Roman conquest.

The pressure of the northerners on the frontier increased in the second half of the fourth century. They overran Hadrian's Wall about 367, raiding the province almost as far south as London. Simultaneous raids were made by Irish from the west and by Saxons from across the North Sea. In 369, however, the invaders were repelled by Count Theodosius (father of the Emperor Theodosius I), who called the recovered northern part of the province Valentia, after the Emperor Valens. This area was probably also known simply as *Recepta Provincia* ("The Recovered Province"), the former part of which name survived as the *Rheged* of the Welsh bards. *Rheged*, indeed, seems to have included territory north of Hadrian's Wall, in the south-west area of Scotland commonly known as Galloway. And it is here that a very important Christian forward movement towards the end of the fourth century had its base.

When Magnus Maximus left Britain with his troops in 383, to promote his imperial ambitions on the continent, the history of Hadrian's Wall as the provincial frontier seems to come to an end. At any rate, no wall-fort has produced a coin dated later than that year. But we referred in our last chapter to the suggestion that before his departure Maximus entrusted the defence of the province—at least of its northern parts—to two Romano-British princely families in that area. For some decades they were remarkably successful in performing this task, and even pushed the frontier of Roman civilization northwards. This success, however, was not one of military enterprise alone; it was closely connected with the Christian forward movement which we have just mentioned.

The prestige of the imperial religion must have been considerable across the border, especially in those parts most influenced by the Roman civilization of the province. That a Christian nucleus existed in Galloway is suggested by the fact that towards the end of the fourth century a bishop was sent to that district. Bishops were not sent, so far as we know, to completely pagan areas. The bishop sent to Galloway was Ninian.

A helpful reconstruction of the circumstances of Ninian's mission has been offered by Dr. W. Douglas Simpson, librarian of Aberdeen University. Shortly after the withdrawal of the imperial troops from Hadrian's Wall in 383, he says, a stable rule, centred on Carlisle, seems to have been organized by a member of one of the Romano-British families already mentioned. The relatively stable conditions of this rule would enable Ninian to carry out his pastoral and missionary work in security. For Ninian was not sent simply to be bishop of the few Christians who were already to be found in Galloway, but to organize a missionary campaign among the Picts, who formed the chief part of the population of Scotland north of the Forth-Clyde line. "It is probably no coincidence," says Dr. Simpson, "that the very moment which saw the collapse of the northern frontier organization of the Roman Diocese[1] of Britain should also witness the inception of a great missionary movement to win for the now Christian Empire the heathen nation of the Picts who were already swarming round the crumbling bastions of the imperial defence. In all likelihood St. Ninian's mission, like that of Ulfilas to the Goths very shortly before, was a detail in Roman policy."[2] No doubt Ninian himself was animated by evangelistic rather than political motives, but under the circumstances his evangelism suited the imperial policy well enough.

The earliest and most reliable account of Ninian and his mission is given by Bede. It appears in the course of Bede's record of Columba's evangelization of the "northern Picts," which he dates in 565. He explains that these northern Picts are divided from the southern Picts by "high and rugged mountain peaks." Then he goes on:

> For these southern Picts, who dwell on this side of the same mountains, abandoned the error of idolatry a long time before, as we are told, and accepted the true faith, when Ninian, a most reverend bishop and most saintly man, preached the word to them. He belonged to the British nation, and had been duly trained at Rome in the faith and mysteries of the truth. His episcopal see, made notable by the name and church of the holy bishop Martin, where Ninian himself now rests in body along with many saints, is now occupied by the English nation. This place, which belongs to the province of the Bernicians, is commonly called *Ad Candidam Casam* ("At the White House") because there he built a church of stone, after a fashion to which the Britons were not accustomed.[3]

We next find Ninian mentioned in a letter sent about A.D. 800 by Alcuin of York to "the brethren of St. Ninian of Candida Casa." Alcuin had learned something about Ninian from a poem describing his great holiness and his many miracles. He therefore sent a silken shroud for the body of "our holy father Ninian," and asked the fraternity to pray for him in the church "of our father the bishop Ninian."

[1] In late Imperial Roman usage a political, not an ecclesiastical, division.
[2] W. D. Simpson, *The Celtic Church in Scotland* (1935), p. 52; cf. his *Saint Ninian and the Origins of the Christian Church in Scotland* (1940), pp. 1ff.
[3] Bede, *Hist. Eccl.*, III, 4. The capital of the north Pictish kingdom evangelized by Columba was near Inverness (see pp. 389, 392).

A third source of information is the *Life of Ninian*, written by Ailred, abbot of Rievaulx in Yorkshire, in the twelfth century. This work, which is largely a conventional record of miracles, has little independent value. It is ultimately based on Bede's narrative, although Ailred says in his prologue that he used an older Life of Ninian which was difficult to understand because it was written in a "barbaric tongue," possibly Old English. (This older *Life* was also used by the author of an eighth-century poem on Ninian.)[1] Ailred represents Ninian as organizing a thorough-going national church north of the border, with bishops and presbyters, dioceses and parishes. This representation is historically false, but it exactly describes what was going on in Scotland under King David I (1135–53), in Ailred's own time. Ailred's purpose was perhaps to grace with a fictitious antiquity David's Romanizing innovations at the expense of the Celtic Columban tradition in Scotland. But a few of Ailred's statements about Ninian do appear to have some better foundation than his work in general: for example, when he tells us that Ninian was the son of a Christian British king; that he learned of the death of his master, Martin of Tours, at the very time when he was engaged in establishing his monastery at Candida Casa; that under his preaching a local prince, named Tuduvallus, was converted. Certainly the date of Martin's death, A.D. 397, agrees well with other chronological indications for Ninian's career.

The late Professor W. J. Watson, who held the Chair of Celtic in Edinburgh University, thought it probable that Ninian was one of the Britons who followed the usurping Emperor Maximus to Gaul in 383, and that after the death of Maximus (388) he stayed on with Martin at Tours. The nine years from the death of Maximus to the death of Martin would afford ample time for Ninian's training at Rome, of which Bede speaks, as well as for some time spent with Martin at Tours. Watson, indeed, thought that Ninian did not go to Rome at all, but received all his training in Gaul, like Patrick a few decades later; but there is no adequate reason for discounting Bede's evidence. It seems clear, however, that it was Martin's influence that counted most with Ninian, when we consider the monastic character of his foundation at Candida Casa.

A further very probable suggestion of Watson's was that Ninian's bishopric, the name of which has not been preserved in any account of him, was the recovered province of Valentia, which included Galloway and Dumfries.[2]

[1] W. Levison, "An Eighth-Century Poem on St. Ninian," *Antiquity*, XIV (1940), pp. 280–291.

[2] W. J. Watson, "Notes on St. Ninian," *The Evangelical Quarterly*, V (1933), pp. 31ff. J. H. G. Meissner suggests that Ninian was a hostage taken to Rome by Theodosius, and sent back to evangelize the territory north of the province of

These suggestions of Watson supplement quite cogently the reconstruction quoted above from Dr. Simpson. But Dr. Simpson is a protagonist of a school of historical thought which has emphasized the importance and extent of Ninian's mission at the expense of the traditional account of the later mission of Columba. Dr. Simpson, to be sure, is much more moderate in his claims for Ninian's mission than some representatives of this school have been. Professor Watson entered the lists as a protagonist on the other side. The school which has laid special stress on the Ninianic mission has unfortunately neglected for the most part to equip itself with a working knowledge of Old Gaelic, indispensable for this study, and has thus laid itself open to incisive attacks by such a master of Celtic philology as Watson was.

Dr. Simpson has argued that the Ninianic mission was not confined to the southern Picts, but penetrated to the far north of Scotland. His argument depends largely on the association of Ninian's name with various sites throughout Scotland. This argument must be used with care. Only where the association of a saint's name with any particular place can be traced back to very early times can we begin to feel safe about drawing historical conclusions. But it seems to be well established that in the days of Celtic Christianity new monastic sites bore the name either of the actual founder or of the founder of the parent monastery. Thus the monastery at Candida Casa was called after Martin, founder of the parent monastery at Ligugé.

Dr. Simpson traces the northward expansion of the Ninianic mission by a series of ancient sacred foundations which he reduces to a "severely censored list" of eight.[1] The first is at Candida Casa itself, the second at Glasgow. (According to the twelfth-century *Life of Kentigern* by Joceline, a monk of Furness, when Kentigern—otherwise Mungo—founded his church at Glasgow about 573, he chose a site where Ninian had consecrated a cemetery.) The third is near Stirling, and from there the line of foundations runs north-east roughly parallel to the Roman line of penetration already traced, via Arbroath and Stonehaven. This correspondence between the two lines has been taken as further support for the view that Ninian's mission was a deliberate part of imperial policy. The legions had once followed this road; since they had been withdrawn, let the missionaries follow it in their turn; perhaps they might succeed where the legions had failed.

But the legions on one occasion, and possibly on two, had penetrated north of the mountain barrier. Did Ninian or his followers

Britain in pursuance of imperial policy (*History of the Church of Ireland*, ed. W. A. Phillips, Vol. I [1933], p. 61).
[1] He adds two more in "New Light on St. Ninian," *Archaeologia Aeliana*, Ser. 4, Vol. XXIII (1945), pp. 78–95.

do so? Bede's language confines Ninian's mission to the south side of the "high and rugged mountain peaks" which divided the southern from the northern Picts. But some scholars of the newer Ninianic school have claimed confidently that the Ninianic mission penetrated to the far north. One of them, Dr. A. B. Scott, found as many as ten Ninianic foundations in the north of Scotland—two in Aberdeenshire, two in Moray, and one apiece in Inverness-shire, Ross, Sutherland, Caithness, Orkney and Shetland.[1] Most of these can be discounted at once. Dr. Simpson, more cautiously, confines his argument to three of these northern sites; and two of these—Temple, in Glenurquhart, near Loch Ness, and Navidale in Sutherland—must be questioned on philological grounds. The only site north of the Mounth which may at all reasonably be regarded as going back to the Ninianic mission is a foundation bearing Ninian's name at Andet,[2] in the parish of Methlick, Aberdeenshire. This site does not take us beyond the Roman line of penetration; in fact, the Romans passed through this district to encamp at Ythanwells. It is also noteworthy that the area between the Ythan and the Don, in which this district lies, bears the name Formartin, a name which first appears about A.D. 800 in the form *Ferann Martain*, Gaelic for "Martin's land." We do not perhaps overstep the bounds of probability if we suggest that the Martin after whom the land was called was Martin of Tours. It may be, therefore, that here we have the solitary exception to the rule that Ninian's mission was restricted to the *southern* Picts.

Some decades after the commencement of Ninian's mission, the territory south of the Firth of Forth was invaded and occupied by the northernmost units of the sea-borne Angles. In due course they formed themselves into the kingdom of Bernicia and expanded steadily westwards. The time came when they penetrated as far as Candida Casa itself. The Ninianic succession there came to an end, but after an interregnum the now Christianized Angles re-established the old religious foundation, which they continued to call by its proper name of "White House"—not in the Latin form but in the Old English *hwit-aern*, which survives to this day in the modern form of the place-name, Whithorn (Wigtownshire). The first English bishop of Whithorn, Pecthelm by name, was consecrated early in the eighth century. He was a friend of Bede, and may have supplied him with some of the information recorded in his *History*.

The English invasion and other disturbances of the fifth and

[1] A. B. Scott, *The Pictish Nation: Its People and its Church* (1918).
[2] The place-name Andet or Annat means "a patron saint's church"; it is "always a sure sign of an ancient religious foundation" (W. J. Watson, *Celtic Place-names of Scotland* [1926], p. 319).

following centuries proved a setback for the Ninianic mission in Scotland. But, whatever doubt there may be about the extent of its northward penetration, there is ample evidence of its extension south-westwards, across the channel that divides Galloway from Ulster.[1]

[1] In addition to literature mentioned above, see also on the subject of this chapter A. O. Anderson, "Ninian and the Southern Picts," *Scottish Historical Review*, XXVII (1948), pp. 25–47.

CHAPTER XXXVIII

THE APOSTLE OF IRELAND

'IRELAND IS SMALL IN SIZE, AS COMPARED WITH BRITAIN, BUT larger than the Mediterranean islands. In soil, in climate, and in the character and civilization of its inhabitants it does not greatly differ from Britain, and where it does, it is for the better. Its approaches and harbours are well known from the merchants who trade with it. Agricola had given asylum to an Irish prince who had been driven from home by a rebellion there, and kept him at hand under guise of friendship lest an opportunity of using him might arise. I have often heard Agricola say that Ireland could be reduced and occupied with a single legion and a few auxiliary units, and that its conquest would be an advantage from the point of view of Britain as well, as in that case Roman arms would be in evidence on every side and liberty would have disappeared from their horizon.''[1]

The writer of these words is Tacitus, biographer and son-in-law of Agricola, Roman governor of Britain from A.D. 77 to 84. It may be thought that, in his estimate of the ease with which Ireland could be conquered and held, Agricola was an optimist. He had no opportunity of putting his opinion to the test, however, and Ireland remained outside the Roman Empire. The coasts of Ireland were well enough known, as Tacitus indicates, to travellers and merchants; and while remaining politically independent, Ireland was considerably influenced by Roman civilization. If the Roman legions did not invade Ireland, the province of Britain did not remain equally immune from occasional raids from Ireland. Settlements of invading "Scots" from across the Irish Sea appeared in the western territories of the province during the fourth century, as we have seen, and it was probably one of these settlements that produced the heresiarch Pelagius.

How exactly Christianity first came to Ireland we can only guess, but it was probably carried over from Britain. Certainly the views of the earliest Irish Christians who find a place in extant records are said to have been tainted with Pelagianism, and this may have been due to the influence of some of their emigrant kinsmen who had been converted to Christianity in the province. There was a strong Pelagianizing current in Britain early in the

[1] Tacitus, *Agricola*, 24.

fifth century. The first clear date in the history of Irish Christianity is A.D. 431, in which year, according to Bede, "Palladius was sent by Cælestine, bishop of the Roman church, to the Scots who believed in Christ, to be their first bishop."[1]

Palladius seems to have been a deacon of Germanus, bishop of Auxerre in France, who visited Britain in 429 to deal with Pelagianism in the British churches. It was possibly during this visit that the attention of Germanus, and of Pope Cælestine, who authorized his mission, was drawn to the condition of the scanty Christian communities in Ireland. If the British Christians were to be redeemed from Pelagianism, it would be better that the Irish Christians should have the same help given them. Possibly some of the more orthodox of the Irish Christians themselves asked for help. In any case, help was given. The deacon Palladius, who had actively assisted Germanus's anti-Pelagian mission in Britain, was consecrated bishop of the Irish Christians.

But within a year after he landed at the mouth of the Vartry, in County Wicklow, Palladius was dead. He had time, during his brief episcopate, to visit some Christian communities in the east of the island from Wicklow northwards to South Antrim and County Down, and to found one or two churches, including one at Donard, in County Wicklow. He probably also established relations with the Ninianic mission in Scotland. How far he succeeded in putting down Pelagianism in Ireland we cannot say. But it is worth noting that the first man to enter Ireland with a commission from Rome was a bishop, not a general, and received his commission from a pope, not from an emperor.

A successor to Palladius must be found, and there was no difficulty in finding one. In the church at Auxerre there was another cleric whose interest in Ireland was much more personal than ever Palladius's could have been. He had already received the inward call to evangelize the Irish, and was indeed on the point of setting out on this business (if he had not in fact already started) when the news of Palladius's death arrived. Now, instead of pursuing his missionary work under the direction of Palladius, he was sent to Ireland as Palladius's successor in the episcopal office. Palladius's interest had been in the Christian communities of Ireland, and his aim was to strengthen the things that remained among them; his successor was enflamed with the ideal of winning the great mass of Irish heathendom for Christianity. His very name declares the measure of his success—the greatest name in Irish history: St. Patrick, the apostle of Ireland.

Patrick was a native of the Roman province of Britain, and as a freeborn provincial he was a Roman citizen. His father Cal-

[1] Bede, *Hist. Eccl.*, I, 13, perhaps following the fifth-century chronicler Prosper of Aquitaine.

purnius and grandfather Potitus were both clerics; their names indicate how thoroughly Romanized the family was, as does his mother's name, Concessa. So also does Patrick's own name (Latin *Patricius*),[1] although he was also known by a British name Succat. His father belonged to the class of citizens who were liable to serve as decurions, members of the municipal council of a Roman town. How he combined his municipal responsibility with his clerical status need not concern us here. Exactly in what part of Britain Patrick's home lay cannot be determined; he himself tells us in the short work entitled his *Confession* that his father's estate was near a place called Bannavem Taberniae, but this place-name is almost certainly a textual corruption and cannot be identified. All we know is that it was near the west coast of Britain. Various locations have been suggested, from the Bristol Channel to the Firth of Clyde; indeed, one more recent writer of independent mind has confidently identified the place with Banavie in Lochaber —but this involves him in the awkward corollary that the frontier of the Roman province ran along the line of the Caledonian Canal![2] Any site farther north than the Solway is unlikely.

Wherever Patrick's home should be located, the district was invaded one day in the early years of the fifth century by a band of Irish raiders, who seized a great number of the inhabitants and carried them across the Irish Sea to be sold as slaves. Among these was the sixteen-year-old Patrick. He was bought by a landowner of Slemish, near Ballymena in County Antrim, and served him for six years as a swineherd. During the hardships of those years, Patrick had ample time for reflection. Although he belonged to a Christian family, he tells us himself that at the time of his captivity he did not know the true God. But during those years, he goes on, "the Lord opened the understanding of my unbelief, that, late as it was, I might remember my faults and turn to the Lord my God with all my heart; and He had regard to my low estate, and pitied my youth and ignorance, and kept guard over me even before I knew Him, and before I attained wisdom to distinguish good from evil; and He strengthened and comforted me as a father does his son."

From that time Patrick's life was marked by intense and persistent prayer, and from time to time he was conscious of an inner monition in which he recognized the divine response to his prayers. It was a monition of this kind at the end of his six years of servitude which incited him to escape from his master and make his way to the sea-coast, to a port where he would find a ship to take him away from Ireland. Sure enough he found the ship of which the inner voice had forewarned him, and the skipper, after

[1] This was also the name of the father of Augustine of Hippo.
[2] P. J. O'Regan, *St. Patrick's Boyhood Home* (Oban, 1948).

first refusing him, consented to take him on board. The ship was carrying a cargo of Irish wolfhounds to the Continent; it may be that Patrick had a way with dogs and so appeared to be a useful person to have with them. The traders landed at some port on the west coast of France, and after spending two months with them travelling through France and Italy, through territory lately devasted by the Vandals and other invaders, Patrick was able to leave them and resume a free life.

A free life, we mean, in that he was no longer subject to the beck and call of fellow-men; but it is plain that he henceforth regarded himself as the bondservant of God. We find him next in the island of St. Honorat, one of the two Lérins islands, off the French Riviera coast. Here was a famous monastery, associated with many illustrious Christian names. Patrick intended to return to his British home ultimately, but he was in no great hurry, for his nearest relatives were no longer alive—killed or captured, very likely, in the Irish raid to which he owed his own captivity. For the present, he spent some years at St. Honorat, where he embraced the monastic life.

After these years at St. Honorat, he returned at last to Britain, and there found some of his relatives who took him to their home as if he were their own son, and besought him never to leave them. But a higher obedience was required of Patrick: "in the depth of the night," he says, "I saw a man named Victoricus, coming as if from Ireland, with innumerable letters; and he gave me one of these, and I read the beginning of the letter, which ran: *The Voice of the Irish*. And while I was reading out the beginning of the letter, I thought that at that very moment I heard the voice of those who were beside the wood of Focluth,[1] near the western sea; and this is what they called out: 'Please, holy boy, come and walk among us again.' Their cry pierced to my very heart, and I could read no more; and so I awoke."

This was Patrick's Macedonian cry; to him "Come over and help us" meant "Come back to Erin." The call was confirmed by further experiences of a similar kind. But a further term of years must pass before he could respond to it. In order, probably, to prepare himself for what he now knew to be his true vocation, he went to the church of Auxerre to study the Christian faith. One reason for his going to Auxerre rather than anywhere else may have been that some special interest was taken there in Irish Christianity. Before

---

[1] There is a difficulty here; the wood of Focluth or Fochlad is in County Mayo, and why should Patrick's old companions call to him from there? J. B. Bury concluded that this district, and not Slemish, must have been the place of Patrick's six years' servitude (*Life of St. Patrick* [1905], pp. 27ff.). E. MacNeill supposed that Focluth was a textual corruption in Patrick's *Confession*, and that the true reading was "the wood of Uluti," which he located near Lough Neagh (*Proceedings of the Royal Irish Academy*, XXXVI [1921-24], pp. 249ff.). But strange things happen in dreams.

long, Patrick was ordained deacon by Amator, bishop of Auxerre, the predecessor of Germanus. But there is ground for believing that his aspirations to carry the Gospel to the Irish were not encouraged by his superiors. A certain lack of polish, which he himself acknowledges, may have been one among a number of reasons why they thought him unsuitable for the task. At any rate, when a bishop was chosen to go to Ireland in 431, it was not Patrick who was sent, but Palladius. But when Palladius died shortly after his arrival in Ireland, Patrick was consecrated bishop in his place, and was at last able to fulfil his heart's desire. He was now over forty years old; some twenty years had passed since he made his escape from Ireland. Those who were beside the wood of Focluth had waited long for the holy boy to come and walk with them again, but now he was on his way. "Thanks be to God," said Patrick, "that after so many years the Lord granted them according to their cry."

Ireland in the fifth century A.D. was divided into a large number of small tribal areas, each of which was ruled by a king. But some of these kings were able to maintain a degree of overlordship over their neighbouring kings, and these overlords may be regarded as provincial kings, each one of whom ruled over one of the "five fifths of Ireland"—Munster, Connaught, Leinster (south of the Liffey), Meath (between the Liffey and the Boyne), and Ulster. There was one overlord for each of the first four, while there were three independent kings in Ulster, which was not unified at this time.

These provincial kings themselves in turn had an overlord, the ruler of Meath, who reigned at Tara, and held the title of "high king" of Ireland. One famous high king was known as Niall of the Nine Hostages; he is reputed to have led raiding expeditions far afield, and to have met his death in the English Channel on his way home from one of these, in 405. (Dr. Gogarty suggests that it was when this very expedition was returning to Ireland that the raid was made on the west coast of Britain in which Patrick was taken captive.[1] That is as it may be; certainly the date is near enough.) To Niall a number of dynastic families in Ireland traced back their lineage; one of these—the Ui Neill or the O'Neills of north-west Ulster—we shall meet later.

When Patrick arrived in Ireland, the high king was Laoghaire (pronounced Leary), a son of Niall, who had acceded to power in Tara in 428, and reigned for thirty-six years. It is recorded that Irish law was codified in his reign; this codification may have been influenced or even suggested by the publication in 438 of the Code of Theodosius II, in which the imperial edicts were gathered together by the leading Roman lawyers. Laoghaire had to decide

[1] O, St. J. Gogarty, *I follow St. Patrick* (1938), pp. 63ff.; cf. Meissner, *op. cit.*, p. 78.

what attitude he should adopt towards the missionary activity of
Patrick and his companions, and settled on a policy of toleration.
But he did not wholeheartedly accept the new faith himself; he
preferred to be buried standing up like his ancestors, he said,
with his face towards the men of Leinster, the traditional foes of
the house of Tara.

In deciding on a policy of toleration, Laoghaire must have gone
counter to the advice of the druids, the custodians of the pagan
lore of Ireland as of other Celtic lands. It may be, indeed, that at
the outset, he was inclined to listen to them and oppose the missionaries; but wiser considerations prevailed with him. The
druids knew that the days of their influence were numbered if
Christianity were allowed free course in Ireland. An old Irish
chant, predicting the coming of Patrick, is attributed to them:

> Adze-head will come
> Over a furious sea;
> His mantle head-holed,
> His staff crook-headed,
> His table in the east of his house;
> All his household shall answer,
> "Amen, amen!"

Ireland, though politically separate from the empire, was not
hermetically sealed off from Britain and the continent, and the
appearance of Christian clerics and the procedure of Christian
worship could easily have been known to the druids; besides,
there were Christians in Ireland itself. But the coming of a
Christian bishop, which they regarded as inevitable, spelt for
them the beginning of the end. The nickname Adze-head probably refers to Patrick's tonsure.

The political power of Rome might be receding, but the very
name of Rome carried tremendous prestige for a very long time,
and Christianity was the Roman religion. Patrick himself was a
Roman citizen, and even if he was not personally consecrated by
the bishop of Rome, as Palladius had been, yet he represented a
church in which the bishop of Rome enjoyed acknowledged
primacy. From the political point of view, in fact, his mission may
be compared to those of Ulfilas among the Goths and Ninian
among the Picts. It is an additional point of comparison with
Patrick that Ulfilas belonged to a family within the Roman Empire
which had been carried into captivity among the people whom he
was later to evangelize.

Though the direct power of the druids dwindled rapidly with
the coming of Patrick, yet in an indirect way it continued to
manifest itself, as may be seen from the later traditions of Patrick's
own activity. In some of these he achieves his success, not by the
power of the Christian message, but by proving himself to be a

mightier druid than the pagan druids of Ireland, and beating them at their own magic games. And it seems plain that a distinctive magic element which characterizes much Celtic Christianity is a survival of pagan druidism. There is a suggestion of it even in the ancient hymn called *St. Patrick's Breastplate*, which—whether composed by Patrick himself or not—is in any case "an interesting document for the spirit of early Christianity in Ireland."[1] One might almost suppose that the Triune Name is here invoked as a supernally potent charm, by which evils of every imaginable sort may be repelled, including "spells of women and smiths and druids" and "all knowledge that should not be known." All the same, it is a magnificent composition. Most people know it best in the abridged English version by Cecil Frances Alexander, which begins:

> I bind unto myself to-day
> The strong Name of the Trinity.

Although Patrick is credited with evangelizing the greater part of Ireland, the chronology of his apostolate is not at all certain. With a company of Gaulish and British assistants, and such ecclesiastical equipment as was reckoned necessary in those days (including doubtless a supply of sacred relics), Patrick landed on the east coast of Ireland and tried first to establish contact with those Christian communities which Palladius had strengthened or founded the previous year. Having thus established some continuity with the work of his predecessor, he sailed north to the coast of Ulster, and put ashore near the entrance to Strangford Lough. He received a welcome from the local magnate, Dichu, whose fortress was at Downpatrick: it has been suggested[2] that Dichu's wife was a daughter of Patrick's former master, and one of the people whose voices he had heard in his dream calling him back to Ireland. However that may be, Dichu listened to Patrick, believed his message and accepted baptism at his hands, and gave him a barn near his fortress to serve as a church building. The later name of this place, Saul, represents *sabhall*, the Irish word for "barn."

But Patrick was eager to visit another place in Ulster—the homestead of Miliucc, his former master at Slemish. He hoped to win him too for Christianity. But Miliucc would have none of Patrick nor yet of Patrick's religion. When he heard of his former slave's approach, fearing probably lest he might be forced to change his religion under the influence of a fearfully powerful spell, he gathered all his property into his wooden house, set fire to it and perished himself on this domestic pyre.

The counties of Antrim and Down were divided at this time

[1] Bury, *op. cit.*, p. 246.
[2] By Bishop M. Fogarty, cited by Gogarty, *op. cit.*, pp. 102, 152, 156.

into two racially distinct parts. The territory of County Down and south Antrim was called Dalaradia, and was populated by people known in Ireland as the *Cruithnich*, immigrants from the the British side of the North Channel. In the course of the fifth and sixth centuries some parts of Dalaradia came under the influence of the monastery founded by Ninian at Whithorn in Galloway, but it is not certain if there was such an influence so early as the time of Patrick. The idea that Ninian himself visited Northern Ireland is largely based on a confusion of his name with that of another missionary, Moinenn. There probably were some Christian communities in Dalaradia before Patrick's arrival, but any earlier evangelization in those parts was overshadowed by Patrick's achievement. Saul, where he instituted his first church in Ulster, was near the south of Dalaradia; and Slemish was near its northern limit. To the north of Dalaradia, in north Antrim, was the territory of Dalriada, populated by Scots. It was from this region that Scots first went by sea to colonize the land to which they later gave their name; the part of Scotland which received their earliest settlements, Argyll, shared the name Dalriada with the part of Ireland from which they set out.

Patrick based his missionary campaigns on the existing social and political structure of Ireland. Wherever he went, he tried to win the local ruler for Christianity. And it was specially important for the establishment of his enterprise to secure the good will of Laoghaire, king of Tara and high king of Ireland. This, as we have seen, he was able to do, and although Laoghaire himself did not become a convinced Christian (even if he rendered a feigned obedience to the new faith), some members of Laoghaire's family were more forthcoming. One of his sons had married the daughter of a British prince, who was probably a Christian. Lomman, a British assistant of Patrick, made contact with this royal pair through their young son. Son and father became Christians, as well as the mother, and the son, Fortchernn, was given to Lomman to be brought up as his foster-son and pupil. The father, Fedilmid, presented his estate at Trim, on the Boyne, "to God and Patrick and Lomman and Fortchernn;" it is one of the oldest Christian foundations in Ireland.

A brother of Laoghaire, Conall by name, lived in another part of Meath, at Telltown, near the Blackwater, and when Patrick visited his domain he accepted Christianity more readily than his brother had done. Like his nephew, he too presented Patrick with ground for a church building, and on it the apostle erected one of unusual size, sixty feet in length, called the Great Church of Patrick. The name survives still in the form Donaghpatrick.

Once a Christian community had been strongly established in Meath, Patrick traversed the breadth of Ireland from east to west, in order to visit Connaught and pursue his missionary work there. It was on his way thither that he is said to have overthrown the great stone idol of Crom Cruaich in the plain of Slecht, near Ballymagauran in County Cavan. Farther west, at Croghan (in County Roscommon), the seat of the king of Connaught, Patrick and his attendants met and baptized two maiden daughters of King Laoghaire, who were being brought up there. (The dynasty of Tara was related to the royal house of Connaught.) The girls plied Patrick with eager questions about the new faith, and Patrick consented to baptize them when they had given satisfactory answers to the questions which he in turn put to them:

Do you believe that by baptism you cast away the sin of your father and mother?
Do you believe in repentance after sin?
Do you believe in life after death?
Do you believe in the resurrection on the day of judgment?
Do you believe in the unity of the church?

To all these they returned answer "We believe," and were baptized and received the Eucharist—"and fell asleep in death," says our record. It does not explain how they died so apparently immediately; perhaps their death was not so sudden after all. If they did die simultaneously while still in their girlhood, it may have happened to them as it did to Bessie Bell and Mary Gray in the ballad——

> The pest came from the burgh town
> And slew them both together——

but the motif of two maidens dying together voluntarily in the hour of their accepting Christianity is not unparalleled in Christian legend.[1]

Patrick spent seven years evangelizing Connaught, concentrating particularly on County Mayo. There lay the wood of Focluth or Fochlad, which he had seen in his vision many years before; there too is the Hill of the Eagle, now called Croaghpatrick, where he spent the forty days of Lent one year and to which a number of remarkable legends of the saint have attached themselves.

Whether Patrick ever paid a visit to Rome, as some of our sources say he did, is a much debated point. But if he did, Bury has shown reason to believe that it must have been at the end of his evangelization of Connaught, about 441, in the second year of Pope Leo the Great. He suggests that Patrick may have wished to to consult the Roman bishop about the choice of a metropolitan see for the Irish Church.[2]

[1] J. B. Bury, op. cit., pp. 141, 307; cf. Meissner, op. cit., p. 147.
[2] Bury, op. cit., pp. 150ff., 367ff.

At any rate, the year 443 finds Patrick in Ulster once more, and the following year marks the founding of the church and monastery at Armagh. He won the respect of Daire, the local king, who allotted him a piece of land for his purpose. And there is every ground for holding that it was Patrick's own intention from the first that Armagh should be his own episcopal seat and the metropolis of Irish Christianity. Prestige was added to the new foundation, it is said, by the depositing there of relics of Peter and Paul, which Patrick presumably brought back from his recent visit to Rome.

The ecclesiastical organization on the continent and in the British province was based on the chief cities of the empire. Each city had its bishop, and these were grouped in provinces under their metropolitan. The social order in Ireland made this form of organization impossible there. Patrick therefore based his episcopal organization on the tribal divisions of the country, and, in the absence of cities, monasteries—villages of small beehive cells grouped round a larger one which served as the church—did duty as episcopal sees. But each monastery was governed by an abbot, who was in practice a much more important person than the bishop who had his see there. Patrick's earliest bishops and other clergy were mostly Gaulish and British coadjutors who came to Ireland with him; one at least was an Irishman by birth, Iserninus, a fellow-student of Patrick at Auxerre and founder of the church at Aghade on the Slaney.

Patrick himself never attained as much proficiency in Latin as he would have liked. His Latin writings show how much truth there is in his own confession of "rusticity" in style, and there were other ecclesiastics who were sufficiently boorish to rub it in. But Patrick had no thought of making any other language than Latin the canonical language of the Church of Ireland, as it was of the rest of western Christendom. This unity of ecclesiastical language gave a cultural unity to the whole of western Europe which could not be matched in the east because of the linguistic diversity of the Orthodox Church.

Patrick's best known Latin work, his *Confession*, was written fairly late in his life, partly to reply to certain attacks that had been made on him (especially by some British clerics), but mainly to rehearse the wonderful dealings of God with him. It is valuable not only for the first-hand autobiographical information which it supplies, but also because of the strong impression it makes of the simple honesty and humility of its author, "an Israelite indeed, in whom is no guile." He will not boast of himself, or of anything that he has done; but he gladly makes his boast in God who has chosen such an unworthy instrument for the conversion of Ireland and has wrought such wonders through him. "Of miracles, in the sense of violations of natural laws, the *Confession* says nothing; but his own strange life seemed to Patrick more marvellous than any miracle in that special meaning of the word."[1] And thus he concludes his testimony:

> But I pray those who believe and fear God, whosoever has deigned to scan or accept this document, composed in Ireland by Patrick the sinner, an unlearned man to be sure, that none should ever say that it was my ignorance that accomplished any small thing which I did or showed in accordance with God's will; but judge ye, and let it be most truly believed, that it was the gift of God. And this is my confession before I die.

Another extant Latin work begins in similar terms, "Patrick, a sinner and unlearned, to be sure, appointed bishop in Ireland"; but it shows that where indignant remonstrance was required, Patrick was perfectly equal to the occasion. This is his *Letter to the Subjects of Coroticus*. Coroticus, from his fort at Dumbarton, ruled the British kingdom of Strathclyde during the greater part of Patrick's episcopate. The incident which called forth the letter was a raid which some soldiers of Coroticus made on the coast of Ulster, similar to the raid in the opposite direction in which Patrick was enslaved forty or fifty years before. Among those who were massacred or taken captive by the British raiders on this occasion were a number of Christians who had just been baptized and confirmed and still wore their white neophytes' robes. Hearing of the outrage, Patrick sent a presbyter to the raiders before they embarked, entreating them to release the captives and return the loot; but they received his request with insults. The outrage was all the greater because the raiders were themselves Christians in name, Patrick's own fellow-countrymen, Roman citizens like himself—but "I do not call them my fellow-citizens or fellow-citizens of the holy Romans," he says, "but fellow-citizens of demons, because of their evil deeds." Perhaps it was not the British soldiers themselves who laid sacrilegious hands on the newly baptized converts, but some of their companions, "Scots and apostate Picts;" but the Britons shared the responsibility for it by doing nothing to prevent it, and Coroticus himself shared the responsibility until he made proper amends.

The Scots mentioned by Patrick in this connexion were probably some who had already crossed the North Channel to settle in the west of Scotland; they seem to have been still pagans. The Picts, however, are described as apostates. The reference will be to some of the southern Picts evangelized by Ninian a few decades previously, who had subsequently relapsed into paganism. So at least Patrick implies; of course he was somewhat biased against them, and no wonder. But the fact that the British soldiers were

[1] Bury, *op. cit.*, p. 197.

in name, though not in behaviour, Roman citizens, is specially interesting; it supports the suggestion already made, that for some decades after the legions withdrew from Britain, far from Roman civilization in the province collapsing at once, it advanced a considerable way beyond the provincial frontier.

We do not know what effect Patrick's protest had. The tone of his letter suggests that he did not really expect Coroticus to release the captives and that he thought there was little likelihood that the British Christians would do their bounden duty and excommunicate Coroticus if he proved obdurate, though he enjoins this course upon them.

While Ulster, Meath and Connaught were the chief fields of Patrick's apostolic activity, there is adequate evidence in ancient records that he visited Munster and Leinster as well. The episcopal jurisdiction which he received on the eve of his departure for Ireland extended over the whole island. But after he selected Armagh as his own see, and organized Ireland as a province of the western Church, he seems to have spent most of his remaining days in the north. About 457 he resigned his position at Armagh, and was succeeded there as bishop by his disciple Benignus. He himself retired to Saul, where he had established his first centre in Ulster twenty-five years before, and there he died on March 17, 461. The anniversary of his death—St. Patrick's Day—remains, of course, the outstanding day in the national calendar of Ireland. His burial-place, Downpatrick, retains his name to this day.

We have already mentioned some of the features of Patrick's singularly attractive personality. Another trait which impressed his contemporaries was his steadfastness. This is illustrated by the story of his dealings with Daire, the prince from whom he obtained the land on which he built his monastery at Armagh. At first Daire would not give Patrick the hill for which he asked, but offered him a site on the level land below. About the same time he sent a servant to Patrick with a bronze cauldron as a gift. Patrick accepted it gravely with the Latin words *Gratias agamus*—"Let us give thanks" (i.e. to God). "What did he say?" asked Daire when his servant came back. "He said *Gratzacham*,"[1] said the servant. Daire, who had expected some more demonstrative expression of gratitude from Patrick, was annoyed and sent the servant to take the cauldron back. Patrick returned it with the same words, *Gratias agamus*. "What did he say this time?" asked Daire. "He said *Gratzacham* again," said the servant. "*Gratzacham* when he received it," said the prince, "and *Gratzacham* when it was taken from him? It is a good word, this *Gratzacham*." And he himself took the cauldron back to Patrick. "Here is your cauldron," he said. "You are a steadfast and unchangeable man." And he gave

[1] This spelling may convey a hint of Patrick's guttural pronunciation.

him in addition the hill that he had previously asked for, the hill of Armagh, on which he built his cathedral.

There are not many figures in history who have impressed their personalities upon a nation so completely as Patrick impressed his on the people of Ireland. Later legend was influenced by the apparent parallel between Patrick and Moses in this regard, and attempted to emphasize the parallel in various ways—by representing Patrick's age at death as a hundred and twenty, by telling how an angel spoke to him from a burning bush, by ascribing to him a forty days' mountain-top vigil, by recording how he beat the magicians in a wonder-working match, and so forth. But Patrick's real greatness is impressive enough without such aids as these. It was he who brought within the orbit of imperial civilization and—better still—of Christian faith a land which had never belonged to the empire politically. And he did so to such good purpose that when darkness fell over a great part of western Europe, as it began to do even before his death, the true light continued to burn brightly in the island of saints and scholars and was carried forth from there to rekindle the lamps that had been extinguished.[1]

[1] See, in addition to literature already mentioned, N. J. D. White, *St. Patrick: His Writings and Life* (1920); E. MacNeill, *St. Patrick: Apostle of Ireland* (1934); L. Bieler (trans.), *The Works of St. Patrick* (1953). Especially since T. F. O'Rahilly's paper *The Two Patricks* (1942), it has been widely, though not unanimously, supposed that the credit of evangelizing Ireland must be shared by at least two men named Patrick, the elder of whom may be identical with Palladius (who in that case lived some thirty years longer than the account on p. 372 allows). See L. Bieler, *The Life and Legend of St. Patrick* (1948) and *St. Patrick and the Coming of Christianity* (1967); J. Carney, *The Problem of St. Patrick* (1961); R. P. C. Hanson, *Saint Patrick: his Origins and Career* (1968).

CHAPTER XXXIX

THE IONA COMMUNITY

OUR AUTHORITIES FOR THE HISTORY OF IRISH CHRISTIANITY during the century that followed Patrick's death are much more sketchy than our authorities for Patrick's life and ministry. It appears that for some time after his death the Church of Ireland continued to be staffed largely by clerics of British or Gaulish origin, so far at any rate as most of the higher offices are concerned. But other influences gradually made themselves felt, and the picture of Irish Christianity by the middle of the sixth century is markedly different from that which we find in Patrick's lifetime.

Some of these differences were not important in themselves, but acquired importance in later years for reasons which will appear in due course. One of these was the style of tonsure.

The tonsure which Patrick wore when he went to Ireland—and which won him the epithet "adze-head" in the druidical prophecy —was the circular tonsure on the crown of the head, common to western Christendom. But the pagan Irish knew another form of tonsure, which was a badge of servitude among them—the shaving of the front of the head from ear to ear. Although Patrick instituted the coronal tonsure among his Irish clergy, it was not long before the old native frontal tonsure was adapted to Christian use and ousted the European coronal tonsure. Authority for this change was carried back into the story of Patrick's life, and a saying was attributed to him, complete with all the circumstantial trappings of a story from real life. to the effect that the frontal tonsure was as valid as the coronal. In consequence, the frontal tonsure came to be regarded as characteristic of Celtic Christianity, and there was some difficulty in the restoration of uniformity when Celtic and European Christianity came into contact again. The Old Irish term describing someone who has the frontal tonsure was *mael* (appearing in modern Gaelic as *maol*); this word appears as an element in several Celtic personal names, indicating that the bearer is the servant of some saint or other. The name Malcolm, for example, is Old Irish *Mael-Coluim*, i.e. "the (frontally tonsured) servant of Columba."

But the really important change which came over the Irish Church after Patrick's death was its reorganization on a thorough-going monastic basis. Patrick's organization, as we have seen, was one of territorial episcopacy, as nearly as possible on the lines which he had known in western Europe. But the absence of cities in Ireland to serve as bishops' sees had led to the use of monasteries for this purpose. This monastic element in Patrick's organization, however, is insufficient to account for the swamping of Irish territorial episcopacy by the monastic system which we find from the following century onwards. From the sixth century the chief figure in the Celtic Church is the abbot, not the bishop. These rulers of monasteries commonly belonged to the same family as the local tribal rulers; it was a regular practice for one or more boys of these princely houses to be sent to the monasteries, there to be brought up as monks and ultimately to take their place as abbots. So completely did the bishop's office become over-shadowed by the abbot's in the eyes of Irish Christians that they could even refer to the Pope as the *abbot* of Rome.[1]

This growth of monastic influence in the life and very structure of the Irish Church cannot be set down simply to the development of certain elements in Patrick's settlement. It must be linked up with influences from outside the island, and from no place more than Ninian's monastery at Whithorn in Galloway. It is not certain that Whithorn had begun to send representatives to Ireland before Patrick's arrival, though it is not at all improbable when we consider how close Galloway is to north-east Ulster, and how abundant was the intercommunication between south-west Scotland and the opposite shores of Ireland. By Patrick's time there were not only Britons on both sides of the North Channel but Scots as well, and the channel united the two territories much more than it separated them.

The influence of Whithorn is shown also by the large number of Irish saints who went there for their training during the century after Patrick's death. It is curious that Patrick's own foundations are largely lost to sight; certainly the outstanding saints of the period after Patrick did not go to them for their education. "There seems good reason for believing that a wave of British influence from Candida Casa, and the region between the Walls, swept over Ireland, and that the Romano-British and Gaulish clergy [installed by Patrick] were replaced by those from the Celtic-speaking, recently Christianized districts."[2]

The latest and most notable of the Irish scholars who went to Whithorn for his education bore the name of Finbarr or Finnian. He seems to have been sent down from college by the authorities at Whithorn because of a trick he played on Princess Drustice, daughter of a Pictish king, who was at the same time a student in

---

[1] See *Tripartite Life of Patrick*, ed. W. Stokes (*Rolls edition*, 1887), I, pp. 30f.
[2] Meissner, *op. cit.*, p. 134.

the ladies' section of the monastery. But he went on from Whithorn to Rome, and after spending seven years there and being
ordained presbyter, he came back to Ireland and established a
great monastic school at Moville, near Newtownards in County
Down.

The chief subject of instruction in Finnian's school, as in the
other schools of Ireland, was the Latin Bible. All the pupils were
expected as a matter of course to learn the Latin Psalter by heart.
But classical literature was also studied, not only Latin but also
(in some small measure at least) Greek. It was due to the Irish
schools that much classical learning was preserved from destruction during the darkness that spread over western Europe between
the sixth and eighth centuries. And as the reputation of the Irish
schools spread farther afield, pupils made their way to them from
other lands—not only from England (after the Anglian conquest)
but from various parts of the continent as well.

Finnian, however, brought back with him from Rome something that had not been seen in Ireland before—a copy of the
Latin Gospels in Jerome's version.[1] This was possibly the book
which gave rise to a famous lawsuit—or it may have been a Latin
Psalter, another of Finnian's literary treasures. Whichever it was,
one of Finnian's most illustrious pupils, paying a visit to the
school in later years, obtained his former master's permission to
examine it. Then, in his eagerness to have a copy for himself, he
began to transcribe it—without obtaining permission to do so,
for (as he later said) he knew quite well that he would not get it if
he asked it. All went well until the transcription was practically
complete, when Finnian caught him in the act. Finnian tried to
confiscate the copy; the former pupil refused to give it up. But the
former pupil was a very distinguished one, and belonged to a very
important family, and Finnian could not simply exercise his
authority as head of the school. The dispute was taken to arbitra-
tion, and the arbiter was Diarmaid, the high king of Ireland, no
less. He heard both sides, and pronounced his verdict. "To every
cow belongs her calf," he said; "to every book, its copy. The copy
belongs to Finnian." The former pupil was annoyed. He had to
return the copy, but he did so under protest. "It is an unjust
decision," he said, "and will bring trouble in its train."

The former pupil was Columba, a member of the royal dynasty
of the northern Ui Neill. He was born at Gartan, in County Donegal, in 521, and gave early promise of quite exceptional gifts. On
his father's side he was descended from Niall of the Nine Hostages,
high king of Ireland at the beginning of the fifth century; on his
mother's side he was related to the royal family of Leinster. He

[1] According to another account he copied it from an exemplar at Whithorn,
brought from Rome by Ninian.

was also closely akin to the sons of Erc who, about the year 500, founded in the west of Scotland an extension of the kingdom of Dalriada in Ulster. This Scottish Dalriada was to prove of special importance, for in course of time it became independent of the Irish Dalriada and its ruling house gradually extended its power until it ruled all Scotland. At this time, however, the two territories constituted the one kingdom of Dalriada.

We have already seen that it was a custom for the princely houses of Ireland to send one or more of their boys to be brought up as monks, and this promising boy, instead of being earmarked for a political or military career (for either of which he would have been quite capable) was sent to study under Finnian at Moville. From Moville, after he had been ordained deacon, he went to Clonard in Meath, to continue his studies under another Finnian, a former pupil of St. David of Wales, and famed as the "teacher of the saints of Ireland." During his time at Clonard he was ordained presbyter. He visited other schools in Ireland, and returned to the north at the age of twenty-five, to found the monastery of Derry. Six or seven years later he founded the monastery of Durrow, in the north of Offaly; and many other foundations in Ireland are ascribed to him, including Kells (Ceannanus Mór) in Meath, which became the chief centre of the Columban order when Iona was devastated by the Norsemen early in the ninth century.

But it is Iona, which we have just mentioned, that is most intimately associated with Columba's name. He took up his residence there in 563, and spent practically all the remaining thirty-four years of his life there.

Columba's departure for Iona is connected with a battle fought in 561 at a place called Culdreimhe, north of Sligo. It was thought by some of his contemporaries that Columba was responsible for this battle—that he had brought it about because of his grievances against the high king Diarmaid, among which the decision about the transcription of Finnian's book may not have been the most important. So serious a view did some Irish clerics take of Columba's part in the quarrel that he was excommunicated at a synod held in Telltown, and although the sentence of excommunication was reversed almost at once, Columba decided to leave Ireland. Some accounts represent him as vowing that he would not return to Ireland until he had won as many pagans for Christ as had fallen in the battle—three thousand all told. However that may be, he set sail for the west of Scotland with a few comrades, and continued to sail until he reached a spot from which Ireland could no longer be seen. Here he landed, and here he founded what was to prove his most famous monastery.

The island on which he settled was called I (pronounced *ee* as in *see*)—the name which it still bears in Gaelic. Columba's biographer Adamnan, in the following century, coined an adjective from this name, *Ioua*, and this was later misread as *Iona*. The error persisted all the more readily because of its resemblance to the Hebrew word *yona*, meaning "dove," which is the meaning in Latin of the name Columba itself.

As this tiny island lay off the coast of the Scottish Dalriada, where Columba's kinsmen were rulers, there was little difficulty in having it granted to him for a monastic foundation; probably the grant had to be confirmed by the Pictish high king, whose vassals the rulers of Dalriada were at this time for their territory in Scotland. And the light that was lit in Iona sent its beams to the farthest corners of Scotland, and farther afield still.

The events of those years mark a change in Columba's inner life as well as in his active career. Some portrayals of Columba which have come down to us represent him as passionate, imperious, unscrupulous and vindictive, the worst type of ecclesiastical statesman. No doubt he could be passionate and imperious; he was of royal blood, and Irish royal blood at that; and we must judge him according to the standard of his own times. But on the other hand a strong impression of reality is conveyed by Adamnan's picture of him as a most lovable personality, full of the purest religious devotion. This impression is confirmed by some of the poems traditionally ascribed to him, which breathe besides a lofty patriotism and a deep love of nature.

These two diverse portrayals of his character may readily be reconciled if we conclude that he underwent a profound spiritual change as a result of the battle of Culdreimhne. The sense of his responsibility for the slaughter there wrought in him intense conviction of sin, and we have ample evidence of the merciless severity with which he ever afterwards subjected himself to penitential discipline.

Even before Columba's mission we have traces of Irish Christian activity in central Scotland. There is a story of an Irish saint, Buitte, passing through Forfarshire on his return to Ireland from the continent in the reign of the south Pictish king Nechtan I (*c.* 457–481); and another story points to early influence exercised in Scotland by Bridget (*c.* 450–524), founder of the monastery at Kildare in Ireland.[1] Bridget's name is widely commemorated in Scotland. A monastery was founded in her honour at Abernethy by a Pictish king about 600. In south and central Scotland and in the Hebrides there are several places called Kilbride (the "cell" of Bridget) or Kirkbride, while other place-names to her memory are found in the counties of Aberdeen, Banff, Moray and Ross.

[1] See A. O. Anderson, *Early Sources of Scottish History*, I (1922), pp. cxx f.; H. M. Chadwick, *Early Scotland* (1949), pp. 9ff.

Three years before Columba's arrival in Iona, the royal house of Dalriada, which had been encroaching steadily on Pictish territory in central Scotland, was decisively defeated by Brude, high king of Pictland. The Scots had to retreat to their Dalriadic territory in Argyllshire, and even there they probably had to acknowledge the overlordship of Brude. This Brude seems to have done more towards the political unification of Scotland than any previous ruler in those parts had done; even the people of Orkney acknowledged him as overlord.

According to certain historians, Columba—politician first and ecclesiastic next—burned to avenge the defeat of his Dalriadic kinsmen on the Pictish king.[1] It is much more likely that, being a wise man, he tried to reconcile the two peoples. To do this effectively, it was necessary to evangelize the northern Picts. And he set about this enterprise in the true tradition of Irish missionary policy by attempting to win over the high king.

There was a further reason for Columba's visiting Brude. He had received Iona from Conall, the Dalriadic king, for the foundation of his monastery; but as Brude claimed to be Conall's overlord, it would be as well to have Conall's gift ratified by him. This is confirmed by Bede's account, according to which it was in consequence of the conversion of the Picts that Columba received Iona.[2]

Brude's headquarters were in the neighbourhood of Inverness, and thither Columba made his way about two years after his landing in Iona. The greater part of the journey could be accomplished by water, through the lochs of the Great Glen, which are now joined by the Caledonian Canal. But Brude was not anxious to see him. For one thing, he was too closely related to Brude's recently vanquished enemies in Dalriada; for another, Brude's druidical attendants were as apprehensive of Columba's coming as Laoghaire's druids had been of Patrick's. Columba and his companions, however, would not be turned away, and in the event he succeeded in establishing cordial relations with the Pictish king and, as Bede says, "turned that nation to faith in Christ by word and by example."[3]

The two companions whom Columba took with him when he went to visit Brude were two Cruithnich, Comgall and Cainnech, whose language was probably closer to Brude's than Columba's was. Both these men had distinguished careers of their own. Cainnech (517–600) not only engaged in evangelistic work in the western isles and mainland of Scotland but founded two monasteries in Ireland—Aghaboe in Leix, and Kilkenny. Comgall in

[1] Cf. W. D. Simpson, *The Historical Saint Columba* (1927), p. 21.
[2] Bede, *Hist. Eccl.*, III, 4.
[3] *Ibid.*

555 founded the great monastery of Bangor in County Down from which in 590 Columbanus set out upon his missionary career in Europe, in the course of which he founded famous monastries at Luxeuil in France, St. Gall in Switzerland, and Bobbio in Italy. Another Irish contemporary of Columba who had a share in the evangelization of western Scotland was the famous St. Brendan, of Clonfert, whose seven years' voyage in search of the Fortunate Islands has passed into legend. But when the story of Brendan is stripped of legendary accretions, there remains good reason for believing that he visited Iceland (where we know on independent grounds that Irish monks did settle before the Norse colonization) and that he even possibly reached some part of the American continent.[1]

Columba and his Iona community were thus by no means the only evangelists at work in Scotland in the sixth century, though they were by far the most influential. And their activity extended right to the north-east of Scotland. Several place-names on Deeside still commemorate the activity of members of Columba's own kindred. One of these, Ternan, has given his name to the parish of Banchory Ternan on North Deeside, while the name of the family of the Ui Neill itself is preserved in the neighbouring parish of Kincardine O'Neil. And if we may believe the tradition preserved in the Aberdeen Breviary (published in 1509–10), Drostan, founder of the monastery of Deer in Buchan, was "sprung from the royal ancestry of the Scots," and would therefore be another relative of Columba. It is perhaps unlikely that Columba himself visited the north-east of Scotland, although one source describes him as accompanying his alumnus Drostan on the occasion of the founding of the monastery of Deer. This source is a note in the Book of Deer, an incomplete ninth-century copy of the Latin Gospel, with notes of grants and translations of charters added in Gaelic in the eleventh or twelfth century. But its story of Columba's personal association with the founding of the monastery is suspiciously similar to the story of his founding of the monastery at Derry, and contains some traits of folklore which do not encourage us in accepting it as historical.

But in all Scotland there was no foundation so influential in prestige and activity as Iona, and when the power of the Dalriadic kingdom revived and extended throughout the land, the authority of Iona likewise spread. Columba is credited with an important contribution to the increase of the power of the Argyllshire Dalriada. When Conall died in 574, Columba was (as Adamnan tells us) instructed in a vision to go and anoint Aidan as his successor.[2] (This Aidan was the son of the king who had fallen in the battle

---

[1] See Meissner, *op. cit.*, pp. 247ff.
[2] Adamnan, *Life of Columba*, III, 5.

with Brude in 560.) Dr. Simpson concludes that the story of the vision was told by Columba as an excuse for illegally foisting Aidan on to the throne, since according to the accepted laws of succession the dead king's cousin Eoghanan was the rightful heir. But Adamnan assures us that Eoghanan was Columba's own choice, and that Columba resisted the àngelic command because he did not wish to anoint Aidan, and in consequence received a blow which marked him to the end of his days. Thus rendered obedient to the heavenly vision, Columba consecrated Aidan as king in Iona. Aidan, who was connected through his mother with the Britons of Strathclyde, was probably the first king in the British Isles ever to be consecrated as a Christian ruler. Tradition alleges that at his consecration he was enthroned upon the Stone of Destiny.

In the following year Columba was present at the Council of Druim Ceata, in County Derry, where (among other questions) the relations between the kingdom of Dalriada and the other Irish kingdoms were settled. The fact that Columba was greeted at this council as an honoured and influential arbiter throws doubt on the story that he had been banished from Ireland twelve years before, instead of leaving it as an act of voluntary penitence. The status of the king of Dalriada, whose territory lay in Scotland and Ireland, required to be regulated. In virtue of his territory in Ulster, he was subject to the high king of Ireland, while he governed his Argyllshire territory as vassal of the high king of Pictland. Aidan regarded the claims made upon him by the Irish high king as excessive. A compromise was reached, by which Dalriada was to serve the Irish high king with military land-forces only, "because military service always goes with the soil" —and these land-forces were apparently to be supplied from the Ulster part of Dalriada only—while it should pay tribute and taxes, and perhaps also furnish naval assistance, to the king of Dalriada, whose headquarters were now permanently in Scotland.[1] This decision was agreed upon largely through the statesmanlike influence of Columba. "On his return from the assembly, Columba had probably little difficulty in obtaining from King Brude a recognition of Aidan's character as independent king over the western districts which were occupied by the Scots of Dalriada."[2]

It is not surprising, therefore, that for political as well as ecclesiastical reasons, the abbot of Iona was looked upon as the most important cleric not only in Dalriada but in the whole of Scotland. Bishops played a very minor rôle as compared with Columba and

---

[1] See A. O. Anderson, *op. cit.*, pp. 83f.; E. MacNeill, *Phases of Irish History* (1920), pp. 197f.

[2] W. F. Skene, *Celtic Scotland*, II (1877), p. 126.

his successors, who were all presbyters only. Columba continued to maintain relations with the high king of Pictland. He paid several visits to Brude in his fortress near Inverness (dealing effectively on one of these occasions, according to Adamnan, with an ancestor of the Loch Ness monster).[1] When Brude died in 585 or thereby, the high kingship of Pictland passed to the ruler of a south Pictish province, Gartnait IV (c. 585–600). Columba quickly established relations with him in his fortress at Abernethy, and is said to have undertaken a mission among the tribes of Tayside. The Christianity which the Ninianic mission had introduced among the southern Picts had already received welcome strengthening from contact with other Irish Christians.

The king of the Britons in Strathclyde also knew of the fame of Columba, and sent him a message at the beginning of his reign, when he was hard pressed by the English kingdom of Bernicia on his eastern border, to inquire whether he would die at his enemies' hands or not. Columba replied that, unlikely as it might seem at the time, he would in fact die a peaceful death; and so it fell out.

The British king was Rhydderch Hael, who reigned from Dumbarton between 572 and 612. He is chiefly of importance in that it was during his reign that the kingdom of Strathclyde was evangelized by Kentigern. The Britons had, of course been Christianized long before; but it is plain from Patrick's *Letter to the Subjects of Coroticus* that a serious lapse from Christian manners had developed in the course of the fifth century. This lapse became a positive pagan reaction until, about 573, Rhydderch Hael, who was a Christian himself, put an end to his insecurity by enlisting the support of another British prince and inflicting a heavy defeat on his enemies. Rhydderch then made it his business to restore Christianity throughout his kingdom, and for this purpose he summoned Kentigern from Wales.

Kentigern, a native of Lothian, had been elected bishop of Cumbria in 543 and did some missionary work in the neighbourhood of Glasgow at that time; but in 553 the hostility of a pagan chief compelled him to seek refuge in Wales. There he visited St. David; there, too, he founded the monastery at Llanelwy in Flintshire which was later called St. Asaph's after his successor. On his recall to Strathclyde by Rhydderch, when he was now about fifty-five years old, he settled at Glasgow and fixed his episcopal see there. Glasgow has ever since been associated with the memory of Kentigern, who is more familiarly known by his pet-name Mungo ("dear friend"). Here, according to his twelfth-century biographer Joceline, he was visited by Columba about

---

[1] Adamnan, II, 27: this aquatic creature, by reason of its mortal bite, was a menace to swimmers in the river Ness, but at Columba's command, issued to it in the name of the Lord, it went into reverse "as though drawn by ropes."

584; if this tradition is true, it must refer to a time when Columba was in south Pictland, on the borders of the British kingdom. Not only did Kentigern thoroughly re-evangelize the Britons of Strathclyde during the remaining thirty years of his life, but missionary activity radiated from Glasgow southwards to Galloway and northwards to Aberdeenshire and even to Orkney. Glasgow Cathedral, where he is buried, is dedicated to him; his mother's name, Thenew, survives in a corrupted form in the name of St. Enoch's Church (and St. Enoch's railway station); and traditions of his life are commemorated by the bell, robin and hazel in the arms of the City of Glasgow.

Columba died in Iona on June 9, 597, at the age of seventy-six. His *Life* was written by his eighth successor in the abbacy of Iona, Adamnan, who was born of the same lineage as Columba himself in County Donegal in 624, entered the Iona monastery as a young man, and became ruler of the community in 679. His *Life of Columba*, however, is not a biography as we understand the term. It is a compilation in three parts, which deal respectively with Columba's prophetic revelations, miracles of divine power, and angelic visions. It is a work "teeming with anecdotes, but the first impression created by that book is one of despair of ever reaching solid historical fact, a concept indeed quite alien to the mind of the 'biographer.' It is from stray hints embedded in a mass of legend that the lineaments of a real person must be described, and the environment in which he lived and worked constructed."[1]

But the lineaments which are descried from the stray hints in Adamnan's work and other sources of information about Columba (mainly Irish) are the lineaments of a very real person—imperious and passionate, no doubt, but one who, having seen with horror the effects of these qualities, forthwith set himself resolutely to "crucify the flesh with its passions and desires" and left behind him the memory of a saint and apostle much more than of a political schemer. The anecdotes which have been preserved about his contacts with ordinary people reveal him as a man of great kindness, shrewd commonsense, and ready accessibility to poor people. He plainly had a commanding personality, and his voice was remarkable for its melodious tone and bell-like carrying power. When he raised his voice on Iona his words could be clearly heard in Mull; when he sang in church he could be heard a mile away; and when he paid his first visit to King Brude, and the court-druids raised a clamour to prevent him and his companions from being heard, he began to sing the forty-fifth Psalm ("My heart is inditing a good matter . . .") in such tones that the

[1] J. H. S. Burleigh, in *The Evangelical Quarterly*, July 1950, in a review of Lucy Menzies, *St. Columba of Iona* (Glasgow, 1949).

thunder of his voice struck terrified silence into the king and his people.[1]

The keen interest in literature and zeal in transcription which had brought Columba into trouble when he copied Finnian's book at Moville continued to take up much of his time in Iona. Psalters and Gospels were required for the many churches and monasteries founded by Columba's community, and he showed his monks a good example in producing beautiful copies of these. The "Battle Psalter" in the library of the Royal Irish Academy is believed by many to be his work; and the Book of Durrow, a manuscript of the Vulgate Gospels in Trinity College, Dublin, was copied from one written by Columba for his own use within the space of twelve days.

A number of poems have come down to us traditionally ascribed to Columba. The accuracy of the ascription is doubtful in many cases. But it seems reasonably certain that he was indeed the author of a Latin poem called from its opening words, *Altus Prosator* ("High Creator"), an acrostic poem, each stanza of which begins with the appropriate letter of the Latin alphabet. This poem, "a miniature *Paradise Lost* relating the Divine Plan of Salvation, goes to show, what Adamnan fails to make clear, that the Bible did have a meaning for Columba besides being a liturgical text and a lucky talisman."[2]

A later legend tells how messengers from Iona to Rome sang this hymn before Pope Gregory the Great (590–604), and Gregory "said there was no fault in the hymn apart from the small extent to which the Triune God was praised in it directly, though He was praised in His creations." When this was reported to Columba, he made up for the shortcoming by composing another hymn, *In Te Christe* ("In Thee, O Christ"). The legend is worth noticing only for its indication of intercourse between Iona and Rome. As for the hymn *In Te Christe*, it is doubtful whether it is Columba's in its entirety, though there is adequate reason to ascribe to him the part beginning *Christus Redemptor Gentium*, which has found its way into some modern hymnals in Duncan Macgregor's translation, *Christ is the world's Redeemer*.[3]

Among shorter pieces ascribed to Columba is a Gaelic prophecy referring to Iona:

Iona of my heart, Iona of my love,
Instead of the voice of monks there will be the lowing of cows;[4]

---

[1] Adamnan, I, 37.
[2] J. H. S. Burleigh, *loc. cit.*
[3] *Revised Church Hymnary*, No. 179. The lines beginning *Deus Pater credentium* appear as No. 454 in the same hymn book, in Macgregor's translation, *O God, Thou art the Father*.
[4] Columba, it is said, would not allow cows on Iona, because, as he said, where there are cows there will be women, and where there are women there will be

But before the world comes to an end.
Iona will be as it was.

Probably this quatrain is a later composition, belonging to a time when monastic life on the island had ceased. In any case, some people to-day like to think that the words foreshadowed the life and activity of the Iona Community of our own day. Whether Columba would have recognized in Dr. George MacLeod and his colleagues the proper successors to himself and his monastic family, who can tell?[1]

trouble of another kind. But not all Celtic clerics were of this mind, as otherwise we should not have found monasteries for both sexes within the one foundation as we do, e.g. at Whithorn, Kildare (St. Bridget's foundation), and later Whitby (St. Hilda's foundation). And though celibacy was a regular feature of the general asceticism of Celtic clerics, it was not obligatory. It is evident from such patronymic surnames as Mactaggart ("son of the priest"), Macpherson ("son of the parson"), Macnab ("son of the abbot") etc., that married clergy were not unknown in the Celtic church. King Duncan I of Scotland—he who was killed in 1040 by Macbeth —was the son of the Abbot of Dunkeld in Perthshire by the daughter of King Malcolm II; it was through his mother that he had a claim to the throne, although Macbeth's claim, through his wife Gruoch, was nearer still.

[1] On Celtic Christianity see also C. Thomas, *The Early Christian Archæology of North Britain* (1971); *Christianity in Roman Britain to A.D. 500* (1980).

CHAPTER XL

EVANGELIZING THE ENGLISH

IN THE YEAR 597, A FEW MONTHS BEFORE COLUMBA BREATHED his last in Iona, a party of clerics from Rome landed in the Isle of Thanet. The leader of the party was Augustine, prior of the monastery of St. Andrew on the Caelian Hill in Rome. They had been sent to England the previous year by Gregory the Great, bishop of Rome (590–604), in order to evangelize the English nation, but had spent considerable time in France before completing their journey.

Gregory's interest in the evangelization of England was later explained by a pleasant tale which tells how Gregory, before he became bishop, saw some fair-skinned boys exposed for sale in the Roman slave-market.[1] On learning that they were pagans, he thought it sad that such heathen darkness should exist within so fair an exterior, and when he was told that they were Angles, he said, "A good name, too, for they look like angels and they ought to be joint-heirs with the angels in heaven." He asked further questions and made further puns on the name of their native province and of its king; people from Deira should be rescued from the wrath (*de ira*) of God, and subjects of King Aella[2] ought to sing Alleluia. And so, not being able to realize his ambition of evangelizing these people in those days, he made it his business to have them evangelized when he was elected to the Roman see.

Whether this story is true or not, a statesman like Gregory must have recognized the importance of evangelizing the English in any case. So long as they remained unevangelized, they formed a pagan bloc cutting off the Christians in the rest of the British Isles from easy communication with Europe. And the sequel makes it plain that Gregory had but little idea of the quality or strength of the Christianity that remained in the western parts of Britain.

If, however, Gregory's interest in England was aroused first by boys from the north of the country, why did he send his delegates to Kent? One reason no doubt was the proximity of Kent to the continent; it was the most convenient part of England to reach from France. Besides, there was considerable intercourse between Kent and the land across the Channel; the men of Kent must have

---

[1] Bede, *Hist. Eccl.*, II, 1.   [2] King of Deira, 560–588.

known something about Christianity already. This is no mere surmise; the king of Kent at this time, Ethelbert (*c.* 560–616), had a Christian wife, Bertha, daughter of the Frankish king of Paris. This Frankish dynasty had been Christian for a century, and when Bertha was given in marriage to Ethelbert, it was stipulated that she should be able to practise her religion freely, and to this end a Frankish bishop, Liudhard, attended her to the Kentish court as her chaplain.

Bertha and her chaplain had already exercised some Christian influence upon the men of Kent; we know from one of Gregory's letters that some of them applied to the Frankish bishops to send missionaries to instruct them in the Christian faith, and Gregory, on hearing this, conceived the idea of having a number of English youths selected to be trained in continental monasteries and sent back to England to evangelize their fellow-countrymen. But before anything could come of this scheme he decided on more direct measures, and sent Augustine and his companions to Kent. What with the Christian influence at the Kentish court already, it was most natural that that part of England should be selected for Augustine's first missionary operations in preference to any other.

Soon after he landed, Augustine sent a message to King Ethelbert to announce his arrival and request an interview. Ethelbert granted an interview, but insisted that it should be held in the open air, as his spiritual advisers told him that he would be less easily overcome by the strangers' magical influences there than if he met them under a roof. Friendly relations were established, however, and Ethelbert allowed the missionary party the use of an old Romano-British church building at Canterbury, dedicated to St. Martin, which Queen Bertha also used for her devotions.

There does not seem to have been any effective opposition to the missionaries from the pagan Saxon priests, certainly much less than the Irish druids offered to Patrick. One reason for this may have been that the old Germanic religion was weakened already through being transplanted from its native soil on the continent to the new environment of England. It did not speak to the condition of men who had settled down to an agricultural way of life in the green and pleasant land to which they had migrated.

The missionaries' behaviour commended itself to the king and his people, and very soon the king embraced the new faith, as also did many of his subjects. No compulsion was pressed upon them, however, for Ethelbert "had learned from his teachers, the authors of his salvation, that the service of Christ must be voluntary and not forced."[1] It is a great pity that this lesson was not more widely taught and heeded in those days—and in other days as well.

[1] Bede, *Hist. Eccl.*, I, 26.

Now that a Christian community had been established in Kent, it was deemed proper that they should have a bishop to be responsible for their pastoral care, and who was so fit to be this as Augustine? So Augustine went to Arles and was consecrated bishop of the English by the bishop of that city, in accordance with previous instructions given by Pope Gregory. Then he returned to England, and sent two of his companions to Rome with the news of the progress of his mission and also with a long series of practical questions on ecclesiastical procedure on which he desired an authoritative ruling.

The messengers came back from Rome in 601, with other assistants and ministers of the Word whom Gregory commissioned to strengthen the missionary party already active in England. Looking forward to the early evangelization of the whole country, Gregory gave Augustine metropolitan authority to consecrate other bishops in England, up to the number of twelve, as the need should arise. Augustine himself was to have London as his metropolitan see. (In point of fact, he never gave effect to this provision, but stayed at Canterbury out of regard for King Ethelbert, and so it has come about that Canterbury remains to this day the premier see of the Anglican communion.) Moreover, when the time seemed ripe, Augustine was authorized to consecrate a bishop of York, who in turn would have metropolitan power to consecrate twelve further bishops in the north of England. And Augustine was to have authority over all these, and also over all Christian clerics in Britain, "in order that from your holy life and speech they may receive a pattern both of true faith and of good life, and by carrying out their duty in the realm of faith and morals may attain to the heavenly kingdom when God so wills."[1]

Some people may wonder whether the multiplication of bishops has any necessary connexion with the spread of Christianity; others may think that Christianity cannot properly spread without them. But at the time of which we are treating the appointing of bishops is a reasonably exact index to the spread of the gospel. For it was not until there was a Christian community of reasonable dimensions in any place that a bishop was appointed to superintend them, and even then the normal practice was for the community in question to ask for a bishop. Gregory's scheme for the appointment of twenty-four bishops in England remained a paper scheme for a very long time; it was not until the reign of Henry VIII that England had so many bishops. Gregory's idea of a second metropolitan at York was first realized in 634, but only for a short time; it was revived in 735 and has continued to our day.

Gregory's intention in giving Augustine authority over all the

[1] Bede, *Hist. Eccl.*, I, 29.

British churches was to bring these churches once again into close relation with Rome, from which they had been severed as a result of the English invasion. From the point of view of liturgy, this policy represented an outflanking of the Gallican church. The British churches used a liturgy akin to the Gallican, but in all the area under Augustine's jurisdiction the liturgy of the city of Rome was imposed. Gregory, however, does not seem to have taken account of the realities of the situation in Britain. The independent churches of Ireland and Scotland were more ready to treat with the see of Canterbury on an equal footing when contact was in due course established between them; but the native British Church which had been driven to the west of the country by the English invasion required the most diplomatic and conciliatory approach. They resented first of all the English conquest (naturally so); they also resented the advent of a new mission from Rome to take over such ancient British sees as those of London and York. It might be said in reply that they had no cause to resent the Roman policy of the evangelizing of the English; that if they themselves had tried to evangelize the English there would have been less need for Gregory to send Augustine to do so. Bede, who manifests a strong prejudice against the British Christians—or perhaps we should now for greater clarity call them the Welsh, as the English did—blames them bitterly and quite unfairly for their failure to evangelize their English dispossessors.[1] It is not easy to try to convert people at the same time as you are trying desperately to ward off their encroachment upon your homes. Once the Christian householder has got the burglar down and is sitting on his neck until the police arrive, he may employ the time preaching the gospel to him; but it is not so easy to do so if the burglar is stronger and has bound and gagged the householder so that he may the more conveniently rifle the household safe. What the British people wanted first and foremost was not the conversion of the English but their eviction. If, after they were sent packing to their original homes, someone went and converted them, that would be so much the better; they might be less disposed to renew their aggressive raids. Of course such hopes were fruitless; the English were now firmly installed, but the Britons may not have realized this so clearly at the time as we do, looking back.

This, then, was the mood of the Britons when Augustine arranged a conference with a number of their bishops. They met in 603 at a spot near the Severn, under an oak which was long after remembered as "Augustine's Oak." Near at hand was the battlefield of Dyrham, in Gloucestershire, where the last British resistance in those parts had been wiped out by the men of

[1] Bede, *Hist. Eccl.*, I, 22.

Wessex about twenty-five years before. The situation, from every point of view, demanded the most delicate handling. Augustine, according to Bede, opened the discussion by telling the British bishops that they reckoned the date of Easter wrongly and "practised many other things contrary to the unity of the Church."[1] (A different system of computing Easter had been accepted at Rome during the time when communications between the British churches and Rome were broken.)[2] The British bishops were unwilling to change their traditions at Augustine's bidding, but were impressed when they saw him restore the eyesight of a blind Englishman whom they themselves were unable to cure, and agreed to consult their people and arrange a further meeting.

This second conference was attended by seven British bishops and a large number of scholars, led by Dinoth, abbot of the great monastery of Bangor Iscoed in Flintshire. On their way to the place of meeting, the British delegation consulted an aged hermit of high repute for piety and wisdom, and asked him whether they should abandon their inherited customs at Augustine's bidding. "Yes," said he, "if he is a man of God." "And how shall we know that?" they asked. "Why," said the hermit, "our Lord said, 'Take my yoke upon you, and learn from me, for I am gentle and lowly in heart.' Well then, if this Augustine is gentle and lowly in heart, we may believe that he too bears the yoke of Christ and offers it to you to bear; but if he is harsh and arrogant, it is plain that he is not of God and we must not heed what he says." "And how shall we tell which he is?" said they. "Why," said he, "arrange that he and his companions come to the place of meeting first; then on your approach, if he rises to greet you, you will know that he is a servant of Christ, and you must listen to him obediently; but if he despises you and refuses to rise in your presence, though you are more in number, then let him be despised by you."

And so it was arranged, and when the Welsh delegation arrived, Augustine kept his seat. No arguments were of any avail after that; he had not shown them decent Christian courtesy. And it is striking that Bede himself, good man, while he records this incident faithfully, does not seem to draw the obvious moral; to him the Welsh were clearly in the wrong because they obstinately preferred their own ways to those which Augustine pressed upon them. And so, when he records a bloody battle which followed some years later (613) at Chester, in which the Welsh were worsted by the pagan Ethelfrith, king of Northumbria, and a number of unarmed clerics were massacred, he concludes complacently that this happened because they ignored the advice and warnings of Augustine, "so that these faithless men learned by

[1] Bede, *Hist. Eccl.*, II, 2.   [2] See pp. 410ff.

the vengeance of temporal death that they had despised the counsels of eternal salvation which had been offered them."[1]

No wonder, then, that the cleavage between the English and Welsh churches lasted for centuries; it was not until 1188 that it was finally overcome.

Augustine returned to Canterbury, and redoubled his efforts for the conversion of the Saxons. King Ethelbert gave him every facility. He presented Augustine with a palace of his own to be his headquarters, and this place, with an old Romano-British church building in the vicinity, became the nucleus of Canterbury's first cathedral. A monastery was also built near the city—later known as St. Augustine's—over which Augustine appointed as abbot one of his Roman companions, Peter by name.

The Christianization of Kent is closely bound up with the publication of a law-code in that kingdom. The traditional laws were revised in the light of the new faith, and written down in the Saxon vernacular. This was the first occasion on which a law-code was drawn up in the vernacular instead of Latin in any of the territories which had formed part of the Roman Empire. Ethelbert's code is a basic document for the study of English social history; it demonstrates that the main part of the population consisted of free peasant land-holders, subject directly to the king and to no other lord.

But Ethelbert's sphere of influence extended beyond his own kingdom of Kent. He enjoyed the title of *Bretwalda* ("Britain-ruler"), which was held by that English king whose predominance was acknowledged by his fellow-kings in the heptarchy, south of the Humber especially. This meant that the faith to which he was converted was treated with respect and favour in the other English kingdoms which recognized his leadership. This was good in so far as it facilitated the expansion of the Christian mission; it was not so good in that some rulers were tempted to yield an external conformity to Christianity without any inward conviction, so that when a shift in the leadership came about, they were quite prepared to renounce Christianity if it seemed expedient.

Of the adjacent kingdoms, Essex was the first to be evangelized from Kent. The king of Essex was a nephew of Ethelbert and this is the first of several instances in the evangelizing of England where this work was helped on by the widespread practice of intermarriage between the royal families of England. The first bishop of London was consecrated in 604; he was Mellitus, another cleric who had come from Rome to join Augustine in 601. The earliest cathedral church of St. Paul in London dates from this time. In the same year a second bishop was appointed

[1] Bede, *ibid.*

in Kent, when Justus, who had also come from Rome in 601, became first bishop of Rochester.

A few months after these appointments Augustine died. He had already consecrated his companion Laurence to be his colleague and successor, so that the see of Canterbury might not be vacant on his death. Laurence tried to establish relations with the Church of Ireland, but the trouble about a different computation of the date of Easter, which had been such an obstacle when Augustine conferred with the Welsh bishops, was equally an obstacle here. Besides, the Irish Christians at this time were very doubtful about the English Christians; they knew that the Britons had pronounced solemn curses upon the English when they invaded their country, and they regarded the English as still under these curses even after their conversion. It may have been for this reason that an Irish bishop, Dagan, passing through Kent (probably on his way to or from the continent), refused to eat with English Christians or even to stay under the same roof with them. Laurence also tried to treat with the Welsh bishops, but without success.

The death of Ethelbert in 616, after a long reign of fifty years or more, together with the death of the king of Essex about the same time, heralded a temporary reversion to paganism in the royal houses of both Kent and Essex. The example of the royal houses was followed by many of their subjects. In Essex particularly, where Christianity was not so firmly established, the situation was serious; the three pagan sons of the late king, who shared their father's realm between them, expelled the bishop of London from their territory because he refused to admit them to holy communion until they had submitted to Christianity in baptism. The three brothers were soon afterwards killed in a fight with the men of Wessex, but it took some time to recover the ground that had been lost in Essex during their rule.

In Kent, after a few years, Ethelbert's pagan son and successor Eadbald followed his father's example and became a Christian. But while he was his father's successor as king of Kent, he did not succeed to the honour of *Bretwalda*. During the closing years of Ethelbert's reign this leadership had been gradually passing to Redwald, king of East Anglia. Redwald had spent some time at the Kentish court and been baptized there, but on his return to East Anglia he showed that he was still a pagan at heart; it is recorded that he maintained a temple in his kingdom where there was one altar for Christian worship and another for the old pagan cult. But Redwald's period of supremacy did not last long; he died a year or two after Ethelbert, and the leadership over the other kings passed for the first time to the Northumbrian king, Edwin.

Northumbria included the two former kingdoms of Bernicia in the north and Deira in the south. The kingdom was first united by the father of Edwin's predecessor Ethelfrith, who added Deira to his own realm of Bernicia and handed on the united kingdom to Ethelfrith in 593. Edwin belonged to the royal house of Deira, and was a son of that Aella who, according to the story, was king of Deira when Gregory inquired about the fair-haired boys whom he saw in the Roman slave-market. He was placed on the Northumbrian throne by Redwald in 617, after the latter had overthrown and killed Ethelfrith. Redwald's idea was that Edwin should rule Northumbria as his vassal, but Redwald himself died very soon afterwards, and the authority of the *Bretwalda*, instead of passing to his successors on the throne of East Anglia, was asserted by Edwin. Edwin then allied himself by marriage with a sister of King Eadbald of Kent, and thus Christianity was first introduced into Northumbria, but that story will be told in our next chapter.

One thing that strikes us in the history of the evangelization of the English is their tolerant attitude to the missionaries. The mission to the English has no roll of martyrs, such as the missionary records of other Germanic nations can show. This is not because the English at that time were imbued with general principles of tolerance and liberalism. But it does suggest that the old paganism had lost its power and appeal and that they were ready to give a fair hearing to the teachers of Christianity.

CHAPTER XLI

ENGLAND TAKES UP THE TORCH

THE ANGLIAN KINGS OF NORTHUMBRIA COULD NOT FAIL TO learn something of Christianity from their Pictish neighbours to the north, and their British neighbours to the west, on whose territory they encroached in south-east Scotland and north-east England. But the first occasion of their accepting Christianity was in 625, when Edwin, king of Northumbria, received in marriage Ethelberga, the daughter of King Ethelbert of Kent. Ethelbert was now dead, and when Edwin sought Ethelberga's hand in marriage from her brother King Eadbald, consent was given only on condition that she should have every liberty to practise her Christian faith.[1] Edwin readily agreed, and when Ethelberga came north to become his queen, she was accompanied by Paulinus, who was consecrated bishop by Justus, Augustine's second successor at Canterbury.

At Easter season of the following year a daughter was born to the royal pair and was baptized by Paulinus at Whitsuntide—the first Northumbrian to be baptized. Some time later Edwin himself, after much hesitation, decided to be baptized, together with his chief priest Coifi and many other leading men in the kingdom. The contrast between their old religion and the new faith was expressed very movingly by one of these leading men while Edwin was consulting with them in the Witan or royal council about the advisability of embracing Christianity. His words, according to Bede, were these:[2]

> Your Majesty: When we consider the uncertain span of time that is ours, the present life of men on earth seems to me as when a sparrow comes to the house and flies through it quickly, coming in at one door and immediately going out by another, while you sit at dinner with your chiefs and attendants in the winter time. The dining hall is warm from the fire kindled in the midst of it, but hurricanes of rain or snow rage everywhere outside. While the bird is inside the house, it does not feel the wintry weather, but when once the tiny space of light and warmth has been traversed (and that takes but a moment), then it returns from winter to winter and is gone from

[1] Traces of a wooden palace of Edwin's were discovered by air photography in 1951 near the Northumbrian hamlet of Yeavering, in the Cheviot hills; excavation has been carried on there since 1953.

[2] Bede, *Hist. Eccl.*, II, 13.

your sight. So this life of men appears for a brief space; but we are completely ignorant of what has gone before or what will follow after. Therefore, if this new teaching has brought us any greater certainty, I think it is right that we should follow it.

Accordingly, Edwin and many of his people were baptized at York on Easter Eve, 627.

Edwin appears to have been a considerate and practical Christian; it is recorded to his credit that all over his kingdom, where springs of water welled forth by the roadside, he ordered posts to be erected and bronze cups hung on them so that wayfarers might quench their thirst in comfort. More than that, so peaceful was his kingdom that (as Bede relates) a woman might walk alone with a newborn infant from one end of it to the other in perfect security. He also brought his missionary enthusiasm to bear on the royal family of East Anglia, and persuaded Earpwald, son and successor of Redwald, to become a Christian. Earpwald's successor Sigbert (631–634) had spent some time before his accession among the Franks, and when he became king he invited a cleric from Burgundy, Felix by name, to come to East Anglia as bishop. He installed him at Dunwich, and there Felix had a successful ministry for some sixteen years.

Meanwhile Paulinus, who had established his episcopal see at York, carried out a long missionary tour in Lincolnshire, in the course of which he founded the first church in Lincoln since the English conquest. His success was such that Pope Honorius (625–638) raised him to metropolitan status. Thus York was now a metropolitan see, as Pope Gregory had intended, but at present only for a very brief spell.

In 633 Edwin fell in battle (at Hatfield, near Doncaster) against the Welsh king Cadwallon, who was allied with Penda, king of Mercia. Northumbria was invaded by the enemy, and Queen Ethelberga with her children had to flee by sea to Kent, escorted by Bishop Paulinus. Paulinus was appointed to the see of Rochester, which had just become vacant, and York remained without a bishop for thirty years. Bernicia and Deira became separate kingdoms again, each under a prince of its own royal house; but both princes were attacked and killed by Cadwallon the following year. Very soon after, however, Cadwallon himself was surprised and killed near Hexham, with a great part of his army, by Oswald, a son of Edwin's predecessor Ethelfrith.

Bede's unfavourable opinion of the Britons finds fresh expression when he moralizes about Cadwallon. It was monstrous, he thought (and naturally so), that Cadwallon, who professed Christianity, should ally himself with the pagan Penda to war against the Christian king Edwin, and by his depredations in Northumbria do such disservice to the Christian cause in that kingdom.

But in fact, he says, the British Christians are so hostile to the English Christians that they will sooner associate with pagans.[1] We should remember, however, that Cadwallon, four or five years previously, had been driven from his own realm in the Chester area by Edwin, who carried his arms as far as Anglesey and the Isle of Man. To Cadwallon the only good Englishman was a dead one, and his policy was to extirpate the English population in Northumbria and recover the land for his own people.

Oswald had spent the years of Edwin's reign as an exile among the Scots of Dalriada, and from them he had learned the Christian faith. When he was established as king of Northumbria in 634, he found that kingdom had for the most part reverted to paganism as a result of the Welsh invasion and the influence of the two princes who ruled for a short time in Bernicia and Deira respectively after Edwin's death, for both of them, although formerly Christian, had apostatized. As he himself had become a Christian among the Scots, he naturally looked to them rather than to Canterbury for help in evangelizing his kingdom. At first they sent a missionary of such an unattractive character that the Northumbrians would have none of him, so that he went back to Iona and reported that the Northumbrians were "untamable men, of a hard and barbarian mentality,"[2] and that it was no use trying to teach them. But one of the monks, Aidan by name, suggested that the fault might be as much his as theirs, and that he should have been more accommodating to the ignorance of the Northumbrians and not tried to feed them with strong meat when they were still too immature to dispense with milk. The brethren, hearing Aidan express himself thus, suggested that he should go to Northumbria himself in response to Oswald's request and practise there what he preached at Iona. Aidan was therefore sent as bishop to the Northumbrians in 635, and Oswald welcomed him and gave him the island of Lindisfarne, off the coast of Northumberland, as his episcopal see. Lindisfarne, indeed, was and is an island only at flood tide:

> For, with the flow and ebb, its style
> Varies from continent to isle;
> Dry shod, o'er sands, twice every day,
> The pilgrims to the shrine find way;
> Twice every day, the waves efface
> Of staves and sandall'd feet the trace.[3]

Aidan quickly proved that his companions at Iona had done wisely in selecting him as their delegate, after the unsuccessful attempt of his predecessor. He was a true missionary, and the

[1] Bede, *Hist. Eccl.*, II, 20.
[2] Bede, *Hist. Eccl.*, III, 5.
[3] Sir Walter Scott, *Marmion*, Canto ii, 8.

Northumbrians, far from showing themselves untamable and un-teachable, flocked gladly to hear him preach. "And there was often a most beautiful sight to be seen, that the king himself acted as interpreter of the heavenly message to his chiefs and attendants, when the bishop, who did not know the English tongue very well, preached the gospel. For the king had of course mastered the Scottish tongue [i.e. Gaelic] perfectly, during his long exile."[1]

Converts were made and baptized, churches were founded, and Christianity was now solidly established in Northumbria. As the work of evangelism advanced, Aidan sent to Dalriada and Ireland for further help, and many other monks from Iona came to join him, so that Lindisfarne quickly became a second Iona, still, however, acknowledging the superiority of the parent monastery in Scotland.

About the same time as Aidan re-established Christianity in Northumbria, the people of Wessex also received the Gospel. Their missionary-bishop was Birinus, who came to England with the approval of Pope Honorius, promising him that he would "sow the seeds of the holy faith in the hearts of those English who lived beyond the others, in parts where no teacher had preceded him."[2] His mission was successful; the king of Wessex believed the Gospel and was baptized, and at his baptism he had no less eminent a sponsor than the Northumbrian King Oswald, who at that time enjoyed the dignity of *Bretwalda*. Birinus was given Dorchester-on-Thames, in Oxfordshire, as his episcopal see. Ten years later Wessex was invaded by Penda of Mercia and its king, Coenwalch, expelled. When he regained his kingdom in 648, he installed as bishop of Dorchester a Frankish scholar named Agilbert, who had spent many years of study in Ireland. About 662 Coenwalch established a second bishopric in Wessex, at Winchester, and here an Englishman, Wini by name, was installed as bishop. Some four years later, Wini, to his dis-credit, provides us with the first example of simony in the Church of England, for he bought his appointment to the see of London.

Mention of the see of London, which lay within the kingdom of Essex, reminds us that that kingdom had by this time been re-claimed for Christianity. After a succession of pagan kings, King Sigbert of Essex was converted through the influence of Oswy of Northumbria, and in 653—thirty-six years after the expulsion of Bishop Mellitus—a Northumbrian Christian, by the name of Cedd, was consecrated bishop of the East Saxons with his see at London. In addition to the discharge of his episcopal duties, Cedd retained responsibility for the direction of a monastery which he founded in 654 at Lastingham, near Whitby, and in

[1] Bede, *Hist. Eccl.*, III, 3.   [2] Bede, *Hist. Eccl.*, III, 7.

which he died and was buried in 664. It was in the vacancy which followed his death that Wini purchased the bishopric of London.

Penda, king of Mercia, whose capital was at Tamworth, remained a pagan so long as he lived. He did not, however, forbid members of his family to become Christians; he said he had no objection to Christians provided that they practised what they preached. He established a dominant position for himself among the English kingdoms, but his dominance did not hinder the spread of the gospel. In 641 he attacked Northumbria and Oswald fell in battle. Deira, the southern part of Northumbria, became a dependency of Mercia, under a Christian prince Oswin, who ruled it as Penda's vassal, But in the north Oswald's brother Oswy succeeded him as king of Bernicia. In 651 Oswy procured the death of Oswin, and three years later he defeated and killed Penda when the latter attacked Bernicia. Oswy now reigned over all Northumbria. With the death of Penda a Christian mission from Northumbria began to evangelize Mercia.

In the meantime, Aidan had died, in 651. He left behind him a pleasant memory for his humility, scholarship, and missionary industry. The royal families of Northumbria showered gifts upon him, but he bestowed them in charity. When Oswin, king of Deira, presented him with a horse to enable him to cross fords without getting his feet wet and otherwise travel more comfortably, he gave the horse, all rich'y caparisoned as it was, to the first beggar who sought alms of him. Oswin expostulated with him: "I have plenty of other horses," he said, "and any one of them would have done to give to the poor; why must you give away that special horse which I gave you for your special use?" "Why," rejoined Aidan, "is that son of a mare more precious in Your Majesty's eyes than the son of God?"[1]

The tradition of asceticism and sound learning which Columba had established at Iona was maintained by Aidan at Lindisfarne, and Northumbria remained a leading centre of Christian scholarship until the Danish depredations of the ninth century.

Finan, another monk from Iona, came to Lindisfarne as bishop and abbot in Aidan's place and held that office for ten years. It was during his bishopric that the famous monastery at Whitby was founded by Hilda. Hilda (the Latinized form of Hild, originally the name of a Saxon war-goddess) was a grand-niece of Edwin king of Northumbria. With other members of that family, she was baptized by Paulinus on Easter Eve, 627, at the age of thirteen. Some years later she resolved to enter the monastic life, and intended to join her sister who lived in a convent near Paris, but at Aidan's invitation she came back to Northumbria, and in 649 was appointed abbess of a small convent near Hartlepool, in succession

[1] Bede, *Hist. Eccl.*, III, 14.

to the founder-abbess. Eight years later she obtained a piece of land at a place which Bede calls by its Old English name Streaneshalch (interpreted by him as "Lighthouse Bay"), but which we know by its later (Danish) name of Whitby. Here she founded a monastery where there were houses for monks as well as nuns (as there were at some other early English and Irish monasteries); the nuns took precedence over the monks and both classes were subject to the rule of the abbess. Very soon the fame of Whitby had become such that bishops began to look to it for their clergy, and Bede enumerates five monks of Whitby who became bishops in the seven or eight decades which separated the founding of the monastery from the time when he wrote his *History*.

It was under Hilda's rule that the poet Cædmon was admitted to the brotherhood at Whitby. Bede tells how this man was completely ungifted in poetry or song, until one night, when he had left a merrymaking party in order to avoid having to contribute to the musical entertainment, he fell asleep in the stable, and saw in a dream a man standing by him who commanded him to sing. He protested that he could not sing, but the command was repeated, and when he asked what he should sing he was told to sing the beginning of created things. "Then he proceeded at once to sing to the praise of God the Creator verses which he had never heard before, and this was their general sense:

> Now must we praise
> The Maker of the heavenly realm,
> The Creator's power and wisdom,
> The deeds of the Father of glory,
> How He, being God eternal,
> Was the Author of all wonders,
> Who first to the sons of men
> Made heaven for the roof of their abode,
> And thereafter created the earth,
> Almighty Guardian of mankind . . .

And when he rose from sleep, he kept in his memory all that he had sung, and later added to it in the same strain further words of song worthy of God."[1]

It was recognized that Cædmon had received a new gift from God and the abbess persuaded him to enter the monastery, where he had ample opportunity for the cultivation of this gift. "And he sang of the creation of the world, the origin of the human race, and all the story of Genesis, of Israel's exodus from Egypt and entry into the promised land, of very many other stories from Holy Scripture, of our Lord's incarnation, passion, resurrection and ascension into heaven, of the coming of the Holy Spirit, and the apostles' teaching. Moreover he composed many songs telling

[1] Bede, *Hist. Eccl.*, IV, 24.

of the terror of judgment to come, the horror of the pains of hell, and the bliss of the heavenly kingdom, and very many others of the divine benefits and judgments, in all of which he made it his aim to draw men away from the love of evil deeds and stir them up to love and zeal for good works."[1]

Cædmon's songs, in fact, constituted a sort of Bible for the people, teaching them the outlines of the Gospel story in their own language, in words which they could easily memorize and sing themselves. A number of Old English poems on these themes have been preserved, and some of them at any rate are probably Cædmon's composition.

But Hilda's monastery was also the scene of an event of a different kind, of great importance in early English history. This was the Synod of Whitby, held in 663.

To begin with, the Roman mission operating inland from Canterbury and the Irish mission working south from Northumbria were largely independent of each other. But with the progress of both missions and the advancing evangelization of the country, they soon made contact with each other, and certain long-standing differences of practice began to cause embarrassment. One of these was trivial enough; it was the style of tonsure adopted by the two groups. Whereas the Canterbury clerics practised the normal coronal tonsure of western Christendom, their Irish brethren cultivated the frontal tonsure, as they had done, if not from Patrick's time, at any rate from the time immediately following his death. One might have thought that, if clerics must be tonsured, it was a matter of indifference how they were tonsured, and that the two traditions might be allowed to continue side by side. But, whatever the origin of the coronal tonsure was, it had come by now to be interpreted as commemorative of the Saviour's crown of thorns, whereas the frontal tonsure could not be accounted for in any similar fashion. The Irish Church claimed St. John's authority for it, but the Roman clerics traced it back to Simon Magus!

There was also a dispute, of which we are not informed in detail, with regard to baptism or confirmation; possibly the Irish Church, like the eastern Church, allowed presbyters to perform the act of anointing in confirmation, whereas the Roman Church restricted this function to bishops.[2]

Of more practical consequence was the difference in computing the date of Easter. The Celtic Christians, of Britain and Ireland alike, used a cycle of eighty-four years which had been in general use in the west at the time when the British Isles were evangelized. But there had been changes since then, and in 525 a nineteen year

---

[1] *Ibid.*
[2] H. Williams, *Christianity in Early Britain* (1912), p. 474.

cycle was accepted at Rome as the proper basis of reckoning. It was this, naturally, which Canterbury and her daughter-churches used. Besides, the Welsh and Irish Christians counted as Easter Day the Sunday which fell next after the spring equinox between the fourteenth and twentieth days of the moon (inclusive), while the Roman computation fixed Easter on the Sunday which fell next after the spring equinox between the fifteenth and twenty-first days of the moon. Nor was the situation rendered less complicated by the fact that the Celts regarded March 25 as the spring equinox and the Romans March 22.

This divergence of reckoning meant that in certain years the two groups of English Christians might celebrate Easter on different dates; thus Bede relates that in one year King Oswy had finished his Lenten fast and was keeping Easter according to the Irish reckoning while his queen, Eanfleda (daughter of Edwin and Ethelberga), who had been brought up in Kent and therefore followed the general western reckoning, was still fasting and observing Palm Sunday. This was an obvious practical inconvenience, and deserved to be corrected on that score alone, but some churchmen regarded the discrepancy as more serious than a mere inconvenience. Bede seems to regard it as almost immoral; for example, in his commendation of Aidan, he explains that he had preferred to dwell upon his praiseworthy qualities, "by no means choosing for commendation the fact that he had imperfect understanding of the observance of Easter, but rather holding this in great detestation."[1] Pope Honorius and his second successor John IV (640–642) sent letters to the Irish Church drawing their attention to this deviation from the general practice of western Christendom, emphasizing an admonition which had already been addressed to them (as well as to the Welsh) by Laurence, second archbishop of Canterbury; but although the southern Irish conformed to the Roman Easter about 634, after receiving Honorius's letter, it was several decades before other Irish Christians followed their example.

Matters came to a head in England, however, in 663, shortly after Finan had died and been succeeded at Lindisfarne by Colman, another monk from Iona. Colman, like his predecessors, kept the Celtic Easter. But there was another Irish cleric in the province, Ronan by name, who had travelled in Europe, and been converted to the Roman reckoning. Besides, the church at York was in charge of an elderly cleric named James, who in King Edwin's

---

[1] Bede, *Hist. Eccl.*, III, 17. We may contrast the more reasonable attitude of the church historian Socrates towards divergences in practice with regard to Easter and other matters: "Since no one can produce a written command as an authority, it is evident that the apostles left each one to his own free will in the matter, in order that each might do what is good neither by fear nor by compulsion" (*Hist. Eccl.*, V 22).

reign had been Bishop Paulinus's deacon, and remained in
Northumbria when Paulinus left; he had continued to observe the
Roman Easter all these years. The disputes between the two
parties of churchmen came to the ears of King Oswy—and indeed,
with the difference in reckoning affecting his own domestic circle,
he could not have been ignorant of it in any case. The chief agitation against the Celtic practice came from Oswy's son Alchfrid,
whom he had made king of Deira under him. Alchfrid's tutor,
Wilfrid, abbot of Ripon, had lived in Rome and Lyons, and
followed the Roman practice. Alchfrid, instructed by Wilfrid,
determined to replace the Irish by the Roman usages throughout
Northumbria; but Oswy was sure that his Irish teachers were
right. The matter had to be settled one way or the other, and a
synod was called at Whitby, to which representatives of both
viewpoints were summoned. King Oswy presided and called on
the abbot of Lindisfarne to speak first. Colman pleaded traditional
custom, and also maintained that the Irish reckoning had the
authority of the apostle John behind it.

Now this was the plea which had formerly been made by the
Quartodecimans in support of their reckoning,[1] and the fact that
it was put forward by the Celtic Church in support of theirs gave
rise to the idea that the Celtic Church was itself quartodeciman
(and therefore heretical on this point, since quartodecimanism had
been forbidden by the Council of Nicaea). Pope John IV, for
example, in his letter to the Irish Christians, charged them with
renewing an old heresy. But this was a mistake; Bede himself
points out by way of mitigating the error of the Irish that at least
they always observed Easter on a Sunday and not (after the
Jewish and quartodeciman fashion) according to the day of the
month, whatever the weekday might be.

When Colman had spoken, Agilbert, bishop of Wessex, who
was present, was invited to speak, but he requested that his disciple Wilfrid of Ripon be spokesman for the Roman side instead
of himself, as Wilfred was better able to express himself in
English. Wilfrid therefore defended the Roman practice with
great vigour and ability. He pointed out that the quartodeciman
practice of John, who "on the fourteenth day of the first month
in the evening began the celebration of the paschal feast, irrespec-
tive of whether it fell on the sabbath or any other day," could not
be invoked in support of the very different Irish practice. But if
the other side invoked John, the Roman side could invoke Peter.
Much more learned argument followed on both sides, as Colman
and Wilfrid invoked great names. Wilfrid allowed that Columba
and the other holy men of Iona were men of God in spite of their
defective practice with regard to the keeping of Easter, but they

[1] See pp. 210f., 276.

could plead ignorance, whereas now that Colman and his associates had the right procedure presented plainly to them, it was sheer sin for them to persist in their deviation. "Your Columba—yes, our Columba too (if indeed he belonged to Christ)—may have been a saint and mighty in deeds of power, but can he be given the slightest preference above the most blessed prince of the apostles, to whom our Lord said, 'You are Peter, and . . . I will give you the keys of the kingdom of heaven'?"

At this King Oswy anxiously inquired: "Did our Lord really say that to Peter?" And on being assured by both parties that He did, and that He had given no comparable authority to Columba, he said, "Well; I must tell you that I am in no mind to go against this doorkeeper, but desire to obey his ordinances in everything, to the best of my knowledge and power. Otherwise, when I come to the doors of the kingdom of heaven, I may find none to open to me, if I earn the displeasure of the one who so clearly holds the keys."[1]

And so, in spite of his former preference for the Irish fashion, Oswy was so moved by the fear of Peter's reaction that he was immediately converted to the Roman reckoning, and the synod accepted his decision.[2] But that did not spell the end of Irish influence in England. That influence did not depend on such comparatively minor questions as the computation of Easter, or varieties of usage with regard to tonsure and confirmation. It depended rather on a whole tradition and outlook and organization and way of life, which was too deeply rooted to be extirpated by such a decision as was made at Whitby.

Colman seems to have taken the decision as a vote of no confidence in himself; at any rate he withdrew from Lindisfarne and went to become abbot of a monastery in County Mayo. But he was succeeded as *bishop* of Lindisfarne by Tuda, a southern Irishman (who therefore had already accepted the Roman reckoning of Easter) and as *abbot* of Lindisfarne by Eata, another Celt, who was already abbot of Melrose. The abbot and monastery of Lindisfarne were independent of the bishop's jurisdiction. Hilda accepted the synod's decision and remained abbess of Whitby.

This was really no victory for the party of Alchfrid and Wilfrid, whose aim was to purge the Northumbrian Church of Irish influence and not simply to impose the Roman computation of

[1] Bede, *Hist. Eccl.*, III, 25.

[2] Outside England, too, there was increasing conformity after this to the Roman practice in the computation of Easter and other matters. During Adamnan's abbacy of Iona (679–704) the Roman practice was accepted by the daughter-communities of Iona; Iona itself held out until 716. Adamnan was greatly influenced by Abbot Ceolfrid of Wearmouth. Another northerner who held correspondence with Ceolfrid was Nechtan IV, king of the Picts, who in 710 went over to the Roman discipline with most of his kingdom. In a few parts of Scotland, as in Northern Ireland and Wales, the older practices survived until the Norman period.

Easter upon it. But Alchfrid died almost immediately after the synod. He had intended to revive the see of York, as the chief ecclesiastical centre of Deira, and have Wilfrid installed as bishop there. But Oswy gave it instead to Chad, who had recently succeeded his brother Cedd as abbot of Lastingham.[1]

Even a saint like Cuthbert, so English in name and so venerated in the Christian memory of Northumbria, represents the Irish rather than the Roman tradition. He was prior successively of Melrose and of Lindisfarne under Abbot Eata, and later became bishop successively of Hexham and of Lindisfarne. But his real desire was to live as an anchorite in the true Celtic manner, and it was as an anchorite that he died on March 20, 687, shortly after resigning the see of Lindisfarne.

One reason for the persistence of Irish influence in Northumbria was the superiority of Irish education to anything that could be had in England, or even in western Europe, at the time. Not only Northumbrian clerics, but even members of the royal house, went to Ireland for their education. Even a cursory comparison of the script of the Lindisfarne Gospels, a manuscript whose illumination is ascribed to Bishop Eadfrith of Lindisfarne (698–721), with the distinctive script of Ireland suggests the debt that England owed to Ireland in the art of lettering. This manuscript has been described as, "next to the Book of Kells,[2] the finest of all existing illuminated manuscripts . . . The inspiration and technique of the work are Celtic, but those who wrought it were English."[3]

It was partly to counter this cultural influence that the joint monasteries of Wearmouth and Jarrow were founded in the later part of the seventh century. Their founder was Benedict Biscop, a Northumbrian by birth, who introduced the Benedictine rule from the continent to his two foundations. They were designed to be centres of Christian learning in the interests of the Roman and continental tradition, amid an environment which reflected the Celtic tradition, and it is necessary to mention only the name of Bede of Jarrow to realize how worthily the founder's aims were realized. It is noteworthy, too, that the most reliable manuscript of Jerome's Vulgate version of the Bible, the *Codex Amiatinus*, now at Florence, was produced at one or the other of these two monasteries. The work was carried out under the direction of Abbot Ceolfrid, probably on the basis of copies which he

---

[1] In 669 Chad was removed from York and became bishop of Mercia (first at Repton and then at Lichfield), while Wilfrid entered into possession at York.

[2] The Book of Kells, so called from the monastery at Kells in Meath, is a seventh- or eighth-century copy of the Gospels, famous as being the most perfect extant specimen of Irish handwriting. It is housed in Trinity College, Dublin.

[3] Meissner, *op. cit.*, p. 219. See also A. A. Luce, "The Book of Kells and the Gospels of Lindisfarne," *Hermathena*, May 1952, pp. 61ff.; Nov. 1952, pp. 12ff.

had brought from Italy, and presented to Pope Gregory II in 716.

There was a revival of Christian culture in the south of England as well around this time. In 668 there came to Canterbury as archbishop a great scholar of Greek provenance, Theodore of Tarsus, consecrated to the Anglican primacy by Pope Vitalian. It is a matter of interest that Theodore was the last non-English archbishop of Canterbury until the Norman Conquest.[1] Theodore's first concern was the reorganization of the Church of England. Under him the English nation attained religious unity long before it became politically one. He convened the first pan-Anglican synod at Hertford in 673. This synod confirmed the arrangements Theodore had already made to subdivide the large dioceses of England into smaller and more manageable areas. Previously the general practice had been to have one bishop for one kingdom of the heptarchy. As a result of Theodore's reorganization there were now sixteen dioceses; Northumbria, for example, had four. Theodore then took steps to appoint suitable bishops to these sees, and he did not overlook the Celtic clerics in filling them; he gave preferment to several of these, but did so in such a way that the unity of the Church of England was strengthened thereby. He saw clearly that the best way to deal with the divergence of traditions in Northumbria was not to try to suppress the Celtic influence, but to control it. During his career as archbishop, and for forty-five years after his death, Canterbury remained the sole metropolitan see in England; it was not until 735 that York was raised once again to metropolitan status.

But Theodore did not confine his activity to diocesan organization. He settled priests in groups in charge of districts which it would be anachronistic to call parishes. He also saw that if the prestige of Irish culture was not to continue undisputed, it was necessary to equal it in England iself. Wearmouth and Jarrow were making a name for themselves in Northumbria, but Canterbury too became an important centre of education under Hadrian of Naples, whom Theodore brought to England with him to be abbot of St. Augustine's monastery. Under Theodore the study of Greek flourished in England, at a time when it was generally unknown in western Europe.

One distinguished pupil of Theodore at Canterbury was Aldhelm (c. 640–709), a member of the royal family of Wessex, who became abbot of Malmesbury about 673 and bishop of Sherborne in 705. He was a great scholar himself, proficient not only in

---

[1] It is also a matter of interest that Theodore was tonsured after the eastern style, and on being appointed to Canterbury had to grow his hair and be re-tonsured after the Roman style.

Latin and Greek but also, we are told, in Hebrew; and through his exertions Wessex became a rival of Northumbria for learning in the first part of the eighth century.

In spite of the relatively late date of the evangelization of the English, therefore, the Dark Ages came to an end in England sooner than they did in many parts of western Europe. English scholarship became deservedly renowned. Bede, to whom we are so greatly indebted for our knowledge of the progress of Christianity in this island, seems never to have left his native province of Northumbria, but his great scholarship won him such widespread fame that we may well consider him one of the great Europeans of his age. The cloister school of York, which owed much to his influence, provided Charlemagne with his great adviser Alcuin (735–804), through whom the court at Aachen (Aix-la-Chapelle) became the centre of a revival of learning which gave direction to the whole course of mediæval culture. Alcuin made a special contribution to Biblical learning by his revision of Jerome's Vulgate text, which he undertook at the commission of Charlemagne himself.

In the more direct work of evangelization, too, the recently evangelized English took a speedy and important share.[1] Wilfrid of Ripon did much more useful Christian service in this way than he did by his agitation against the Irish computation of Easter. In the winter of 678–679 he began missionary work among the pagan Frisians, and thus became the first foreign missionary of the Church of England. A little later, from 681 to 685, being prevented by the Northumbrian king from performing his episcopal duties at York, he visited the last remaining pocket of paganism in England, the kingdom of Sussex, and turned its people from idolatry to Christianity. His work among the Frisians was carried on by his pupil Willibrord (c. 658–739), who in 695 became first archbishop of Utrecht. Another missionary who undertook evangelistic work among the western Germans about the same time was Boniface (c. 675–754), a native of Wessex (traditionally of Crediton in Devonshire).[2] His labours won for him the title "the apostle of Germany," for it was he who planted Christianity in the territories east of the Rhine, becoming first archbishop of Mainz in 732. Towards the end of his life he resumed missionary work among the Frisians, where he had assisted Willibrord in earlier days, and there he met his death in a pagan attack in 754. He is buried at Fulda (where he founded an abbey in 744).

It has been said that Boniface was the last foreign missionary to go out from England for nearly a thousand years. Probably this is too sweeping a statement, especially when we make

[1] See C. H. Talbot, *The Anglo-Saxon Missionaries in Germany* (1954).
[2] See G. W. Greenaway, *Saint Boniface* (1955).

allowance for the many Christians who have acted as "unofficial" missionaries when business of one kind or another took them to other lands.[1] But it is appropriate that we should conclude our survey of the rise and progress of Christianity in those early centuries A.D. by remembering our own fellow-countrymen who took up the apostolic torch and carried the light to the Gentiles. The virility of the Christianity which was planted in these islands in those days proved itself by the missionary spirit which animated our ancestors. The evangelistic enterprise of those centuries has remained an honourable heritage for all the nations of the British Isles; and English, Welsh, Irish and Scots have never proved more worthy of that heritage than when they have most energetically carried the same liberating message to the uttermost parts of the earth.

We have already dwelt upon the many handicaps of their own creation which Christians had to overcome from the fourth century onwards in the prosecution of their proper business in the world. There were other handicaps too; the decline of imperial power in the west and the barbarian invasions might be looked at in that light. But handicaps of that kind Christianity took in its stride, showing once again that it was organized for catastrophe and never revealed its true qualities better than in times of general disaster. Christianity was not so tied to the imperial power that it was forced to share the decline of that power. On the contrary, all that was of value in Roman civilization was preserved by Christianity and carried over into the new world that followed the Dark Ages. The barbarian nations of Europe one by one in quick succession accepted the Christian gospel; the Gentiles came to the light.

It is not to the policies of ecclesiastical statesmen that we look for the truest evidences of pure Christianity in these centuries, nor yet even to the debates and decisions of ecumenical councils. We do not go so far as the late seventeenth-century writer who said that "the true church in any generation is to be found with those who have just been excommunicated from the actual church"; but the genuine spirit of Christ is sometimes to be found in unlikely quarters. That, after all, is what we might expect when we consider that Christ Himself was regarded as scarcely orthodox either in belief or in practice by the leaders of His own religious community.

We have tried, however, to follow the main stream of Christian progress in these pages, and in so doing we have found proof enough that the spirit of the Servant was vigorously alive in those

[1] The English-born bishop Henry of Uppsala directed missionary activity in Finland about the middle of the twelfth century.

centuries. We may think of the apostolic labours of Patrick, or of the unwearying toil of Bede, as he maintained his output of Christian learning to the end, dictating with his dying breath his Old English translation of St. John's Gospel. It was the single-minded service of men like these, and of many more whose witness was less public than theirs, that kept the true light shining through the darkness that covered the peoples of the west after the collapse of imperial authority in these lands. Professor Kenneth Scott Latourette has presented the story of the expansion of Christianity as a pattern of advance and recession; and the first and greatest recession, following the initial Christian advance, he dates in the four and a half centuries which began about 500. In each period of recession, however, he traces the beginnings of the next period of advance; and we have seen in our closing chapters how clearly such signs of promise appeared during that first recession.

In those days the redeeming message of Christianity burst as a great light on the people that walked in darkness. How it appealed to them may be judged by the words of the councillor at the Northumbrian court, quoted on pages 404f. His parable of human life is all too apt a picture of the life of many of our own contemporaries. But where Christian men and women are prepared to take up and carry forward the commission of the obedient and suffering Servant, the issue is not in doubt: the nations will come to His light.

Note. The approximate thirteenth centenary of the birth of Boniface (p. 416) was commemorated by three Paternoster Press publications: J. C. Sladden, *Boniface of Devon: Apostle of Germany* (1980); T. Reuter (ed.), *The Greatest Englishman: Essays on St. Boniface and the Church at Crediton* (1980); D. Keep, *St. Boniface and his World* (1980).

POSTSCRIPT

A WORD MAY BE ADDED ON PRIMARY SOURCES. For Part I the main source-book is the New Testament. An evaluation of the historical quality of its contents may be found in my inquiry *Are the New Testament Documents Reliable?* (first published in 1943). In addition the writings of Josephus are indispensable for the Jewish environment of the period, and those of the Roman historian Tacitus for the Gentile environment.

For Part II the chief authority is the church historian Eusebius, bishop of Palestinian Cæsarea in the earlier part of the fourth century, whose *Ecclesiastical History*, written about 324, traces the progress of Christianity from the coming of Christ to the reign of Constantine. For the latter part of this period Eusebius is an increasingly reliable authority; for the earlier part, especially for the century following A.D. 70, his sources were inadequate. Yet he had access to sources (even for that obscure century) which are not available to us, and he has made us his debtors by his copious quotations from them in the course of his work. The Christian literature which has come down to us from the period between the apostolic age and Constantine is not historiography, but it does contribute in various ways to our knowledge of the advance of Christianity during this period.

For Part III we have a much greater number of authorities. Many of the leading Christian figures of this period provide us with the stuff of history in their voluminous writings. But among historical writers properly so called there are three to whom we are specially indebted. For the events from 313 to 324 we continue to have the information provided by Eusebius in his *Ecclesiastical History*, and for the career of Constantine we have the same writer's *Life of Constantine*. A later historian, Socrates of Constantinople, took up the *Ecclesiastical History* where Eusebius left off, and carried the story from the Council of Nicaea in 325 down to 439. Socrates wove several first-hand sources into his work, which is characterized by sound judgment and accuracy. He has a moral to point; layman as he was, he wished to demonstrate the deplorable effects of ecclesiastical controversy. It must be admitted that he had no need to depart from the due proportion of historical narration in order to find abundant evidence of the harm caused by such controversy. Then, for the later chapters of our book we are immensely indebted to the *Ecclesiastical History of the English Nation*, written in Latin by the Venerable Bede, monk of the monastery at Jarrow-on-Tyne and one of the finest scholars of his day (*c.* 672–735). This, the first major literary work composed by an Englishman, carries the story of Christianity in Britain from Roman times down to 731, and is marked by those features which distinguish the true historian from the mere annalist. By far the greater part of his *History* deals with the period which began with the coming of Augustine to Canterbury in 597, and for that period it is an authority of incalculable value.

The reader will find useful collections of source-material in C. K. Barrett, *The New Testament Background: Selected Documents* (1956), J. Stevenson, *A New Eusebius: Documents illustrative of the history of the Church to A.D. 337* (1957), D. J. Theron, *The Evidence of Tradition* (1957), and (for the closing period of our study) W. Levison, *England and the Continent in the Eighth Century* (1946).

INDEX